Women of the Sacred Groves

Women of the Sacred Groves

Divine Priestesses of Okinawa

Susan Sered

New York   Oxford

Oxford University Press

1999

Oxford University Press

Oxford   New York
Athens   Auckland   Bangkok   Bogotá   Buenos Aires   Calcutta
Cape Town   Chennai   Dar es Salaam   Delhi   Florence   Hong Kong   Istanbul
Karachi   Kuala Lumpur   Madrid   Melbourne   Mexico City   Mumbai
Nairobi   Paris   São Paulo   Singapore   Taipei   Tokyo   Toronto   Warsaw

and associated companies in
Berlin   Ibadan

Copyright © 1999 by Susan Sered

Published by Oxford University Press, Inc.
198 Madison Avenue, New York, New York 10016

Oxford is a registered trademark of Oxford University Press

Library of Congress Cataloging-in-Publication Data
Sered, Susan Starr.
Women of the sacred groves : divine priestesses of Okinawa / Susan Sered.
p.   cm.
Includes bibliographical references and index.
ISBN 0-19-512486-3; ISBN 0-19-512487-1 (pbk.)
1. Women—Religious life—Japan—Okinawa-ken.
2. Okinawa-ken (Japan)—Religious life and customs.
3. Women priests—Japan—Okinawa-ken.   I. Title.
BL2215.04S46   1999
299'.56—DC21   98-17673

9 8 7 6 5 4 3 2 1

Printed in the United States of America
on acid-free paper

Preface

The Ryukyus are a chain of some seventy islands located where the Pacific Ocean meets the East China Sea, south of Japan and east of China. The largest and best known of the Ryukyu Islands is Okinawa—famous for the bloody battles fought there between the American and Japanese armies during World War II.

The Ryukyu Islands are the only known place in the world where women lead the official religion. Women are the acknowledged religious leaders within the home, within the clan, within the village, and—until the dismantling of the Ryukyuan Kingdom by Japan approximately 100 years ago—within the kingdom.

In 1994 and 1995 my family and I lived on Henza, a small island off the coast of Okinawa. We came to Henza to find out firsthand what it is like to live in a culture where women communicate with and embody the divine on behalf of the entire community of men and women. This book is my attempt to share with Western readers a culture which, in many ways, turns on its head some of the most basic paradigms of our own culture.

I thank the residents of Henza for allowing me to live in their village and for teaching me about their culture. I especially thank the *noro* and *kaminchu* who permitted me to attend their rituals.

I wish to express my gratitude to Teigo Yoshida of Tokyo for his ongoing encouragement and advice and for helping arrange my trip to Okinawa. I also wish to thank Takashi Tsuha and Masanobu Akamine of the University of the Ryukyus for their help in choosing a field site, getting settled in Okinawa, and making sense of my data. Special thanks to Yoshimi Ando, also of the University of the Ryukyus, for working together with me in sorting through and analyzing the population records of Henza, for so kindly serving as my link to other Okinawan scholars since my return to Israel, and for his spirit of true collegiality. Kurayoshi Takara, a historian at the University of the Ryukyus, spent hours teaching me about Okinawan history and generously helped me overcome the disadvantages of not being able to read many of the relevant historical sources.

With insight and laughter, Fran Markowitz discussed this manuscript with me. Judith Plaskow's encouragement and suggestions were immensely helpful. I thank Teigo Yoshida, Kaja Finkler, Laurel Kendall, Patrick Beillevaire, Dafna Izraeli, Sam Cooper, Pamela Feldman, Diane Jonte-Pace, Judith Lorber, David Murray, and Harvey Goldberg for reading and commenting on the manuscript. Special thanks to Eyal Ben-Ari for so generously sharing bibliographies, contacts, and ideas.

I extend my sincere thanks and love to my Okinawan family, Kuni and Kanshun Okutara. I am grateful to Kumi Yamada for her assistance with the fieldwork. Thank you to Noriko Goeku for her friendship and for helping my family survive in a new environment. I will never forget you.

And to my Israeli family—Yishai, Barak, Yoav, Asher, and Shifra—I offer my admiration and appreciation for their courage in accompanying me to a remote island.

Portions of some of the chapters in this book have appeared elsewhere in different form. Part of chapter 11 has appeared in the *Journal of the American Academy of Religion*; part of chapter 7 has appeared in *Ethos*.

This project was funded by the Israel Foundation Trustees, the Japan Foundation, and Bar Ilan University's Research Authority.

All photographs are my own.

S. S.

Jerusalem
January 1998

Contents

Appendixes

Women of the Sacred Groves

Introduction

Eight middle-aged and elderly women enter the *kami-ya* (village shrine). They sit on tatami mats on the floor and chat. Gradually, the conversation ceases. One of the women instructs a male assistant to light incense and place it on the altar. This woman, flanked on either side by her associates, turns toward the set of three rocks arranged on the altar and pours sake (rice wine) over the rocks. All of the women kneel, press their hands together, and quietly murmur prayers. The eight women then file outside, where a bus provided by the town hall drives them to the beginning of a trail that leads into the jungle. They begin their ascent, single file, the male assistant walking in front in order to clear away vines and look out for poisonous *habu* snakes. After fifteen minutes of steady climbing, they pause at a clearing. The male assistant walks on. The women take out five-piece white robes from the bags they have been carrying and quietly don the robes. *The eight kami-sama* continue their trek into the increasingly dark jungle, finally reaching the sacred grove. There are two stone benches where they sit and weave crowns of leaves and vines to put on their heads. One of the kami-sama goes further into the sacred grove, stopping at a small stone altar on which rest six conch shells. She squats in front of the shells, prays briefly, and "feeds" rice and sake into the opening of each shell. She then joins her fellow kami-sama at the benches, taking her place on the center seat. The male assistant pours sake for each kami-sama; they pray briefly and quietly. The eight kami-sama rise and begin their journey back to the bus. The bus driver takes them to the edge of the village, and the kami-sama walk to the village square, where they are met by clan members and by the village headman, who bows and pours sake for each kami-sama. Clanswomen provide food and drink for the kami-sama. After a small meal the kami-sama rise, take off the white robes and hang the crowns of leaves on special nails in the village square.* Eight middle-aged and elderly women then walk home to prepare food for their families, to weed their vegetable gardens, and to do their housework.

---

*The Japanese word *kami* is usually translated as 'god'. However, since *kami* encompasses a much larger range of meanings than does the English 'god', I prefer to translate it loosely as 'divinity' or 'spiritual energy' (cf. Kitagawa 1987: 44–45). *Sama* is an honorary suffix added to names or titles.

The power of patriarchy—or of any other strongly embedded hierarchical form of cultural organization—lies less in specific expressions of inequality than in the taken-for-grantedness of that inequality. Patriarchy, as feminist scholars such as Mary Daly (1978) have explained, takes hold of consciousness, of thought patterns; it persuasively presents an oppressive status quo as natural, universal, biologically ordained, and inevitable. In the presentation of patriarchy as inescapable—as essentially good and right—religion has a crucial role. Religion, through emotionally compelling rituals and stories, constructs a view of reality from which it is nearly impossible to fully escape.

As an anthropologist who lives with and studies non-European societies, my own research efforts have been aimed at exploring religious cultures in which women are the leaders—the paradigm-builders and maintainers. Although most historical and contemporary religions are indeed governed by men, there are, scattered throughout the world, a small number of well-documented religions that are led by women. Examples include *zar* possession religion in Africa; matrilineal spirit religion of northern Thailand; *nat* religion in Myanmar (cited as Burma in the literature); shamanism in Korea; Sande secret societies in west Africa; ancestor religion among the Garifuna of Belize; Candomble and Macumba in Brazil; Christian Science, Shakers, and Spiritualism in the United States, Mexico, and Great Britain; the contemporary Feminist Spirituality movement; and the indigenous religion of Okinawa (Ryukyu Islands). These religions are dominated by women in the sense that the majority of members and leaders are women and that they are independent of any kind of overarching male-dominated institutional framework.[1]

Few if any traits are shared by all of these religions: leadership by women does not automatically lead to particular kinds of religious beliefs or rituals. As I argued in *Priestess, Mother, Sacred Sister: Religions Dominated by Women* (1994), this finding is consistent with the feminist and the social scientific understanding that gender patterns are culturally constructed and therefore vary from society to society. There is no reason to assume that women cross-culturally, any more than men cross-culturally, are attracted to certain religious modes as a function of their biological sex.

There is, however, a structural position shared by all but one of these women's religions. With the exception of the indigenous religion of Okinawa (Ryukyu Islands), all known religions led by women are comprised only of women and/or are considered marginal, subordinate, or secondary in the societies in which they are located. Only on the Ryukyu Islands do women lead the official mainstream religion—Okinawan women are the acknowledged and respected leaders of the publicly supported and publicly funded indigenous religion in which both men and women participate.[2] Okinawa is the only known society in which women's religious endeavors are neither reactive to nor a consequence of those of men; men do not oversee, define, circumscribe, or persecute women's religious leadership in Okinawa. For this reason, Okinawan ethnography is an especially intriguing case study of the intersection of gender and religion.

This book looks in depth at one Okinawan village, Henza, in an effort to understand the links among religious beliefs, gender roles, and other aspects of community life. I make no claim that Henza is a 'typical' Okinawan village. Indeed, villagers enjoy talking about the ways in which Henza is different from other Okinawan villages—most particularly in terms of Henza's scant and meager supply of land and the resulting dependence upon the ocean for subsistence. Despite this disclaimer, in many (but not all) matters, my findings are consistent with those of anthropologists who have studied other Okinawan villages.

In Okinawan villages such as Henza, priestesses (*noro* and *kaminchu*) perform rituals on behalf of the community. Some of these rituals take place in the jungle, in the sacred grove, where villagers cannot see. Other rituals take place at the village square, in full sight of the community, and with the assistance of the village headman. Each clan has several priestesses who pray for the clan at public and private ceremonies. Within the household, the senior woman is responsible for rites directed toward the household kami-sama. In addition, a variety of independent practitioners—*ogami* (prayer) people and *yuta* (shaman-type practitioners)—communicate with kami-sama and ancestors on behalf of village families. These practitioners, almost all of whom are women, include both unpaid lay grandmothers and well-paid professionals.

Over the centuries, women's religious preeminence in Okinawa has endured through a range of political structures and political changes: decentralized villages, warring feudal chiefdoms, a centralized monarchy, occupation by a foreign power, and annexation by another foreign power. It has survived extensive culture contact with Buddhist, Shinto, and Christian missionaries. And it has coexisted with Chinese ancestor worship, American cinemas, and Japanese schools (see Kerr 1958; Haring 1964). There does not seem to be one unique social or historical backdrop to women's religious leadership in Okinawa (or anywhere else).

Okinawan women's religious preeminence should not be treated as an unsullied bubble that hovers over shifting political and economic realities, however. Gendered religious roles can only be understood in the context of a variety of social and cultural patterns that compose a constantly changing, lived reality. My approach in this book is a three-pronged one: I treat rituals and ritual roles as constituted and shaped by long-standing cultural themes and patterns, by specific historically discernable social forces, and by the individual personalities of the particular people who perform the rituals and fill the roles at any given time (cf. Geertz 1973).

What elements of Okinawan social arrangements support, sustain, give form to, preserve, and inspire women's religious activity? How do Okinawan religion and other aspects of Okinawan social arrangements enhance, reflect, and conflict with one another? What other cultural or social elements have tended to cluster with women's religious preeminence? As we shall see in the chapters that follow, in Henza this cultural cluster includes village endogamy, extended male absence, a central role for women in subsistence work and commerce, lack of substantial inheritable property, marriage and childbirth patterns that enhance women's longevity, weak political structures, aversion to hierarchy and rules, and strong social integration among women. It is crucial, however, to clarify that other East and Southeast Asian societies are characterized by some or many of these same features (including significant religious roles for women; cf. Karim 1995; Errington 1990), and thus the presence of a religion led by women should not be seen as an automatic corollary to any specific social structural arrangement but rather as one part of a complex, multilayered, and nonstatic cultural configuration.

Henza cultural thinking and activity tend to mitigate against the reification of social and cosmological categories. Although certain rituals seem to play with the idea of construction and deconstruction of shifting dualistic structures, in village ideology male and female, death and life, leader and laity, good and bad, and human and kami-sama are not understood as natural or essential polarities. Divinity is not perceived as a discrete entity situated outside of everyday reality, but rather as a vague spiritual force potentially present anywhere. Divinity can be summoned into immediacy through ritual, and Henza culture includes a wide variety of old and new, communal and personal, formal and idiosyncratic rituals. In Henza, humans can be kami-sama, and human kami-sama can be plain old housewives; there is no ontological distinction between divine and human. The (Japanese) word which can be roughly translated as god (kami-sama) is neither masculine nor feminine, neither singular nor plural; and nothing in Henza liturgy or material culture serves to portray kami-sama as one or the other.

Despite its small population (approximately 1800), Henza is home to a large number of ritual leaders and experts, almost all women, whose various spheres of expertise and authority are not regulated or clearly delineated. In general, in Henza rules of social behavior are not codified or reified, and divergence—as long as it is not aggressive—is barely noticed. The notion of cosmic prohibition does not exist: When I naively tried to elicit a list of taboo foods from villagers, the closest they could come up with was "maybe poison."

Although Henza men and women tend to engage in different activities, villagers do not describe this arrangement as existentially meaningful, universal, or absolute. Men who wear women's clothing at rituals elicit no social response, nor do women who take on roles that are usually filled by men. In Henza, the reality of women's religious leadership demands no explanation, interpretation, excuse, or mystification. Concurrently, although most political leadership is in the hands of men, the reality of men's political leadership is not bolstered or justified via gender beliefs or rules.

Nonhierarchical complementarity—including gender complementarity—is a pervasive pattern in Henza ritual, social life, and cosmology. In a variety of contexts, villagers explain that the living help their ancestors and the ancestors help the living, that men go to sea and women work on the farms and that both are necessary, and that there are both male and female kami-sama just as there are male and female people. Many Henza rituals strive toward social and cosmic harmony, toward smoothing out or clearing up rough spots, and toward dramatizing themes of complementarity and balance.

Doing Gender

Feminist scholarship has devoted a great deal of attention to deconstructing sex and gender as natural or universally constituted categories. Although this literature is, by now, familiar to most anthropologists, I wish to clarify how I use the term 'gender' throughout this book.[3] Gender is not an immutable fact of life or state of being, but rather an expression of social processes. What Judith Lorber (1994) and Sherry Ortner (1996) call "doing gender" or "making gender" begins with the cultural construction and acknowledgment of conceptualizations that designate essential differences. These differences are most often thought to be biological (what we call sex) and tend to be perceived as dichotomous (Harding 1986). Perceived essential differences are potentially gravitational, drawing to themselves—gendering—other sorts of cultural material. This process can be thought of as the naturalization of gender through reference to supposedly immutable biological characteristics. To take a somewhat extreme example of doing gender, Maurice Godelier explains that among the New Guinea Baruya:

> The differences of form, substance, and bodily function, the anatomical and physiological differences that arise from the different functions of the sexes in the process of the reproduction of life—supplies a steady stream of material from which are fashioned the messages and explanations that serve to interpret and justify the social inequalities between men and women. It is as if sexuality were constantly being solicited to occupy every nook and cranny of society, to act as a language to express, and as a reason to legitimize, the facts of a (mainly) different order. (1986: xii)

The amount and content of gendered material varies from culture to culture. In some cultures (such as Okinawa), very few traits are recognized as gendered; only external genitalia or pregnancy are perceived and acknowledged as essential differences, whereas other attributes and roles, even if they sometimes tend to be associated with men or with women, are understood to be temporal or local rather than essential. In other cultures (like the Baruya of New Guinea), many traits are gendered—are associated with or assimilated into a perceived core of essential and dichotomous difference. A well-known expression of the latter pattern is found among the East Asian cultures that elaborate upon and find meaning in the yin-yang dichotomy. In these cultures, categories of perceived essential differences seem to have the power to attract myriad symbols, attributes, and roles, making them look as if they are biological, inherently meaningful, and dichotomous.[4]

Differences that are envisioned as being absolute (for example, black and white or good and bad) are particularly compelling; binary distinctions leave no gray area, no room for doubt, and no room to negotiate. The construction of two and only two sexes or genders leads to cultural understandings in which men and women are not only essentially different but also antithetical and mutually exclusive types of beings. A popular form of this kind of thinking is represented in contemporary American culture by books like *Men Are from Mars, Women Are from Venus* (Gray 1992) in which men and women are characterized as species from different planets who need an interpreter in order to learn how to communicate with one another![5]

The perception and acknowledgment of differences that are believed to be rooted in nature (naturalized differences) are a precondition for hierarchy—for systematic, permanent distinctions in access to power and prestige. If everyone is the same, there is no basis out of which hierarchy can develop or be sustained. The more that differences are perceived to be absolute and natural, the more forceful and self-sustaining the hierarchy. As Elizabeth Colson explains, "Hierarchy implies something institutionalized which governs relationships *over time* between individuals who *consistently* accept placement in a system of ranking . . . it involves *legitimation* as well as pecking order" (1993: xv–xvi; my emphases).

In the case of gender hierarchies, gender ideology provides that legitimation. Peggy Reeves Sanday defines gender ideology in this way:

> Ideology refers both to a system of thought that guides and legitimates social action and to attempts to create a transcendental order by legitimating the power of that order. . . . Viewed in these terms, gender ideology can be defined as (1) the system of thought that legitimates sex roles and customary behavior of the sexes, and (2) the deployment of gender categories as metaphors in the production of conceptions of an enduring, eternal social order. (1990: 6)

Gender ideologies are ideologies of difference that elaborate and legitimate the attribution of a range of traits, roles, and statuses either to men or to women. Gender ideologies are how societies establish and justify the links between bodies, laws, emotions, customs, and behaviors; between sex and gender. We can ask how strong, how compelling, how total, and how persuasive the ideological links are in specific societies. In the late-nineteenth- and early-twentieth-century United States, for example, the thick link between sex and gender was reflected in medical, political, and religious discourses that claimed that voting and higher education are "naturally" male activities and liable to cause gynecological malfunction in women. Women who did not adapt to contemporary gender patterns ran the risk of being subjected to gynecological surgery intended to correct their "abnormal" bodies (Ehrenreich and English 1979). In Okinawa, as I shall show in this book, the ideological bonds linking gender to sex are exceptionally thin.

Cross-culturally, people and groups of people tend to be ranked according to intangible social or religious values (like purity or sacredness) that transcend, encompass, and outlast day-to-day and tangible political or economic realities (Dumont 1970). Drawing upon the ideas of Louis Dumont, Sherry Ortner argues that gender is first and foremost a prestige system—a system that is, by its very nature, hierarchical and encompassing vis-à-vis other principles of social organization. According to Ortner, "Gender is . . . a system of discourses and practices that constructs male and female not only in terms of differential roles and meanings but also in terms of differential *value*, differential 'prestige' (1996: 143)."[6]

Because strong and long-lasting gender hierarchies are prestige systems that rest upon persuasive ideologies, we can easily understand why so many cultures augment naturalizing gender ideologies with religious beliefs in the gendered order of the cosmos, beliefs in gendered creation, beliefs in divine decree regarding sexuality and sex roles, and beliefs that define purity and pollution, good and evil, and sacred and profane in gendered terms. Cross-culturally, gender is likely to be reified both through reference to immutable biological characteristics and through reference to cosmically ordained religious ideologies. The "natural" and the "su-

pernatural" serve as complementary tools for naturalizing and sanctifying difference, prestige, and hierarchy.

Okinawan religion is unusual in that it does not embrace or advance an elaborated gender ideology. Male-dominated religions typically devote a great deal of effort to idealizing men's superiority and women's religious subordination: Women
are less rational (Islam), women are more tied to this world because of their role as
mothers (Buddhism), women are the cause of original sin (Christianity), women
are polluted because of menstruation and childbirth (Hinduism and some Japanese religions), and women are by definition private rather than public beings (Judaism). These ideological efforts, one could argue, are necessary to counteract the
empirically observable reality that women and men are far more similar than different and to rationalize the truly irrational male dominance of social institutions.
These ideologies play key roles in creating and upholding the prestige systems that
we call gender.

Women-led religions also tend to devote a great deal of energy to idealizing
women's religious leadership: The northern Thai believe that women have softer
souls that are easier for the spirits to penetrate (Tanabe 1991), members of Afro-
Brazilian religions surmise that men's involvement with money and alcohol
interferes with their spiritual prowess (Lerch 1982), and Spiritualists interpret
women's suffering as making them more sensitive to spiritual forces (Moore 1977:
121). Attention to gender ideology, to explaining why women can be religiously
dominant, is a crucial reactive task in cultural situations in which the official
and normative religion is dominated by men (as it is in Brazil, Thailand, and so
forth). This task is unnecessary in Okinawa, and Henza villagers are surprised—
sometimes to the point of disbelief that such gender differentiation exists—when
asked why all their religious leaders are women. Villagers offer no ideology to promote or enforce gendered social roles. *Kami-sama* are not called upon as arbiters of
gender arrangements.

Judith Lorber has astutely argued that the paradox of gender is its ubiquitousness; it is hard to find a society that does not create gender as a cultural category
and infuse it with singular potency. Societies seem to need to work hard *not* to reify
gender. As I show throughout this book, a noteworthy pattern in Henza culture is
the ritual construction followed by the ritual deconstruction of dualities. In a variety of settings, binary categories—like male and female—are very obviously and
artificially created, only to be shattered. That villagers repeatedly see dualities publicly constructed and deconstructed seems to serve as a kind of prophylactic
against the naturalization of hierarchical differences that occurs in so many other
cultures.

The ritual described at the beginning of this introduction is a key example: Before the eyes of villagers, women both become and unbecome *kami-sama*, a ritual
process that deconstructs any notion that there may be ontological differences between human and divine. To take another example, as we shall see in detail in
chapter 12, for the annual tug-of-war ritual (*tsuna-hiki*), the village that for other
purposes is divided into five hamlets temporarily divides itself into a male half and
a female half, a division that has no relevance in any sphere of life except the tug-
of-war (for example, there are no marriage rules regarding parts of the village, no

subsistence patterns or stereotypical personality traits regarding halves of the village, and so forth). One rope is supposedly male and one is supposedly female, but the difference is far from obvious—the "female" rope has a slightly larger loop at the end. Henza villagers explain the success of the winning team in terms of how many people on each team came to pull in a particular year, rather than in terms of any sort of biological or cosmological factor.[7] I see these and other rituals as devices for playing with categories such as gender: for putting gender on and taking it off, and thus mitigating against its naturalization. These rituals defuse the pull of sex-gender gravity.

In a broader sense, I suspect that Henza villagers are intrigued not only by the making and unmaking of gender but also by other manifestations of order and disorder. A variety of rituals express some sort of concern with situations characterized by too much structure; these rituals experiment with and ultimately deconstruct order, categories, and structure. Concurrently, disordered situations seem to be experienced both as problematic and in need of ritual treatment and as spaces in which growth and transformation—and especially spiritual growth and transformation—are possible. The embrace of disorder as a socially and cosmically positive state nourishes the absence of reified social categories in Henza.

How This Book Is Organized

The first section introduces what I call "divine dis-order"—the easygoing interactions, porous social boundaries, and minimal rules and hierarchy—that characterize Henza's social ethos. I use the hyphenated "dis-order" not in a negative sense but to indicate the absence of rigidity in the social order in Henza. Following Clifford Geertz, I use the word "ethos" to mean "the tone, character and quality of [a people's] life, its moral and aesthetic style and mood; it is the underlying attitude toward themselves and their world that life reflects" (1973: 127). It is, of course, axiomatic to contemporary anthropological thinking that individuals and groups, in varying ways, embrace or resist the multitudinous patterns that comprise a culture's ethos. However, diversity does not nullify the tendency of cultures to emphasize and define themselves in terms of certain clusters of attitudes, conceptualizations, relationships, and ideals. Given the sustained and often forceful culture contact that Okinawa has had with China, Japan, and the United States, I would not expect all aspects of Okinawan culture to fit snugly into one overarching ethos. Still, I do think that a society, such as Henza, which maintains a discrete identity and sense of cultural integrity, is able to absorb foreign or new elements into its own ethos and to reject, modify, or reinterpret elements that are strongly inconsistent with that ethos. It is in this multidimensional and dynamic sense that I, like Geertz, use the notion of cultural ethos.

Chapter 1 explores the theme of divine dis-order in terms of interpersonal relationships and village social organization. Villagers share a group identity of being *yasashii*. This term, in Henza, is used in broader ways than in standard Japanese, where yasashii simply means 'easy' or 'gentle'. For Henza villagers, being yasashii encodes easygoingness, nonviolence, having a "good heart," avoiding quarrels

and conflict, not being pushy or having strong opinions, and tolerance of difference. These personality traits reflect and are reflected in a variety of social stances
and cosmological beliefs. For example, villagers almost never say that a certain behavior or opinion is absolutely right or wrong, there are no taboos, and hierarchy
is usually temporary, and insignificant. People are believed to be naturally good
and healthy, villagers rarely complain about ill health, and life expectancy is unusually long.

Chapter 2 considers divine dis-order on cosmological planes and explores villagers'unsystematized and noncompulsory understanding of *kami-sama*. Kami-
sama are felt to be totally immanent, and villagers describe no ontological distinction between humans and kami. Kami-sama are never depicted by villagers as
powerful. Power over others is neither respected in social and political relationships nor worshipped in kami. The kami do not make rules for behavior or punish
or reward people. All kami are understood to have the same rank—there is no
"chief" kami. Although some kami are thought to be male and some to be female,
there is neither content nor meaning associated with kami's gender identity; male
and female kami do not have male or female roles or personalities. Villagers seem
to hold a vague belief that both male and female kami, like male and female people, are necessary, but this ideology is not particularly elaborated upon.

The three successive chapters address questions of gender. In chapter 3, I
demonstrate that not very much is done in Henza to "make" gender and that
whatever gender differences villagers acknowledge tend to be explained in terms of
socialization rather than of nature. Although men and women typically do different jobs, there is a great deal of flexibility; men sometimes do jobs that women usually do, and vice versa. Marriage is fairly loose, and virginity is not considered a
value. Villagers sometimes say that "men are boss," but male dominance—such as
it is—seems to be limited to the formal political domain. Men hold political leadership roles, but the Henza village council and headman in actual fact have very little power. The fundamental gender pattern in Henza is one of complementarity.

In chapter 4, I suggest that women more than men are involved in extensive
and intensive forms of social integration. In chapter 5, I analyze men's subsistence
and ritual roles in terms of the motifs of death and absence, and women's subsistence and ritual roles in terms of motifs of food and presence. These constellations,
villagers explain, are a result of specific historical and economic forces; they are
not intrinsically male or female traits.

The discussion of women and presence in chapter 5 leads to closer considera-
tion of the priestess role which I interpret as the embodiment or actualization of
divine presence. The third part of the book examines the priestesses: who they are,
what they do, how they fit into the general cosmology of the village. Chapter 6 is a
descriptive chapter that details what happens at priestesses' rituals. I explain that
the word most commonly used for priestess is kami-sama and that this usage
should be understood literally: There is no ontological difference between kami-
sama and humans—the priestesses are embodied kami-sama. A subtheme in this
chapter is the pivotal role of food in rituals that enhance relations among people
and between people and the cosmos. Chapter 7 considers how priestesses become
kami-sama; I present three narratives in which priestesses tell how they came to

take on their ritual role. In their narratives, illness—divine dis-order (*kamidaari*)—is both a sign that one is meant to sit the priestess role and a means of opening oneself up to a sort of fusion with kami-sama. Chapter 8 follows the experiences of one woman who was initiated as a priestess during the year that I was in the village. Her experiences illustrate the gradual process of becoming kami-sama.

The fourth section of the book addresses questions of power. Chapter 9 offers a theoretical look at issues of power and religious leadership. Perhaps because the very meaning of being a priestess—being kami-sama—is potentially problematic in a society that avoids allowing power to be accumulated in the hands of any particular category of people or *kami*, many aspects of the priestesses' rituals deconstruct power in various ways. Chapter 10 brings in other ritual actors—*yuta* (shaman-type practitioners) and *ogami* (prayer) people—paying particular attention to the ways in which power is diffused among priestesses and other ritual actors.

The final section opens up broader questions that arise from the intersection of gender and religion in Henza. Chapter 11, the pivotal chapter in the book, presents a series of conversations, incidents, rituals, and anecdotes in which villagers showed me that they do not recognize—or perhaps that they do not wish to recognize—gender as a salient cultural category. When villagers were asked why priestesses are women or why headmen are men, their answers were consistently situational, sociological, or trivial; ideological or naturalizing reasons were never offered. Chapter 12 looks at a series of examples of "gender bending," playing with gender, and the deconstruction of gender as a social category.

A brief overview of Okinawan history, an introduction to Henza, and a note on methodology are found in the prologue. A glossary and "cast of characters" are found in the appendix. For the reader who is interested in parallels between Okinawan and Japanese culture, I have included some references and explanations in the end notes.[8]

In this book, I look at ideology, social relationships, family relationships, village organization, age and aging, ideas about illness and health, cognitive categories, socialization of children, subsistence work, and the life stories of religious leaders, as well as at more ephemeral aspects of the cultural ethos.[9] Because Henza religion is embedded within other social frameworks and forces, I am convinced that all of this is necessary for us to understand Henza religion as it is lived by real people in a real village in the 1990s. Yet I see the ultimate significance of this book as lying beyond Okinawa or even Asia. Like other social scientists, I understand religion to be a linchpin that holds social life together; religious ritual has the extraordinary power to make forms or ideas seem "really" real or true (Geertz 1973). If, as many would like to believe, God is in His heaven and all is right in His world, current patterns of oppression appear to be both immutable and benign (Daly 1973). A case study, even of a small village like Henza, provides proof that male dominance of the religious sphere is not universal, not axiomatic, and not necessary. Henza villagers offer an alternative vision of a world uncolored by assumptions about God the Father who creates, commands, and punishes His children and a renewed hope that women and men can move beyond the hierarchical paradigms that oppress the spirit and constrain the imagination.

Okinawan History, Henza Village, and Methodology

The following overview of Okinawan history is intended to give the reader a context for the ethnographic material presented in this book; it is in no way meant to be comprehensive.

Okinawan history is somewhat well known from the fifteenth century on. A great deal of information has been gleaned from letters and reports of Chinese and Japanese visitors. A primary source of information about Okinawan culture is the *Omoro Sooshi*, a collection of songs and rituals written down in the sixteenth and seventeenth centuries in the Okinawan language using a phonetic Japanese script (see Drake 1995 for a more detailed discussion of the *Omoro sooshi*).

Until approximately the fourteenth century, the Ryukyu Islands, including Okinawa, seem to have been characterized by small, autonomous communities, each of which may or may not have had a chieftain or head priestess. Gradually, on the main island of Okinawa, these autonomous and sometimes warring communities were consolidated into three kingdoms: north, south, and central. In the fifteenth century, the central kingdom headquartered in the town of Shuri extended its rule over the entire island and then over the rest of the Ryukyu Island chain.

In the Ryukyu Kingdom, a male descendant of the first king was the political leader; a female relative (typically his sister) was the chief priestess (Takara 1994). The rank and prestige of the chief priestess (*kikoe okimi*) were nearly equal to that of the king. One act of the new central government was to institute a system of noro priestesses, one in each village, who served as links between the villages and the central government. The noro typically did not come from the founding kin group of the village but rather from a family with links to the Shuri government (W. Lebra 1966: 109). It was the noro's task to bring the first fruits of the rice, wheat, millet, and sweet potato harvests to a regional religious leader, who then brought them to Shuri (W. Lebra 1966: 115). The noro was given land of her own, and although she had children, she did not marry. Household and kin group priestesses did not become absorbed into the centralized noro system, nor did a variety of other ritual practitioners. The rituals and songs of village and clan priestesses were not unified under the kikoe okimi (Drake 1995).

The ruling family in Shuri had close links with China and Japan.[1] These links were, to varying extents, both voluntary and involuntary. As a small island chain located between two major powers, Ryukyuans had no choice but to pay tribute, both politically and through taxation, to China and Japan. At the same time, the Shuri government embraced certain aspects of foreign, especially Chinese, culture. The upper classes imported Chinese ancestor worship and Buddhism, "but there is little evidence that the practice of these imported rituals was known beyond the Shuri-Naha complex of settlements. Throughout the countryside and on the adjacent islands the ancient pantheism and rituals of the *noro* priestesses remained predominant" (Kerr 1958: 110). Although the royal class provided some support for Buddhist temples, there was no wide base in popular support (Kerr 1957: 219).

During the early years of the Ryukyuan Kingdom, trade with cities and countries throughout Asia was extensive. In the seventeenth century, in the wake of changes in Japanese society, the Satsuma clan of Kyushu (southern Japan) obtained control over Okinawa's ocean trade, foreign affairs, and certain aspects of internal administration. Villages became hard pressed to pay taxes, and, whereas sea-based work had been central in the subsistence economies of many islands and villages, "domestic agriculture assumed paramount importance in Okinawa after 1610" (Kerr 1957: 169). Most land was owned communally by the village, and each village as a whole had an assigned quota of agricultural products to provide. "This system of accepted mutual obligations has left its stamp upon the Okinawan character, for it fostered a deep sense of social obligation, of group responsibility in maintaining the welfare of community members who suffered economic hardship" (Kerr 1957: 196–197). Under the Satsuma, the power of the Ryukyuan king and chief noro were gradually eroded, and Confucian rites and ceremonies were promoted. Efforts—for the most part unsuccessful—were made to undermine the autonomy of the local priestesses.[2]

In 1879, Japan officially annexed Okinawa, bringing about a number of changes in Okinawa's economic structure. Rice and subsistence agricultural land was rapidly converted into cash-crop sugarcane fields, and Japanese businessmen held a monopoly on the sale of sugarcane and on the sale of wholesale goods for the Okinawan market. In 1989, a Temporary Land Readjustment Bureau was created with the mandate to convert the traditional communal land (nearly 76 percent of the total land) to private ownership, and lands assigned to support village noro became the private property of the noro's family, registered in the name of the male "head of household." As a result of losing their land, most noro are now married.

Schools were built, and during the twentieth century formal education became widespread in the villages. The educational system took the lead in the program of Japanization of Okinawan culture (Kerr 1957:47). Because of high population density on Okinawa and the lack of lucrative natural resources, the Japanese government encouraged migration to the outer Ryukyu Islands and to other countries. Extensive migration significantly disrupted the traditional household structure in the villages during the twentieth century. Although many aspects of Japanese culture did catch on, state Shinto was not welcomed by Okinawans.

World War II was a turning point for Okinawa. "No prefecture contributed so little to the preparation for war and its prosecution through the years, but none suffered as much in widespread misery, in loss of human lives and property, and in ultimate subservience to military occupation" (Kerr 1957: 463). During the bloody battle for Okinawa, fought between Americans and Japanese on the backs of Okinawans, the majority of Okinawans killed were civilians. The American occupation, beginning after World War II and lasting until 1972, was a time of economic stagnation for Okinawa. Since its reversion to Japan, the economy has picked up, yet Okinawa continues to lag behind other Japanese prefectures in terms of economic development. Currently, the United States military occupies 20.1 percent of Okinawa Island (Okinawa Prefectural Government 1993). Despite the continuing American military presence (or perhaps because of it), ties to Japanese cultural institutions have been strengthened, and Okinawans, to some extent, identify themselves as Japanese (on Okinawan ethnic identification, see Angst 1996; on Okinawan attitudes toward Japan and the United States, see Taira 1997).

The origin of women's religious dominance in Okinawa is lost in the mythical mists of time, and a detailed historical investigation is outside the parameters of this study. Still, I do wish to point to contemporary nat worship in Myanmar, matrilineal spirit cults of northern Thailand, shamanism in Korea, and women *miko* in Japan as possible remainders of more extensive women's religious roles throughout Southeast Asia, Korea, and Japan, roles that contracted when and where either Buddhism or Confucianism was adopted as the state religion (Yusa 1984; Kim 1982; Furnivall 1911; Spiro 1967; Cohen and Wijeyewardene 1984).[3] Although Buddhism reached Okinawa as early as the mid-thirteenth century and was later given royal patronage, Buddhist priests made little effort to propagate Buddhism among the common people. As I said previously, when the Ryukyu Islands were unified into the Ryukyuan Kingdom, village priestesses were incorporated into the centralized *noro* framework. As a result, in Okinawa, Buddhism competed with a highly organized, kingdomwide system of priestesses structurally able to withstand foreign religious domination.[4] Beginning in the seventeenth century, the Satsuma fostered Confucianism in Okinawa (Sakihara 1981). During the twentieth century, Christian missionaries of various denominations have endeavored to convert the local population, and Japan continues to encourage the establishment of Shinto shrines. The Ryukyuan Kingdom and the centralized *noro* system have disappeared, yet world religions continue to make little impact in Okinawa, and women continue to predominate as village and clan priestesses (Anzai 1976).[5]

Introducing Henza

Henza Island, located fairly close to the east coast of the main island of Okinawa, is home to one village—also called Henza—built along the southwestern shore. The rest of the rather mountainous and jungle-covered island has been rented out for the last thirty years as storage space to a Japanese oil company. Although villagers continue to envision themselves as living on a poor and isolated island, that picture reflects past rather than present reality. Because of rental revenues, many villagers nowadays are relatively affluent, and transportation to the main island of Okinawa has improved significantly. Village architecture shows the recent change from a subsistence to a cash economy; approximately half of village houses are traditional wooden shacks, whereas the other half are modern, cement structures. Houses are built close together on a few streets running parallel along the coast.

Henza is a coral island, and the land is not especially good for agriculture, although women do seem able to coax several annual crops out of even the smallest gardens. Village women continue to farm on garden patches located in or near the village; in the past, gardens were spread over the entire island. Traditionally, village men were fishermen or seafarers, and many older village men spent months or years away from the village. Nowadays, as a result of overfishing during the American occupation and of the attraction of safer land-based jobs, few village men go out to sea.[6] Still, fishing and seafaring remain central to Henzan identity.

Currently, there are approximately 1800 residents in Henza. The village is divided into five neighborhoods, each of which elects representatives to the village council. In former days, the village was divided into three neighborhoods, east, west, and center. The village council and headman (elected, rotating roles) are responsible for administering rental money from the oil company, for arranging villagewide rituals and events, and for keeping track of who lives in the village. Villages like Henza constitute the smallest type of unit in the Japanese political system. The village headman has no power outside of the village; he does not represent the village at the level of the district or prefecture.

Villagers market both fish and agricultural products through a cooperative organization. There are close to thirty small grocery stores in the village, providing part-time employment for many village women, and the current headman has made efforts to prevent a large supermarket from moving into the village. A post office and postal bank are located in the village, and the small grocery stores carry a fairly wide range of products. To go to the doctor, dentist, or bank or to buy clothes, furniture, or tools, villagers must go off the island. The headman was not able to give me an estimate of what percent of village income is generated by the oil company, but he told me that the village receives 400 million yen (approximately $4 million) annually in rent. According to the original contract signed in 1968 between the oil company and Henza, the annual rent was $100,000.

A school has been located in the village for nearly 100 years; schooling was one of the earliest Japanese cultural elements to have been embraced in the village. The sole language of instruction in the school is Japanese, and young villagers no longer speak fluent Okinawan. Middle-aged and elderly villagers speak both Japanese and Okinawan. There are very few professionals in the village; almost no village members attend or have attended college. On the other hand, all villagers know how to read, and many are interested in politics and culture.

Village endogamy has been and continues to be normative. The village ideal (although not always the reality) is to live in patrilocal households, in which the eldest son inherits the house and the role of caring for the ancestors. In fact, most village household arrangements diverge from the ideal. In Henza, as in the rest of Okinawa, birth rates are high, divorce rates are high, and life expectancy is long. Many village households consist of one elderly woman or of grandparents, an adult daughter, and her children. Every Henza house has a *hinu-kan*—shrine of the hearth deity—in the kitchen; the senior woman of the household is responsible for praying at the *hinu-kan*. Each household in which a member has died has a *butsudan*—a shelf on which is placed the *ihai* (tablets with names of patrilineal ancestors), and bowls for incense, drink, and food.[7]

The kami-ya—village shrine or 'god house' where priestesses carry out periodic rituals—is located in the center of the village, facing the village square. Certain rituals are carried out at sacred groves (*utaki*) located in the jungle on mountains in the areas now rented by the oil company and at other sacred sites such as springs and ports around the island.

Each Henza villager belongs to a *munchu*. Munchu, loosely translated as 'clan', comprise the descendants of an ancestor who lived a few hundred years ago. Typically, the ancestor is an important man who came from the north or south of Okinawa to live in Henza. Clan members know very little about their ancestors; older and more active clan members may know approximately when the clan founder came to the island and from where. Although munchu membership is through the male line, women serve as clan priestesses, and married women remain in their natal clans. The primary (and pretty much only) function of clans is to pray to clan ancestors on pre-set dates. Each clan has a clan house in which the ancestral altars are located. Nowadays, some of these houses stand empty except for ritual occasions.

Possibly the most telling observation that I can make about Henza's religious life is that it is omnipresent: Rituals, ritual preparations, altars, ritual experts, and spiritual experiences are key foci of village life. Almost every day it is possible to find some sort of public or semipublic ritual being performed in the village, in addition to the many private rituals that go on behind the scenes.

Okinawan rituals are historically very rich—often including ancient nature elements, Ryukyuan Kingdom elements, Chinese elements, and modern Japanese elements. Continued commitment to the Chinese lunar calendar (especially for ritual purposes), rather than the Japanese solar calendar, is a component of village identity. Holidays such as New Year that are shared with Japan are acknowledged briefly on the (Japanese) solar date but celebrated extensively on the lunar date.[8] Grave making, house building, and other private ceremonies are celebrated on days considered to be auspicious according to the Chinese calendar.

There seems to be a great deal of choice regarding when rituals are performed and even if they are performed at all. Indeed, it is rare to find two people who carry out exactly the same ritual repertoire. Similarly, the words of prayers are idiosyncratic; there is no formal liturgy, and each villager prays as he or she wishes. There is no ritual overseer in the village whose role it is to enforce conformity.

Villagers, including the ritual experts, usually cannot explain "the meaning" of rituals, although they find it interesting to speculate and look in reference books. In discussions of rituals, villagers are comfortable with ambiguity and obscurity. Henza's ritual world is not classified in any way, yet it does seem to me that there are several themes that appear again and again in a variety of forms in village ritual life.[9] Among the most prominent themes in Henza ritual are group solidarity (with the living and with the dead), bringing kami-sama into immediacy (for example, in the bodies of priestesses), dealing with out-of-place items, and the ritual deconstruction of cultural constructs. These themes are examined in detail throughout this book.

A variety of ritual experts are in Henza. The major categories are kaminchu (priestesses), yuta (similar to shamans, they mediate between villagers and ancestors or gods), ogami or "prayer" people (who represent or speak for villagers in a number of rituals), and male assistants to the priestesses.[10] Subsumed under the English word *priestess* or the Okinawan word *kaminchu* are several ritual roles. First, there is the noro—the chief priestess—who, during the time of the Ryukyuan Kingdom, was appointed by the Shuri government but now is distinguished because, in the words of villagers, she "is the one who does for the whole village [rather than for one clan]." The noro has a small group of associates—the village priestesses—who accompany her at all village rituals. In Henza there are four of these, each a member of a specific clan.[11]

One priestess from each of the approximately one dozen largest or oldest clans in the village accompanies the noro to the sacred grove and to the kami-ya (village 'god house') several times each year. Then there are the clan priestesses, known in Okinawan dialect as *ukuringwa*, of whom each clan has several. The clan priestesses pray at their clan houses on the first and fifteenth of each month and at other clan occasions such as memorial days and pilgrimages. The noro, her associates, and the clan priestesses are all referred to as kaminchu (literally, people who do "god things," kami people).

Today, as was most probably the case before the Ryukyuan Kingdom, priestesses of different villages have no relationship, hierarchical or otherwise, with one another. Each village has its own kami; the kami of one village have no reason to become involved with another village. According to what villagers told me, the Shuri government's noro system only reached Henza about 250 years ago, and with the dismantling of the kingdom 100 years ago it began to decline.[12] Thus, the centralized noro system should not be seen as the paradigmatic Henza religious pattern.

Villagers usually discuss history previous to the twentieth century in terms of the history of their own clans. According to local versions of village history, in the very distant past there were a small number of households on the island. During the period in which the Shuri government conquered the rest of Okinawa, other clans, particularly clans from the northern part of Okinawa, escaped to Henza and settled there. Most of the large clans in the village continue to maintain some sort of ritual link with the place from which their ancestors came. Changes during the twentieth century are more likely to be discussed on the village level: the erection of the first school building; the building of the causeway connecting the island to the mainland; the encouraging or forcing of villagers to serve in the Japanese army during World War II; emigration due to economic stresses; and the institution of the Japanese land registration system that resulted in priestesses losing their hereditary land. The villagers with whom I spoke were interested in discussing the ways in which global and Japanese political and social changes during the past hundred years have affected their lives, their rituals, their subsistence activities, and their household membership.[13]

Despite a large American military presence on the main island of Okinawa, only a few Henza islanders have had contact with the Americans. In general, villagers would like the Americans to leave Okinawa. Their feelings about Japan are more ambivalent: They recognize that the Japanese economy benefits them, they consider themselves Japanese citizens (which indeed they are), yet they retain a strong Okinawan identity. Even more than an Okinawan identity, they boast of a strong village identity, and villagers reiterate that Henza's dialect and customs are different from those of other Okinawan communities. I was told, for instance, that as a result of seafaring, Henza has been more influenced by Chinese culture than have many other Okinawan villages. In comparison to other islands of the Ryukyus and other villages on the main island of Okinawa, relatively few Henza residents have emigrated, and many traditional religious structures have been preserved, albeit often with changes in form and meaning. The new affluence of the village has had an impact on the importance that villagers accord to agricultural and other rituals.

Anthropologists who study Ryukyuan culture emphasize the high level of local variation (e.g., Mabuchi 1968: 138). Especially in recent years, the rate of cultural change has been uneven, affecting some areas more and some less, and affecting different villages in different ways. Villages and islands located farther than Henza from the urban sprawl of the main island of Okinawa have undergone drastic demographic changes, bringing in their wake transformations of household makeup, as many young people have left to look for jobs and a more modern lifestyle. In more urban areas, the priestess system has declined, and *yuta* are increasingly popular. My observations in Henza may differ even from observations made by anthropologists in other, rather similarly situated, Ryukyuan islands and villages, both because as a woman anthropologist I had access to certain events not open to men anthropologists and lacked access to other events that may have been more accessible to men anthropologists, and also because villages do indeed differ from one another. The centralization of the noro system did not, as I pointed out earlier, entail uniformity in ritual performance. It is, of course, axiomatic that my own research agenda and life experiences affected my choice of events to observe, the way in which I saw those events, and how I interpreted them. (References to studies of other Okinawan villages are included in the end notes).

Methodology

The ethnographic material presented in this book was collected during 1994–1995, when my family and I lived in Okinawa. Nine months of that year we lived in Henza; during the other three months, we visited Henza for major rituals and observed rituals in other villages on the main island of Okinawa. In the summer of 1996 and again in February 1998, I returned to Henza for another two months.

My primary research goal was to spend as much time as possible with the priestesses in order to explore their role in rituals and in daily life and in order to gain insight into their own understanding of their role. During the year, I interviewed at length (and often more than once) each individual in the village who had some sort of religious leadership role. I collected over a dozen life histories of priestesses, shaman-type practitioners (yuta and ogami people), and other ritual experts. Many of these interviews I conducted together with an interpreter, Kumi Yamada, who grew up in a nearby village and who has relatives living in Henza. A great deal of my time in the field was spent attending the many public and private rituals that took place in the village. The rituals that I was privileged to see included funerary rituals, ancestor rituals, clan rituals, agricultural rituals, fishing rituals, New Year's rituals, *obon* rituals, and a ritual for the initiation of a new priestess, among others.

On a daily basis, I circulated through the village, chatting with people in the streets and often being invited into their homes. In these daily perambulations, I frequently was accompanied by Mr. Kanshun Okutara, my colleague, adopted grandfather, and dear friend. Mr. Okutara, now eighty years old, is a native of Henza, lived in Chicago for thirty years, and was willing to use his excellent English to help me out when my Japanese proved insufficient. Mr. Okutara is also an aficionado of Okinawan folklore and shared with me his vast knowledge of village history and folklore.

Living with my family in the village involved me in a range of day-to-day interactions, especially with the local nursery school that two of my children attended. A fair amount of my time was spent observing children's activities. My time with the children was balanced by the time I spent with the local senior citizen's club.

The headman made available to me village census records. With the help of Professor Yoshimi Ando, a sociologist at the University of the Ryukyus, I used the records to compile demographic data to which I refer in chapter 3.

Although I had studied Japanese before coming to the field, when I first arrived in Okinawa, my knowledge of Japanese was perfunctory; with the patience and encouragement of villagers, it improved throughout the year. Because of my initially weak language skills, I made great use of a tape recorder: I would record conversations and then listen to them again, sometimes with the aid of an interpreter. Working this way turned out to be fortuitous because it has allowed me to cite exact comments made by villagers rather than the types of summaries often found in ethnographies. Given that the intellectual context for this project is the study of religion and gender rather than Japanese studies, my less-than-rudimentary Japanese literacy has not proven to be an overwhelming drawback. Henza priestesses do not have a literate tradition or a corpus of sacred texts; the books that have been left unread by them (and by me) were written by outsiders or by members of the Okinawan (mostly male) literary elite. Although there has been a school in the village for many years, the priestesses among whom I carried out my research do not seem interested in reading; they know how to read headlines and advertisements, but I rarely saw them reading a book or newspaper. As much as possible, I have tried to compensate for my poor Japanese literacy through lengthy discussions with sociology and anthropology professors at the University of the Ryukyus.

Throughout this book, I quote the comments of many different villagers. Henza does not recognize codified rules of behavior; there is no official or institutionalized cosmology; there are very few well-known folk tales; there is no leader or group of leaders who can be said to represent village opinion; and villagers' own life experiences vary enormously. By quoting a variety of villagers, I endeavor to convey at least some of the range of ideas that I heard expressed in the village. After I left Henza, as I began to go through my field notes and interview transcripts, I saw that a great deal of the time my questions had elicited particular sorts of answers. Although, like all anthropologists, I encouraged my informants to speak freely and at length, and I tried to avoid asking leading questions, I am convinced that my word choice and my subject choice led villagers to say things that they might not have said or that they may have said differently without my questions. In order to allow the reader to judge for him- or herself how much weight to give particular remarks, and in order to help the reader share in my own experiences of excitement—and of bewilderment—in the field, I present excerpts from some of my encounters with villagers in the form of dialogue.

I wish to clarify from the outset that the parameters of this study are quite modest: I have tried to look at questions of gender and religion in the specific setting of one particular village at one particular point in history. This book attempts neither a historical reconstruction of traditional Henza culture nor an overview of gender patterns throughout the Ryukyu Islands. I set out to see how women's religious leadership plays out in a contemporary village context: As an anthropologist, I do not see village life in the 1990s as less "authentic" than village life in previous decades or centuries. Cultures always shift and transform, and anthropologists have no need to privilege the past. Yet the present does, of course, rest upon past patterns and experiences, and so far as it was possible within the parameters of this study, I have noted issues of historical change, usually through the eyes of contemporary villagers. I leave it to others to document Henza history in a more orderly fashion.

Henza villagers, especially older villagers, speak a mixture of standard Japanese, "indigenized" Japanese, and their local Okinawan dialect. Often, all three are mixed together in one sentence. For the sake of clarity, I have chosen to transliterate most words in their standard Japanese spelling. The exceptions are words that seem to have a substantially different meaning in Okinawa and words that are used often by villagers to talk about key ritual constructs. (For example, I follow the villagers' lead in spelling the word for chief priestess *noro* but spelling the word for clan *munchu*.) I have not changed the names of villagers, with the exception of a small number of cases in which I felt that the anecdotes or conversations that I was reporting would be likely to cause distress to individuals or to Henza as a whole. I was specifically asked not to use a pseudonym to disguise Henza's identity—villagers are proud of Henza and happy to see Henza receive publicity.

Henza villagers are known by a mixture of family names, personal names (in Japanese and Okinawan), and nicknames; in addition, women are sometimes known by the family name of their natal family and sometimes by the family name of their husband's family. For this book, I decided to use the name that I was given when a particular villager was introduced to me.

The word over which I have deliberated the most is *priestess.* The women who are called priestesses in most English-language ethnographies of Okinawa are usually called kami-sama (deities) by people in Henza. Villagers, unlike the writer and readers of this book, however, usually know whether the reference is to, for example, Mrs. Shimojo (a human kami-sama who lives over on the next block and was seen just yesterday at the beauty parlor getting a permanent and whose granddaughter has a new dog) or to a disembodied kami-sama associated with the sky or the ocean. With some misgivings, in order to avoid confusion in this text, I have chosen to follow the lead of other anthropologists and distinguish linguistically between priestesses and kami-sama in most of this book. The word *kaminchu*—kami-people—is sometimes used by villagers to refer to the same women whom, in English, I call priestesses; I use the words *priestess* and *kaminchu* interchangeably.[14]

Finally, having written so many pages about how *I* understand Henza religious culture, it is in order to say a few words about how Henza villagers perceived my work and my family's presence in their village. Because Japanese scholars tend to treat Okinawa as a kind of living museum of Japanese history, Henza, like many other Okinawan villages, has had its share of Japanese researchers who came to record aspects of village life. These researchers typically came for periods ranging from one day to two weeks. When my family and I arrived, rented a house, enrolled our children in the local nursery school, and showed no signs of leaving in the immediate future, villagers did become curious about who we were and why we had come. From the beginning, we made a point of explaining that we are not Christian Americans but Jewish Israelis. We thought that a non-Christian and non-American identity would help us integrate into a society that had felt the unwelcome presence of Christian missionaries and American military bases. Although some villagers did not seem to understand or care about this "subtle" distinction (few villagers had even heard of Israel or Jews), other villagers were fascinated by our food laws (*kashrut*), which often became the topic of intense discussion when I was served the ubiquitous pork and seafood at the many ritual and social events that I attended. Similarly, Middle East politics had never been a topic of concern to Henza villagers, but as some of our village friends became attached to us, they began to listen to reports of terrorism and war in the Middle East and then became quite worried for our safety. In the wake of photographs that I had shown them of Bedouin women wearing robes that cover their faces and bodies, a few of our friends urged us to leave our young daughter behind with them rather than take her back to a dangerously war-torn region in which women are horribly oppressed.

Like all anthropologists in the field, we experienced ignorance of even the most basic rules of social intercourse, and I am sure that our behavior was a source of great amusement to villagers. In particular, my husband's "unemployment" (that is, his role as chief housekeeper, shopper, and child-care provider) evoked curiosity. One conversation that stands out in my mind occurred toward the end of our stay. A few women whom I had come to know quite well mustered up the courage to ask me, very politely, whether in my country there were *some* men who work or whether all of them were like my husband (who, in fact, had very graciously left his job as a computer engineer in order to make my research in Okinawa possible). This diffidently asked question has served to remind me that I, like all anthropologists, make up part of the context that I am studying.

And so, it is to my husband, and to all women and men who have the curiosity and the courage to question gender patterns, that I dedicate this book.

PART I

DIVINE DIS-ORDER

ONE

Divine Dis-order

On Social Planes

"Okinawans like to use the word *tege—tege yasa*. This is a special Okinawan word; Japanese don't say this word. It means something like 'I don't mind' or 'almost' or 'it's not good and it's not bad but that's okay.'" (Kumi Yamada—Okinawan friend, key informant, and interpreter)

Yasashii

Social relations in Henza tend to be easygoing, nonhierarchical, and, for the most part, without rigid rules or reified classifications. For Henza villagers, the ubiquitous term *yasashii* (lit. 'easy') encodes positive valences of dis-order: a broad attitude of tolerance toward deviance and difference, indifference to categorical opinions and prohibitions, and rejection of ambition, authority and pushiness.

Although Japanese-English dictionaries tell us only that yasashii means "nice" or "gentle," in Henza, being yasashii is the single most important personal quality for women and for men (cf. T. Lebra 1984: 137); it conveys profound cosmological and communal connotations and it is a central element of village identity. Villagers often comment that "nothing ever gets done here," "nothing here is ever organized well," "nothing ever starts on time," and "no one ever knows exactly how to do things correctly." These comments, however, are rarely made in a plaintive manner. To the contrary, depending on the speaker and the situation, these sorts of remarks are made either as simple statements of fact or with a certain amount of pride. Dis-order is not seen as bothersome but rather as a group expression of being yasashii. According to Mrs. Yasamura, "Henza people are all yasashii; there are no people with bad hearts here." A bad heart, other villagers explained, is what causes people to hurt other people. As we see in the next chapter, in the context of a cosmology without a punishing deity, a "bad heart" is the ultimate symbolic statement of cosmic disharmony. "There are no people here with bad hearts" suggests that the normal, natural, existential state of being in Henza is yasashii.

Yasashii for Mrs. Yasamura means more than amiability—it means absence of malice; it means essential goodness. Her comment that all Henza people are yasashii is one that I heard many times. Whether or not she really meant that there is not one single non-yasashii person in Henza is irrelevant. What is important is her perception of Henza as a community of yasashii people, her sense of Henza villagers sharing a common existential state of being yasashii. Mr. Okutara clarified that Henza villagers are intrinsically good; those who act bad do so because of unusual circumstances. When I asked him to describe a bad person he answered, "There are no outstandingly bad people here. There is a little stealing here and there, but not really bad people. There are some people without a father or whose father died in childhood, and their mother can't control them and they give their mother a bad time, and drink a lot of sake." Mr. Okutara echoes accepted village wisdom in blaming sake—the excessive consumption of which villagers clearly understand to be a function of external political and economic forces—rather than human nature for bad behavior (especially of men; see chapter 3). According to Mrs. Noriko Goeku, even immoderate sake drinking is not a reason to say that an individual or his family is bad. "Only if they are violent do people say they are a bad family."

In contrast to my own observation that Henza boys aged fourteen or fifteen sometimes seem sullen and unruly, villagers claim not to notice that this is so; or, like Mrs. Shinzato—one of the most respected middle-aged women in the village—they explain:

MRS. SHINZATO: Henza children are yasashii. Nowadays at schools in Japan there is a big issue about groups of children picking on and beating up one child. Henza doesn't have that problem, Henza children are yasashii.

SUSAN: How about fourteen-year-old boys? They seem pretty nasty.

MRS. SHINZATO: They are at a rebellious stage. So their language is bad. But their hearts are not bad, just their mouths.

In the following conversation, Mr. Miyezato clarifies that people in the village naturally are good and healthy; it is only when they eat unnatural foods that they act bad.

SUSAN: Do boys get horrible at fourteen?

MR. MIYEZATO: No, it's just that all the children are spoiled nowadays. It might be because they eat bad foods, not natural foods. Look at the grandmothers and grandfathers of Henza, they are so healthy.

Villagers are cognizant of their easygoingness.[1] On many occasions, villagers asked me how I liked Henza, and when I answered "very much," the rejoinder was typically, "Yes, Henza people are yasashii." I was told repeatedly that Henza residents are especially yasashii, more so than mainland Japanese or even Okinawans from other islands. I quickly learned that the most direct route to pleasing Henza villagers was to praise their community for being yasashii. Yasashii as a communal value and not merely as an individual personality trait emerges clearly in the following anecdote. One morning Mr. Hikoski and I discussed what it means to be a good person. Mr. Hikoski, in his early sixties, is one of the few villagers who has had extensive contact with Americans (on the military bases) and spoke to me in a mixture of English and Japanese. As we talked, I offered him the following examples:

SUSAN: In America a good person is rich, in Israel a good person is intelligent. What do Henza villagers think?

MR. HIKOSKI: A good person is yasashii and does good things.

SUSAN: What kinds of good things?

MR. HIKOSKI: Respect everyone's rights, want peace in the world, be yasashii.

In his comments, Mr. Hikoski linked being yasashii to attitudes that we in the West would see as communal values of social idealism: respect for everyone's rights and world peace. The three examples of "good things" offered by Mr. Hikoski are significant—they all suggest that being good has to do with not intruding upon others physically (through war), socially or politically (through infringing upon their rights), or personally (by being pushy—not yasashii). Henza children rarely play with war toys.[2] According to Mrs. Hokama, "We try not to give the idea of guns to children, so they don't sell toy guns in the store here." For Henza villagers, war is a foreign intruder that breaks the physical and social integrity of their good island (see the tale of Ashtray Rock in chapter 5).

Being yasashii, apparently, is deeply rooted historically in Okinawan culture. In the late fifteenth century, during the reign of the great Okinawan king Sho Shin, private ownership and use of arms were done away with. All weapons were brought to Shuri and stored in a central warehouse (Kerr 1957:105–107).[3] George Kerr, writing about Okinawa in the sixteenth century, comments that "the Okinawans had no zealots in their midst with burning faith to propagate by fire and sword. They shunned quarrels; they could afford no wars, for they had no strength in manpower and no surpluses to be spent on arms. From this position of weakness they had perforce to learn accommodation" (1958: 90). Okinawa never developed the samurai culture that is so central to Japanese cultural pride and identity. Joy Hendry's description of samurai warriors who "valued deprivation and rigorous discipline in the interest of building an impenetrable inner strength of spirit," for whom "relations between them were based on hierarchical principles . . . and loyalty to the ultimate leader was a paramount virtue" (1995: 13) is totally alien—indeed anathema—to Henza's cultural ethos.

According to Kerr, during the Sino-Japanese War and during the Russo-Japanese conflict, Okinawan "women went daily to the Shinto shrine of Nami- no-ue [lit. 'on the wave'] or to the Buddhist temple Enkaku-ji to pray that sons and husbands would be unfit for military service. These things did not endear Okinawans to the military leaders at Tokyo" (1957: 460). As World War II approached, "manifestations of extreme nationalism—the mass hysteria which swept Japan along the road to national defeat—were unpopular in Okinawa. The common people could not afford the 'voluntary' contributions; they had no traditions glorifying war and the fighting man" (Kerr 1957: 462). The entire Japanese historical-cultural constellation of zealous patriotism and militarism during World War II, followed by military defeat, economic triumph, and an emphasis on achievement and allegiance to one's company, are not part of Okinawa's historical-cultural experience. Although some Henza villagers were drafted into the Japanese army, villagers did not and do not identify Japan as their ally and America as their enemy in the War. To the contrary, villagers see themselves as assaulted by both sides, as forced to participate actively and passively in a war literally fought on their backs. Villagers told me that before and during the War, Henza people did not want their sons to go to fight, and (according to Mr. Tamura) many sent their sons away to avoid the Japanese draft.

Groups of Okinawans have protested and demonstrated against the continued presence of American military bases on Okinawa.[4] When Okinawa's Governor Ota testified before the Japanese Supreme Court on July 10, 1996, in the wake of his having refused to sign documents in lieu of Okinawan landowners that would allow the forcible acquisition of their land for the use of United States military bases, he began his remarks with his view of the Okinawan cultural ethos, a view almost identical to that of Mr. Hikoski.

> What I would like to say before anything else is that among my people, the longing for peace is very strong. . . . For ages, the Ryukyu Kingdom had been widely, even abroad, known as an unarmed land of courtesy. . . . On the basis of the above historical background, the [late] Professor William Lebra . . . concludes that the cultures of Japan and Okinawa are fundamentally different. That is, in contrast to Japan's 'warrior culture,' Okinawa is notable for "absence of militarism." Other scholars define Okinawan culture as a 'feminine culture' (josei bunka) or a 'culture of moderation' (yasashisa no bunka). . . . In this way, my prefecture is dedicated to a way of life that shuns and abhors armed conflict. (Translated by the editors of *The Ryukyuanist*, Newsletter No. 35, Winter 1996–1997)

Only after his description of Okinawa's yasashii culture did Governor Ota move on to describe the history of occupation of Okinawan land and the hardships that the occupation causes to Okinawan population and to plead for reduction of the American military presence.

Being Easy

Being yasashii means being easy with life, not pushing oneself forward, not trying too hard. Several villagers told me that Henza people are not ambitious and that this lack of ambition distinguishes Henza from other places. (In only one instance was this comment made to me in the form of self-criticism or complaint.) In the course of my stay in Henza, I indeed met young and middle-aged men and women who had almost completed qualifications that would allow them to move into an upwardly mobile career but who had chosen to remain in a lower status, easygoing job. Of course, ambitious individuals tend to leave the village and pursue jobs in Naha (the capital of Okinawa Prefecture) or other Japanese cities. Emigration in search of better job opportunities is particularly pronounced among young women.

Pushing oneself forward in the sense of showing off or bragging is discouraged in Henza (cf. Rohlen 1989; T. Lebra 1976 on Japan). Individuals (both men and women) do take leadership roles; for example, each women's *usudeku* (ritual dance) group has a leader, and many village men have served as headman. Still, leaders are not expected to be loud, overly assertive, bossy, or "above" other people. Villagers do not expect the headman to tell people what to do; his role is more as a representative of the people than as a leader. The rotating nature of the headman position is indicative: Each headman serves for a year or two, then someone else takes over. Similarly, as I show in chapter 9, priestesses are not leaders in the sense that we recognize in our own culture: The priestess does not stand up in front of a room and vocally "lead" the laity, teach, or direct them.

Leadership in Henza is a function of rich social networks rather than of being assertive, (self-consciously) talented, or domineering. This notion was expressed well by Mrs. Shimojo, the woman who is believed by villagers and priestesses alike to be the most knowledgeable priestess in Henza. At the end of a long visit to Mrs. Shimojo's house, I thanked her and complimented her for knowing so much and explaining things so clearly. She answered, "My house is in a location where people can easily stop by all the time." Her response explicitly—and modestly—situated the source of her knowledge in village social interactions rather than in her own efforts.

While bragging is not considered yasashii, talented individuals are much admired in Henza; gifted dancers, singers, and drummers are the pride of the community. Within my first few days in Henza, numerous people rushed to call my attention to the specially talented individuals who live in their village. Henza villagers love to perform; from a young age, children are encouraged to get up in front of audiences and sing and dance. At village events, there are typically performances by groups of villagers and by individual villagers, and it is never a problem to find enough people to perform; rather, the problem is tactfully limiting the number of performances. Stage fright seems to be unknown in Henza: Children, old people, men, and women all perform at weddings, celebrations, and village events.[5]

Yasashii means not pushing oneself forward; it does not mean either shyness or utter conformity. Everyone knows that Mrs. Hokama is especially interested and expert in traditional music, and she is not embarrassed or reluctant to acknowledge that people know this. Villagers recognize that individuals have different abilities, and those abilities are respected and honored as long as they are expressed in an easygoing manner. To take one example, a village man who is a gifted dancer comes drunk to most communal events, and, uninvited, likes to stand up in front of the crowd and dance. His dancing is tolerated and even appreciated unless it clearly interferes with another activity, such as someone else's scheduled dance performance or the headman's speech.

The flip side of self-aggrandizement is complaining, and, indeed, villagers do not gripe or whine very much. This does not mean that villagers have Pollyannish delusions about the world. Older villagers remember well the suffering and bombings during World War II and the periodic food shortages before and after the war. The issue is one of consciousness—to what extent identity, interactions, and social status revolve around experiences of evil and suffering. Just as villagers do not show off regarding success, they do not show off regarding suffering.

Growing Up Yasashii

[The new baby] is discharged from the darkness
It observes the light of the world
Thus helping the mother's life
The baby's birthing is celebrated
The baby born last night.
When it becomes about seven years old
I will have a horse barn [for a boy]/storage barn [for a girl] built
The baby is newly born into a prosperous world
It shall brighten the ancestors forever.

(traditional song sung at birth of new baby, recorded by Mrs. Nae Hokama, translation by Mr. Kanshun Okutara)

I open this section with the traditional song rejoicing in the birth of a new baby because the words of this song encapsulate villagers' attitude toward children and, indeed, toward life. By being born the baby helps its mother; during birth, the baby is already urged to be cooperative (by coming out easily) and, upon birth, is immediately praised for its helpful attitude. The new baby is straightaway educated about its connection to the ancestors, and it is told that the world that it has been born into is a prosperous one.

Following Paul Riesman (1992), I do not treat child-rearing practices as leading to the formation of particular modal adult personalities. Rather, I see these practices as part of the same cultural ethos that is expressed in interpersonal relationships of all sorts. Henza children are held almost constantly until approximately one year of age. Although it is usually the mother who holds the baby, in extended family households, the grandparents also hold the baby, as do older siblings (cf. Maretzki and Maretzki 1966; see also T. Lebra 1976 on Japan). The transition away from being held is gradual, and by four years of age children are seldom held or hugged, nor do they seem to solicit physical attention of this sort. In traditional Okinawan houses, the entire family sleeps on futons next to each other in one room. In more modern houses, older children sleep in their own room, but babies and young children sleep with their parents.[6]

Henza children begin to attend nursery school at two or three years of age, and sometimes even younger, although in most cases adults who assumedly could take care of the children are at home. Villagers believe that it is good for children to be in a social environment. From a young age, children are usually seen hanging around together in groups. I rarely saw children involved in individual play.

Henza parents in general seem relaxed about their children's health, an attitude that makes sense considering that Okinawans have the longest life expectancy in the world. Babies and young children seem to cry very little. This is both because they are held so much of the time and because they are rarely reprimanded or told "no." Many of the frustrations of young children in the West arise when concerned parents and teachers prevent them from engaging in dangerous activities. Henza children are rarely hindered from doing something because it is dangerous. At the nursery school, for example, a favorite activity is climbing up the drainpipe on the outside of the building. The teachers do not try to stop the children; rather, when very young children climb the pipe a teacher simply stands at the bottom to catch whoever slips off. Children are taught from a young age that the village is a safe place. Children two and three years old can be seen riding tricycles around the village, although there are quite a few cars on village streets. I often would see children playing in construction lots and other kinds of places that Western parents usually deem as unsafe. Young children rather freely enter village houses and help themselves to food and treats. We found that although village children were intrigued by us (strange-looking foreigners), they were not afraid, and felt quite comfortable coming into our house, invited or uninvited, and looking around.

Small children's sense of the world being filled with good things is enhanced by the practice of gift giving. Henza adults constantly give food, candy, and money to children. On one typical morning in the village, the post office attendant blew up balloons and gave them to my children; a shop owner gave them each a handful of candies; a woman who works in the kitchen at the nursery school saw them from her house, called to them, and threw them a bag of chips over her wall; and a neighbor who stopped by to talk to me gave them 1000 yen (approximately $10). According to one woman who now lives in Henza but who was born in Japan, "People in Henza, unlike people in Japan, are always giving money to children. Like if they don't have anything else to give a child they say, 'Sorry, I don't have anything' and give the child 1000 yen."

Not only are children rarely reprimanded, but also young children are seldom instructed in "proper" behavior. Until approximately age three or four, children are not seen as truly cultured beings; that is, they do not seem to be expected to stay tidy, use household furnishings properly, refrain from grabbing, or speak politely.

Nursery school teachers share this noninstructional approach to young children. In the nursery school, there is almost no structured play: no puzzles, building blocks, crayons, paints, Lego blocks, matching games, or anything similar. The children spend most of the day running around, climbing furniture, playing tag and hide-and-seek. Although adult villagers, men and women, are expected to be soft-spoken, young children typically screech in loud, shrill voices. No one suggests to them that they quiet down. I never in the course of a full year saw a teacher raise a voice to a child. Both in the home and at nursery school, corporal punishment is rare. Parents and teachers gradually socialize children primarily through setting a personal example of proper behavior and very secondarily through talking to the children and explaining to them what is right. On several occasions, I heard villagers blame an adult's undesirable behavior (usually drunkenness) on a faulty upbringing; but the prevailing attitude seems to be that unless something goes very wrong, children are born and grow up naturally to be good and healthy.

One structured activity that does exist at the nursery school is preparing for performances. Approximately every two months, the nursery school is involved in some type of party or celebration to which parents and other villagers are invited.

The children perform traditional and nontraditional songs and dances at these events, and a great deal of nursery school time is spent in rehearsal. From a young age, children are taught complicated dances and drumming and are expected to enjoy getting up in front of an audience. In contrast to the incessant running around and screeching during normal nursery school hours, at these public events the children are expected to sit quietly, sometimes for up to two hours, listening to speeches by adults and watching performances by other groups of children. Most of the children do manage to sit quietly (sometimes with the help of a teacher's firm hug.)

The contrast between the almost total lack of structured activity in nursery school play and the long rehearsals and patient listening at celebrations demands comment. What I call the lack of structured activity in nursery school is actually an absence of emphasis on competitive games (such as lotto) and on cognitive development (no one is concerned with preparing the children for success at school). In contrast, in the performances at celebrations, the children are socialized into becoming part of the village community: They are taught how to be good performers[7] and how to be a good audience. They are taught to be relaxed in front of a group, and they are taught to be patient and tolerant. In other words, they are taught the essentials of being yasashii.[8]

Conflict

Perhaps because I have spent most of my adult life in a culture (Israel) in which arguing is common and often even relished,[9] I was struck by how little arguing goes on in Henza. It was difficult to get villagers to talk to me about the issues that cause quarrels or the ways in which they settle quarrels.

SUSAN (desperately searching for anecdotes): If two women disagree, like if one sold fish and the other one says, "The fish was bad and I don't want to pay you"—how would that kind of thing usually end?

MRS. HOKAMA: Ha ha ha. I don't think anyone would buy rotten fish.

The paradigmatic folk, religious, national, and children's stories with which Westerners are familiar tend to revolve around themes of conflict and opposition—in particular, of good versus bad (think, for example, of Cinderella). In a variety of contexts, Henza villagers show that they prefer to blur opposition and strong opinions in favor of just going along with or getting along with others (cf. Hendry 1995 on Japan).[10]

SUSAN: In Israel we have a lot of stories in which good and bad fight each other. How about in Okinawa?

MRS. ADANIYA (eighty-two year old, locally recognized expert at old-time stories): Not so much. The heart is different here from in mainland [Japan]. That is a big country. Okinawa is so small, so Okinawan people are close to each other in their hearts. It is easy for other people to get along with Okinawans. Like you, Susan, are used to me and I am used to you too. Okinawan people have a lot of those feelings.

Mrs. Adaniya's description of the moral superiority that accompanies Okinawa's structural subordination (vis-à-vis Japan) is, from a cross-cultural perspective, a well-known stance. In American society, for instance, women—structurally less powerful than men—are commonly thought to be kinder, more devout, and less likely to commit criminal acts than men (see Janeway's 1981 discussion of the powers of the weak.) Still, I believe that Ms. Kumi Yamada summed up village attitudes correctly when she explained that "people here don't like it if either side [in an argument] is too strong, right or left. There are always village people who think both ways." Indeed, in reference to a dispute over land in which one side to the dispute clearly seemed (to me) to be in the right, Japanese-born Kuni Okutara told me in exasperation that village people "don't want to take sides, they ignore these things."[11]

I did not see any fights or loud arguments during my year in Henza.[12] According to Mr. Okutara, even when people act in a way that others do not like, villagers are unlikely to say anything. "People don't want to get involved because that creates trouble, bloodshed." When there are disagreements, whether within families or between friends, clan members or neighbors, other villagers will be more likely to help those who are quarreling find a compromise that will resolve the quarrel than to actively take sides. To my great frustration as an anthropologist, gossip—although ubiquitous—also tends to be rather easygoing and low-keyed (thus I was deprived of one of our greatest sources of ethnographic information). It was almost impossible to learn secondhand about problems, deviancy, or unacceptable behavior. Villagers told me that they spend lots of time talking about other villagers because everyone knows everyone else. Yet, according to one man, "It doesn't go too far. It is more jokingly, to entertain the group."

I am well aware that the fact that villagers rarely quarrel in noticeable ways does not mean that there are no undercurrents of friction, nor does it mean that villagers do not repress and brood over feelings of anger or conflict. In the particular sphere in which I concentrated my research efforts—the ritual work of priestesses—I heard more than occasional murmurs of discontent regarding the level of expertise of the current chief priestess (noro). These murmurs, however, never erupted into any kind of unpleasantness; priestesses did not stop attending rituals conducted by the noro; there was no fission. Rather, the issue seems to be dealt with primarily through quiet and subtle efforts on the part of the more experienced priestesses to teach the current noro some of the rituals in which she lacked proficiency. Did certain of the priestesses brood over this state of affairs? One very elderly priestess—who had been the best friend of the previous (deceased) noro—did brood, and villagers told me that she is "a bit crazy." We see, then, that one way of dealing with conflict that threatens to get out of hand is to redefine it as unnatural or sick rather than to enter into the content of the conflict. Individuals who make a practice of exhibiting dissatisfaction, anger, aggressiveness, or strong opinions receive little positive reinforcement in Henza and are likely to be seen as "frightening" or "sick." The message, of course, is that the "natural" way for humans to be is harmonious.

In many societies, including our own, labeling deviant or unpopular behavior as "sick" or "crazy" serves not only to censure that behavior but also to justify discrimination against, repression of, and sometimes physical restraint of individuals who engage in such behaviors. Although my information in this area is limited regarding Henza, my sense is that "sick" or "crazy" people remain in the village and go about their lives relatively unhindered unless their "sickness" or "craziness" becomes violent. Families with "sick" or "crazy" members eventually will seek advice from a shaman-type practitioner, whose judgment generally shifts the blame for the behavior from the specific individual onto the shoulders of a variety of relatives and ancestors who had committed ritual or moral errors.[13]

If conflicts are rarely expressed openly, one might assume that they are repressed, held inside. This seems to be the pattern in Japan, where, according to Margaret Lock (1987), internalized feelings of conflict often take the form of chronic illness or depression. In Okinawa, however, as we shall see later on, there is very little illness. Unlike Emiko Ohnuki-Tierney's (1984) Japanese informants, many of whom complained of the kinds of chronic illness that seem to be associated with emotional distress, my informants almost never complained of headaches, stomachaches, or the like, and they say that it is rare for villagers to miss a day's work because of illness.

Henza village is not Utopia; villagers do feel angry, insulted, and cross, and conflicts ripple both under and over the surface. Yet in comparison to other cultures with which I am acquainted (see Swartz, Turner, and Tuden 1966 on conflict cross-culturally), Henza villagers seem to have developed both social patterns that make it fairly easy to avoid situations that lead to conflict and a cultural ethos that discourages expression (either directly through fighting or indirectly through illness and complaining) of conflict.

The Question of Hierarchy

As we have looked at a variety of manifestations of being yasashii, the focus until now has been upon informal relationships. The yasashii cultural ethos also permeates organizational and ideological realms of Henza: Village life is characterized by an absence of significant hierarchical structures and absolute taboos or prohibitions. In later chapters, I argue that these patterns are closely tied to women's religious leadership.

Certain hierarchical patterns and expressions can be found in Henza. Among the priestesses, for example, there are clearly defined roles, with the noro at the top, then the titled priestesses who regularly accompany the noro, then the dozen or so clan priestesses who pray at the sacred grove on certain dates, then the regular clan priestesses, and finally the ritual servants of the clan priestesses. Similarly, in the secular sphere, the village has a headman and a village council, and these roles are recognized as prestigious roles (for example, municipal dignitaries will be served drinks at public gatherings where everyone else brings their own drinks).

The more important issue, to my mind, is the social meaning of status and hierarchy. In line with their belief that the locus of reward and punishment for human behavior is the human heart rather than some outside agency, human or cosmic, Henza villagers do not usually engage in the kinds of structured, hierarchical relationships in which a superordinate (whether divine or human) tells a subordinate what to do. Thus, for example, neither the noro nor the headman see it as their role to prevent one of the male ritual assistants from showing up drunk at village rituals.

To take what at first seems to be the clearest instance of hierarchy—the priestesses—we find that outside of the context of the specific rituals performed by priestesses, this hierarchy has no social meaning. Several priestesses told me that in their daily lives they are not treated with special respect by villagers, a claim that is indeed borne out by my own observations. The relationship between yuta and priestesses is relevant to this discussion. On the one hand, priestesses are a publicly recognized, official group of religious practitioners, whereas yuta are private practitioners who are paid for their labor; the former are called kami-sama, whereas the latter are not. On the other hand, I have been told by priestesses that yuta are higher than they are because the yuta see and hear spiritual things that priestesses cannot see and hear. As a result, yuta have a critical role in choosing the priestesses. When I accompanied Henza's chief priestess on a visit to a *yuta*, the priestess treated the yuta as a superior; for example, she bowed lower, talked more quietly, and so forth. If these same two women had met in a context in which the priestess was conducting a ritual on behalf of the village, I assume that their positions would be reversed—that the yuta would bow lower and speak more quietly. These kinds of situation-dependent interactions serve to sabotage conventional notions of religious hierarchy.

Temporary, shallow, situation-specific status also characterizes the position of those who serve as headman or on the village council. These positions are rotating, and once a villager has finished the term he or she also loses the position in the social hierarchy. Moreover, as in the case of the priestesses, outside the context of municipal events the headman and village councilmen are indistinguishable from other Henza villagers. When a village official finishes his term of office, his status does not, in the words of one villager, "follow" him.

In an evening conversation with the women at the local beauty parlor, one middle-aged woman who had lived part of her life outside of the village compared Henza's social uniformity to the more "polite" culture of Shuri (the old capital and residence of the king). "Henza dialect doesn't have many respect words, so it is a harsh language. All age groups talk the same. They don't use polite language for older people." Elderly people in Henza are praised for their longevity and treated well but not with veneration or reverence. My guess is that the distinction here is between institutionalized hierarchy—rules for how subordinates and superiors must be differentiated in speech, dress, and behavior—and social recognition of individual talent, which as I said earlier is embraced in the village. Advanced age is seen by Henza villagers as a talent or skill in much the same way that musical ability is. It earns the individual admiration and attention but does not grant social status or "respect words."

When I assert that hierarchy is unimportant in Henza, I make three somewhat separate claims. First, I claim that there are few apparent differences among villagers in terms of status or rank. Second, I claim that when differences exist, villagers tend to minimize or ignore them, much in the way that gender differences are minimized and ignored (as discussed in chapter 12). Finally, I claim that such hierarchical differences as do exist are situation-specific; outside of the particular context in which an individual's status is germane, marks of status tend not to be evident.

Henza, like most of Okinawa, appears to be economically egalitarian. It is hard to tell who is poor and who is rich. There are no obvious differences in clothing style, and houses tend to look uniform from the outside. According to George Kerr, although Okinawan society during the Ryukyuan Kingdom was divided into aristocratic and peasant classes, the gaps were never very large, at least in part because the gentry were also the artisans and craftsmen. "The Okinawans never quite brought themselves to believe in the existence of uncrossable social lines and often found occasion to make exception to rules they laid down for themselves after Chinese or Japanese precedents. Peasants lived in utmost poverty, but at the same time there were no extremes of wealth among the gentry" (1957: 192–193). Although official ranks were established and distinguished by certain rules of dress during the time of the Ryukyuan Kingdom (Sakihara 1981: 9), the system of rank never caught on in Henza. In general, Okinawan culture and religion are far less hierarchical than are those of Japan.[14]

On many occasions, I was told that Okinawans are not economically ambitious. Automobiles and household appliances are relatively inexpensive; villagers are not particularly interested in foreign travel; the Japanese welfare system provides an economic net for those who are sick or unemployable, and so families do not feel a need to accumulate money as a safeguard for future problems or disasters; a cash economy is relatively new on the island; and a great deal of food continues to circulate through gifts and exchange.[15] In villages like Henza, gardening, fishing, and foraging guarantee a steady and desirable food supply for rich and poor alike. As one villager told me, "The old lady digging over there in her garden could be rich and we don't know it."

Traditionally, the clan system did represent a somewhat hierarchical framework. For example, the Nakada clan, which had connections to the Shuri government and to the noro's family (*nunduruchi*), were relatively high status. Yet when I asked villagers whether it ever happens that one of the families of a couple who want to be married might disapprove of the other family, the consensus was that this never happens. "What families want for their son is a girl who can work in the fields." When I asked Mr. Shinyashiki in what way rank was manifested, in marriage or behavior, he explained that it was not manifested, that actually "it all leveled out."[16]

The current egalitarian ethos is consistent with the traditional system of land redistribution. One woman in her seventies explains how this system worked in her mother's time:

Land is divided according to how many people there are, even girls get land. The girl takes land with her and gets married. And everyone knows that the land belongs to her. Also boys. And second and third sons also. Until my mother's time they had this land distribution. [Susan: so the land belonged to the village?] I think so. My mother got land and it was her land and she worked it, she had her own *hatake* [vegetable garden] given to her by the village. When people reached a certain age they got land, and however many people were born that year, that is who the land was divided among.

When the individual was no longer able to work, either because of old age or death, the land reverted to the village. In the words of one elderly villager:

> There were no rich people really, only a few families. If you show you are rich, wear nice clothes, act snobby, people will say you are stuck up and will exclude you from things. So people try to blend in. If you show you are rich, bad things will happen to your family, because people won't like you. But there really weren't differences. Everyone got 36 *tsubo* [a unit of measurement] in the village land redistribution. Only the noro had more.

In Henza, land redistribution did not mean that all families had equal amounts of land. Families with strong connections to the Shuri king had more land; other families had less. Still, and this is the crucial point, the traditional land redistribution system ensured that all families had access to land, that the amount of land owned by a family reflected at least to some extent the number of mouths to feed in the family, and that the notion of private ownership and inheritance of land was relatively undeveloped. As anthropologists such as Marvin Harris have shown, in cultures in which there is substantial land to pass on as inheritance, it is common to find women's freedom curtailed in order to ensure that they bear heirs for the correct paternal line (1985: 498–500). This pattern, with its accompanying social rules and prohibitions, did not occur in traditional Okinawan society.

Earlier I made the distinction between actual lack of hierarchy and villagers' perception of lack of hierarchy. At various village events, I tried to ask why some people sit inside the kami-ya and others sit outside or why some sit on chairs and others on benches. On almost every occasion, the answer I received was that there is no distinction; "It is just that the kami-ya is small and not everyone fits inside," or "There are not enough chairs so some people sit on benches." However, to me it did seem that there were certain people who fairly consistently sat in the "better" place (usually civil servants or people who had some official role in Henza, such as Parent-Teacher Association committee members). I am not sure that it is productive to debate whether villagers really could not see that there was some kind of hierarchy in action or whether they see hierarchy but choose to deny it. In any case, the effect of their rhetoric is the same—to minimize hierarchy and differential social status.

"Maybe You Don't Like This Food, But I Do"

Henza people in those days [when I was young] were told not to become policemen. It is okay to be a thief, but not a policeman. That means that policemen tie up people, and they beat you if you do something bad. The thief doesn't have things, and that is why he steals from someone who has—it isn't so bad. Even though you steal [that is okay], but not to tie up people or beat them [like policemen do]. In Henza they didn't have that kind of thing, to tie up criminals, like they have on the main island.[17] That is why we don't have many policemen in Okinawa. There are only three people who are policemen; in comparison, there are 100 people who are teachers. (Mr. Shinya, school principal)

Henza villagers recognize illegal behavior in terms of Japanese law and American occupation law, and they recognize bad behavior in the sense of non-*yasashii* acts; they do not, however, identify a category that we might call absolutely forbidden or cosmically prohibited behavior.[18]

SUSAN: In my religion we have the Ten Commandments, not to steal or. . . .

MS. KUMI YAMADA (interrupting): No, here it depends upon the situation. For example, during the War people stole things from farmers at night to survive, and this is okay.

SUSAN: Is murder always bad?

MS. KUMI YAMADA: That is the heaviest one. But it depends whether the person who was murdered was bad.

SUSAN: How about adultery?

MS. KUMI YAMADA: It depends. Not always bad. Maybe the husband is missing like in a war, or maybe he is a fisherman who is away for a long time.

In this conversation, Ms. Kumi Yamada presented an articulate overview of situational ethics: She explained that there is no particular act that is always bad—actions need to be evaluated in the interpersonal contexts within which they occur.[19] Rigid laws are incompatible with being yasashii.

In an exchange that took me quite a while to unravel, Mrs. Adaniya and I discussed whether it is proper to lie to avoid hurting someone's feelings. Actually, to be honest, *I* discussed whether it is proper to lie to avoid hurting feelings. For Mrs. Adaniya, it is so obviously desirable to lie to preserve harmony that she jumped far ahead of me and talked about whether there "really" is one objective truth at all. Specifically, I had asked her whether it is right to say that you like food that someone else cooked even if the food is not tasty. In other words, I was positing a situation in which food really is not tasty and in which one must decide whether or not to tell the cook. The more interesting issue for Mrs. Adaniya was that there is no such thing as food that is absolutely, unconditionally, and universally not tasty and that imposing her notions of tastiness upon me would be a breach of interpersonal relationships. "Maybe you don't like this food, but I do." This conversation encapsulates two fundamental themes in village discourse: first, that different people have different and legitimate tastes, preferences, talents, and opinions; second, that getting along with others (being yasashii) overrides any absolute notion of right and wrong.

Because absolute or cosmic prohibitions of one kind or another are found in so many, and in so many different sorts, of cultural frameworks (cf. Durkheim 1963; Douglas 1966; Paige and Paige 1981), I interpret their absence in Henza as a significant part of the broader pattern of social "easiness" (*yasashii*).[20]

In many cultures, there are prohibitions on women's activities during menstruation. Mary Douglas has suggested that where gender status is ambiguous these prohibitions tend to be more extensive (1966). Paige and Paige have argued that menstrual prohibitions are more extreme in societies that are based on unstable and perishable wealth (such as salmon fishing) and in which "men can build up factions from a core group of kin but can never rely on automatic kin-group support" (1981: 220). Both Douglas's symbolic model and Paige and Paige's political model have to do with issues of status and structure: Menstrual taboos clarify social relationships in societies in which social relationships tend to be cloudy. Although Henza fits both the Douglas and the Paige and Paige models for societies with extensive menstrual taboos (ambiguous gender status; unstable food source, fishing; and lack of automatic kin-group support), there are no menstrual taboos in Henza. Unclear social relationships (whether between men and women or among men) are yasashii, nonproblematic, and not in need of clarification or order (cf. Yoshida 1990).

Henza priestesses continue to carry out their ritual roles while menstruating. The only exception concerns a situation in which menstruation would cause the priestess discomfort. According to Mrs. Shimojo, "It used to be that in March when they [noro and kaminchu] went to the ocean for the *hama ogami* [beach prayer ritual], they didn't go if they were menstruating, but nowadays they do. They didn't go because they used to go into, under the water. But now [because some coastal land has been dried and reclaimed] they don't have to do that, so they go."

Henza men and women, young and old, were surprised to hear that in my (traditional Jewish) culture there is a prohibition on sexual relations during menstruation. "In Henza there are no rules like that," remarked one woman in her thirties. During pregnancy, villagers told me, there are certain foods that one tries to avoid eating (for example, little grapes without seeds), but these mostly seemed to be interpreted by villagers in terms of health or "sympathetic magic." No activities were or are prohibited during pregnancy. There are no taboos surrounding the effluvia of birth.[21] Women stay inside and rest next to the fire after giving birth, but again, this is interpreted in terms of health, not pollution, and when for economic reasons a woman cannot afford to rest after birth, no cosmic sanctions are expected. It is simply seen as unhealthy. There is no word in Okinawan dialect that can be translated as either 'pollution' or 'purification'.[22]

In most societies (perhaps in all societies), there are certain groups of people whom an individual may not marry. In some societies, the rules and taboos are so broad as to exclude all but a narrow category of potential marriage partners. According to Henza villagers, on the other hand, people are free to marry whomever they want. Distant cousins, neighbors, friends, clan members and nonmembers, and newcomers to the village are all considered appropriate marriage partners. Nowadays, first-cousin marriage is infrequent, but in the past it was a more common option. There is also some evidence from villagers that in the past there was no actual prohibition on brother-sister marriage; rather, it was seen as an undesirable and low-status type of marriage entered into by poor families. Sexual relations between parents and children were not mentioned by villagers when I asked if there are any forbidden sexual connections, and when I asked specifically about it, the reaction was surprise and shock: No one would do such a thing. The point is that there is little attention to the issue of with whom one is allowed to have sexual relations or whom one may marry; there is no explicit category of forbidden sexual relationships that can be enumerated; and there is no notion of divine or cosmic punishment for sexual relationships that are considered undesirable. The only negative consequence of undesirable sexual relations (that I heard reference to) is that in villages in which close cousins tend to marry, there are high numbers of handicapped children.

Villagers do not talk about sexual activity in terms of firm prohibitions. Premarital sex is allowed, preserving virginity is not a social value, and extramarital sex—if discreet—is not considered essentially evil or wrong (if indiscreet, it is considered tactless). William Lebra writes that "There is virtually no strong moral condemnation of adultery per se, but repeated involvement in extramarital affairs and neglect of family responsibilities does invoke censure. Particularly reprehensible is the squandering of family resources on a paramour, for this impairs the survival and continuity of a family" (1966: 35). This should not be taken to mean that there are no norms regarding sexual activity. Sexual encounters are expected to be discreet and preferably limited to one's spouse or, for young people, a serious boyfriend or girlfriend. As one widow in her late forties explained to me, if she were to be seen visiting with men, people in the village would talk about her and it would make her uncomfortable to know that she had become the object of gossip. However, she clarified, village gossip would not lead to ostracism, punishment, accusations of harlotry or witchcraft, or a social stigma being placed upon her daughter. In short, while there are rather clear expectations regarding sexual behavior and even a fair amount of scrutiny of the sexual activities of others, village identity, morality, and pride do not seem to be expressed in terms of sexual rules or prohibitions.

Turning to a final example of a widely distributed prohibition, anthropologists have argued that through food taboos societies distinguish themselves from other societies (they are the ones who eat crickets, we are civilized and eat locusts). In Henza there are no forbidden foods.[23] When I tried to ask Mrs. Hokama whether there are any foods that people in Henza believe one should not eat, her answer was, "You mean like poison?" Henza villagers believe that their varied food consumption is in part responsible for their longevity and good health. A good diet is considered to be one in which dozens of kinds of food are eaten on a daily basis. If food taboos indeed are a means of setting off or delineating groups, we can perhaps reason that the absence of food taboos, like the absence of menstrual and sexual taboos, is consistent with Henza's nonhierarchical and non-reified social organization.

Naturally Healthy

Okinawa is an exceptionally healthy society. Japan has the highest life expectancy of any nation in the world today, and Okinawa has the highest life expectancy of all Japanese prefectures, despite being the poorest prefecture, having the highest birth and lowest economic and education rates, and being afflicted with a difficult climate and topography.[24] Old people in Okinawa generally look and act *genki* (lively) and tend to be proud of good health. Even within this larger Okinawan context of normative healthiness, Henza residents believe that their island village is particularly healthy, and health rather than illness is understood to be the normal human condition throughout the life cycle.[25] As quoted in the first section of this chapter, Mr. Miyezato attributes the non-*yasashii* behavior of fourteen-year-old boys to their consumption of nonnatural foods and the health and longevity of village old folk to their consumption of natural foods. Being *yasashii*, in other words, is linked to a more general understanding of health as the natural state of the physical world.

Different cultures posit a variety of sources of illness: sorcery or witchcraft, germs, humoral imbalance as a result of environmental stress or incorrect foods, the presence of a disease goddess (this is the south Indian model), divine punishment for sin, somatization of guilt feelings, and more. Despite ubiquitous requests for health in Okinawan prayers, villagers do not particularly elaborate upon the causes of illness. Thus, for instance, although great use is made of modern medical facilities, germs are not seen as the ultimate cause of illness. According to Ohashi et al. (1984), Okinawans are aware that not everyone exposed to germs gets sick and that modern physicians cannot cure all illnesses. Villagers believe in healthy habits, but what constitutes healthy habits is not explicitly spelled out. Varied food consumption is said to be linked to good health, but this link is vague and implicit; humoral theories—which constitute a highly elaborate cultural system of health and healing—are not known by the villagers. Although there is a traditional role that can be roughly translated as sorcerer (*ichijamaa*), villagers are vague about what sorcerers actually do, and no one was able to tell me any specific stories regarding sorcerers (although this does not seem to be the case in other Okinawan villages; cf. W. Lebra 1966: 92–93). No one claimed to know of any sorcerers, nor are villagers afraid of sorcerers. Human manipulation of the supernatural for evil purposes is not a salient cause of illness in Henza society. Not even lay sorcery, such as the evil eye or other forms of domestic magic, is part of the Henza yasashii worldview. In short, illness does not seem to be seen as either inherent to the human condition or omnipresent in the form of supernatural threat.

Nor are those popular Western sources of illness, sin and guilt, considered relevant to the state of one's health in Henza. As we see in the next chapter, villagers have assured me that kami do not punish bad actions either in this world or in the next, and feelings of guilt are not prominent in Okinawa's yasashii culture. I have heard people express regret for past conduct, but long-lasting guilt feelings seem to be rare. In the case of regret for misconduct toward someone who has since died, the individual is offered a variety of socially acceptable channels for rather thoroughly "expiating" guilt feelings. The typical funerary sequence is so lengthy, elaborate, and costly that it well enables descendants to finish the sequence with a conscience cleared of any earlier misdoings. The absence of a discourse of guilt (whether phrased as shame or phrased as sin) is one way in which Henza seems to differ dramatically from mainland Japan (see Creighton 1990).

Discourses of guilt arise when an external authority—a higher being (parent, teacher, priest, king, or god)—declares that there is a right way and a wrong way to act, talk, look, think, feel, or be. I interpret the absence of guilt discourse in Henza in terms of the egalitarian yasashii ethos. The "healthy" stance of Henza villagers reflects their perceptions of the human body, male or female, as clean and whole, of death as unfrightening, of social interactions as easygoing and nonhierarchical, and of the cosmos as holistic rather than bifurcated. This constellation merits particular attention because it brings together aspects of the *yasashii* ethos that are not evident in Japanese culture.

Okinawans complain of ill health at a rate significantly lower than that of Japan as a whole (Okinawa Prefectural Office 1994: 241). Emiko Ohnuki-Tierney characterizes the Japanese as inordinately concerned with minor illness, extremely frightened of serious illness, and inclined to avoid accepting death even in case of a diagnosis of an obvious terminal disease. This Japanese concern with the causes and symptoms of disease is paralleled by enormous attention to treating illness, attention that includes charms and amulets, visits to temples and shrines (many of which specialize in particular illnesses), Chinese medicine, and Western biomedicine. Ohnuki-Tierney cites a recent study of housewives in the Kyoto, Osaka, and Kobe areas in which 88.1 percent of the women questioned described themselves as suffering from some type of illness (1984: 53).[26]

In Japan, guilt seems to serve as one of the mediating links between the ubiquitous presence of rules and hierarchy, on the one hand, and high rates of illness (and even higher rates of perceived illness) on the other. Margaret Lock interprets the high rate of illness in Japan, especially minor chronic illness, as a nonconfrontational tactic for dealing with group and interpersonal conflict. She argues that somatization often is a form of "self-aggression that represents an attempt to induce changes in the behavior of the people affecting one's life. . . . In Japan several aspects of the cultural heritage . . . serve to reinforce a tendency to somatize" (1987: 136). Because people (and especially women) in Japan are discouraged from the direct expression of their emotions and needs, somatization and talking about physical symptoms become ways to express one's distress and convey it to others. Lock notes that "women themselves, therefore, tend to welcome medicalization of their problems; many of them actively seek out professional care and willingly imbibe medication for problems that they believe originate in social conflict" (1987: 151).[27]

The entire cultural package of stress, conflict, guilt, and illness does not seem to characterize Okinawan villages. Kaja Finkler (personal communication) has suggested that the low rate of illness and perceived illness in Henza may be related to the more general low levels of conflict in the society. As she shows in regard to Mexican women, anger and ensuing illness "are interpretations of the world involving social relationships that have gone awry" (1994: 18). Additionally, Finker demonstrates that in Mexico the threat of sickness is a form of social control: It is believed that if you get angry, you will get sick; therefore, you try not to get angry. In Okinawa, in contrast to both Japan and Mexico, the largely egalitarian and *yasashii* ethos precludes the sorts of structural stresses and conflicts that would tend to be reflected in illness either as an expression of guilt or anger or as an expression of social control. (I return to the issue of illness as an expression of being "out of place" in chapter 7.)

Conclusion

> Henza people pray to be healthy, that is all [that they pray for]. They don't pray for things like to be smart, just to be healthy. They pray for strong legs so as to stand, to be healthy, so that the legs can step on the ground. (Mr. Shinya, school principal)

Despite the conviction that villagers are naturally healthy, on almost every occasion in which I asked a priestess or a lay woman what she was praying for, the answer was "health." In the prayers that I have recorded, the word "health" (kenkoo) is heard more than all other requests and wishes (such as for prosperity, peace, etc.) put together. Even in situations where it looks as if the purpose of a prayer is something else, priestesses insist that health is indeed the theme.[28] The emphasis on health reaches an almost absurd level in exchanges such as these:

> A few days after a funeral at a graveside ritual conducted by a male shaman-type practitioner, I asked a group of women to explain to me what the man was saying in his prayer. "We don't understand the exact words," they said, "but it is just 'you should be healthy.'"

> Dead People's New Year is a day on which recently deceased are visited at their graves, a meal is shared, and relatives pray. I asked a woman in her mid-thirties to tell me the words of her prayer. She answered, "I hope you are healthy."

Obviously, a dead person cannot be healthy in the sense that Westerners mean, just like priestesses praying only for health and nothing else makes little sense given the generally excellent health and outstanding longevity in the village. Health, for Henza villagers, seems to be a metaphor suggesting a diffuse and extensive sense of personal and social wholeness, harmony, and easiness—being yasashii. Health signifies that people, things, and spirits are in an easy relationship to one another—not intruding on each other's turf.

Certainly, not all Henza villagers are mellow, harmonious people who never bicker, quarrel, argue, fight, feel guilty or jealous, or suffer from illness. However, Henza culture does encourage its members to avoid the kinds of strong opinions that can lead to arguments; to avoid the kinds of absolute ideological stances that can lead to according more importance to rules than to relationships; to avoid the kinds of prohibitions which, when trespassed, lead to guilt, shame, recriminations, and illness; to avoid the kinds of social trespassing that can lead to altercations; to avoid the kinds of exhibitions of status and hierarchy that can lead to jealousy, quarreling, or accusations of sorcery; to look down upon war and violence; to cultivate a conversational mode that leads to agreement and compromise; and to re-spect a fairly wide range of exceptional (nonaggressive) talents and handicaps. This ethos is introduced when a baby is born and receives praise for being coopera-tive; is reinforced through expectations of family, friends, and neighbors; and is re-flected in the yasashii cosmology to which we turn in the next chapter.

As I discuss in the following chapters, the *yasashii* ethos has important implica-tions for the ways in which gender is "done" in Henza. First, the cultural ideal of interpersonal interactions is one that men and women equally can hope to attain: Being easygoing is not dependent upon musculature, freedom from the demands of pregnancy and lactation, or any other physiological (or perceived as physiological) characteristic. Second, a large range of talents and proclivities are respected and tolerated in both men and women. Neither men nor women are limited to a small number of mutually exclusive roles, personalities, hobbies, or skills, and those who deviate from common social patterns, including gender patterns, are not scorned or harassed. Third, absolute opinions or ideologies, including notions about gen-der, are less salient than are specific relationships or interactions. Fourth, hierar-chy, including gender hierarchy, is weak and, when it exists, tends to be situa-tional, temporary, fuzzy, and minimized. Fifth, cloudy social relationships are not experienced as problematic, and control of women (or women's bodies) is not used to create social order. And sixth, the notion that people are naturally healthy and that the human body is not polluted, painful, sinful, or in need of moral, medical, or cosmetic modification holds equally true for men and for women. Gender, when it is "done" in Henza, is done in a yasashii way.

Henza's yasashii social arrangements are consistent with what we know about social patterns in other contemporary societies characterized by a gender egalitar-ian cultural ethos. For example, regarding the Vanatinai, a relatively egalitarian people of New Guinea, Maria Lepowsky submits that "societies that are sexually egalitarian tend to place little emphasis on other forms of social stratification such as class, rank, or age grading" (1990: 177). More specifically:

[The] Vanatinai example suggests that sexual equality is facilitated by an overall ethic of respect for an equal treatment of all categories of individu-als, [and] the decentralization of political power. . . . Sex role patterns and gender ideologies are closely related to overall social systems of power and prestige. When these systems stress personal autonomy and egalitatian social relations among all adults, minimizing the formal authority of one person over another, gender equality is possible. (1993: 306)[29]

TWO

Divine Dis-order

On Cosmological Planes

"In the old days Henza was called *kami*'s country because there are many things here related to *kami*." (Mrs. Adaniya, eighty-four years old)

"Henza's religion is the natural one, that came up in the natural way, but now people from mainland Japan come and say, 'What are these people doing?' Even if I explain that this is the natural way, the custom, they don't understand." (former village headman)

MRS. ASATO: The Agaregusuku [east sacred grove] kami-sama is a male kami-sama, it is big, its body is muscular, very hairy.

SUSAN: How do you know, have you seen it?

MRS. ASATO: Yes. Hairy arms like a monkey's arms. There is no one like that kami-sama now born in Henza, with that type of body. So giant.

SUSAN: Does he have a name?

MRS. ASATO: I don't know. The Irigusuku [west sacred grove] kami-sama is a woman, also big, and white. Agaregusuku kami-sama wears a black hat like *uzumaki* [wrapped around like a water cyclone]. The hat doesn't have a visor. This is the kind of hat that Ryukyu kings wore. The kami-sama was very tough looking, muscular.

SUSAN: How did you know it was the Agaregusuku kami-sama?

MRS. ASATO: I didn't know anything at that time. He came through the yard. He came and washed his hands and feet, so I thought that the water that we [ritually] put out on the first and fifteenth of the month, that is what it is for, so kami-sama can wash hands and feet. He washed his feet. The entrance [to the yard] was there [to the south], but he didn't come through the entrance, he came from the east and washed his feet over there in the east side, and then came in.

SUSAN: How did you know this was the Agaregusuku kami-sama?

MRS. ASATO: Because he came from that direction [east]. And the one who comes from Irigusuku is the white one, with a round face. In Henza there is no one so white like that. Round face and white face and white clothes. Like a priestess wears.

45

SUSAN: So you saw both kami-sama?

MRS. ASATO: Yes. Agaregusuku kami-sama wears a black hat and black clothes.

SUSAN: Was this before you became a priestess?

MRS. ASATO: Yes. I had nothing to do with priestesses at that time. I was a regular person. Irigusuku kami-sama was wearing the kind of decoration called *haya duru* that is put on top of the ritual tug-of-war rope. On her hat, like the kind of elaborate hat worn in traditional Okinawan elegant dancing. When I saw her I thought she was wearing the haya duru.

SUSAN: Do you think other people will see those things too?

MRS. ASATO: I don't know.

The ethnographer's task is to represent faithfully, as best she can, what she sees and hears. This understanding of the ethnographic mission places me in something of a dilemma. Henza villagers, on all sorts of occasions, refer—often in vague ways—to many different kami-sama (deities). As a Western intellectual and writer, my own inclination is to organize these kami-sama into categories: nature deities, location deities (sacred grove kami-sama, ocean kami-sama, house kami-sama, hearth kami-sama), occasion deities, individual people's deities, clan deities, yuta's deities, and deities that are in particular materials (wood, shells, etc.). Henza villagers, however, do not recognize these or any other categories. Villagers conceptualize kami-sama neither as related to each other (hierarchically or in any other way) nor as belonging to different groupings. Henza villagers use one multivalent word—kami-sama, which is, like all Japanese nouns, singular and plural and genderless—and they provide no sense of organizing kami-sama by age, appearance, gender, job, power, or realm of action.

My task is further complicated by the fact that it is at best misleading and at worst utterly fallacious to write that "Henza villagers believe" or "Henza villagers say." Henza villagers express a broad range of ideas about kami-sama (and anything else), and no one particular person is believed to officially represent Henza's views. Various religious experts and lay people find significance in various aspects of kami-sama, and all of their views must be taken into account if one wants to get a sense of Henza's cosmological repertoire. This point is well made by Mrs. Asato in the passage with which I opened this chapter. In our conversations, Mrs. Asato was eager to talk about kami-sama whom she has seen, yet she was clear that what she talks about is her own experience; she neither knows nor cares whether other villagers see the same kami-sama.

Many aspects of Henza's cosmology are similar to Japanese cosmology; readers familiar with Japanese religion should not expect to find great novelties here. The culture contact between Okinawa and Japan has been so long and complex that few if any Okinawan institutions are uninfluenced by Japan.[1] On the other hand, there are differences in emphasis, and although a comparison of Japanese and Okinawan religion is far outside the scope of this book, I do draw attention to some of the more interesting of those differences.[2]

". . . So Be Good for Goodness' Sake"

Mrs. Noriko Goeku, one of my closest friends in the village, joined me in a discussion of human behavior—why people do good things. In this conversation, Noriko and I were on totally different conceptual planes—neither of us understood what the other one was saying (a situation typical of anthropological fieldwork!).

SUSAN: Do Okinawan kami-sama give rules about how people should act?

NORIKO: No.

SUSAN: Then why don't Okinawans steal or do bad things?

NORIKO: Because of the police. [Note: in small Okinawan villages doors are unlocked, there is negligible police presence, and although there is plenty to steal, there is almost no theft.]

SUSAN: What if the police don't see, what stops someone?

NORIKO: A good person doesn't steal.

SUSAN: Do kami-sama see what people do?

NORIKO: No.

SUSAN: Do kami-sama punish?

NORIKO: No.

SUSAN: What about after you die, do bad people get punished?

NORIKO: No. After someone dies people only say good things about that person; it is not good to say bad things about that person.

SUSAN: Do good people and bad people have the same things happen to them after they die?

NORIKO: Yes.

SUSAN: For example, Christians believe that good people are rewarded and bad people punished after death, and Buddhists have different kinds of reincarnations for good and bad people. What do Okinawans believe?

NORIKO: Same for everyone. But you can only say good things about someone who is dead.

SUSAN: Do Okinawans believe in heaven and hell?

NORIKO (with sudden understanding): Oh yes, at Christmas, Santa Claus rewards good people!

SUSAN: Is that why people are good?

NORIKO: No.

SUSAN: Do people here believe that if you do bad things you will be punished on earth, for example, through sickness?

NORIKO: Sort of, people think for example that you had a car accident because last week you did a bad thing.

SUSAN (with excitement): Oh, so kami-sama do see and punish?

NORIKO: No!

SUSAN (with mounting frustration): So where does the punishment come from?

[Pause in the conversation.]

SUSAN: Is it automatic?

NORIKO: I think so. For example, someone's grandchild is sick and the yuta gives a judgment that it is because that person did something bad. But it is not caused by kami-sama, but automatically.

SUSAN: So if you can't tell your children that if they are bad kami-sama will punish them, how do you teach them to do good things?

NORIKO: Well, maybe sometimes we spank the child. But not very much. Mostly, we talk to the children a lot and explain.

SUSAN: Well, what if the child asks why, for example, not to steal?

NORIKO: I would say that I have lived longer and know more whereas the child has only lived a short time. Actually, we teach more by personal example than by talking.

SUSAN: Do you tell children things like, if you do bad things no one will like you?

NORIKO: No. It's not like that. You do good things because you have a good heart, for yourself, not because of friends or kami-sama.

As Noriko demonstrated in this conversation, the concept of kami-sama concerning themselves with people's behavior is irrelevant and incomprehensible. When pushed against a wall by my awkward and bumbling questions, the only example of a powerful "god" that she could come up with was foreign—Santa Claus! But since there are no Christians on Henza Island and Noriko herself knows next to nothing about Christmas or Christ, her Santa Claus remark should not be interpreted in a Christian context.

Henza villagers do not celebrate Christmas in any way except for an annual party at the local nursery school. These parties are part of the education ministry curriculum and are embraced by the nursery school staff, who, like most other villagers, enjoy any reason for a party. A few months before this conversation with Noriko, I had participated in one of these Christmas parties (two of my children were attending the nursery school, and Noriko has had three children attend the nursery school in recent years). The program consisted of children performing Okinawan-style and Japanese-style dances and songs. At the climax of the party, the head teacher stood up in front of the room full of children, teachers, and parents and, microphone in hand, asked in an upbeat voice:

TEACHER: Who's been good this year? I hear bells ringing. Children, who is coming now?

[reverberating silence]

TEACHER: Children, who has been good this year?

[silence]

TEACHER: Who can expect a toy as a reward for being good?

[silence, except some bored chair shuffling from the younger children]

TEACHER (with a big smile and simulated excitement in her voice): Who is that coming, listen, there are bells.

[silence]

TEACHER: Santa Claus!

Into the midst of the politely silent room (silence is a typical Okinawan reaction to confusion or incomprehension) walked one of the fathers, dressed in a red Santa Claus costume and carrying a sack of toys. A few of the children cried a bit at the sight of a big red man with a bushy white beard, but most children quickly figured out that what they were supposed to do was to rush to the front of the room and reach out their hands for toys. This Santa Claus, then, is Noriko's sole association to the question of whether kami-sama reward and punish people's behavior. In fact, Noriko literally believes that one should be good for goodness' sake ("because you have a good heart, for yourself") and not for God's sake.

In our conversation, Noriko volunteered only one bit of information without my prodding her: It is not good to say bad things about someone who is dead. She attempted to move our discussion away from reward and punishment at the hand of kami-sama (my Western concern) to proper behavior on the part of the living toward the dead (her Okinawan concern). On the famous Kohlberg scale of moral development, Noriko expressed a higher level of ethical development than I. Whereas I was talking about behaving well in order to obey laws and avoid punishment by a higher authority, Noriko was talking about universally recognized principles of justice and mutual respect that the individual is capable of interpreting and applying him- or herself (Kohlberg 1981; Gilligan 1982).

I find Noriko's volunteered comment significant for another reason. Words are understood by Henza villagers to have the power to call kami-sama into being; that is one of the meanings of ritual.[3] If we look closely at Noriko's words, we see that "living people only say good things about dead people" came in answer to a question about punishment after death. For Noriko, saying bad things about the dead would in itself constitute a punishment—it would call something bad, something undesirable, into being. The ability to punish the deceased lies in the hands (or mouths and hearts) of the living and not in the hands of the kami. But because, as we shall discuss below, the deceased also affect the fortunes and misfortunes of the living, this ability is reciprocal. Noriko's worldview here is looser than the classic Buddhist circular view of cause and effect: Each cause simultaneously has an effect and is an effect.

There is an expression, *bachi ga ataru*, which means, it comes back to you. . . . People don't really think about it, whether bad things happen automatically or because of kami-sama. *Bachi ga ataru* means, like, for example, when I am pregnant, if someone says bad things about it and then she gets pregnant and the baby has red marks on it, it is because of what she did. But kami-sama didn't do it to her. (Ms. Kumi Yamada)

Mr. Miyezato is one of the male assistants at the rituals of the village priestesses:

SUSAN: Why do Okinawan people do good things? Do kami-sama punish and reward?

MR. MIYEZATO: If you don't pray at the altar when you should, or something like this, your family will not be lucky. Get sick. Also, if you do bad things, bad things will happen to your grandchildren.

Mr. Miyezato is suggesting here that, through ritual, Henza villagers can tap into something called "luck." But note his avoidance of the word "punish" or an explicit statement of involvement on the part of kami-sama. He has clarified that one's actions have results—bad things can happen to one's grandchildren. What he has not spelled out is the mechanism. I believe that he has not spelled out the mechanism because I had set the conceptual stage in our conversation by talking about kami-sama punishing and not about cause and effect and the power of human actions and words.

Mr. Hikoski, unlike most other villagers, has had extensive contacts with foreigners. He contends that people avoid doing bad things because kami-sama will punish them:

MR. HIKOSKI: Just like Christianity.

SUSAN: What is the punishment, is it in the next world after you die?

MR. HIKOSKI: No.

SUSAN: In this world? What kind of punishment, like bad things happen?

MR. HIKOSKI: No, you feel bad in your heart. That is the punishment kami-sama give for people doing bad things, that people feel bad in their heart.

Mr. Hikoski's remarks do not mean that Henza villagers believe that the only reason to behave well is for one's own inner sense of peace and contentment. To the contrary, feelings in the heart cause behaviors which bring further events into being. As Noriko has explained, people do good things because they have good hearts (on a "clean heart" as the arbiter of human behavior in Japanese mythology, see Pelzel 1974: 24). In all of these comments, the locus stays firmly in human behavior.

I quote now at some length from Mr. Shinya, the local school principal. In this excerpt, we see a theme that is crucial to Okinawan understandings of kami-sama: There is no ontological difference between kami-sama and humans. Kami-sama are not all-powerful beings who demand obedience to a set of laws. Rather, kami-sama are an ongoing and integral part of the household who encourage good behavior by their benevolent presence. I began by asking him why people in Henza do good things and whether kami-sama punish people who do bad things:

No. In Okinawa we respect ancestors. People will think that the ancestor who dies is a kami-sama. On the other hand, in other countries ancestors are not kami-sama, the Christians have a Christian god, it is not someone in direct relationship to you that you pray to. In Okinawa, kami-sama is your parents or grandparents or great-grandparents, someone who is directly related to you. Your ancestors look at you, they see you, they are watching you to see that you do good things. That is what we are taught here. But there is nothing like if you do the wrong thing there is a punishment. Always grandparents are taking care of you, looking after you, so be good. The education from a long time is that from the household altar [butsudan] the grandparents are looking at you. There is direct educational teaching in the house because there is an altar. That is the main part of how we teach. That is a bit different from mainland Japan. It is not like someone who is not related to you is directing you, it is in the family that you are taught. Kami-sama is in your altar.

Mr. Shinya, a professional educator, is most comfortable using educational jargon, but his ideas are typical of Henza's cultural ethos. He stresses the importance of the closeness between people and kami-sama, a closeness that is expressed in terms of family relationship (the kami-sama are near relatives), in terms of location (the altar is in the house), and in terms of ontological substance (people become kami-sama when they die). It is this natural closeness, rather than the power and authority of a transcendent God, that leads to naturally good behavior on the part of Okinawans and natural benevolence on the part of kami-sama (see also W. Lebra 1966: 31ff. on supernatural punishment).

Okinawan culture is highly empirical—villagers are unlikely to believe wholeheartedly in something that they cannot see. The answer to my cosmological questions was often "I don't know, I never met/saw/heard one."

I now cite one of my favorite conversations with Mrs. Tanahara:

SUSAN: You told me that the hinu-kan [hearth kami-sama] goes up to the sky on December 24 to report about your family. When it returns, does it punish you if you did bad things during the year?

MRS. TANAHARA: No! [She seems to think this is a ridiculous question.]

SUSAN: Christians have a "good god" and "bad god," is it like that here?

MRS. TANAHARA: No. Everyone goes to heaven [tengoku] they don't go to jigoku [hell; tengoku and jigoku are Japanese words.]

SUSAN: Are there any bad kami-sama?

MRS. TANAHARA: I haven't met such a one, so I don't know.

People behave well because they have good hearts, because they are embedded in relationships with ancestors and descendants, and because they understand that "what goes around comes around." I find it interesting that villagers believe that good things are contagious—that is why it is good to get a gift or some food from a person who has lived long (aiakari)—but bad luck is not contagious; one does not need to be afraid of coming near someone who is unfortunate (this does not seem to be the case in mainland Japan; see Befu 1974: 211).

Villagers do not devote very much intellectual or ritual energy to evil spirits, demons, witches, divine punishment, guilt, sin, or cosmic pollution. There is little preoccupation with dangerous forces: People are not particularly afraid of other people, ancestors, or spirits hurting them.[4] In fact, the nonhuman creature I heard mentioned most frequently—the kijimuna, a kind of hairy ocean-dwelling tree sprite—is not bad but rather playful, amusing, or at worst, annoying; he is known for trying to befriend humans and catch fish for them (but because he eats one of the eyes no one really likes the fish he catches).

A term I did hear fairly often is warui koto (lit., 'bad things'). Warui koto refer to what, in English, is encompassed by several distinct linguistic and conceptual categories: insects, nasty spirits, misfortune, misdeeds, and illness. In conversation, it is common for villagers to switch back and forth among the several meanings:

SUSAN: Why do you throw ocean water around the house?

MRS. SHIMOJO: Ocean water is salt water and that is used to clean [kiyomeru] one's own house. It used to be that there were snakes and roaches, those warui koto, so that those small animals won't come into the house, that is why we did it. We threw salt water onto the ground.

I had seen Mrs. Adaniya and other villagers use salt to cure various physical ailments (for example, she rubbed salt on my daughter's abdomen to ease a stomachache). Even more commonly, villagers sprinkle salt on the hands and body after attending funerals in order to keep the recently departed away. I asked Mrs. Adaniya:

SUSAN: Where do warui koto come from?

MRS. ADANIYA: What?

SUSAN: For example, why do you use salt?

MRS. ADANIYA: For example, if in this house there is death or accidents or illness, if someone had these warui koto, to get rid of it [oharai], that is what the salt is for.

SUSAN: Why do warui koto come?

MRS. ADANIYA: If you are honest and serious, no one will hate you and say warui koto about you. You have to build up good relationships with others also. If you don't have good relationships with others, if when you are alive you do warui koto, it could be that there will be a message through your grandchildren [something unfortunate will happen to your grandchildren] while you are alive. When you do warui koto a spiritual thing [rei][5] will come to your grandchildren.

SUSAN: How do you get rid of warui koto, salt?

MRS. ADANIYA: Salt, yes. In my case, I say, "From now on, I won't have bad thoughts about other people. I won't do warui koto." If warui koto happens to me, through the hinu-kan I say, "I won't have bad thoughts, I won't do warui koto."

This dialogue is complex. The impression created is that speech can call warui koto into being: Because you do bad things, people may say bad things about you, and that can cause bad things such as death or accidents or illness to come into your house. In Mrs. Adaniya's conception, there is no ontological distinction between misfortune and misdeed—between bad thoughts and words and things—and salt can get rid of all.

According to Mrs. Adaniya, the misdeed may be located with the ancestor and the misfortune with the descendant. Yet the interesting point is this: The ancestor's misdeeds may reappear as misfortune for the descendants but may also reappear as misdeeds by the descendants that turn into misfortune for the ancestors. Several other villagers elucidated this idea, starting from different points in the potential sequence. According to Noriko, when someone is born handicapped, the yuta will say that this is because the ancestors are unhappy or neglected by their descendants. According to Mrs. Shimojo, there once were lepers who would go around Okinawa and beg for food. "When there was low tide they would cross the ocean to come here. Because they need food to survive. The people from Henza, if they don't give food to those people, maybe their grandchildren will turn to be like that too. So they gave them food, a bit of money or rice." In other words, the ancestors' misdeeds can bring misfortune to the descendants (the ancestor was stingy, so the descendant becomes a leper), but the descendant's misdeeds (neglecting the ancestral altar) also brings misfortune (both to the ancestor who is neglected and to the descendent who is born handicapped). In these analyses, misdeeds and misfortune bounce back and forth between ancestors and descendants; the one who suffers the warui koto is not necessarily the one who did the warui koto. But in the end, it is really all the same, because, of course, descendants become ancestors who continue in a relationship with their descendants.

Henza villagers do not posit a concept of higher-order beings who punish mortals for bad behavior or who capriciously cause suffering in this world. Their worldview emphasizes that "what goes around comes around," that goodness generates goodness and badness generates badness, that what constitutes goodness and badness is, for the most part, situation-dependent and that health and goodness are the norm. Bad things materialize when people do bad things, such as saying bad things about neighbors or neglecting their ritual duties toward their ancestors. Local religious culture provides rituals and techniques for taking care of these kinds of misfortune-causing problems. The central cosmological and existential concepts in village culture are not good and bad in the sense of rules originating with and adjucated by a god or gods, but rather interpersonal harmony and responsibility that are generated by and mediated through human agency.

Immanence

Okinawan religion has been described by previous ethnographers as more concerned with ritual than with cosmology (W. Lebra 1966: 43, 46, 204). I am not convinced that this assessment is true. On the one hand, when I asked villagers to tell me about festivals or ceremonies, their answers typically dealt with the exact date or precisely who attends the event. On the other hand, the calendrical and personnel details came in response to questions that, from the start, concerned ritual. When I spoke to villagers about kami-sama, they were interested in discussing matters of cosmology.

Henza villagers do not seem to have a notion of "god" (or gods) as a discrete entity (or entities). Kami-sama can more accurately be described as a kind of spiritual state or energy. The *noro* priestess, like several other villagers with whom I spoke, uses the word *dempa*—electric wave—to describe the presence of kami-sama.[6] Kami-sama becomes germane when it is concentrated in a particular place, time, or person. The way to concentrate *kami-sama* is through ritual. Rituals can be seen as techniques for actualizing kami-sama.[7] In the conversation cited at the beginning of this chapter, for instance, we see that Mrs. Asato assumes that kami-sama came because she had put out the semimonthly bowl of water in her yard: Her ritual brought the kami-sama into being. Without ritual, kami-sama has little relevance to human beings: It remains diffuse, potential, but not a describable presence. This means, of course, that rituals are far more than social dramas (Turner 1969) or cultural performances (Geertz 1969); they are the means by which kami-sama comes into a perceptible state of being.

Kami-sama are potentially accessible through rituals and visions; many villagers have seen kami-sama, and all villagers engage in harnessing or concentrating kami-sama through ritual. Villagers refer to the kami-sama of particular rituals: kami-sama of *ama goi* (a rain ritual) or kami-sama of February *umachi* (an agricultural ritual). When these rituals are performed, kami-sama is called into being.

I cite here one of the most interesting comments I heard during my stay in Henza. At a ritual to transfer the hearth deity (hinu-kan) from her old house to her new house, Mrs. Shinyashiki, at the direction of an ogami person, (a kind of ritual expert; "prayer" person) placed three piles each of three sticky rice cakes in front of the hinu-kan:

SUSAN: Why do you do this?

MRS. SHINYASHIKI: Only kami-sama know.

MRS. SHINYASHIKI'S SISTER-IN-LAW: Only the person who *does* kami-sama knows.

In the eyes of Henza villagers, kami-sama do not "do"—they do not punish, reward, create, or know—they are not discrete entities capable of action or knowledge. If we take Mrs. Shinyashiki's sister-in-law's comment seriously (as I believe we should), we learn that kami-sama is "done"—kami-sama is a verb rather than a noun.[8] I would venture to suggest that the reason that ritual is so important in

Okinawa is because ritual is, literally, "doing" kami-sama; ritual gives form to kami-sama, conceptualizes kami-sama, materializes kami-sama, conjures kami-sama; ritual transforms kami-sama from a verb of potentiality to a noun of actuality.

Henzans are more concerned with experiencing than with believing matters having to do with kami-sama. For instance, a great deal of attention is given to the exact path or route on which priestesses or other villagers walk at particular rituals. The similarity to native Australian religion is striking: Henzans, like native Australians, *walk* the stories or spiritual energies that Westerners *talk*.

My suspicion is that previous ethnographers, in claiming that Okinawans are not interested in cosmology, picked up on the Okinawan style of cosmological discourse, and in particular, the lack of doctrines, dogmas, and tenets in that discourse. Members of world religions generally believe that their own religious beliefs are absolutely true, are true for everyone (that is the meaning of a world religion), are unchanging, and are codifiable. None of this is the case in Okinawan cosmology, a fact that may tend to make Okinawan cosmological discourse invisible and inaudible to Western observers. Westerners generally speak about, pray to, and write about a deity who is, in some manner, a separate entity—named, unique, powerful, and nonhuman. This deity creates, commands, and judges; the ultimate arbiter of human action is the nonhuman God. For Okinawans, divinity is so totally embedded within humanity and human experience that the notion of a deity who rules, rewards, and punishes is incomprehensible; the ultimate arbiter of human action is the human heart and community.

Kami-sama are immanent in this world and this world's creatures. Josef Kreiner explains that, "[There] is a very strong belief in one entirety, made up by this world of men and the Other World. The deity . . . resides all year round with the people and is always among them. In the words of an old priestess of the Okinawan island of Kakeroma: How could life exist in this world even for one moment, if the deity would not stay with us every moment!" (1968: 114). As a cosmological stance, total immanence fits well with the "naturally healthy" worldview described in the previous chapter. Kami-sama potentially can be anywhere: in the toilet, in the pigpen, in the kitchen, in the altar, in the mountains, in the ocean, in castles, in the stars, in animals, and in humans. Villagers cannot go anywhere that is not somehow associated with kami-sama; the entire Henza universe is, in some way, imbued with *"kami-ness."* Kami-sama *are* whatever they are kami-sama of.[9]

The immanence of kami-sama is illustrated, to my mind, by one of the more striking differences between Okinawan and Japanese prayer behavior. In Japan it is customary to begin and end prayers with noise (clapping of hands or ringing a bell) that serves to call the kami-sama (Ashkenazi 1983: 63). These sorts of loud attention-getting ritual practices are very rarely done in Henza, suggesting, I believe, that for Henzans kami-sama is already present—or at least very nearby. Henza priestesses and shaman-type practitioners sometimes rub their hands together gently before they begin to pray, and prayers are begun by quietly reciting the word *utooto*, which means, according to Mrs. Shimojo, "We are going to start praying. *Hajimimashite* [pleased to meet you]." One priestess, Mrs. Jana, explained that putting the two hands together is to get all of the people who are praying together to pray as one. "Utooto—for everybody; people who do utooto have to have those feelings inside, for everybody to get together." On an energetic or spiritual level, according to Rikki Horowitz, a Western healer, with whom I discussed this issue, clapping hands serves to dispel negative energy and disperse stagnant energy, whereas rubbing or pressing hands together raises and focuses energy. My sense is that Henza villagers understand kami-sama to be present everywhere but in a very diffuse way. Ritual such as pressing hands together does not summon or dispel spiritual forces the way it does in Japan (cf. Blacker 1975: 35ff.; 107ff.), but rather it focuses or concentrates kami-sama so that kami-sama can be related to. In this context, I am struck by a passage from the *Omoro sooshi* (recorded in the sixteenth and seventeenth centuries) in which the ritual behavior of the chief priestess of Okinawa is described in this way:

> She presses her hands together, concentrating
> shining, in the southwest corner of the castle
> incandescent inside the castle shrine

(Nakamoto, Minoru, and Drake 1985: 33, as cited in Kawahashi 1992: 45).

The kinds of ontological distinctions commonly made in the West (human versus divine; inanimate versus animate; living versus dead)—distinctions which presuppose that one entity can only have one ontological status—are not relevant to Okinawan worldviews.[10] The hinu-kan can be a functional stone used for placing pots on the hearth *and* it can be the hearth kami-sama; *ryugu* (cf. Blacker 1975: 75) can be the world of the ocean kami-sama, or it can be, as one villager put it, "the kami-sama who died in the ocean," or it can simply mean ocean; a priestess can be a person *and* she can be kami-sama; certain priestesses can be women *and* they can be male kami-sama.[11] These kinds of multiple identities are not perceived as problematic, and therefore do not elicit attention, diagnosis, interpretation, or exegesis.

Henza priestesses (*noro* and *kaminchu*) are most commonly referred to as kami-sama. As I will discuss in greater detail in chapter 6, this is not a mere turn of phrase—the priestesses *are* kami-sama.[12] Both the priestess, a matrilineal descendant of the ancestor, and the ancestor, a matrilineal forebear of the priestess, are kami-sama. The relationship between the kami-sama and priestess is not hierarchical—the *kami* does not possess or control her. Rather, they are assimilated into one another. The priestesses who go to the sacred groves are descendants of the founding families of Henza. The clan priestesses are descendants of other Henza clans. Each priestess is assimilated to a kami-sama who is an ancestor who is also, in some way, the essence of the clan. Thus on several occasions I also heard villagers use the term kami-sama to refer to the clan. This usage suggests that the clan is in some way an embodiment of kami-sama, that in the collectivity of the *munchu* the clan ancestors are present.[13]

The kami-sama who appear to villagers in visions are typically dressed like priestesses, and villagers give offerings to the priestesses (embodied kami-sama) in the same way that they give offerings to ancestors and other (disembodied) kami-sama. The identification among ancestors, historical figures, priestesses, and kami-sama in village cosmology is illustrated by the comments of Mrs. Asato that opened this chapter: The male kami-sama is described as dressing like a Ryukyu king and the female kami-sama as dressing like a kaminchu. My own fieldwork was constantly complicated by (what I understood to be) the dual usage of the word kami-sama. We would begin conversations in which I would ask about the ocean kami-sama or the Irigusuku (sacred grove) kami-sama. The villager would tell me some rituals associated with these kami-sama. In my next question I would ask the names of kami-sama, and the villager's answer typically would be a list of the current priestesses ("Oh, yes, Mrs. Ishikawa, she lives in Okinawa City now"). The point is of course, that the two uses are my perception, not theirs. Villagers generally refer to the priestesses simply as kami-sama and do not make linguistic distinctions between kami-sama who are living, embodied humans residing in Henza and kami-sama who are not.

Henzans pray and perform rituals in a variety of locations around the island. Water sources, particular points along the coast, and certain groves of trees are all understood to be especially filled with *"kami*-ness." Certain key rituals of the noro and her associates are carried out at the west and east sacred groves, Irigusuku and Agaregusuku. Villagers talk about the identity of the kami-sama associated with the west and east sacred groves in concrete, historical terms. According to the village priestess, Mrs. Ishikawa: "The king, the one of Nakijin, Oezato, Shuri, Nakagusuku, or one of those places, I am not sure which king that was, or the descendant of the king, visited Henza and got women pregnant and left the children to be born here [*umiotosareru* 'to be born in various places'], and those children are the clan kami-sama, and are prayed to. The children who died here, they are the ones who are prayed to." According to Mrs. Adaniya, "Izena Aji [*aji* means 'chieftain'; Izena Aji probably lived in the fifteenth century] was the one who originally built Irigusuku and Agaregusuku. . . . That is the island kami-sama [*shima no kami sama*]. . . . There was a time that only two or three houses were in this village, those are the ones who go to [pray at] Irigusuku and Agaregusuku, the original people in this village."14

We learn a few things from these accounts. First, some of Henza's most important ritual places are associated with Izena Aji, a figure who lived in the historically traceable past, not in the mythological beginning of time. Although this figure is sometimes described as the kami-sama of the island, only certain clans send priestesses to pray at the groves—the clans who lived in Henza when Izena Aji built the shrines; other clans are neither forced nor encouraged to acknowledge the kami-sama of the oldest clans. Second, the clan kami-sama are simply the children of knights who sowed their seed in Henza a few centuries ago (cf. Tanaka 1977: 48). There is no moral or dramatic story associated with them.15 I asked one of the priestesses which kami-sama is at the sacred grove, and her answer was, "It is Mrs. Kamura's [the noro's] mother's mother's mother's mother's long-time-ago kami-sama." Significantly, neither the kami-sama's name nor story were mentioned, but rather the name of the person who currently has a relationship with the kami-sama. Finally, not all Henzans even associate the sacred groves with historical figures—for many villagers the groves are significant simply because of their geographical location near certain water sources or because of their trees (it is forbidden to pick leaves or flowers in the sacred groves—except the ones that the priestesses use for their crowns—or to urinate in the groves).

"They All Have the Same Rank"

Kami-sama in Henza does not carry the connotations of power or rank that we in the West normally associate with God—kami-sama does not stand outside of or above human reality.[16] The stance of absolute immanence has profound effects upon interpersonal relationships. If an old peasant woman who, in her everyday life, looks like any other old peasant woman is actually kami-sama, then in fact anyone and everyone is or may be, in one way or another, kami-sama. Not surprisingly, abuse—whether of children, women, handicapped people, or the elderly—is most uncommon in Henza.

Dominance of any sort does not seem to be part of Henza's cosmology. Unlike in mainland Japan, former kings are not salient to the religious life of Henza, and religiously inspired political ideologies have not been part of Okinawan cultural experience (cf. Kitagawa 1987: xvii, 49, 53–57, 74). In comparison to Christian, Hindu, and Buddhist deities who boast unique personalities, associated myths, and the ability to perform miracles (Powers 1995: 162–163; Parrinder 1982; Hick 1993; Williams 1985), Okinawan kami-sama are amorphous and powerless. The ability to perform miracles implies that the deity holds some sort of power that is not held by "regular" human beings and that, in some way, lies outside of nature.[17] This kind of conceptualization of the deity is not found in Henza.

Indeed, kami-sama do not really "do" anything. We saw in the chapter-opening dialogue that when the kami-sama appeared to Mrs. Asato, their appearance was striking, and she is still, many years later, impressed and fascinated by their presence. Yet when they came to her yard, they neither said nor did anything. The contrast to nineteenth- and twentieth-century Marian apparitions is striking; Mrs. Asato's kami-sama neither had a message for humankind nor showed any special powers (for example, healing).

Unlike in Western religions in which an important function of gods is creation (most of the religions with which we are familiar have creation myths of one kind or another, and these myths often contain laws for human behavior), Henza villagers do not speak of kami-sama as creators. More generally, villagers know few myths or legends of any kind.[18] In response to my question about kami-sama and creation, one of the village priestesses, Mrs. Ishikawa, answered, "I don't know. We don't know those things. Like how Henza was formed, or things like that." On other occasions when I asked elderly Henza villagers about how the world was created, their answers, typically after a great deal of thought, comprised bits and pieces of modern astronomy and Darwinism.

The absence of mythology reflects the absence of an idealized past in villagers' accounts of Okinawan and local history. Although there has been a great deal of change, both religious and nonreligious, over the past 100 years, villagers rarely claim that the old days were better or that people used to be more spiritual or moral (although they do say that people used to worry less before there was cash).

According to Ms. Kumi Yamada, "Ancestors are good and bad—long time ago people were not better than today's people." The absence of an idealized past, together with the absence of a codified cosmology, sustain the *yasashii* social patterns described in chapter 1. For Henza villagers, there is no one right way to do things.[19]

> Narratives of origin tell people what kind of world it is, what it consists of, and where they stand in it; they make it seem natural to them. . . . Origin myths, precisely because they hook individual identities to ontological realities, are not substitutable; they describe the natural and supernatural orders that people often fight over and are willing to die for. (Yanagisako and Delaney 1995: 1–3)

In Henza, the absence of elaboration of mythologies or rules that claim divine origin means that social arrangements—and most especially patterns of power—do not tend to become naturalized or idealized.

The past for most Henza villagers is the recent past—World War II or perhaps slightly before the war. Even the most loquacious elderly villagers—women and men who enjoyed talking to me about anything and everything—came up with surprisingly few stories when I asked them to tell me folktales. The same one or two stories tended to come out after I did a fair amount of memory jogging (after the first blank response to my general question, I would ask if they knew any stories about families, lovers, kings, spirits, ghosts, fishermen, etc.). The thin repertoire suggests to me that villagers are disinterested in explaining how things got to be the way they are, in teaching the next generation idealized behavior patterns, and in generating a social or cosmological ideology.[20]

Henza kami-sama are neither models of good nor models of bad. (This is true of deities in certain other women-led religions as well; on the nat of Myanmar, for example, see Spiro 1967.) There are no great benevolent lords or thoroughly evil devils. Most are somewhat fair to middling, yasashii sorts of divinities—depending on how they are treated. Unlike the Greek, Roman, Hindu, and Japanese models of polytheism with which we are well acquainted (see Pelzel 1974 on Japanese mythology and its meaning for human behavior), Henza kami-sama do not have personalities or elaborated mythologies. Although clan members know snatches of the history of their clan kami-sama, kami-sama are usually unnamed and without idiosyncratic personalities. There are no statues or visual representations of kami-sama.

Unlike in Western liturgy, Okinawan prayer seldom refers to any deity by name. I asked Mrs. Ikene, an ogami person:

SUSAN: Which kami-sama are they [that you say in your prayer]?

MRS. IKENE: They come from above, I don't know what kind.

Here is a conversation with one of the men who assists the *noro:*

SUSAN: Who is Henza's kami-sama, does it have a name?

MR. MIYEZATO: It used to have a name a long time ago. I don't know it. Now we just say kami-sama.

Kami-sama do not have relationships, hierarchical or otherwise, among themselves. On one occasion, Noriko Goeku and I read through a Japanese-English collection of Okinawan folktales published by a Japanese bank. In one story ("Kajimaya"), there was a character called, in English, "Almighty God" (in Japanese—*erai no kami-sama*). Noriko was astonished to hear this terminology. "There are many kami-sama, like Katsurengusuku kami-sama and Nakagusuku kami-sama, but they all have the same rank, there is no first ranking one." Kami-sama do not serve as a prototype for power relations among humans.

According to one yuta, Mrs. Uyealtari, "Henza does not have a main kami-sama; each individual clan has kami-sama." Some people might believe certain kami-sama to be especially relevant, yet there is no notion of hierarchical nesting. The kami-sama associated with Irigusuku and Agaregusuku are not on top of, over, or in charge of the clan kami-sama. Social arrangements of kami-sama are similar to those of the clans—in Henza, there is no chief clan, and headman is a rotating job, but some clans are informally understood to be larger, older, more prosperous, or more active than others. Unlike in Japan, where many people pray to Amaterasu, the sun kami, Henzans recognize no one kami who is significant for all Henzans.[21]

According to Mrs. Adaniya, "A family that has someone who died in the ocean will believe in the ocean kami-sama. I don't have an ancestor who died in the ocean. That is why I pray mainly at Irigusuku (west sacred grove) and Agaregusuku (east sacred grove)." Clan kaminchu only pray to their own clan kami-sama, not to those of other clans. Each kami-sama is given offerings at a particular altar in the munchu house; each priestess is associated with one kami-sama and not with any other.

Although the world is imbued with "kami-ness," specific kami-sama are understood to be highly localized, and, therefore, kami-sama are prayed to in particular places.[22] Villagers devote a great deal of ritual attention to reporting relevant information to kami-sama. Here is how one priestess talks about building houses for her adult children:

> When you buy property, like when you build a new house, you have to report to the kami-ya of that area. If you don't report, the kami-sama will say that there was no report. That's very important, just like registering at the city office. That's how it is done in Okinawa. You have to report to the kami-sama, and then the kami-sama protects everyone.

Okinawan prayers, both of priestesses and of shaman-type practitioners, inform kami-sama of who is speaking, where, when, and why. Take the following excerpt from a prayer by the ogami person, Mrs. Ikene, at the occasion of the opening of a new building to be used for funeral ceremonies at the local cemetery:

> Today is the eighteenth, it is a good day, we are waiting for kami-sama to come on such a good day. The people of Henza built this place together. We have food and sweets, and seventeen packets of incense here. It did not used to be like this, but the society changed so we have to follow those changes so that is why we had to build this building.[23] So the people who go to another

world can go through here. The carpenters built this using materials. So kami-sama, help make my prayer go through. So prayers will go through well, so this place will be okay, even though it is something new. So headman and village committee and everyone will be of one mind. We prayed at this place last November [she turns to the headman to clarify the date] before we began to build, and everything went smoothly, and now it is completed. This is the wish of the village people, that the dead people should go through here to the other world. People from different houses will all go through here to the other world. The money from renting land to the oil company paid for this building. . . . The concrete was brought by. . . . the wood came from. . . .

Conspicuous in this prayer is the amount of explanation and detail. Mrs. Ikene's prayer reveals that kami-sama need to be told the date, the nature of the food and incense offerings, the reason for the gathering and the identities of the people at the gathering, the history of the event, the amounts and sources of money concerned, and with what materials the building was constructed. To my mind, this litany of informative details suggests that kami-sama are not expected to know these things without being told. Note also that the only request made of the kami-sama ("help make my prayer go through") does not reflect a cosmology of power or dominance.

Villagers do not understand kami-sama to be omniscient, omnipresent, or omnipotent. Going back to my Santa Claus conversation with Noriko, kami-sama do *not* "know when you are sleeping or know when you're awake." Henza's kami-sama are dis-ordered; that is, they are nonhierarchical, unclassified, vaguely conceptualized, all over the place but not omnipresent, and somewhat nebulous until called to order by ritual. They are not only dis-ordered but also disinterested in giving orders—Henza's kami-sama do not order doctrines, rewards, or punishments. Henza's kami-sama confound our Western notions of a natural order in which human, culture, nature, and deities are ontologically distinct orders of being.

> To think about religion, even for those of us who have "no faith," is to be influenced by the assumptions and attitudes of the Christian tradition. In this tradition, religion is ultimately about accepting and submitting to authority. . . . As Nietzsche pointed out a long time ago, our faith is the faith of the dog that gets beaten and takes that as proof that his master loves him. . . . My sense of the Manjaco [an African society] was that they did not have this kind of faith precisely because their religion was not hierarchical. This means that the Manjaco act as if the spirit-human relationship depended on a social contract that a people writes or rewrites according to its civic interests. . . . Manjaco can be skeptical about the utility of this contract. (Gable 1995: 254)

In writing about the Manjaco of Africa, Eric Gable challenges Western notions of the relationship between humans and deities, specifically the notion that this relationship is necessarily hierarchical. The questions that this leads to are both social and conceptual: Does the lack of a human-divine hierarchy mean that humans are empowered and that the divine is disempowered? Does the lack of human-divine hierarchy reflect or produce a lack of hierarchy among humans? Does the lack of human-divine hierarchy imply a more pervasive lack of existential or ontological difference? As I understand Henza society, the answer to these questions is "yes."

Gender of the Deities

In a statistical analysis of 312 societies around the world, Ronald Stover and Christine Hope (1984) found a clear relationship between monotheism—which is almost always the belief in one male god—and gender inequality. In a very different sort of study, Judith Ochshorn has uncovered an interrelationship between the rise of monotheism and gender inequality in ancient Near Eastern religions. "Where there was a polytheistic pantheon and cultic practices directed toward its propitiation, the presence of both sexes in the priesthood, in cult, and in popular religion was almost universal" (1981: 108; see also Lerner 1986). Writing about the Greco-Roman world, Ross Kraemer further suggests that:

> There is conceivably some relationship between monotheism and the exclusion of women from Jewish and Christian priesthood, an exclusion that carries over to monotheistic Islam as well. When divinity is perceived to be one, and the gender of that divinity effectively presented as masculine in language, imagery, and so forth, perhaps only the sex which shares that gender is perceived as able to perform priestly functions. Conversely, among the Greeks and Romans both the gods and their clergy came in two genders. (1992, 197)[24]

Almost all women-led religions relate to many spirits, gods, or ancestors—even in cultural contexts in which the mainstream religion is monotheistic (see Sered 1994). This is true, for example, of Afro-Brazilian religions and of Black Carib religion (Catholicism is the mainstream religion of Brazil and Belize), of North American Spiritualism and contemporary American and European spiritual feminism (Christianity is the mainstream religion of the United States and Western Europe), and of the zar cult (Islam is the mainstream religion in the Sudan).[25] Two women-led religions, the Shakers and Christian Science, do not fit this polydeistic pattern. Because both of these religions are committed to staying within the Christian tradition, repudiating monotheism would be unthinkable. Shakers and Christian Scientists, however, have rejected purely masculine monotheism—both of these religions developed a theology of a male-female or mother-father deity (see Bednarowski 1980). Significantly, neither of these groups replaced the male god of mainstream Christianity with a female goddess; rather, they developed a theology that blurs gender boundaries. And, indeed, a close look at the genders of the deities in polydeistic women-led religions—including that in Okinawa—shows a fairly even split between male and female. Women-led religions do not substitute male dominance with female dominance but rather with models of nondominance (power diffused through many male, female, genderless, and bigendered deities).[26]

When asked to describe or to tell about a particular kami-sama, Henza villagers occasionally mention that the kami is male or female. However, unlike in Hindu and Greek mythology, where the gods have stories attached to them in which socially constructed gender notions are relevant, in Okinawa there is no elaboration of the gender of the deities, and villagers do not always even agree about the gender of a particular kami-sama (cf. Mabuchi 1968: 137). When mentioned at all, the gender of kami-sama was alluded to in short comments like this one about Futemma Shrine (one of the best known shrines on the main island of Okinawa): "I heard from my mother and grandmother that this is where the woman kami-sama lives." Other kami-sama that I have heard labeled as female are the Katsuren Castle kami-sama and the ryugu kami-sama (ocean kami-sama). More often, however, no gender is mentioned in association with kami-sama.

The hinu-kan (hearth deity) is said to be the *onna no kami-sama* (*onna* means female). Because of Japanese syntax, this statement is open to two interpretations: It could mean that the hinu-kan is the kami-sama that women pray to (the women's kami-sama) or it could mean that the hinu-kan is a female kami-sama. I am convinced that both meanings are understood by villagers and perhaps even overlap, but neither is seen as particularly relevant. The elastic use of the words *onna no kami-sama* is illustrated in the following comment by a middle-aged village woman. She was explaining to me that her children go to events of their father's clan, and she goes to those of her own clan. "I go to my own, onna no kami-sama, but if there is time I also go to otoko no kami-sama [*otoko* means male], to my husband's and children's, I go." In this instance, the notion of male and female kami-sama refers neither to the gender of the person who prays nor to the gender of the kami-sama but to which side of the family the kami-sama is associated with.

Returning to the passage cited at the beginning of this chapter, we find that, like other villagers, Mrs. Asato mingles or fuses the two uses of onna (or otoko) no kami-sama. Not only is the Agaregusuku kami-sama a male kami-sama, but Agaregusuku belongs to (is associated with, is prayed at by) the (human) male kami-sama—her brother, Mr. Shibahiki, who used to wear black robes when performing his ritual roles. Irigusuku belongs to (is associated with, is prayed at by) the (human) female noro, who wears white robes. In short, associated with each sacred grove is a kami-sama who appears in visions and a kami-sama who appears in the flesh—and both look the same. The kami-sama who prays and the kami-sama who is prayed to intermingle, overlap, and merge.

My sense is that villagers lean toward a belief that there is a cosmic need for both male and female kami-sama, although, unlike in Hindu or Greek mythology, the kami-sama are not understood to be married or even related to each other:

MRS. TANAHARA: On September 9 kami-sama comes down to the east yard, and Henza's descendants are protected by kami-sama.

SUSAN: What kami-sama?

MRS. TANAHARA: Male kami-sama and female kami-sama. There have to be both, male and female. Because of that. They come down from the sky.

SUSAN: Is there a name for these kami-sama?

MRS. TANAHARA: [Just] male kami-sama and female kami-sama, because of men and women. Just say "kami-sama" and you know [what it means].

I discussed the same question with Mrs. Uyealtari, a yuta:

SUSAN: Do male and female kami-sama say different things?

MRS. UYEALTARI: Yes, they are not combined into one kami-sama. I am man-blood-related [the kami-sama to whom she relates are from her father's rather than her mother's clan] so I ask the [or a] man kami-sama. If you are a woman-related kami-sama, the [or a] woman kami-sama will tell you things.

SUSAN: What is your male kami-sama's personality?

MRS. UYEALTARI: Very old chief. He teaches, with a beard like this (long). White kimono type clothes. And a stick.

In these passages we see the theme of complementarity: that both male and female are necessary, a theme that also appears in rituals such as the tug-of-war (see chapter 12). There is, however, very little elaboration of kami-sama's gender (as Mrs. Tanahara says, "just" male and female). In Mrs. Asato's remarks, quoted at the beginning of this chapter, we saw that what distinguishes male from female *kami-sama* is clothing—not role or personality. Similarly, Mrs. Uyealtari offers the barest stereotypical description of an important man from the old days. The only way in which male and female kami-sama are differentiated is visually: The kami-sama that villagers see in visions and dreams are usually dressed in Shuri court men's or priestess's clothing. Mrs. Uyealtari explains that the gender of kami-sama is relational and not intrinsic: If the kami-sama is from one's father's family, one sees it, or experiences it, as male. And finally, we see a pattern that we will return to in chapter 12, the pattern of gender crossover: Mrs. Uyealtari is a woman, but she is male-kami-sama related.

R.W. Connell (1987) identifies two widespread practices for constructing and reifying gender. *Cognitive purification* produces shallow, unidimensional, "neat," stereotypic, dichotomous representations of male and female. *Naturalization* (see the introduction to this volume) legitimates gendered social patterns by identifying them with the physical body and the physical world. In many cultures, gendered gods and mythic figures are particularly effective instruments for both practices. Gendered deities are models of the natural and inescapable gendering of the universe. Gendered deities "prove" that gender is ontologically true. Gendered deities are also models of the fixed and restricted qualities assigned to each gender. Unlike one's neighbors and friends, deities are not usually observed engaging in the multitudinous tasks and interactions that, despite gender roles and ideologies, reveal the reality that both men and women are capable of expressing a sizable range of traits. Quite to the contrary, a fixed number of costumes, feats, relationships, and skills is associated with particular gendered deities. Gendered deities thus naturalize gender in an idealized, frozen, "purified," and narrow sense. In the many societies in which deities are believed to hold or represent some sort of extraordinary power—power to create, power to punish and reward, power to perform miracles—any characteristic of the deity, including gender, acquires some of the aura of that power. In Henza, the sparsity of gendered attributes and the fuzziness and flexibility of gender identity associated with kami-sama—in a cosmological context in which deities are not powerful—suggest that gender naturalization and cognitive purification practices are relatively limited in scope and effect.

PART II

QUESTIONS OF GENDER

THREE

Gender in an Egalitarian Society

In the old days men were stronger. Men went out at night and got money, and so we could buy rice. The men brought money for this, so men were stronger. Women were only in the garden to grow sweet potatoes to eat. Men had money. A woman could not earn money. I feel so sorry when I talk about old life stories. Always we did hard jobs. (ninety-two-year-old village woman)

SUSAN: Do boys and girls speak differently?

MRS. SHINZATO: Boys are strong and girls are weak. They are raised from a young age that way, boys to be strong and girls to be kind. Boys are strong and girls are yasashii. If girls get to be strong, the mother will say to be yasashii yasashii. From right after birth. Mother educates that way.

These two comments are good examples of sociological approaches to the study of gender. The first provides a historical and economic gender analysis: Men were stronger because of their economic role; there were no cash jobs available for women, and that fact gave men social strength. The second comment emphasizes the process of socialization. I had asked Mrs. Shinzato a general question: Do boys and girls speak differently? My question certainly allowed room for an essentialist answer. Instead, Mrs. Shinzato chose to discuss the socialization process: Boys and girls speak differently because they are educated from right after birth to do so.

Cross-culturally, hierarchies, including those of gender, are constructed out of building blocks of belief in differences among people or among groups. When differences are naturalized, hierarchies tend to be especially rigid and durable. As American and European feminists have learned, even when governments attempt to legislate equality, if an ideological foundation of belief in difference exists, hierarchy is sustained. Significantly, it is often in severely patriarchal cultures that we hear the claim that women are not subordinate—"just different" (Hawley 1994).

In Henza, villagers insist that there are few innate differences between men and women, even though men and women often do engage in different activities. Men's and women's activities are understood in pragmatic rather than naturalized terms, and they are not arranged into a hierarchical schema but rather conceptualized in a complementary manner. Men's work and women's work are equally necessary for survival.

The downplaying of gender differences—and especially of innate differences— is a theme that runs throughout this book. In this chapter, organized around the life cycle, we see that cultivation of gender differences takes place only during a particular period in the life cycle (the years of fertility), and that religious involvement is strongly linked to life-stage both for village men and for village women. Moreover, as I discuss at the close of the chapter, villagers (in general and women in particular) tend to be aware and critical of even minor manifestations of gender inequality. Henza gender discourse is characterized by a dual assertion that, I argue, functions to undermine hierarchy. First, differences between men and women are said *not* to be innate or meaningful. Second, specific instances of inequality between men and women are exposed, articulated, analyzed, and publicly critiqued. This two-pronged discursive motif prevents the transformation of gendered social roles into permanent or reified gender ideology.

Gender ideologies are simultaneously a means for the reification, public legitimation and enforcement of gender roles, and a means of private legitimation, interiorization, acceptance, and re-forming of the self as gendered. The negligibility of gender ideology in Henza means that neither of these processes occurs to any great extent. Gendered cultural patterns are present in Henza, yet the villagers with whom I spoke consistently interpreted these patterns not as manifestations of gender ideology, but rather as outcomes of historical forces, economic pressures, and influence from other societies. These kinds of sociological understandings of gender are a far lighter load to carry—and a far simpler conceptualization to reevaluate and deconstruct—than are the sorts of gendered ideologies that are found in so many other societies.

Sherry Ortner has argued that although few if any cultures are unfailingly egalitarian, in a small number of known cultures *most* important social processes are egalitarian. In these societies, "Egalitarian prestige orders are culturally dominant and relatively deeply embedded," yet neither totalistic nor immmutable (1996: 147). Reviewing three societies that have been presented as gender egalitarian in the ethnographic literature (Andaman Islands, the Wana of Central Sulawesi [Indonesia], and the Meratus of Kalimantan [Indonesia]), Ortner finds that, "In all three cases there is a lack of formal ideology about male superiority; in all three cases there are extensive patterns of gender equivalence and equality; in all three cases there is a tendency not to use gender as a conceptual or social organizational principle at all. Very few things are limited to men simply because they are men, or to women simply because they are women" (1996: 175).[1]

Henza's gender arrangements are consistent with those found in the other egalitarian societies overviewed by Ortner. Having said this, however, I wish to clarify that I do not believe that any society has gender patterns, ideologies, or a gender ethos that is consistently maintained by all subgroups, throughout all historical periods, or even by individuals throughout their life cycles. In this chapter my aim is to present the experiences and gender beliefs of some contemporary Henza villagers. These experiences and ideas are, unsurprisingly, not uniform. Still, I do think that taken as a whole Henza is characterized by a relatively egalitarian gender ethos deeply rooted in the cultural imagination and actively expressed via tangible cultural practices. For the most part, those notions and practices that run counter to the egalitarian ethos tend to be understood by villagers as having originated outside of Henza, an understanding that does seem to fit the historical record.

Boys and Girls Both Come from the Same Place

There was the same celebration for a boy baby as for a girl. At one week. And then a month later there was the first walk ritual and mother and baby came out of the house for the first time. (traditional midwife)

In Henza, girls my age are like boys. They aren't like American or Israeli girls. They don't sit around talking about makeup. They play volleyball. (Barak Sered, twelve-year-old boy)

Children at Henza's nursery school do not behave in a noticeably gender differentiated manner. All of the children spend great parts of the day running around, screaming (usually with joy), and climbing on furniture and on each other. Boys and girls wear the same clothes; most girls do not have long hair or ponytails.[2] At children's performances it is not uncommon to see a child wearing the costume worn by the other gender in order to even up the numbers of drum players (boys) and castanet players (girls).

Teachers in the local nursery school intimate that gender is not a particularly relevant social category for adults dealing with Henza children.

At age three, boys and girls behave the same; at four or five they begin behaving differently. At that age girls play with dolls or play house. Boys play fight—they act out superheros or ninjas. Soccer is usually played by boys but sometimes by girls. [Who hits more?] Usually boys but sometimes girls. [Crying?] Boys and girls the same, but girls a bit more. [Stronger?] Boys are weaker. Actually, physically they are the same, but girls' spirits are stronger. Girls talk better so they attack verbally. [Do you encourage boys not to cry?] The government gives a booklet on how to teach and they say not to tell boys not to cry. But maybe it used to be that boys were told not to cry. A lot of the differences seem to begin at about age three and up. Up to three boys and girls play together, but after that separately.

In this discussion with two teachers, we went through a list of characteristics that I had observed to be somewhat gender-linked in Henza. For each characteristic, I asked if there is a difference between boys and girls. For each characteristic the teachers answered that one sex is "more," but the other sex is also "sometimes like that." In other words, the teachers consistently shied away from any kind of dichotomous ideological or general statement about gender differences. Finally, I asked the teachers whether children laugh when a girl plays with or like a boy (or vice versa) and whether children ever say to a boy, "stop acting like a girl"? The answer was "No!"

The teachers account for gender differences among older children in terms of the influence of grandparents who tell boys and girls to behave differently. According to the teachers, gender differences are neither innate (young children are all the same) nor desirable (they as teachers do not encourage gender differences) but rather a carryover from an earlier and less enlightened historical period.[3]

Remarks by elementary and junior high school teachers reflect the same approach as that of the nursery school teachers.[4] One morning in the teachers' room, I asked in a general way if there are differences in boys' and girl's behavior. Here is the first response to my question: "When they work on the school [model] farm the work is divided by sex. The school divides it that way because girls can't do the work that needs more strength. Sometimes girls want to do that work and it is okay, they can." Two points bear notice. First, the answer to my open question about behavioral differences was rather trivial—the division of labor during the very few hours each month the children work at the school farm. Second, even though the school divides that work by sex, girls nevertheless can do a job deemed appropriate for boys when they want to.

Another theme that emerged repeatedly in conversations with elementary and junior high teachers is that girls are better at schoolwork in every subject, including math.

> At other schools [in Okinawa] it is the opposite, the boys do better. Henza parents have a different mentality. In other schools, boys already decide that they want to go to university. Henza boys never think about university. This used to be a village of fishermen. We did a project in the school asking the students if they want to go to university, and only a few girls and no boys said that they want to go. . . . Until the second year of junior high, girls are stronger than boys because they speak better and more and boys cannot reply. Girls are on the student council. Boys go to play soccer instead! (school principal, Mr. Shinya)

I draw attention here to the teachers' understanding of gendered behavior among the children as local and temporal rather than innate: In other villages, at other ages, patterns differ.

Parents of school-aged children generally attribute differences among children to factors other than gender. Noriko Goeku told me that her twelve-year-old daughter likes to study, but her thirteen-year-old son does not. "Usually the first child is a slow type, and the second is very strong, boys and girls." Noriko has organized her three older children, two girls and a boy, with a rotating chart of household tasks: bring in laundry, wash cups, bathe baby brother. All three children take turns at all three jobs. Of her two daughters, who are less than two years apart in age, one is active and likes balls and bikes, whereas the other likes to learn to cook and sew from her mother and to play with dolls.[5] (Despite this one family's experiences, I do believe that there is an overall tendency to expect girls to be given responsibility for household tasks at an earlier age and to a larger extent than boys; cf. Maretzki and Maretzki 1966).

Until junior high school, girls and boys continue to act and dress similarly: Both have short hair and spend their free time at sports. As in the rest of Japan, during school hours junior high children wear a uniform: skirt, blouse, and jacket for girls and a jacket and slacks for boys. High school girls seem somewhat quieter than boys and show more interest in babies and young children. On the other hand, when I told a local mother that in Israel teenage girls are more subdued than boys, she answered that "here boys and girls are equally *genki*" (lively).

I note here a conversation with an elderly clan priestess. What interests me in this exchange is the ideological stance of equality even when in specific situations villagers realize that there is inequality.

SUSAN: Do boys play more freely?

MRS. ADANIYA: In Okinawa boys and girls are the same, both are free.

SUSAN: I see that in Henza boys ride bikes and girls don't so often.

MRS. ADANIYA: In that one area boys are freer.

Both parents and teachers say that boys, and especially brothers, sometimes engage in physical fights but that girls argue verbally. Boys' fighting is not seen as in any way positive, and, indeed, villagers maintain that girls and women tend to embrace the general cultural value of yasashii more than do boys or men. In various families, either a brother or sister will be considered the strongest child; that strength is manifested in terms of will or personality—not brawn. Parents seem encouraging of their children's individual preferences for career and hobby. Residents are proud and supportive of the village school's championship girls' volleyball team. One middle-aged couple with four grown children, three boys and a girl, made a point of showing me their daughter's university graduation picture and certificate; they also showed me a picture of her posed at a computer that appeared in a Japanese newspaper, because she was the first woman to be hired by a company that had previously hired only men.[6]

Neither boys nor girls are expected to express interest or to participate in most religious events, and very few children attend even exciting and colorful rituals like *san gatsu* (third-month ritual). A variety of explanations are offered for this arrangement. To begin with, children are believed to be disinterested in ritual. "Children don't have the mind for religion. They don't have the spirit to pray, they haven't built it up yet." Or, "Children are noisy, so we don't tell them to come." Specifically concerning funerals, one woman in her thirties told me, "I heard from the older people that if it is close family children can go, but otherwise children are pulled by the dead person, so they don't take children to funerals."

Older people do not teach either boys or girls about kami-sama or encourage children to take an interest in ritual. For example, on one occasion when I was visiting Mrs. Shimojo, a village priestess, her granddaughter, a girl of about ten, came into the room as we were discussing a ritual that had taken place the day before. Mrs. Shimojo shooed the girl out of the room without introducing her. On another occasion, I attended the *umi ogami* (ocean prayer) ritual at the kami-ya. Men sat on the kami-ya porch and ate fish and played the samisen. Children (mostly boys) were playing in the yard across from the kami-ya, but no attempt was made to involve them in the ritual, nor were they offered any food, although plenty was left over, and normally everyone loves to give food to children.[7]

Okinawans follow the Chinese twelve-year cycle in which each year is associated with an animal name. Each thirteenth year, all those born in that animal year celebrate the beginning of the next cycle. Several Henza villagers were eager to tell me that in the rest of Okinawa only girls are given a special celebration at age thirteen, but in Henza boys' thirteenth year is also celebrated. Here is how one elderly woman talks about this: "Boy and girl both come from my body, I can't have a fa-vorite of one or the other. It is the parents who do the celebration, it is their heart. That is why in Henza we have parties for both boys and girls. But there are two dif-ferent songs, one for boys and one for girls."

Young Adulthood and Early Middle Age

Teenage girls and boys rarely engage in the kinds of gender-enhancing cosmetic practices (makeup, high heels)[8] that we Westerners are familiar with, nor do vil-lagers perform any of the gender-enhancing bodily procedures that we find in many other cultures: no foot binding, no clitoridectomy or infibulation, no circum-cision, no ear piercing.[9] Gender is not ritualized (for example, there are no menar-che or menstruation rituals.)[10] In many societies, initiation and puberty rituals serve as gendering rituals—rituals in which a child is ceremonially, symbolically, and socially turned into and recognized as a male or female adult (see Roscoe 1995: 220–221). The absence of puberty or initiation rituals in Henza can be in-terpreted as evidence of an absence of interest in socially constructing gendered beings (cf. Lepowsky 1990: 190, 196). This interpretation fits well with Henza's traditional lack of ceremony surrounding marriage (see the discussion later in this chapter): Cross-culturally, wedding ceremonies tend to highlight gender as a salient social category.

Among women aged from approximately twenty-five to forty-five years, there is more concern with "feminine" appearance. During these years women may grow their hair long and wear lipstick and dresses. These rather minor gender-enhancing practices coincide with the years of active fertility,[11] suggesting that during the years in which sex is salient in terms of organizing one's social role, women cultivate gender differentiation in their outer appearance. During other periods of life (actually, during most of one's life), gender differentiation is not en-hanced through clothing or bodily procedures.

Just as there is little concern with gender ideology, there also seems to be little ideological concern with sexuality (cf. Bleier 1984). Sexuality is not discussed fre-quently; young people become interested in sexual relations at a relatively late age;[12] there is no belief that people are unable to control their sexual impulses, there is no obsession with visual representations of sexuality (as there is in the United States); there does not seem to be much concern with appropriate or inap-propriate sexual behavior;[13] premarital sexuality is well accepted; and sexual at-traction and interactions are joked about in a light and easygoing way (at ritual events like weddings and young men's *eisaa* dancing there is a certain amount of explicit sexual humor, although nowhere near as much as the Embrees described in the Japanese village of Suye Mura in the 1930s; see Smith and Wiswell 1982: 80–84).[14]

One young woman told me that she thinks men generally like women who are "cute" (young, innocent, and—from what I can deduce from her description—androgynous looking). An older man told me that he thinks men like "women who are active and like to do things." Another middle-aged man told me that men like women who work hard. Similarly, when I asked women what kind of men they like, the answers never included strongly "masculine" traits (developed musculature, sexual prowess, good earning capabilities). Rather, women say that they prefer men who are *yasashii* and who do not drink *sake*.

SUSAN: In the old days did men make all the decisions?

WOMAN IN HER SEVENTIES: No, my mother made the decisions. Women took care of the family, men went out to make money.

SUSAN: Nowadays women live longer than men. How was it in the old days?

MRS. ADANIYA: Same as today. But a human's life depends on kami-sama. Men were a bit weak because they had to support the family and go to the boats, which is harder work than women did. Women are always under the [roof] of the house, but actually life depends on *ten* [heaven]. Each person has his/her own destiny.

In Henza, both men and women are involved in productive labor. Traditionally, men went to sea and women produced food in their gardens and foraged for seafood at the shore. Women's work provided most of the food for Henza households and certainly provided the most reliable source of food (fishing, especially long-distance fishing, is an erratic source of food). Even today, villagers estimate that women's gardening and foraging provide approximately half of the family's food.[15]

In fishing communities, women's work encompasses processing and marketing of fish, agricultural labor, domestic responsibility, and more (cf. Ram 1991). Ethnographic studies of fishing communities have found that "among those fishing groups where men are absent for long periods, women are held to play a proportionately greater role in managing both the household and the local community" (Nadel-Klein and Davis 1988: 5). In a study of a Portuguese coastal community, Sally Cole found that "women of maritime households managed the household economy and were visible in the parish as they went about their work harvesting seaweed and selling fish. By contrast, women of wealthy agricultural households were rarely seen; they remained secluded in the home while their husbands supervised the agricultural production of the household" (1991: 45). William Lebra has observed that within Okinawa, women generally occupy a higher status and play a larger role in community affairs in fishing villages than in agricultural villages (1966: 152). When men are absent, women—by necessity and by choice—engage in a wider range of activities.

Henza men went to sea—often for months or years on end. Although villagers continue to describe themselves as an island of fisherfolk, in fact, few Henza men nowadays go to sea; most work for companies such as the Japanese oil company located on the island.[16] A few men work in the Japanese civil service. Older men typically do not work. Young and middle-aged women nowadays work in stores, restaurants, schools, offices, and companies. Middle-aged and older women work in gardens and foraging. Very few Henza women work only inside the home. Quite a few middle-aged and older women pick up part-time jobs, such as collecting money for water or gas bills. Both men and women work on road crews (although far more men than women are employed in road building) and on gardening crews. A fair number of Henza men are unemployed or underemployed, and it is not unusual to see men of thirty or forty years in T-shirts sitting at home during the day. Only very old and sick women do not work at all.

What is most apparent to the observer of village life is the visible role of women in commerce.[17] Despite its small population, Henza boasts approximately thirty grocery stores, almost all of which are owned and run by women. A Henza woman runs one of the largest locally owned businesses, the hotel. A woman drives the baked-sweet-potato truck. Women own a small sewing factory, several beauty parlors, and a barber shop. The role of women in commerce in the village today is consistent with the traditional role of women as fish traders.

To what extent were men's and women's economic roles flexible in the past?[18] There were, and still are a few, wholesalers who bought fish from fishermen and sold it in the village and on the main island. Wholesalers could be men or women. Women were and are involved in seafaring, although to a lesser extent than men. According to one informant, although men usually did not work in the gardens, at harvest season men helped in the fields. Similarly, although housekeeping is typically done by women, during busy cleaning seasons such as before New Year's and *obon* both men and women pitch in and work.[19]

A number of studies have described the Japanese "ideal womanhood" as characterized by full-time, selfless nurture of others (husbands, children, parents, in-laws). This kind of nurture, according to Susan Long, "involves physical proximity [i.e., staying home], the maintenance of social harmony [i.e., avoiding conflict], and undivided attention to the needs of others" (1996: 172). As Margaret Lock points out, "Japanese women are still judged first and foremost by their roles as 'good wife and wise mother,' and although they are well educated there is virtually no possibility of their developing a sense of an independent identity after they are married. Finding gainful employment other than in a factory is extremely difficult for a married woman, and is in any case socially frowned upon" (1987: 143).[20] My sense is that Henza women are not expected to devote themselves in this kind of unrestricted and full-scale way to the needs of others. Almost all women with whom I spoke—of all age groups—engage in a variety of work and leisure-time activities outside of the house. Perhaps somewhat surprisingly (and in contradiction to patterns in most other women-led religions; see Sered 1994), there does not seem to be an elaborated ideal of motherhood or an ideology that praises or privileges maternity. But more important, I doubt whether Henza villagers would postulate that there is any such thing as "ideal womanhood." An "ideal" anything rests upon fairly unambiguous beliefs in a "right way" to be or behave, whereas Henzans seem to accept and praise a rather wide range of personality types and behavioral patterns (see chapter 1). An "ideal type" is an ideological construct grounded in an explicit moral code (not found in Henza culture), mythology (which is not part of Henza culture), a legendary past (not found in Henza culture), or a conscious agenda for building a certain type of society in the future (not found in Henza culture). In sum, I would suggest that not only do Henza women differ dramatically from the "ideal type" of woman described in the literature of mainland Japan but also that the very notion of an "ideal type" would be incomprehensible to Henza villagers.[21]

Neither young men nor young women are expected to be interested in religion. One woman in her twenties told me that she knows that her mother and grandmother pray at the hinu-kan but that is all she knows; she does not know why they pray, how they pray, or what the hinu-kan is. Older women do not make efforts to teach young women what will assumedly be their future religious role.

There are and were in the past very few women who became kaminchu in their twenties. When women in their twenties express interest in religion, it is often interpreted in the context of emotional disturbance, physical illness, or social problems. Mr. Ginjo explains, "Young kaminchu typically get sick often and so they are not married." There is now in the village only one youngish woman clan kaminchu, and she is unemployed, unmarried, and spends most of her time at the hospital (no one was clear about what she does there). When I asked villagers if I should talk to her about how she became a kaminchu, the response was that she would not be able to tell me anything interesting or sensible. Mr. Shinya put it this way: "Among ogami (prayer people) and yuta (shaman-type practitioners) there are no young people. Maybe there are some, but before they become one [a yuta or ogami person] they become a little funny in the head. When they are young they are strange and when they get older they do this, and it is okay. Then they become well."

Women in their thirties may be expected to accompany older women on trips to the yuta or to serve ritual meals at the clan houses, but they seem to try to keep their distance and not actually join in the rituals. At ritual meals, women in their thirties typically serve food and tea to the older people in the main room and then go back to the kitchen to eat outside of the ritual context. Women of this age may claim that they are frightened by yuta and kaminchu business. Most men in this age group are equally unconcerned with religious practice, but, like the women, do carry out the small tasks they are called upon to do.

Women who do not live with mothers or mothers-in-law pray at their household hinu-kan twice each month, and there is a strong village consensus that young women continue to carry out this ritual. Similarly, young men who are responsible for an ancestor altar (butsudan) generally carry out their duties. In an informal way, some few men and women in their thirties or forties begin to move into positions of greater religious activity. I noticed one woman in this age group serving food at a clan gathering, and then a few weeks later I saw her accompanying an older woman relative who was praying with an ogami person at the kami-ya. At the kami-ya she sat a bit behind, reflecting her lower status or lower level of involvement, but my impression is that she was interested and even participating in the ritual. This kind of helping role, then, seems to constitute for some women a developmental stage in religious activity. Similarly, at clan gatherings, a few men in this age group may unobtrusively volunteer to help the kaminchu carry ritual accoutrements, light incense, or pour sake, and my sense is that it is often the same men who tend to volunteer repeatedly for these tasks—reflecting, I suppose, a greater interest in religious rituals.

Marriage and Family

Henza's kinship arrangements are, according to villagers' descriptions of the model family type, patrilineal and patrilocal. The expressed preference is for the eldest son to stay in his parents' home, bringing his wife in to live with them, raising children in their house, and eventually inheriting the house and ancestor tablets and beginning the cycle over again with his own eldest son. In reality, like other Henza social arrangements, family and household arrangements are not uniform. Table 3.1 ("Household Type")[22] shows that only a small minority of village households even approximate the model.[23] Nowadays, most children, young adults, and middle-aged villagers live in nuclear-family households, and most old people live either alone or with a spouse. The most significant relationships within households tend to be among women; many Henza households can be considered matrifocal.

In the past there were socially recognized ways for young men and women to spend time alone together, and virginity at marriage was and is not considered a social value.[24] According to one woman now in her nineties, young people would meet and make parties in the evening at the beach on the other side of the island. If a young man and woman liked each other, the young man would begin to "visit" the young woman at night at her parents' house. This arrangement could continue for a period of several years.[25] Usually, young couples would know each other well before settling down into a more permanent relationship.

It was common for young men and women to have several sexual partners before holding a ritual called *ichigomui* in which both families acknowledged that the couple has been sleeping together (cf. Ouwehand 1985: 101ff.). According to Mr. Masamitsu, "Ichigomui is the first talking. They don't need to register that they are officially married. After ichigomui, if they break up, it is just breaking up, not official divorce. It happened sometimes that they did ichigomui, and then they changed their mind later and said I don't want to marry this person. They did ichigomui a lot." Some time after ichigomui, a second ritual—*sakemui*—was held. Also a small-scale ritual, sakemui consisted of a meal brought by the family of the man to the household of the woman. As Mr. Tamura explained, "The man brings food to the woman's house, and they eat together, and because we ate together, they say, we are now relatives." A final ceremony—a kind of procession from the woman's house to the man's house (*nibichi*)—was held only rarely because "nibichi is for people who have money. In Henza there were a couple of houses who could do nibichi."[26] According to Mrs. Hokama, "Women used to have their first and second child at their mother's house. . . . Nowadays it is mainland Japan's custom that until marriage they don't get together. Then after the marriage they live together. It used to be that if they liked each other he would live with his parents but frequently come to visit her. The parents agreed to it also. And then he could sleep at her place."

According to villagers, first birth typically took place when the woman was anywhere from eighteen to twenty-five years old. Extended periods of breast-feeding helped space babies. The women who are today in their eighties and nineties did not experience the pattern of repeated, closely spaced pregnancies that often

Table 3.1 Household Type

Household Type	Number	Percentage
Husband and Wife	57	11.7
Nuclear[a]	182	37.3
Stem[b]	56	11.5
Augmented Nuclear[c]	21	4.3
Augmented Stem[d]	21	4.3
Siblings only	2	0.4
Other[e]	37	7.6
Single	110	22.5
Don't Know	2	0.4
Total	488	100

[a] Also includes single-parent households.

[b] Grandparent(s) + parents + children.

[c] Includes nuclear or husband-and-wife households with additional resident(s).

[d] Grandparent(s) + parents + children with additional resident(s).

[e] Mostly grandparent(s) + grandchildren, or stem families with divorced spouse.

characterizes agricultural societies. The notion of a father forcing his daughter to marry is unknown in Henza.[27]

Traditionally, Okinawan marriage was endogamous; that is, people married within the village. According to Professor Akamine, the rate of endogamy throughout Okinawa is approximately 90 percent.[28] In Mrs. Hokama's words,

People liked to stay on Henza Island and marry people from the island, because of the tax at the time. There was a tax that the island had to pay. If there were more people each person had to pay less. As a village they wouldn't let the people out.[29] They had a custom that you should do for the village. After I graduated from high school, a few people from outside Henza wanted to marry me, but I didn't want to go out. And there is a custom not to go out of the village.

Anthropological understandings of extended-family households often draw upon descriptions of traditional China and India, where a young bride enters a new family as a low-status stranger; she has not yet proven herself as a fertile mother of sons; she is unacquainted with the customs of the household; and her parents do not live nearby, so she has no one to protect her from an abusive husband or in-laws. In Henza, the position of daughters-in-law is rather different. By the time a woman goes to live in her in-law's house, she is usually already a mother; she has proven her fertility and she enters with the status that ensues from being the mother of children (cf. Sacks 1979). Given village endogamy, her natal family is nearby to offer her protection and to visit with her, and she is likely to already know her in-law's household customs.

One informant told me, in the context of a conversation about a woman in her eighties, "Everyone here (in Henza) has been married twice." The marital bond was and is not perceived as a rigid or sacred structure, and thus it is easy to dissolve. Okinawa Prefecture has the highest divorce rate of any Japanese prefecture, including the urban prefecture in which Tokyo is located (Okinawa Prefectural Office 1994). The flexibility of marriage-type arrangements is reflected in the absence of a traditional divorce ceremony. Okinawan divorce is bilateral—either spouse can initiate divorce. When a divorced couple had been living with the husband's family, the wife was expected to move out.[30] Nowadays, in nuclear-family households, it is more common for the man to move out and the woman to keep the children. Apparently, women living without husbands is not a new phenomenon in Okinawa. According to the 1955 *Population Index*, "Marriage offered permanent sanctuary for only a minority of the women of the Ryukyus. Widowhood was frequent. . . . Separations were also rather frequent. . . . The widowed and the separated accumulated among women, disappeared among men [through remarriage]" (Taeuber 1955: 251)[31]

Because in Okinawan society only the eldest son inherits, subsequent sons live with their wives' families (not uncommon in the old days), establish new households in the village, or emigrate. Villagers say that there is a large number of never-married people, especially men, in Henza.

A leading expert on Okinawan kinship, Professor Higa, believes that although Okinawan ideology is patrilineal, reality is and was bilateral (personal communication). The substance of kinship—blood—is understood to link an individual equally to his or her mother and father; thus maternal and paternal relatives are treated alike and addressed through the same kinship terminology (Tanaka 1977: 37; see also Ouwehand 1985: 88ff.). Prolonged village endogamy, the prevalence of "premarriage" sexual contacts, and the high rate of divorce create a social situation in which most villagers are related to one another in a variety of cross-cutting ways. This reality confounds ordered conceptions of kinship structure.[32]

A number of scholars have argued that patrilineality and patrilocality in Okinawa are rather new (Ota 1989; W. Lebra 1966). Generally, Henza villagers who told me about more egalitarian marriage experiences were in their late seventies or older. A different picture emerges from informants in their late sixties. These informants describe arranged marriages, immediate residence in the man's house, a low status for young brides, and high fertility. According to a Henza woman who used to work as a nurse, "During the war women were told to have as many babies as possible, not to have abortions.[33] In fourteen years I had seven children, one every two years."

Mrs. Shinzato (in her early seventies) tells that:

MRS. SHINZATO: [Before the marriage] we didn't know each other, the parents arranged it. [In my day] the parents decided. . . . They would get married at once, before the bride had a chance to get pregnant. Nowadays they marry at twenty-five or more. In the old days at seventeen or eighteen they married.

SUSAN: But you married at twenty-nine?

MRS. SHINZATO: I was late.

Mrs. Shinzato's experiences seem to represent a transitional stage in which Japanese and Western norms of virginity, young marriage, patrilocal residence, and arranged marriages had partially taken hold in Henza. Still, note that she herself married in her late twenties. Another woman of about the same age also told me that girls married young in her day, but she herself married at thirty! In Mrs. Shinzato's day, the traditional land redistribution system that had protected women's access to land had broken down, and new Japanese laws required that property be registered in the name of a male "head of household"; but there were as yet few paid employment opportunities for women. It is important to understand that this stage was truly transitional—nowadays, marriage customs have, in a modified form, returned to a pattern highly congruent with the "old" old ways. [34] According to Mrs. Shinzato,

In my day there was no money and no food, therefore you had to depend on your husband. So women couldn't earn money, men had power, and the woman had to put up with whatever he did, she had to stay with him because she couldn't earn her own money. Nowadays, women have jobs and men have jobs and there is nothing to worry about having food, and they fight and divorce. You can live alone, there is more independence.

Premarital childbearing has also once again become normative. Of the two weddings that I saw during my time in Henza, one was that of a pregnant bride and one that of a bride who had a six-month-old baby. In both cases, the bride had been living with her parents until the wedding, and there was no stigma attached to premarital motherhood. [35]

Cross-culturally, it is not uncommon for peasants to describe their culture or social structure in a manner that bears a strong resemblance to that of the elite yet to live in the way that fits their own subsistence and spiritual needs. According to Professor Akamine of the University of the Ryukyus, patrilineal-patrilocal ideology before the twentieth century was adopted by the Shuri-connected upper classes and only filtered down slowly and partially to the peasant periphery. Patrilineal-patrilocal ideology did reach Henza—both in the eighteenth and the twentieth centuries—yet other aspects of Henza social and economic life mitigated against the full implementation of this ideology. First, strict patrilineal and patrilocal kinship is a poor fit with extended male absenteeism; when men are not there they cannot run things. And in times of need, when men are gone, women return to their natal homes. Second, women's large and autonomous contribution to subsistence ensures them a good measure of domestic authority. [36] Third, village endogamy tends to dilute either matrilocality or patrilocality because spouses are often cousins. Fourth, the fact that the noro inherits her position matrilineally means that villagers continue to recognize the matrilineal descent principle, thus preventing the institutionalization of pure patrilineality. Fifth, the large difference in life expectancy (see the later discussion) between men and women has meant that many households, now and in the past, have a female head. Sixth, the absence of significant inheritable property took (and takes) the urgency away from strict patrilineality. In fact, Henza patrilineality pretty much comes down to inheritance by the eldest son of the ancestor tablets and shelf (*butsudan*). Seventh, the conjugal unit is not seen as particularly sacred; divorce rates are high, and the strongest emotional links are often between mothers and daughters or between sisters. Eighth, the "winner takes all" inheritance rule by which only the eldest son inherits creates a situation in which subsequent sons are unable to live out the patrilineal and patrilocal ideal.[37] Patrilocality typically was the case only when a woman married a first son; second and third sons would be likely to live with the wife's family or set up a new household. And ninth, as I argue throughout this book, Henza culture typically veers away from any kind of strict categorization. Even without the kinship and household details outlined in this chapter, we could have expected to find few "rules" and many "exceptions."

Late Middle and Old Age

> Women pray hard and joke hard. Men only talk if they drink alcohol, women can talk without alcohol. (Mrs. Yasamura)

In Henza, most women aged fifty or fifty-five and older cut their hair short (many put in permanent waves) and generally wear culottes or baggy trousers; from a distance, it can be difficult to tell whether an elderly villager is a man or a woman. As in many other cultures, old women may engage in kinds of behavior that are more typically associated with men (Gutmann 1977).[38] For example, old women in Henza sometimes smoke and drink, whereas young and middle-aged women generally do not. Similarly, old women tend to speak in louder and deeper-pitched voices than young and middle-aged women. Whereas young and early middle-aged women often try to avoid outdoor work (they say it is bad for their skin), older women work outdoors, both in their gardens and at various kinds of building construction. An image that has stayed with me is that of an oldish woman wearing pants and a towel on her head with a hat on top of it. With her were a man in his twenties, a boy in his teens, and a four-year-old boy. The oldish woman took the lead as they used sledge hammers to knock down a shed in their yard.

Older villagers, like children, rather easily wear clothes usually associated with the other gender. This is not perceived as cross-dressing. For instance, I attended a senior citizens' club recreational event in which several local groups performed. One group consisted of four elderly men and four elderly women. All wore the same costume, pants and karate style shirts (a typical men's costume). However, the dancing was in the style usually done by women. Food and beverages were served at the event, and although serving food is typically a woman's job, one man was among the food servers and another old man helped serve the drinks (to both women and men). Beer was offered to everyone, and although drinking beer is not considered usual for Henza women, many of the women drank cans of beer. The clothing, the dancing style, the choice of servers, and the choice of beverages at this event were "yasashii"—easy; I doubt that anyone in the group perceived the events of the day as an expression of "gender-bending."

There are more women than men over age fifty-five in the village, reaching a ratio of more than two to one by age eighty (see table 3.2, "Sex Distribution by Age"; Table 3.3, "Age Distribution by Sex"; Table 3.4, "Percentage of Household Type by Age for Men"; and Table 3.5, "Percentage of Household Type by Age for Women"). Note the large number of women over age seventy living in single households. Because Henza villagers who cannot care for themselves typically move to an old-age home, we can assume that most or all of these women manage their own households. Relatively few older women live with their sons and sons' families; approximately twice as many older women live on their own as live in extended families. In short, Henza women can expect that, whatever their living arrangement when young, they will eventually manage their own households. Although ideally the eldest son inherits his father's property, mothers often outlive fathers by a good fifteen to twenty years, and nowadays the legal title passes to the wife at the husband's death. In actual parlance, Henza villagers refer to children as having inherited their mother's house.[39]

Table 3.2 Sex Distribution by Age (%)

Age	Total	Male	Female
95–99	100.0	11.1	88.9
90–94	100.0	26.7	73.3
85–89	100.0	29.4	70.6
80–84	100.0	30.0	70.0
75–79	100.0	40.2	59.8
70–74	100.0	39.0	61.0
65–69	100.0	42.3	57.7
60–64	100.0	50.0	50.0
55–59	100.0	46.7	53.3
50–54	100.0	60.3	39.7
45–49	100.0	56.7	43.3
40–44	100.0	56.0	44.0
35–39	100.0	55.2	44.8
30–34	100.0	53.7	46.3
25–29	100.0	61.7	38.3
20–24	100.0	54.8	45.2
15–19	100.0	50.0	50.0
10–14	100.0	55.7	44.3
5–9	100.0	37.3	62.7
0–4	100.0	58.8	41.2
Total	100.0	49.0	51.0

Table 3.3 Age Distribution by Sex

Age	No. Total	Male	Female	Percent Male	Female
95–99	9	1	8	0.1	0.9
90–94	15	4	11	0.5	1.3
85–89	51	15	36	1.8	4.2
80–84	50	15	35	1.8	4.0
75–79	97	39	58	4.7	6.7
70–74	100	39	61	4.7	7.0
65–69	104	44	60	5.3	6.9
60–64	90	45	45	5.4	5.2
55–59	60	28	32	3.4	3.7
50–54	68	41	27	4.9	3.1
45–49	104	59	45	7.1	5.2
40–44	134	75	59	9.0	6.8
35–39	116	64	52	7.7	6.0
30–34	82	44	38	5.3	4.4
25–29	47	29	18	3.5	2.1
20–24	115	63	52	7.6	6.0
15–19	166	83	83	10.0	9.6
10–14	140	78	62	9.4	7.2
5–9	102	38	64	4.6	7.4
0–4	51	30	21	3.6	2.4
Total	1701	834	867	100.0	100.0

Whereas Okinawan men's life expectancy is about the same as the life expectancy of men in Japan as a whole, Okinawan women's life expectancy is significantly higher (see *Okinawa Women's Report,* Okinawa Prefectural Office, page 240):

1990	*Men*	*Women*
Japan	76.04 years	82.07 years
Okinawa Prefecture	76.67 "	84.47 "

Villagers confirm that women's longer life expectancy is not a new phenomenon, that also in the old days women lived longer than men. Their observations are borne out by demographic studies.[40] According to the *Population Index* of 1955 (Taeuber 1955), during the first half of the twentieth century:

The pattern of mortality by sex in Okinawa Prefecture differed greatly from that in most other regions of Japan. The childhood mortality was only a fraction of that in other agricultural prefectures. At ages 12 and 17 the mortality of males was above that of females; at age 22 and all later years, the mortality of females was considerably lower than that of males. Perhaps the characteristic patterns of excess female mortality in the majority of the

Table 3.4 Percentage of Household Type in Which Men Are Living (by Age)

Age	Hus & Wife	Nuclear	Stem	Other	Single	D.K.	Total
0–14	0.0	64.4	25.3	10.3	0.0	0.0	100
15–19	0.0	51.8	33.7	14.5	0.0	0.0	100
20–24	0.0	58.7	25.4	14.3	0.0	1.6	100
25–29	0.0	58.6	34.5	3.4	0.0	3.4	100
30–34	0.0	56.8	34.1	9.1	0.0	0.0	100
35–39	0.0	81.3	15.6	1.6	1.6	0.0	100
40–44	0.0	60.0	28.0	5.3	6.7	0.0	100
45–49	3.4	62.7	27.1	1.7	5.1	0.0	100
50–54	4.9	63.4	17.1	4.9	9.8	0.0	100
55–59	14.3	46.4	21.4	3.6	10.7	3.6	100
60–64	13.0	39.1	28.3	8.7	8.7	2.2	100
65–69	20.5	52.3	20.5	2.3	4.5	0.0	100
70–74	32.5	22.5	30.0	2.5	12.5	0.0	100
75–79	35.9	25.6	17.9	7.7	12.8	0.0	100
80–84	33.3	20.0	40.0	6.7	0.0	0.0	100
85–89	20.0	26.7	53.3	0.0	0.0	0.0	100
90–94	0.0	60.0	40.0	0.0	0.0	0.0	100
Total	7.4	54.4	26.7	7.2	3.8	0.5	100

Japanese areas but an excess male mortality in Okinawa reflect the higher status of women and their different economic role in Ryukyuan culture. (p. 252)

Villagers offer social rather than biological explanations for the difference in life span. According to one woman, "Old men die earlier. Women live longer. Maybe because of the *sake*." According to a middle-aged man, "before the war average life expectancy was fifty years. And men would go on dangerous jobs, on boats, and to different countries where they might get sick and die. To Singapore, Philippines. . . . Nowadays, in the seventy and eighty age group there are one or two men for each ten women."

The significance of gender differences in life expectancy has been explored by G. William Skinner (1993) in an extraordinarily subtle and insightful analysis of conjugal power in Tokugawa Japan. Skinner defines the husband's power (relative to the wife's) in terms of several factors, including the wife's age at marriage and the age gap between husband and wife. "Low husband power" is correlated with late marriage for women and a small gap in spousal ages; "high husband power" is correlated with early marriage for women and a large gap in spousal ages. Following the life courses of 360 couples in a Japanese village, he found that among couples characterized by low husband power, women were long-lived vis-à-vis their husbands. Typically, these women married at a more mature age and thus would

Table 3.5 Percentage of Household Type in Which Women Are Living (by Age)

	Type						
Age	Hus & Wife	Nuclear	Stem	Other	Single	D.K.	Total
0–14	1.4	48.3	37.4	12.9	0.0	0.0	100
15–19	2.4	49.4	41.0	7.2	0.0	0.0	100
20–24	0.0	63.5	23.1	13.5	0.0	0.0	100
25–29	0.0	55.6	38.9	5.6	0.0	0.0	100
30–34	0.0	50.0	47.4	2.6	0.0	0.0	100
35–39	0.0	57.7	25.0	15.4	0.0	1.9	100
40–44	6.8	45.8	39.0	6.8	1.7	0.0	100
45–49	2.2	60.0	31.1	4.4	0.0	2.2	100
50–54	0.0	59.3	29.6	7.4	3.7	0.0	100
55–59	18.8	34.4	31.3	6.3	9.4	0.0	100
60–64	20.0	46.7	15.6	11.1	6.7	0.0	100
65–69	23.3	38.3	25.0	3.3	10.0	0.0	100
70–74	16.1	33.9	25.8	4.8	17.7	1.6	100
75–79	15.5	24.1	15.5	8.6	36.2	0.0	100
80–84	11.4	22.9	20.0	8.6	37.1	0.0	100
85–89	8.3	16.7	22.2	11.1	41.7	0.0	100
90–94	0.0	21.1	26.3	10.5	31.6	10.5	100
Total	7.4	44.0	30.1	8.8	9.2	0.6	100

have been emotionally and practically well equipped to stand up to their husband and mother-in-law. Among high-husband-power couples, women's life expectancy decreased vis-à-vis men's. These women not only married younger, but the gap in age between the husband and wife was larger—leading, Skinner argues, to a more hierarchical relationship. And finally, among couples in which the age differential is very great and the husband had predeceased the wife by many years, the widow's life expectancy turned out to be quite long. The freedom of widowhood, according to Skinner, tends to increase life expectancy for women. Skinner concludes that "unrelieved powerlessness and structural vulnerability to oppression—and, we must assume, to the consequent overwork and physical hardship—are in the long run life-negating. The data . . . on conjugal power . . . [indicates] that the experience of wielding effective power within the family is life-enhancing" (1993: 259). Skinner's statistical study complements my qualitative observations in Henza: Women's delayed marriage and lengthy widowhood—both of which grant women a high degree of autonomy—should be considered factors in the exceptionally high life expectancy of Okinawan women.

Villagers typically describe old women as *genki* (lively, spunky), and younger relatives are proud of their genki grandmothers. In one of my very first conversations with Noriko, when our mutual language skills were still very poor, she went to great effort to tell me that her mother-in-law is seventy-six and still runs a store for fishermen. "And she drives a truck! Every day, on the sea road, to bring the fish.

She doesn't have a license, and she drives fast. It frightens me. But she is so genki. And she smokes!"

According to the woman who owns the local beauty parlor, "Old women here don't stay home, they don't like to. They go outside and do something. They don't have something inside of their heart to worry them, so they just go out. They go to the senior citizens' center, singing and dancing. Or to the vegetable garden. . . . They like to look nice and get permanent waves before festivals like san gatsu." Most Henza women live in close proximity to female relatives of their own age cohort; sisters and cousins visit one another on a daily basis. Elderly women and widows are not social isolates. They control their own finances and immediate living spaces, and they engage in daily interactions with female kin. Elderly women are not a marginal fringe of Henza; women aged sixty-five and older make up 32 percent of Henza's female population (see table 3.3).

In Henza, widowhood is not perceived as a time of misery but as a time of independence. According to one woman in her fifties, "Once you are widowed you can do anything you want, you don't care what he [husband] thinks." Old women and widows continue to work in their gardens and attend a variety of dance and cultural groups. Several women told me that now that they have free time they have learned new skills, such as playing the samisen or koto (string instruments). Talented elderly women, such as Mrs. Okuda, who dances, and Mrs. Hokama, who sings, receive a great deal of respect and attention from villagers. At parties and celebrations when they perform, their age is always announced, followed by enthusiastic applause. Undoubtedly, the freedom that women experience during widowhood is made possible both by the safety net of the Japanese welfare system and by the recent affluence brought about through renting land to the oil company on the island. At the same time, the absence of restrictive gender ideologies means that widows can use their newfound prosperity to engage in a wide range of activities, including religious ones.

Although some older women are very involved in religious rituals of various sorts (both inside and outside the house and the village), other elder women are only marginally involved. Religious activism, beyond the level of tending home altars, seems to be a matter of choice among middle-aged and elderly women (see chapter 11 for further discussion of age and religious activism).

At large rituals such as major clan gatherings or san gatsu, it is common for middle-aged people to attend the beginning of the ritual gathering and then leave part way through, with only old people staying until the end. Old people spend a great deal of time discussing matters of lineage and how people in the village are related to one another. Because the religious system is integrated into the clan system, these conversations overlap discussion of ritual and religious leadership. And because so much of the ritual life of the village is associated with funeral and postfuneral ritual, old people (who tend to have more peers who die) attend far more rituals than do young people.

By late middle age many women begin to become expert in religious activities. One woman now in her eighties told me, "I have been praying since I was forty years old." It is typical for kaminchu to become initiated in their late thirties or early forties but to begin actively doing kaminchu work in their fifties or sixties.

The transition is gradual. Mrs. Shinzato (in her sixties), in 1995, joined the core ritual group of older women at the san gatsu festival, yet she sat toward the edge of their circle, was quieter than the others, and left earlier. When one considers that there are between twenty and thirty clans in Henza and that each clan has several kaminchu, it does seem that being a clan kaminchu should be viewed as a life stage for a significant portion of Henza's women. This life stage, as we shall see further on, brings a certain amount of status and economic resources.

For women, old age often means that household duties become fewer, leaving more time for ritual involvement (cf. T. Lebra 1984: 269). Widows are free of the burden of providing meals for their husbands, and even women whose husbands are still alive may find that being an active kaminchu leads to husbands taking on a greater role in the house. I noticed that in houses of priestesses (especially village level priestesses), the husband seems to be more helpful than in other households: Both the noro's husband and Mrs. Ishikawa's husband served me tea when I came to visit, something that I did not see in other Henza households. Several of the priestesses' husbands sat with us during conversations and seemed to feel knowledgeable about and involved in their wives' religious roles. Because the decision to become kaminchu typically follows years or decades of illness (see chapter 7), the husband may express relief that since the wife has begun to sit as kaminchu, her health has improved. According to Mrs. Ishikawa, "I pray for my husband and my children, so yes, he is encouraging [of my priestess work]. You can't do this on your own, you need to be hand in hand with your husband." The only complaints from husbands concern times when the wife neglects household duties.[41] Kaminchu learn to prepare their husbands' food in the morning before going to the kami-ya or utaki, and that way avoid conflict over neglecting the house. Because of potential conflict with husbands, some kaminchu seem to delay becoming active until their husbands have passed away.

Some old women take upon themselves informal ritual expertise roles such as singing the wakareru utta [funeral laments]. At most funerals, a group (not an organized group but a group nonetheless) of elderly women sit a bit away from the tomb and sing traditional funeral songs, after which the family of the deceased gives them gifts of food. In the old days, according to one woman, "The Buddhist priest did not come to funerals. Within the family it used to be that an old person lit six multiplied by two, that is, twelve incense sticks. And that person prayed and said, 'Now we have this person to go into your [the ancestors'] place so please lead this person into the grave.'" I asked the elderly Mrs. Adaniya if in the old days a priest performed wedding ceremonies. Her answer, "No, old women did this ceremony. Those old women pray for the family that she is going to marry to, bring her good life and good luck." Until about thirty years ago, there were few professional yuta. Divination, communication with the dead, and other rites now performed by yuta used to be performed by old women known loosely (and perhaps only in retrospect) as yutaobaatachi. This compound plural noun literally translates into "grandmother yutas." I have also heard villagers refer to utooto-obaa or "praying grandmothers" who seem to have done much of what is now done by the paid ogami people (see chapter 10).

A series of birthday celebrations is held for very old people. At the eighty-eight-year-old celebration, a special song is sung: "If you reach eight-eight the surface of your face is wrinkled like waves. You have gray hair on your head but your eyesight is better and you are getting younger." The lyrics of this song portray eighty-eight as a time of continuing power and health. At these parties, the old person is photographed, and the photograph is hung up on the wall in a prominent place in the house, often on the beam dividing the main room of the house. As a result, the old person—even after death—remains a noticeable presence in the house. Because most Henzans who reach the age of eighty-eight are women, most of these pictures are of women. Given that ancestors are considered to be kami-sama, one wonders how the presence of these photographs affects the way children perceive the divine.[42]

Are Men the Boss?

Occasional comments by villagers—by some men and more women—that "men are the boss" intrigued me because it was difficult to see manifestations of male dominance in village life. What is the sphere that men control? Clearly not the economic sphere, where women dominate local commerce and have provided most of their family's food. Until less than 100 years ago, moreover, land was periodically redistributed, and the noro seemed to be the only individual who truly owned her own land. Clearly not the sexual sphere, where women as much as men control their own bodies. Clearly not in the educational system, where more girls than boys go on to good high schools and universities. Clearly not the social sphere, where more women than men engage in communal interactions (see chapter 5). Clearly not the religious sphere, where women are the acknowledged leaders. And clearly not the symbolic sphere, where there is no ideology of female inferiority.

In many cultures, male superiority is expressed through physical violence and control of women. Although in Henza domestic violence is neither common nor condoned, it does exist. Village women's complaints about men's behavior is typically linked to excessive alcohol consumption.

SUSAN: Are there bad men here?

MRS. HOKAMA: Those who drink sake.

SUSAN: Are there bad men in Henza?

BEAUTY PARLOR OWNER: Yes!!! Bad men drink sake, so the wife takes the children to go with her to her own mother's house.

———

SUSAN: Do men here hit their wives?

VILLAGE WOMAN (in her nineties): Yes, some did hard beatings. Men who like to drink.

Women disapprove of men staying out all night drinking: They say that some men waste too much money on sake and that when they come home they throw things and are abusive to their families. Although men do not seem to consider alcohol consumption a social problem, women clearly consider it a problem and a gender-linked problem. There is a consensus among Henza villagers that only men drink to excess. Villagers have told me that excessive drinking in Henza is recent; until several decades ago, people did not have enough cash to buy significant quantities of sake. The point I am stressing here is that women interpret a great deal of men's aggressive behavior not as an innate sex-linked characteristic but as a by-product of excessive drinking, which itself is understood to be linked to specific economic and historical circumstances. In the women's comments, men qua men are not perceived as violent—alcohol is the relevant factor.[43]

In general, levels of male violence, including sexual violence, toward women are low.[44] Henza women are not afraid to go out at night; the threat of male violence does not constrain their activities. Recall that the beauty parlor owner quoted above explained that the wife of a drunken abusive man will take her children and go to her own mother's house. Henza women are rarely stuck hopelessly in situations of domestic abuse—they do have culturally condoned alternatives.

Unlike in many other societies, in Henza there are no real constraints on women's freedom of movement.[45] As long as a woman keeps her property in good condition, neighbors do not criticize her for going out. Women are busy with ritual events, women's club (fujinkai) meetings, and social gatherings with friends and relatives. In light of Okinawan women's longevity, they have many years of their lives in which they are not involved in the process of reproduction and are free to engage in a wide range of other activities. Put more generally, Henza society does not seem to be driven by gender-related power interests that could—and do in other societies—lead to control of women or of women's reproductive capabilities: There is no substantial amount of land to be passed on patrilineally; there is no shortage of workers that clans or families seek to correct through producing and controlling as many offspring as possible; there is no ongoing warfare that demands large human and economic resources; and there are no classes or castes that endeavor to preserve their "purity."

One woman in her thirties speculated that what women mean when they say men are the boss is that men don't do much of anything—"They just sit there." Women, in contrast, work hard preparing food, raising children, and growing vegetables on their farms. These same activities, I suggest, provide women with a great deal of control over economic, social, and emotional resources. Much of women's work involves the production and distribution of food. As shown in chapter 5, food is the most important material that links humans and kami-sama, descendants and ancestors, and humans to each other in Henza society. Providing food through horticulture and seashore foraging, serving food, being responsible for food, manipulating food, and controlling food distribution are not menial tasks.

Takie Lebra describes some of the manifestations of patriarchy within Japanese marriages: tyranny on the part of the husband, violence, on-stage male dominance, an expectation that wives will provide "round the body care" for husbands, and total dependency of men upon women's household labor. This extreme dependency, according to Lebra, can lead to a kind of household matriarchy in that "it gives the wife leverage to wield power by making her [domestic] services indispensable. . . . *Patriarchy and matriarchy, far from being mutually exclusive, can be reciprocals of one another*" (1984: 134; my emphasis). I believe that Lebra's insight here is a crucial one. Patriarchy and matriarchy can be reciprocals of one another because both revolve around an axis of power. In Henza, where gender roles are fairly flexible and where power and hierarchy are far less salient than in mainland Japan, it would be less likely for a household to develop patriarchal or matriarchal patterns.

To an outsider such as myself, the one realm in which men do seem to be the boss is the political realm. The significance of that arrangement is, however, diminished by the fact that Henza is a tiny island in a backwoods prefecture. The political decisions that affect people's lives are made in Tokyo, not in the Henza town hall. The village headman is indeed male, but the headman role has little historical depth in Henza, and his main function is to represent the villagers in rituals in which women priestesses are *kami-sama*! Still, villagers are aware of the power of the Japanese state and aware that almost all those who embody or represent that power are men. Men "bosses"—albeit foreign ones—are the ones who decree how much of Okinawan land will be occupied by American military bases, who decide to fight wars on Okinawan territory, and who control most of the links to the wider Japanese economy.[46]

Although, as I said, the political realm is the only cultural arena in which I, as an outsider, discern the presence of male dominance, it would be inappropriate to ignore the reasons for and implications of villagers' assertion that "men are number one." In line with Mary Hawkesworth's insistence that "feminist theory begins with the insight that any construction of gender must be treated as problematic rather than given" (1990: 45), my claim that Henza is characterized by an egalitarian gender ethos does not release us from looking seriously at rhetorical references to male dominance or from taking seriously the fact that it is men—albeit not local men—who make the decisions that determine Okinawa's political and economic present and future.

According to Professor Takara of the University of the Ryukyus (personal communication), the ideological complex of male supremacy is relatively new on Okinawa—it was imported from China by the Shuri aristocracy and never fully reached peasants in outlying villages and islands. During the eighteenth century, in the wake of Chinese influence, formal patrilineal ancestor worship and the butsudan were introduced, whereas previously there had been a more free style of prayer to a variety of gods and ancestors. Professor Takara explains that, beginning in the eighteenth century, "the family boss was the man, with the second boss being the eldest son. Shuri worked through propaganda to make this the system. Before the eighteenth century things were more equal, and there are records of women who were family head. There is documentation of women owning property and women being clan head." Returning to Henza, I would suggest that "men are the boss" is an aphorism that has—in a cursory way—seeped into village discourse from the Chinese-influenced Shuri elite. The analysis offered here is the same one that I offered earlier in this chapter when we looked at kinship ideology. I suggested that the patrilineal-patrilocal ideal is a reflection of the imported Chinese ideology adopted by the Shuri elite and superficially picked up in villages such as Henza where that ideology, for a variety of reasons, did not become rooted in social reality until it was forcibly institutionalized by the Japanese during the past 100 years. Because Henzans know both that men really are bosses in Japan, China, and the United States and that male political dominance has been forcibly imposed on their village via Japanese law, I suspect that the idea of men as boss is, in the eyes of villagers, less an authentic village tradition than a foreign import.[47]

When Henza women say that "men are number one," they say it with a note of humor in their voices, not with the resonance of fear, frustration, and pain that is heard in the voices of women who live in true patriarchies. Women, like any subordinate group, need a certain amount of freedom in order to perceive and dare to vocalize opposition to their own oppression; patriarchy has the insidious power to both possess and prepossess. The lack of free choice and of alternative options that characterizes patriarchy makes it difficult for women to give voice to—much less carry out—significant resistance.[48] In a truly patriarchal society, a dissatisfied woman has nowhere to run to in order to escape an unhappy or even dangerous situation. Perhaps not surprisingly, contemporary Western feminism emerged at a time in history in which middle-class women had political rights, access to higher education and jobs, a reasonable chance of surviving childbearing, and as much food as their male siblings. Feminist consciousness is unlikely to emerge in situations in which women lack the freedom to gather autonomously or to speak out or even think their own thoughts. In Henza, where gender arrangements are not naturalized and where women can marshal a wide range of social, economic, and ritual resources, they are able to say "men are the bosses" with a mixture of humor, criticism, anger, and condescension in their tone.

FOUR

Gender Separation
and Social Integration

SUSAN: Are bad people usually men or women, or are men and women the same?

MRS. HOKAMA: Fights are usually men against men. Women even though they think [bad thoughts], they don't fight.

SUSAN: Describe a good woman in the opinion of Henza people.

BEAUTY PARLOR OWNER: Yasashii and someone who likes to take care of other people. Henza women work hard, they go out to work and come home and take care of the house and of the family. Men have more physical strength. But in the mind, in the heart, women are stronger. Men just go to work and then like to sit down.

MRS. SHINZATO: Men are incompetent and they don't do anything right and they are so lazy.

MRS. OKUTARA: You yourself should be headman. You are always so busy.

SUSAN: What is Mrs. Shinzato busy with?

MRS. OKUTARA: Helping her daughter here and her daughter there. Whenever there is a funeral in the family she goes and cooks and helps out.

Gender Separation

Gender separation[1] can provide women with their own sphere in which to function independently or it can mean that women are excluded from arenas of power and prestige. Although a great deal has been written about the implications of gender separation, sometimes stressing the positive implications for women and sometimes the negative (cf. Reiter 1975), anthropologists are lacking a cross-culturally applicable schema for evaluating when and why gender separation is an expression and a tool of male dominance and when and why it is an expression and a tool of true gender complementarity and women's autonomy. In sorting out the ramifications of gender separation, I see four key issues that need to be addressed.

The first issue is that of control. In some gender-separated cultural settings, women do not exercise autonomy over their own sphere; although men and women are separate, men supervise women's activities. This model is well-known to Orthodox Jewish women, who, in their highly gender-segregated culture, are in charge of cooking, but whose cooking laws (*kashrut*) are supervised by male rabbis. The second issue concerns ideology. In some cultural settings, gender separation is grounded in ideologies of male and female essential difference. Ideologies of essential difference are typically phrased in biological (naturalized) terms; not surprisingly, the ideologies that underpin gender separation often make reference to women's menstrual impurity or to their uncontrollable sexuality. As a corollary, women and the women's sphere tend to be culturally defined as inferior to men and the men's sphere, and women and their sphere tend to be seen as in need of male control. A third and somewhat related issue concerns enforcement. In the wake of a potent ideology of essential difference and "proper" gender domains, gender separation in some societies is total and enforced. An individual whose personal inclinations would lead him or her to seek, for example, professional fulfillment in the other gender's sphere cannot do so without incurring social condemnation. The final issue has to do with access to the public sphere. In some cultural settings, gender separation means that women are denied admittance to the public sphere—even in the form of all-women gatherings. The result is that women's ability to make or influence decisions that affect the society at large is extremely limited.

In cultural situations in which women truly control the women's domain, in which women's interactions are not limited to the immediate domestic environment, and in which there is no ideology of difference or inferiority and no significant enforcement of gender separation, a separate women's sphere can provide women with an autonomous base for social integration and socially acknowledged authority. This, as we shall see, is the situation in Henza. Socializing in Henza tends to be in all-male or all-female groups. Both men and women, however, have access to the public sphere; women's social interactions are not limited to domestic environments; men do not supervise women's activities; there is no ideology of women's existential inferiority and none that leads to the perception of gender integration as dangerous; there are no rules prohibiting gender-integrated socializing; and crisscrossing between men's and women's domains is commonplace and unproblematic.

Gender separation in Henza is subsistence-related. Henza men traditionally were fishermen and sailors. Fishermen would go out on boats by day, returning in the evening. Sailors would go away for longer periods of time (weeks or months). Mr. Shinyashiki, the man in charge of land registration at the Henza town hall, estimates that before the war, when Henza's population was approximately 3000, there were in the vicinity of 700 sailors.[2] Unlike the men, women stayed in the village, working in the fields, foraging at the beach, and occasionally selling fish.

We start here with a woman I met on the street one morning. She looked to be in her late seventies and was carrying a bucket of gardening tools.

SUSAN: Tell me about work in the fields.

WOMAN: I work on my [late] husband's land.

SUSAN: Did he tell you what to plant?

WOMAN: No, I am in charge, I do what I want. . . . Before I was married I went to mainland Japan to work to make money—it was fun. . . . Then I came back here. My husband went to Spain eight times. He was away a lot.

This woman's life conforms to a common Henza pattern: trip to mainland Japan to work, her husband an absentee seaman, autonomous work in the garden, widowhood. Young women of her generation often went to mainland Japan, where they experienced a period of independence from parental supervision and small-village norms. They typically worked in all-women factories or other gender-separated institutions, and they remember that as a pleasant interlude in their lives.[3] When they returned to Henza (in order to have children), they married men who spent many of their middle years away, either on sailing vessels or working in distant countries. This informant expressed surprise when I asked her if her husband told her what to plant in her garden—the garden is her responsibility and she has authority over it, just as the woman fish trader controls her own profits and finances. Like many village women, she is now experiencing a prolonged period of healthy widowhood in which she has little contact with men.[4] Her life story exemplifies the first of the criteria that I suggested for gender separation that empowers women: lack of male supervision over women's activities.

A woman did not usually sell the vegetables that she raised, but if she did, the money was hers and she didn't have to tell the husband. Usually the money is used for the family. So she doesn't need to give the money to the husband. But usually they eat the vegetables. The money from the husband's fishing was his money, he doesn't need to give to the wife. Every day the wife would ask him for the money the family needs. (Mrs. Hokama)

Villagers offer no ideological foundation for gender separation. I asked one elderly man why men and women sit separately at ceremonies. "That is a custom, like dogs and cats each do their own things." In general, at Henza ceremonies, meetings, and celebrations, men and women sit in single-gender groups, although not absolutely separately. For example, at funerals distant relatives sit in the yard in separate groups. The immediate family sits inside the house, men and women together. Out on the street, friends and neighbors wait to come into the house and pay last respects—that is, burn a pinch of incense in front of the body. While waiting out on the street, people tend to cluster, chatting in single-gender groups, but once they get on line to pay their respects men and women mingle.[5] Significantly, in this context, when villagers are physically close together on very crowded lines leading up the narrow path to the house and actively engaged in a religious ritual of lighting incense, men and women mix. This observation supports my claim that we are not talking about a genuine taboo (as is the case in, for example, the Middle East or parts of Melanesia) but rather a preference to be with one's own peers. An ideology of female pollution is not at work here.

The point about socializing is important, because it suggests that gender separation in Henza reflects preference and not rule. On several occasions, I passed crews working in public gardens. Typically, these crews were made up of both men and women. Twice I happened to see gardening crews at their lunch breaks. Once, I saw that the three women were sitting together, and, quite a distance away, two men were sitting together. Another time I saw the women sitting in the van eating and the men sitting outside eating under a tree. In both instances, before and after lunch the crew worked together, men and women side by side doing the same jobs. Thus, even when men and women do the same work, they may elect to socialize separately.

While gender separation is common, it is neither absolute nor consistent. On many occasions I found that although a room was generally divided by gender, several individuals could be found on the side on which the other gender predominated, and this was not seen as interesting or worthy of comment. For example, at an evening PTA meeting the room was clearly set up in advance for men to sit at the tables farthest right—only these tables had ashtrays—but some women chose to sit among the men and some men sat among the women. Similarly, at most activities of the local senior citizens' club men and women sit separately, yet afternoon croquet is composed of a mixed group. And to take a final example, my male research partner, Mr. Okutara, and I once attended a women's *usudeku* (dance) group together. This group has no men among its members, and the women sat with their legs stretched out, many with their thighs showing (this is not common in public gatherings). Yet no one thought it problematic that Mr. Okutara attended with me, and the women were unconcerned about uncovering their thighs with a man in the room. At one point in the evening they dragged him up to dance, in exactly the same way that they dragged me and a few of the "lazy" women up to dance. In short, sexual or bodily modesty or purity does not seem to be an underlying ideology bolstering gender separation. On the occasions on which I saw mixed-gender socializing, both men and women appeared at ease, and there was a great deal of easygoing joking.

Informants have made clear to me that, as an outsider who attends many celebrations, I was receiving an exaggerated picture of gender separation in Henza. According to one informant, "In regular married life you can sit wherever you want, but when you go to events [ceremonies or gatherings] men and women sit separately. In everyday life men and women sit together." And, indeed, at smallish events such as engagement parties in which the immediate families of the bride and groom gather first at the bride's house and then at the groom's, the seating is likely to be mixed. Similarly, at village festivals (see, for example, the description of the tug-of-war in chapter 12), men and women mingle.[6]

Women and Social Integration

The Westerner studying Okinawan society can be handicapped by his ethnocentric focus on the individual, for the basic units of Okinawan society are families, kin groups, and communities—not individuals. The individual, as such, establishes identity only through membership in these groups. Consequently, the primary responsibilities of the individual are to the group; and ideally group interests take precedence, where there is a conflict, over individual self-interest. The group, in turn, is accountable for the action of individual members; this is true for both supernatural and social orders. (W. Lebra 1966: 42)

One of the underlying principles of [Okinawan] domestic ritual is that the *kami* and ancestors are in league with the family and must be informed of all that transpires. The significance of this partnership cannot be overemphasized. (W. Lebra 1966: 201).

SUSAN: Do Henza women help each other a lot?

BEAUTY PARLOR OWNER: Yes, they do. Too much helping each other! If something happened in the family and you need help, even if you don't ask they come and help you!

As I said at the beginning of this chapter, gender separation can be a two-edged sword, endowing groups of women with social power or preventing women from having access to power in the public realm. I have argued that in the Okinawan case the fact that gender separation is not bolstered by any kind of ideology means that there is a fair amount of flexibility in the system, that women's sphere is not defined as subordinate, and that women have equal access to the public realm. We shall now look more closely at the content and structure of women's and men's domains. I shall show that Henza women engage in more frequent, more multilayered, and longer-lasting social interactions than do men. For women more than for men, social, religious, economic, and kin connections overlap. Both formal meetings and informal gatherings ensure an extraordinarily high level of social integration among Henza women.

Henza women socialize in a variety of kin and non-kin-related contexts: in the beauty parlor, stores, and clinics and on the street. Women's vegetable plots are scattered throughout the residential village, so even while gardening women frequently stop and chat with passersby. A great deal of work, such as cutting and drying radishes (daikon), is done in the front yard of the house, promoting socializing. In the evening, the beauty parlor owner sits inside the shop with the door opened, folding towels. Women passing by drop in for a few minutes or longer and catch up on the day's events. In the course of my fieldwork, I found that during almost every visit to the house of a villager, another woman, often a sister or cousin, stopped by for a few minutes to bring some vegetables or to share a message.

Women and Kin: Matrifocal Households

SUSAN: Are there stories that people like to tell children?

MRS. ADANIYA: Not really. Just *oya kookoo* [loosely, children helping and respecting their parents for the effort they made in raising them]. In Okinawa, stories that we have a lot of are oya kookoo. The daughter-in-law will take care of her mother-in-law, like I do for my mother-in-law. To let her go to another world [by praying for her at the butsudan after she dies].

————

Parents and children and brothers and sisters are like one. Before your husband come your parents, brothers, and sisters. (Mrs. Shinzato)

Henza households are, for the most part, matrifocal: Mothers are the focus of the household; the most emotionally significant ties are among women household members; the structurally, culturally, ritually, and affectively central role of mothers is seen as legitimate; and women control key household economic resources (cf. Tanner 1974).[7]

Mrs. Hatsu, now in her late seventies, says that soon after she married, her husband went to the war and she stayed in her parents' house. When he returned from the war he moved in with her. "I had three brothers. My brother served nine years in the military and died in the war. His wife had two children and died, so that is why I stayed with my parents, the two grandparents and the two children, and they had a lot of farming property. My parents died at ninety-two and ninety-three, had a long life." Another very old Henza woman, dressed in baggy trousers and an undershirt, explains that when she was younger her husband went to Singapore for eight years. She stayed in her parents' house, and that is where she continues to live. She raised her children there, and she raised the children of her older sister (who died young) together with her own. Her husband sent her money from Singapore. In both of these stories, we see themes common to Henza household arrangements: women raising the children of maternal relatives; male absenteeism; a household organized around a core of related women. Many Henza women report extended periods of time in which their husbands were away, and they either lived in their own parents' household or ran independent households. Although absentee married men would intend to send money home, in reality their financial offerings were few and far between. Women necessarily relied upon each other for material assistance during the long periods in which men's financial contributions were sporadic.[8]

Even today, it is not uncommon for Henza men to work and live off the island while their wives and children stay in the village. In quite a few families, a daughter is the only child who has stayed in Henza. Often this daughter is divorced and has returned to Henza with her children in part so that her parents (her mother) can look after her children while she works, either on or off the island. Grandmothers seventy and eighty years old cook, clean, and do laundry for grandchildren, and many of these grandmothers are proud of their daughters' professional accomplishments. Traditionally, relationships between mothers and daughters remained strong even when the daughter married and moved to her husband's house. One ninety-year-old woman told me that she would visit her mother every day.

A strong relationship between mothers and daughters is one of the backbones of Henza. In the past, women typically remained in their parents' homes until bearing their second child. The postpartum woman would rest next to the fire for a few weeks after birth, and her mother and sisters would take over her household duties. Often the husband's sisters would help out in the postpartum woman's garden. Now, either the young women go to their mother's houses after giving birth or their mother and often their sisters come to their houses to help out, cook, and do the laundry (this is also true in Japan; see Ohnuki-Tierney 1984: 186–187). Informants tell me that the placenta used to be buried behind the house, and the umbilical cord was preserved. Apparently, until about eight years ago the hospitals continued to give the umbilical cord in a box to take home.[9] Preserving the umbilical cord symbolizes the permanent and intimate relationship between children and their mothers.

Even in those Henza households that are patrilocal, the core relationship tends to be between mother-in-law and daughter-in-law.[10] One woman fondly reminisces about how her mother-in-law took care of the garden plot because she herself did not like that kind of work or how her mother-in-law had been very supportive of her teaching career and did the farming so that she would be free to teach. Although this is probably not a typical situation, the eighty-six-year-old local dance expert (Mrs. Okuda) told me that when her children were young she did not work in the garden; her mother-in-law did the gardening in her place. "I couldn't make rice either, I don't know how to cook. I can't make *popo* [a kind of pancake] now."

Mrs. Adaniya lives with her daughter-in-law, son, grandchildren, and granddaughter's baby. The three generations of women seem to have a close and pleasant relationship, and all take care of the baby and spend time together. The daughter-in-law works sporadically next door at the grocery store that they own, but she spends a great deal of her time coming in and out of the house to talk to her mother-in-law and daughter. In contrast to traditional China, where the mother-in-law is portrayed as highly emotionally involved with her son and threatened by her son's relationship with his wife, in Henza households the relationship between mother and son often seems rather distant, whereas the relationship between mother-in-law and daughter-in-law tends to be warm and friendly.

Some older women recall feeling unhappy in their husband's houses; they remember having to work very hard and not getting along well with their in-laws. My own observations in Henza today are somewhat different, possibly because nowadays, if the mother and daughter-in-law do not get along, the daughter-in-law will leave, with or without her husband. In recent years, both in Japan and in Okinawa, aging women have become vulnerable to the willingness of their sons and especially their daughters-in-law to take care of them (cf. Hendry 1981). While I was in Henza, the elderly Mrs. Okuda, who lives in a house together with her son, daughter-in-law, and grandchildren, became angry at her daughter-in-law and decided to leave. (Mrs. Okuda's conflict with her daughter-in-law is longstanding. Her son, caught between his mother and wife, seems to make an effort to stay out of the feud.) Although Mrs. Okuda has been for several years now dependent upon her daughter-in-law to cook and wash for her, Mrs. Okuda had other options when the situation at home became intolerable. In another city in Okinawa, she has a daughter and granddaughter who live together. The daughter was divorced when the granddaughter was young, and Mrs. Okuda had lived with her daughter and taken care of the granddaughter for a number of years.

The granddaughter is now an optometrist, and Mrs. Okuda may move in with her. After spending a night at a hotel and discussing her problem with a number of close women friends, Mrs. Okuda returned home, and everyone seems to be satisfied with how things worked out—Mrs. Okuda is especially proud of her independence and tells everyone who will listen that she slept in room 205 at the hotel!

Villagers say that in the past men were more eager than women to get married. Still today, villagers say that many women choose not to marry, whereas men usually do want a wife. The fact that women both in previous generations and today are less eager to marry than men are suggests that women's natal families fill their social and emotional needs in a way that men's natal families do not. One woman, unmarried and in her mid-thirties, mentioned to me that she had recently seen in a newspaper article that Okinawa has a very high rate of never-married people. In her opinion this is because "in Okinawa if you are not married you still have family to help you, to bring you vegetables, and to ask how you are." I never heard men make similar comments. In general, for women far more than for men, kin and social ties cross-cut.

I asked Henza women whether they are closer to daughters or to sons. All said they are closer to daughters, although, according to formal patrilineal ideology, a married daughter belongs to a different family from her mother. I asked one woman in her thirties who already has three children if she wants more children. "No. Umh, if it's a girl it's okay, but if not, I don't want another." Several villagers told me that in Henza, unlike in China, eldest sons are not spoiled by their parents—they are treated the same as the other children. Whether or not this is true (and I think it is true), it is significant that this is what people claim to be true.

I asked youngish middle-aged women: To whom do you feel the closest, with whom do you discuss your problems? By far the most common answer was sisters.[11] Other women told me that for financial help they would most likely go to their mothers, for emotional support to their friends. Contrary to reports of earlier anthropologists (Mabuchi 1964), I found that most women do not seem to feel particularly close to their brothers, nor do they expect their brothers to help them; they report much more extensive contact with their sisters. Traditionally, women's religious duties were connected to their brother's rather than their husband's houses, a situation that recently has been changing in Henza.[12]

Women customarily provided most of the family's food, and women continue to purchase, prepare, and serve food, manage the household's finances, superivse children's educational activities, take responsibility for the family's health care, and clean and maintain the house. Maretzki and Maretzki have noted that Okinawan women are believed to have responsibility for caring for children, and that fathers, although not forbidding figures to the children, spend less time at home that any other member of the household. "Contact with the father is, therefore, only sporadic and is not affected by a special desire on the part of fathers to spend time with children" (1966: 150). Henza fathers can sometimes be found taking children to the park or the beach—frivolous activities; mothers are the ones that children rely on to sustain the family.

Women's Gatherings in the Public Domain

Traditionally, one of the most important extradomestic frameworks for women has been *usudeku* groups. Groups meet throughout the year, twice each month, to practice the usudeku dances that they perform on the days following the obon festival. One woman usudeku dancer told me that usudeku dancing was held on the days after obon as a send-off for the ancestors who have returned to their world after a three-day visit in the village. "The dancing is a gift from the live people to their ancestors." Another woman told me that it was done so that the king from Shuri could pick the prettiest women of the village to bring back with him to the royal court. The general opinion in the village is that it was done to show seafaring menfolk how nice it is to return to the village for obon. Usudeku dancing is performed in the village square in front of the kami-ya, in the yards of several old village families, and in the lot in front of the town hall. The women are given gifts by the village in honor of, or in thanks for, their dancing. Thus, usudeku dancing has a clear public component.

In terms of social integration, the meetings and rehearsals are more salient than the public performance. For the purposes of usudeku, the village is divided into three groups: east, center, and west. I was told that even though women who marry may leave their parents' home, they usually choose to stay in their natal family neighborhood's usudeku group.[13]

> MRS. HOKAMA: One woman was born in [the] west but she married a man in the east, and their house is in the center, but she goes to west usudeku. But sometimes she comes here to the center group.
>
> SUSAN: Do all women come to usudeku groups?
>
> MRS. HOKAMA: Even if you don't dance, you go to your group that you like, and help them with singing and see the dancing. Each person has her own preferences regarding which group to go to. My parents were born in center and I also go to center group. If you belong to the center, even if you don't dance, you still go to the center and not east or west.

Usudeku strengthens ties with friends and neighbors and keeps married women in an ongoing extradomestic framework together with their own sisters and childhood friends. Even today, when few young women are interested in usudeku, the groups continue to offer middle-aged and older village women an important forum for aesthetic and ritual expression. Usudeku dancing is complex and highly stylized. What most struck me about usudeku, however, was how much fun the meetings and rehearsals are. For several hours twice each month, women get together and laugh, chat, sing, eat, and dance in a socially legitimate and valued context.

In Okinawa, like in Japan, individuals may belong to a *mo-ai* (a sort of free loan club). In Henza, women far more than men belong to mo-ai, and the women's mo-ai have become assimilated into or grown out of the usudeku groups. According to Mrs. Hokama, "We did not used to have mo-ai, but recently we got it together so that the [usudeku] group won't fall apart. If you are in a group, you have a group awareness." Nowadays, at twice monthly meetings, the women take care of both mo-ai and usudeku matters. They collect money for the free loan collective, they go on one or more picnics or trips each year, and they practice their dance performances. The assimilation of mo-ai into the traditional usudeku neighborhood groups underscores the convergence of social and ritual endeavors among women.

A great deal of women's socializing takes place in the context of ritual activities More women more than men participate in almost all ceremonial gatherings. In particular, Henza women meet regularly at funerals and memorial ceremonies. Friends and relatives gather at the home of the deceased daily for the first week after a death, once a week for the next seven weeks, and then once a year. Except on the day of the funeral, women form the core at all of the memorial gatherings,[14] and "it is the bilateral-multilineal—rather than agnatic relatives of the deceased" who participate in funeral and memorial rituals (Mabuchi 1976: 110). The cumulative effect of these ceremonial gatherings, almost all of which include a communal meal, is near constant opportunities for women to share their thoughts, problems, plans, and opinions with one another and to make their thoughts and plans visible to the village as a whole.

The fujinkai, or women's association, is make up of married women of about sixty-five years old and younger. The fujinkai helps organize village events such as sports day, haari boat racing, and tsuna-hiki (ritual tug-of-war). They also have monthly meetings, parties, lectures, and trips. The fujinkai is well-rooted in Henza, and it provides a long-term ongoing forum for women to meet. Of the three most active women in the fujinkai, one has worked at the Henza town hall for many years, one began to work there during my year in the village, and one was just elected as the first woman on the village council. Fujinkai activism, far from marginalizing women, serves as women's chief passport into Henza's male-dominated political domain.

The senior citizen's association, roojinkai, is extremely active, both at the village level and at the district level. The roojinkai organizes parties, classes, trips, and lectures. For example, during my year in Henza they arranged for a bus to take villagers to a bone-collecting ceremony in the southern part of the main island (many Okinawans killed during the war were never buried properly), they held a huge gala New Year's party, and they provided a forum for senior citizens to learn to play musical instruments. Given the uneven demographic distribution in Henza (see table 3.2), the roojinkai is made up almost entirely of women.

All villagers belong to patrilineally organized clans (munchu), of which there are approximately two dozen (ten or so main ones and other smaller ones) in the village. My claim that Henza households are matrifocal and that Henza religious life is led by women may seem to fit poorly with the formal patrilineal munchu organization in the village. Yet a close look at the meaning of the munchu in Henza reveals that the clans have few functions aside from ritual occasions at which women hold the key roles (cf. Matsuzono 1976: 240). The munchu are concerned almost solely with ancestral beliefs and cult and not with the organization of daily life.[15] When I asked the male administrative head (sekininsha) of one of the larger munchu what the munchu does besides organize ceremonial events, he had trouble answering. He, like other villagers, explains that munchu members are not expected to particularly help one another. The munchu do not have a moral function in the sense of monitoring or controlling the behavior of clan members, nor are they associated with marriage rules. Occasionally, the munchu may get together to support candidates in local elections, and the munchu may come to the aid of a member falsely accused in a criminal case. Clan members, especially older and middle-aged ones, are proud of their clans and boast that their clans have many teachers or musicians or politicians. In the course of my fieldwork, I found that it pleased villagers enormously when I praised their clan's generosity, food, size, importance, or high spirits. But aside from these few situations, clan membership cannot be seen as a particularly significant basis for social organization in the village.[16]

The primary function of the munchu is to carry out rituals connected to the founding ancestors and *kami-sama* of the clan. All of these rituals are attended by many more women than men, and women perform the ritual prayers. Women are the clan priestesses, and at the smaller rituals (for example, the bimonthly prayer at the house in which the munchu altar is located) only women attend. Even at medium-sized ritual occasions it is common for only—or mostly—women to attend. For example, on the *umachi* days, when the priestesses who represent Henza's oldest clans pray at the kami-ya and the sacred grove, women of the clans gather at the village square across from the kami-ya. Clanswomen also prepare meals for the priestesses to eat at the clan houses after the prayers. Although men are allowed to attend the meals, in reality very few do. At larger rituals, such as the clan's New Year prayers or pilgrimages, men do attend, but the majority of participants are women.

For example, the 1995 *seimeisai* (annual ancestor memorial day) ritual of one of Henza's larger munchu was made up of about ten women and five men. At a site next to their ancestral tombs, clan members spread out mats and trays of food. After a clan priestess prayed, a communal meal was eaten. The seating on the mats was vaguely separate, with the women sitting closer together and talking among themselves more than the men. Although the formal ritual and meal took only about an hour or two, seven of the women had spent part of the day together preparing food for the ceremony, thereby more than doubling the amount of time they spent with fellow clan members.

It is not uncommon for women to attend events both in their own clan and in their husband's. Some women say that they go to represent their husbands, who are too busy to attend. Other women say that when something especially good has happened, such as a child passing a major examination, they will go both to their own and their husband's clans to thank the ancestors and kami-sama. And finally, some women claim that in their husband's munchu there aren't enough people to cook the ritual meals and attend the rituals, so they choose to attend in order to "help out." In fact, women are likely to have cousins and friends in their husbands' clans as well.

Gatherings of this sort foster women's cohesiveness more than they do men's. As I said earlier, married women do not move to their husbands' clans. Membership in her father's rather than her husband's munchu provides a woman with an identity and a group affiliation of her own. Munchu involvement is a means for women to continue to strengthen their ties with their natal families. Somewhat ironically, the patriclan is perpetuated by the ritual practices of its women members, who constitute the core of clan activists.

Taken together, kin associations, neighborhood associations, clan gatherings, ritual groups, and age group associations ensure women an extraordinarily high level of social integration. With very little effort, women villagers are involved in daily networks of interaction and exchange. Unlike in societies in which women meet privately for coffee klatches, Henza women's gatherings are institutionalized, public, visible, and (often) sacralized, and therefore an important and acknowledged part of the social and power fabric of the village.

Men's Social Interactions

Henza men are a sort of hang-around population. They don't do anything. They just sit there. (Mr. Okutara)

The material presented in this chapter paints a picture of Henza women as involved in extensive and intensive daily projects of social integration with other women. On the whole, men are less involved in these projects. Men's kin ties are less socially and emotionally salient. They do not have a men's association parallel to the fujinkai; they do not belong to neighborhood-based economic-ritual groups like the women's mo-ai–usudeku groups; and they do not attend family or clan rituals nearly as often as women do.

On the face of it, the most salient social groupings for men should be the family and the clan; as we have said, Henza kinship ideally is patrilineal and patrilocal, and clan membership is, both ideally and in practice, patrilineal. Three factors mitigate against the kinds of strong fraternal bonding often found in patrilineal, patrilocal societies. First, women live appreciably longer than men. Therefore, an adult man and his family are more likely to be living with his mother than with his father, and, as I pointed out above, because of village endogamy and general appreciation of yasashii relations, the key social bonding in the household is often between the mother-in-law and daughter-in-law or mother and daughter. Second, because of the Okinawan inheritance pattern by which the eldest son receives the house and the younger sons move out, it is very rare to find adult brothers living together.[17] And third, because the clan ritual experts are women priestesses, women are more involved than men in clan activities.

In Henza, men typically sit in a row and women sit in a circle. Women's seating style encourages conversation, and men's discourages it. One of the very few gender differences that villagers recognize is that "women talk more than men." In other words, women more than men engage in the verbal exchanges that are the foundation of human society. Henza women typically go out in groups, and it is rare to find a woman at home alone for an entire morning; friends and relatives constantly come and visit. Men, on the other hand, spend far more time alone;

when men do get together, it is often to play a board game such as *go* that involves hours of sitting in near silence. In short, not only the quantity but also the nature of socializing is rather different: men's is more formal, women's is more continuous. It seems to me that each mode offers certain advantages in terms of social power. In the following paragraphs, I discuss some forms of social interaction engaged in more commonly by men.

First, the local political institutions are run by men. The village council is made up of men (the first woman was recently elected), and they meet on a regular basis in order to discuss issues of village importance. The headman, two other men, and two women work at the local town hall, and each day at about 11:00 A.M. a few elderly men drop by for tea and chat. These meetings provide men with a sense of being part of the communal enterprise of governing Henza. Some men are involved in local politics, which, especially at election time, leads to a great deal of social interaction.

Second, most men work outside the home and engage in some social interactions at their workplaces. Traditionally, men went out on fishing boats in groups, and the men who shared a boat also shared a feeling of group identity.[18] Fishermen belong to a fishermen's association, a group (nowadays with a small membership) that has both economic and ritual functions.

Third, some men meet and drink at bars in the evening. The more common pattern of male drinking, however, is for men to drink at home by themselves. Sometimes male co-workers eat lunch or dinner together at restaurants. Although these events can be highly social, at other times each man reads a book while eating and almost no conversation takes place. Villagers agree that men in groups tend to be quieter than women.

Fourth, young men spend a period of about six years as members in the *seinenkai*—young adults' association. The seinenkai is composed primarily of men, although nowadays some young women do join.[19] Their principal activity is preparing for and then performing eisaa dancing at obon season (see chapter 5). In addition to eisaa dancing, which many of the young men find coercive, the seinenkai helps make the large rope used for the annual village tug-of-war and contributes to the playful atmosphere at the san gatsu ritual.[20] All of these activities are seasonal and short term.

The seinenkai is relatively new in Henza, and over the past fifteen years it has disintegrated and re-formed several times. I was told that in the past young men were too mobile for a successful seinenkai to carry on. Both village men and women say that men have difficulty sustaining an ongoing organization. Seinenkai membership is terminated at age twenty-four.

Previously I stated that men do not belong to mo-ai–usudeku groups. That is not entirely correct. When I asked a group of women at the women's mo-ai–usudeku group if men have mo-ai (free loan groups), their initial response was "no," but then they added, "They have something like it, but with friends at work." I see this response as significant for several reasons. The initial negative answer suggests that, at least in the eyes of village women, men's groups are not really comparable to women's groups—a distinction that, I suspect, reflects the fact that the men's groups are only mo-ai whereas the women's groups also have a strong ritual component (usudeku dancing). Their second response underscores that the women's groups are neighborhood-focused and permanent, whereas the men's groups are composed of colleagues, and therefore are more temporary.[21]

Gifts and Gift Giving

Henza is an easy (yasashii) place to live; even people you don't know can come to funerals or weddings. You know just a little bit about a person and you go there. We grow and exchange vegetables so it is easy to live here. (village woman)

We turn now to one of the most important instruments of social integration: gift giving.[22] In Henza the most common gift by far is vegetables—a women's gift. Henza women work in gardens and grow vegetables. Many women grow more than their families can eat, and they give the excess to neighbors and friends. On several occasions, I asked women if they ever sell their surplus. The women were surprised and somewhat offended by my question—they give away, they do not sell, their vegetables. It is important to understand that many Henza women are involved in small-scale commerce: grocery stores, fish selling, and so forth. Commerce as a mode of work is not distasteful to Henza women. Vegetables, however, are different. They are a unit of social integration, not a unit of market exchange.

Many village women specialize in gathering or processing certain kinds of food. For example, some women collect large amounts of particular seaweeds during the appropriate season and give it out as gifts. Some women make their own pickles or dry and process taro root. Other women work long hours in their gardens producing surplus cabbages or carrots. Several women told me that they make an effort to give vegetables or other foods to families that they know do not have enough, although on many occasions I also saw women giving gifts of, for example, cabbages to friends who had their own gardens full of cabbages.

Gift giving is constant. It is rare for one woman to drop by another's house empty-handed or to leave empty-handed. The amount of gift giving is economically significant. Goods are in constant circulation, both necessary items like food and unnecessary items like hand towels (villagers often have closets full of unopened packages of hand towels that they have received as gifts).

Gifts are recycled. If woman A brings woman B lettuce from her garden, and, while they are chatting, woman C drops by, woman B may very well give woman C some of the lettuce she just received. All three women involved witness the transaction. The term commonly used is *morai-mono*—received things. In other words, it is clear that things circulate; there is no pretense that you are giving something original. Gifts are typically given in the context of "I have so much, let me give you my extra" and not "I am giving you a rare commodity." When Mrs. Okuda wanted to give me some fruit, and I said, "No, thank you, you have given me so much already," she got up and took me to the refrigerator to show me that enough was left for her family.

Gifts are reciprocated quickly. If I would bring a bottle of sake to a neighbor whom I had come to interview, I would leave with a bag of fruit or cookies. I felt that villagers were a bit uncomfortable when it was not possible to reciprocate immediately. (This may be because as a foreigner I was not truly absorbed into their social networks.) Although reciprocity is the norm, it is on an informal level; no one keeps records of gift giving. These informal gifts are almost never gift wrapped.

All of what I have said so far leads me to treat women's informal gift giving in Henza as a form of exchange; the continuous circulation of gifts constitutes an interdomestic, women-dominated village economy.[23] More formal modes of gift giving (see the following discussion) are engaged in by both men and women, but the daily, informal exchange of food items is a women's activity. As in the South Indian fishing village studied by Kalpana Ram, women's domestic economy of gift giving provides critical subsistence security during the long absences of their menfolk at sea. Village women clearly articulate that gift giving establishes relationships of obligation: Someone who gave me a gift can expect me to help her. I asked one Henza woman if men also exchange gifts. She found the question so incongruous that it took her a minute to answer. Finally she remarked, "Well, you don't really know what to give them." (I refrained from saying that men eat the same cabbages as women.) After more discussion, she acknowledged that men might sometimes give each other wine or beer. But the interdomestic subsistence economy (my words) is a women's endeavor.

A second type of gift giving, carried out at ritual occasions such as funerals and weddings, involves men and women equally. At Japanese-style ceremonial gatherings, money placed inside of a special envelope is given by the guest to the host upon arrival. Upon leaving, the guest typically receives beautifully wrapped soap powder or towels (at funerals) or kitchenware (at weddings). This kind of gift giving involves keeping precise records of who gave how much. At weddings a table will be set up outside the wedding hall. As guests arrive, they stand on line in front of the table, where several young relatives collect envelopes with money from each guest. At funerals the same thing is done—envelopes are collected, names are written down, and (afterward) the amounts given are recorded. The value of the return gift is calculated in light of the expected size of the gifts received (thus the return gift at weddings is more valuable than at funerals). The size of future gifts is adjusted in accordance with the past history of gift giving between two households.

This kind of gift giving can be economically significant. For example, I visited Mrs. Shimojo on Dead People's New Year. Her husband had died during the previous year. By the time that I arrived at her house, approximately 6:00 P.M., the pile of money-filled envelopes on the butsudan looked to me to number at least 100, and many more people (especially women) were still coming. The average gift was 1000 yen. There was no return gift given out to visitors, and rather small amounts of food were served. During the first year after a death, there will be approximately twelve occasions on which visitors will pray at the butsudan and leave money. This practice unquestionably serves to provide economic assistance to families who, because of a death, have lost a source of labor or income.

The third kind of gift giving in Henza is the typically Japanese formal gift giving at the New Year and the obon festival. For these occasions, nicely arranged and wrapped packages of canned goods purchased in a special gift department of the supermarket or department store are given to relatives (and more rarely to other people) in the context of a ceremonial visit. According to villagers, people eat such staples as oil, rice, and canned meat for a good few months after obon and the New Year from these gifts. These gifts, like most other gifts, are first put on the butsudan and then consumed by the family. Although women will be more likely to use the gifts and to buy the gifts, the actual giving is usually done by men—they are the ones who do the bulk of the obon and New Year visiting.

At occasions of ritual importance (New Year's and obon) and at times of special financial need (funerals and weddings), villagers give gifts. These gifts, associated with both men and women, are formal, precisely calculated, and wrapped. In contrast, the daily vegetable exchanges engaged in by women are informal, uncalculated, and unwrapped. Within the broad context of women's overlapping kin and social ties, and given the true economic significance of their food exchange, these "gifts" serve to consolidate extradomestic ties among women (cf. Hauser-Schaublin 1995 on men's structured and women's informal exchanges among the Abelan of Melanesia).

Conclusion

We have reviewed in this chapter some of the forms of social integration engaged in by Henza women. We have seen that women's social ties include mother-daughter, sisters, mother-in-law–daughter-in-law, cousins, friends, neighbors, fellow munchu members, and fellow members of the women's association, usudeku groups, and mo-ai. The level of social integration among women is higher than among men. On the streets of Henza, women are more visible than men, women exchange gifts more than men, women cook and serve food more than men, women shop more than men, and women exchange information among themselves more than men. Women's social ties are remarkably multilayered: The same two women may be relatives, belong to the same neighborhood group, attend fujinkai or roojinkai activities together, meet at memorial gatherings and clan rituals, exchange vegetables or sea products with one another, and reminisce about their old days as classmates. The women whom I would meet at religious rituals have almost all known each other since childhood. They know each other well and get together often. They know each other's talents, and in the context of celebrations, rituals, and women's organizations, they encourage one another to express those talents. Women's social integration cross-cuts public and domestic realms and is culturally approved and esteemed.[24]

Michelle Rosaldo, in her classic essay "Women, Culture, and Society: A Theoretical Overview," argued that women's position tends to be strong in societies in which women have extensive extradomestic ties with other women. Whereas women's social isolation is associated with control by men of the labor, reproductive abilities, and mobility of individual women, extradomestic ties provide women with access to resources during periods of male absence, and they "add social and moral value to an otherwise domestic role" (1974: 39). Extradomestic social groupings provide women with a power base for improving their status through explicit economic or social demands and through exchange of important information.

Extradomestic ties allow women opportunities to develop communal understandings of problems (such as physical or sexual abuse) that for a woman alone in an isolated household unit appear personal and insoluble and to develop communal understandings of the events that are most important in women's lives. Even in cultures in which reality is defined and interpreted by men, women's groups enable women to generate alternative understandings and paradigms.[25] In Henza, where the primary extradomestic groups are composed of women, women define and interpret reality for the village; women's understandings of the world are the "mainstream" ones; women more than men successfully attain and embody the highest social value—being yasashii.

Twenty-five years of gender-sensitive ethnography has, in my assessment, confirmed Rosaldo's uncovering of cross-culturally widespread patterns of men's domination of public communal domains and women's (relative) restriction to private domestic domains (see also Ortner 1996). In Henza, in contrast, women go out of the house to socialize more than men do; women are seen as more social beings than are men; women work in the village, which is the locus of social interaction; and women control the most salient social paste used in both secular and ritual life—food. Men go out to sea, a more solitary occupation; and the ocean is associated—by both men and women—with antisocial values (the sea is dangerous, threatening, and foreign; see chapter 5). If Michelle Rosaldo is right (and I think that she is) in her conclusion that women's status tends to be higher in societies in which they can meet together as a group, we can see in women's *usudeku* and other group activities the structural basis for and expression of women's high status in the Henza religious system.

In Henza, women's extensive and intensive extradomestic ties and their ritual relationships overlap and interpenetrate. The relationship between women's activity in the public sphere and their preeminence in the religion is a chicken-and-egg situation. On the one hand, many of the occasions at which women meet are religious occasions: ceremonies, festivals, memorial services, clan events, *oharai*. Religion provides women with numerous venues for social contact and integration. On the other hand, in order for women to run a public religion, they need to be able to meet frequently in nondomestic contexts. This is the way in which Okinawa differs, for example, from rural Spain (Christian 1972) or the Middle East (Sered 1992). In those societies, women may be very pious, they may pray and fast more than men do, but that does not translate into publicly recognized leadership of the communal religion. In rural Spain and the Middle East, each woman's religious endeavors are linked to her own particular domestic world, and women are discouraged (sometimes forcibly) from spending large amounts of time outside of the domestic framework. In Henza women are not only permitted to go out as often as they want but they are actually encouraged to meet with other women in a variety of public contexts. In many parts of the world, a woman who goes out frequently is considered a loose woman or at the very least a gadabout and neglectful wife and mother, and male-dominated religions often serve to reinforce these ideas. In Henza, a woman who does not go out often to visit, chat, give gifts, and participate in rituals is considered unfriendly and not yasashii.

Cross-culturally, although the ability to get out of the house and meet with other women is a prerequisite for the existence of an autonomous women's religious stream, when women are restricted to meeting solely in ritual settings, the religion is likely to provide only sporadic assuaging of individual illness or unhappiness (for example, Afro-Brazilian religions or zar religion; cf. Burdick 1990, Lewis 1975). When women—as is the case in Henza—are also involved in multifaceted ongoing relationships with one another, the religion is likely to offer women as a group long-term and collective structural advantages (for example, the Sande societies of West Africa; see Bledsoe 1980). It is in these kinds of situations—when women's religious activism is part of a larger context of social and economic ties—that women's religions can serve as a socially acknowledged base for women's empowerment.

What I am describing here coincides with Ross Kraemer's (1992) use of Mary Douglas's group-and-grid theory to interpret levels of women's religious power in the Greco-Roman world. Briefly, Douglas (1970) developed a system of cultural analysis in which human social experience is described in terms of two factors: group and grid. Group refers to the degree to which individuals feel themselves to be part of a community, to the degree to which the individual is incorporated in the group in shared households, work, resources, and leisure-time activity. Grid refers to the extent to which rules and regulations govern an individual's activities. Kraemer concludes that, in the Greco-Roman world, a strong group and low grid constellation is correlated with increased religious authority and options for women. When women are well incorporated into associations of some kind, and when rules and hierarchy are relaxed, women become more religiously visible (1992: 199). This, with one refinement, is the configuration that I suggest characterizes Henza: Henza culture is generally nonhierarchical and unconcerned with rules and law, and group identity and social integration are highly developed. But more than that, as we have seen throughout this chapter, the lives of Henza woman far more than the lives of Henza men manifest what Douglas calls high group. Women rather than men embody and sustain domestic and nondomestic communal ties.

I do not know whether the pattern of women's extradomestic social integration in Okinawa arises out of the need for women to leave the domestic enclosure in order to work in the gardens, out of the need to handle their own affairs when men are absent, or out of a traditional ethos of communality. Either way, it functions to support and sustain a network of women's religious leadership unparalleled anywhere in the contemporary world. To my mind, the benches in the *utaki* (sacred grove) serve as a symbol of the links between women's high level of extradomestic social integration and their role of religious leadership. At the entrance to the *utaki* stand two large stone benches upon which the village priestesses and priestesses from the major clans sit "to discuss things" (their words) on the days of certain rituals. During the many centuries in which the priestesses would meet and talk at the utaki, village men had no equivalent public body that would meet regularly to talk over matters of village concern. One wonders to what extent the fact that women and not men formed the ongoing, public, communal framework in the village has mitigated against the kinds of male cultural domination found in almost every other known society.

FIVE

Women and Men and Ritual

The social interactions described in the previous chapter blend into the ritual lives of men and women in Henza. The first part of this chapter focuses upon women's involvement with food and food rituals—both of which serve as fundamental media for social integration with other villagers and with ancestors and deities. The second part of the chapter overviews men's ritual repertoire. I shall suggest that women's rituals—and especially food rituals—highlight and strengthen the theme of *presence*; men's rituals—and especially rituals involving the ocean—revolve around the theme of *absence*.

Women and Food

In Henza, food is women's business. Traditionally, men's fishing activity was a sporadic food source; most food came from women's horticulture and shore foraging. All food preparation is done by women; very few men cook at all. The markets were and still are run by women.[1] Almost all food serving is done by women. Food is a resource that women control, and food-oriented rituals sacralize women's everyday activities of cooking and serving. A hinu-kan (hearth deity) can be found in every Henza kitchen. The hinu-kan functions in a loose way as a sort of intermediary between the household and other kami-sama. Giving offerings to and praying at the hinu-kan are women's affair.

In the absence of food taboos, food is considered to be an essentially good thing; not only is it necessary for survival but it is also tasty. In public and semipublic contexts, villagers almost always seem to have something in their mouths. One of the village school teachers told me that in the teachers' room the staff eats all day, and I must say that my own observations bear this out. Any time a villager visits another house, something is served. Food is not only eaten with gusto but it is also talked about with gusto (cf. Smith and Wiswell 1982: 82 for a Japanese parallel). I think that if I had to choose the single most important Japanese word for an anthropologist doing fieldwork in Okinawa to learn, it would be *oishii*—delicious.

Food plays a—perhaps I should say *the*—central role in most Henza rituals. Village ritual life revolves around food. Food is the most common ritual means used to relate to kami-sama, and food is regularly put out for ancestors and for kami-sama. After funerals, food and chopsticks are placed on the household altar. One villager explains: "Kami-sama comes down like this, and then eats. Because kami-sama will come down, that is why we stand the chopsticks up." Food is offered on the butsudan; food is served at ceremonial occasions and informal gatherings; food is shared after or during almost every ritual, whether at the household, clan, or village level. During holidays like obon the village is teeming with people (usually women) carrying plates of food to each other (men are more likely to be seen carrying wrapped store-bought gifts).[2]

At funerals, food, slippers, and a walking stick are given to the deceased to be used on his or her journey. Right after the funeral, the elderly women who have sung the traditional laments are given gifts of food by the family of the deceased. Postfuneral rituals are composed almost entirely of eating. During the first days after a death, the family stays home while friends, relatives, and neighbors visit and bring food and eat. The deceased is also understood as needing food. Several times during the first week after the funeral, the family of the deceased gathers at the grave, prays, spreads out platters of food, and eats in the company of the deceased. The food eaten by the living participants and shared with the deceased consists of sake, sweets, tofu, squid, tempura, seaweed, and other popular food items. Villagers say that the purpose of these meals is to keep the deceased company, but I emphasize that the means by which the deceased is kept company is eating. Once each week for seven weeks following a death and then once each year afterward, as well as on Dead People's New Year, *shiimi* (memorial days), and other special days, rituals are held in which incense is lit, short, informal prayers are quietly said, and large meals are served. On these occasions, food functions to maintain ties between the living and the dead, ties which are negotiated by women, who prepare and serve food.

SUSAN: Henza people put food on the butsudan two times each month. Do the ancestors really eat it?

MRS. YASAMURA: Yes. That is why we tend to give food that the dead person liked.[3]

The mechanism by which kami-sama or ancestors eat is understood by Henza villagers to consist of somehow sucking out the essence or the goodness from the food. Thus food put on the butsudan is said to rot more quickly than food left out on the table, and some villagers feel that food placed on the butsudan does not taste as good as food straight from the table or refrigerator. Other villagers explain that the ancestors eat the steam from the food. The word *usande* refers to taking food off the altar to be eaten by living humans; doing usande—and who exactly does the usande—are key components of village ritual.

Something happens to the food when it is put on the altar. Not only do kami-sama or ancestors eat it (or suck out its essence), but they also put something into the food—something spiritual, something desired by villagers, something of the kami or ancestor's own essence. By eating food put on the kami's altar, the noro and her associates receive *kami*-essence; regular villagers who eat food off the ancestor altar receive ancestor-essence.[4] At rituals, food is placed on the altar not only to feed the kami-sama or ancestor but also to enable the embodied participants in the ritual to eat food that was "touched" by the disembodied participants. Through the act of placing food on the altar and then eating it, the ancestors or kami-sama and the villagers engage in an act of exchange that reinforces their association and identification with one another.

Food is understood to be so attractive to souls and spirits that when one's soul has become lost, food can be used to bring it back. As a corollary, the symptom of soul-loss is absence of appetite.

> When you are surprised, your *mabuya* [approx. soul or life-force] goes out. When I am surprised and then scream, my mabuya will go away from me, and I must go to where that happened to call it back. I might ask an ogami person to call the soul back. When human beings are very surprised, they lose their appetite and feel down. That is the case of the mabuya being away from you. Rice, soup, salt, water: we take these foods to go and call the mabuya back. The person [who this happened to] has brothers and sisters and they come to eat with the person at the butsudan. The ogami person prays "mabuya mabuya, come back come back." Then they lead the mabuya with a towel and put it into the person's chest. That is mabuya *gumi*. (Henza villager)

Eating is the most significant act of solidarity in Henza. Whom one eats with, who serves the food and who provides it, who is served and who is provided with food are crucial social forces. Moreover, as we have seen, the "who" includes not only humans but also ancestors and kami-sama.[5] In Henza households, live family members eat with their ancestors; in clan rituals, current clan members dine with other clan members and with clan ancestors (indeed, practically the only thing that clan members do together is eat); in the noro's rituals, she and her associates dine with the village kami-sama. During a ritual visit to the utaki, I asked the priestesses (who had just eaten a large, leisurely meal at the kami-ya) to explain to me why they were now eating again. They explained that this second meal consists of fish, and they eat fish in the utaki "because this [place] is the ocean kami-sama."

Food is given to people, to ancestors, and to kami-sama. A vital part of the work of the priestess (and especially of the noro) is to eat food provided by the village. As is shown in detail in the next chapter, at many ceremonial occasions eating seems to be the entire point of the ritual. For example, at *hama ogami* (ritual in which the village is protected from "bad things" that come from outside the island), the priestesses begin at the kami-ya, where they say a very short prayer, following which they chat with one another and eat large balls of rice. When they finish eating, they lie down to rest. One gets the feeling that the eating was strenuous—the eating constitutes the ritual work of the priestesses. During the next stage of hama ogami, the priestesses go to the sacred grove, pray briefly, chat some more, and are served cakes. They then make a round of the village ports, praying in front of trays of meat. Finally, they proceed to the town hall, where they are served large bowls of meat soup. In hama ogami, priestesses ritually protect their island by eating food provided by the village. In this case, as in other rituals that I describe in chapter 6, it seems to me that the socializing and eating with each other and with the kami-sama *are* the ritual.

One of the roles of the priestesses' male helpers is to supply food for the priestesses and to ritually serve the food to them. At some rituals, the food is purchased through the municipal budget and prepared by employees of the town hall. Certain families traditionally give food to the priestesses at *shinugu* or other ritual occasions. At new-house rituals (*yanusuji*), the focal event is the seven-course feast served the priestesses. A traditional role of the noro and other village leaders was to supervise food preparation for certain rituals.

Although the noro of each village is (now) independent of any sort of formal intervillage association, once each year the Henza noro gathers with noro of surrounding communities. At this gathering, the main event is a shared meal. The ceremonial occasion at which the noro meet is the day in January on which, during the time of the Ryukyuan Kingdom, priestesses collected taxes in the form of food (mostly grains), which they then passed on to Shuri. Today, on a particular date in the month of January, the noro and her associates—like noro from other nearby islands—still carry eggs and cooked food to the *kami-ya* of the noro of a larger village on the main island of Okinawa. As each noro arrives, she places her food on the altar and prays for a few minutes. Then she sits down to spend the day eating and chatting with the other noro. (The eggs are taken later to Shuri by the noro of the larger village). At least in its current form, food (both the offerings sent to Shuri and the lengthy meal shared by the noro) functions as the principal vehicle for creating any sort of solidarity among noro of various villages.

The food of Okinawan rituals is served in large, not token, portions (at many ritual events, plastic bags are distributed for taking home leftovers). In general, the type of food is not significant. In contrast to the traditional Jewish cultures with which I am familiar, in which each holiday is associated with special, symbolic foods (see Sered 1992), Henza villagers generally do not associate particular symbolic meanings with particular festival foods.[6] The ritual importance of food lies less in what kind of food is eaten than in who eats it and with whom.

Okinawan food rituals have a great deal in common with food rituals in other religions that are led by women (cf. Sered 1994). The foods used in women's religions are not served in small, symbolic portions; unlike the sip of wine and wafer at Catholic Church Eucharist ceremonies, in women's religions we find large quantities of elaborately prepared food (see, for example, Kerns 1983: 154–156 on the Black Caribs of Belize; Desroche 1971: 210 on the Shakers). As in Henza, the food rituals of other women-led religions are public and communal. They involve both the supernatural and the natural domains, and both gods and people eat. Food rituals create bridges between this world and other worlds; sharing food emphasizes good relationships with the living and the dead and the spirits. Food rituals in women's religions dramatize social ties rather than transcendence, and that is why tasty, cooked food (rather than, for example, animal sacrifice) is so important.

Offering a variety of delicious and attractively prepared delicacies to the ancestors or kami-sama is a way of domesticating the deity, of making the deity present, of drawing the deity into one's familiar circle. In the elaborate food rituals of Henza, the accent is on socializing with kami-sama and ancestors; immanent deities are invited to partake of tasty meals. In Okinawan religion, kami-sama and spirits and ancestors all join in communal, human experiences, experiences that—in the context of food-oriented rituals—are organized and mediated by women.

Men and Ritual

MRS. SHIMOJO (speaking to Susan): Only ask us [women kami-sama] because the men don't know anything, they only assist [at rituals].

Despite Mrs. Shimojo's remark, women do not hold a monopoly on ritual activity in Henza. We shall now look at the primary spheres of men's ritual interest.

Death Rituals

SUSAN: Does the noro pray at funerals or when someone is sick?

NORO: No! I don't take care of *bad* things, only *good* things.

Men far more than women are responsible for ancestor and death-related rituals. Because the official kinship system is patrilineal, men are in charge of ancestor worship. The eldest son inherits the butsudan, and it lies on his shoulders to take care of it. Teigo Yoshida has noted that in Okinawa men are far more involved in rituals that take place soon after death; the more time that elapses, the more that women become involved (personal communication 1992).

Nowadays bodies are cremated, so many of the rituals dealing with the actual corpse have disappeared. One or two days after a death, the remains are brought back from the crematorium on the main island, and a special, elaborate altar is set up in the deceased's house. The immediate family sits inside the house and acknowledges visitors who come to pay respect to the deceased by lighting incense and saying a short prayer. During this time a (male) Buddhist priest chants and rings a bell inside the house. The mourners proceed to the cemetery, where the priest conducts a prayer service. The remains typically are carried to the tomb in an urn by the closest male descendant; if there is no appropriate male descendant, a female descendant carries the remains. Men of the family open the family's tomb, and one or two men go inside to rearrange the older urns in order to make room for the newcomer. Although the entire family prays during the Buddhist service, men stand closer to the grave and take a more prominent role even in such small things as giving out token gifts to those who came to the funeral.

On the night after the funeral, three young male relatives gather outside the deceased's house for a ritual called *hohai*. One young man holds a stick, one holds a torch, and one a bucket. The one with the stick comes inside the house and hits three of the supporting poles of the house seven times each while saying "ane ane" [trans. unknown]. The young men then light the torch and run down the street to the cemetery, shouting "hohai hohai." They leave the stick and other accoutrements at the cemetery and return by a different route to confound the spirit who might follow them home. When they return home, the woman family member who is tending the butsudan gives sake to each of the three young men.

Three days after the funeral, relatives go to the ocean and build an arch under which they walk while throwing a piece of metal over their shoulders. The salt from the ocean is believed to keep away spirits. Like hohai, the *su-bane* (also pronounced *su-bari*) ritual is aimed at helping the dead spirit stay away from its living relatives. Although women do participate in su-bane, men have the dominant role of building the arch, and men direct the ritual action.

Men are also prominent in obon—the late summer festival at which ancestors come from the grave to spend three days with their families. Men lead the annual household obon rituals, and most particularly, they make the little sugarcane "boat" on which money, food, and incense are burned and sent back with the ancestors. A major element of obon involves visiting and giving gifts. When relatives and friends visit one another during obon, the host who sits and chats is usually a man, as are most of the guests. Women of the household spend much of obon in the kitchen preparing and serving food. Similarly, at *shiimi* (*seimeisai* in Japanese)—memorial days in which families go to the cemetery to visit their ancestors—men perform the main rituals of burning incense and money, placing cups of sake and water and big trays of food at the door to the tomb, and calling everyone to pray.

Blood Rituals

SUSAN: Are there any rituals that involve killing an animal?

MR. SHIBAHIKI: *Ame tabore*, also *hama ogami*. Pig. Kill the pig, ask them to bring the bowl.

SUSAN: Is killing the pig a job for men?

MR. SHIBAHIKI: Shiidu [a male ritual role] will cut the pig, and Tobaru [another male ritual role], all men.

Ame tabore—a rain ritual—is the only ritual that I have ever heard villagers spontaneously categorize as a "men only" ritual. I never saw ame tabore, both because women do not attend and because it is a ritual that is only performed in years of severe drought.[7] Ame tabore involves the sacrifice of a goat. Men dance around the goat's head, which is placed next to pots of water, and then they eat soup made from the goat meat. Here is how Mr. Tamura describes ame tabore:

We go to a place in the mountains and circle around it [the goat] seven times. We sing a song: "ame tabore, ame tabore" [please rain, please rain]. And then we come down from the mountain. We go to a river and pick up some water from there and carry it and go to the *nunduruchi's* [noro's] place. And then all the important men of the village get together there and say to have rain. And then we grab a little boy, and there is a big bowl with water, and we push down the boy into the water to sit down in the water. If Henza does *ama goi* [ame tabore], strangely, it brings rain. Four years ago they did this and it rained.

Mr. Yamashiro, who has organized ame tabore, fills in a few more details:

> Up there [in the mountains] they kill the goat and bring it to the river and clean it and go someplace to cook it. The goat is usually male—there is more meat on male goats. They decorate the cooked food with the head. There is a big water bowl and little bit of the juice of the goat is put in, and the boy is dumped in it in front of the kami-ya. The boy doesn't like to be the one who is dunked. Henza's ame tabore is very famous. [Neighboring] islands have their own ritual, but if Henza doesn't do it, it won't rain.

Ame tabore is a flamboyantly blood-oriented ritual, incorporating a theme of symbolic human sacrifice.[8] Unlike priestesses' rituals, which have to do with preserving health—"good things"—ame tabore is performed in response to danger (drought)—a "bad thing."

Shima kusara, which used to be conducted on December 24 of the lunar calendar, centered upon men killing a pig, from which bits were given out to families as a kind of "good luck" charm. A pig bone was hung in the entrance to the house in order to keep out illness. Shima kusara was performed during the coldest time of the year when, according to some of the older villagers, certain diseases were prevalent.

Another ritual with some of the same elements is hama ogami—beach prayer—a ritual at which arches are placed along the shore of the island in order to keep away "bad things." The noro and kaminchu pray at hama ogami, but men have an important role in it. Nowadays at hama ogami a pig is no longer killed, but large platters of pork are placed on the shore as each arch is made. The headman and a few other men accompany the noro during hama ogami, but, according to Mrs. Jana, "It used to be that there were men all over there at hama ogami, but now there aren't very many men. They don't have the kami-sama's mentality now."

Finally, at the traditional grave-making ritual (since graves hold many bodies, this long and elaborate ritual is not done very often), the head of a pig—killed by a man—is put outside the new grave.

Fishermen's Rituals

SUSAN: Are there any rituals only men do?

MR. TAMURA: Only the ocean events. *Tairyo kiga*. To have a lot of fish to catch. Twice a year, February and August, umi ogami [ocean prayer]. Fishermen prepare sake and a fish meal and then go to the noro, and the noro prays for them.

Most men's rituals are related to fishing or to the ocean. Some of these rituals have now disappeared because few local men are still fishermen; other rituals have been transformed from profound expressions of the dangers and unpredictability of fishing to lighthearted villagewide festivals. Significantly, I was told on a number of occasions that although not many Henza men still go to sea, they continue to think of themselves as fishermen and sailors. In other words, the men's rituals are linked not only to their subsistence work but also to their identity as seafarers and fishermen. This distinction will become critical when the association between men and absence is discussed later in this chapter.

Hatsu-gyo was the first fishing of the new year. One villager explained, "And they would bring the fish to the house and invite relatives, and give away fish, and say that today we share so that throughout the year there should be a lot of fish." The (women) noro and kaminchu did not attend.

Umi ogami is attended by the men of the local fisherman's organization. The head fisherman has a small ritual role in the ceremony. With the exception of the noro and her associates, all the participants are men.

San gatsu (third-month) festival rituals incorporate a number of ocean themes and ceremonies. The exciting climax of san gatsu is a procession, mostly of men, to a small island off the coast of Henza. According to Mrs. Jana: "San gatsu ritual is to catch the fish at the ocean and eat. There is no property, not much farmland in Henza, so the men go to the ocean to get fish. At san gatsu the fish is speared and there is a song: Poke and pull, poke and pull."

Haari boat racing is traditionally a men's ritual. According to Mrs. Hokama, "It used to be for fishermen, to compete east and west [sides of the village]. In those days almost every house had someone doing an ocean job. . . . There were no other jobs for men except at sea. Women did farming. Men went to the mountains to bring wood and sell it. They sold it in Naha or Itoman. There were many seamen."

Nowadays, haari has become more of a villagewide recreation. Teams representing various Henza subgroupings race one another to the accompaniment of drumming and cheering. Almost all competitors are men (although some women do join the teams). During the year that I was on the island, members of the Henza young adults' association (*seinenkai*) organized competitions of sumo wrestling after the boat races. The wrestling was all in very good spirit, except for a final round that involved two young men who came from outside of Henza.

Many local men seem intrigued both by competition and by fighting. Bullfighting, *habu* snake fighting, chicken fighting, and dogfighting are all popular in Okinawa (in Henza there is only chicken fighting and dogfighting; bullfighting can be seen in a nearby village). According to Mr. and Mrs. Okutara, "Okinawan men will [watch] fight[s of] anything that moves." Still, Okinawa is a relatively nonviolent society, and in Okinawan bullfighting, for example, there is no bloodshed. Two bulls try to push each other out of the ring (like sumo wrestling), but no one is hurt.

Eisaa

In Henza the men are out of the house all the time, in fishing business or *yanbaru-sen* [boats], and they are not always at home, and the woman protects the house, and the men are not available for eisaa dancing [at obon season]. Twice a year, at obon and New Year's, the men come home. So at that time women do dancing to welcome them. (Mr. Tamura)

Unlike women, Henza men tend not to be around for long enough to organize and rehearse their own ceremonial dancing. Young men's eisaa dancing[9] at obon season, which is popular in many Okinawan villages, has taken place only intermittently in Henza. Eisaa dancing in Henza is less self-sustaining than women's usudeku dancing. It is linked to the number of young men on the island (that is, whether young men need to leave to work) and to the presence of a few young men who are interested in taking the initiative to organize it. Young men join the *eisaa* group toward the end of high school and move up through the ranks of dancer, dancer with drum, costumed dancer, and samisen player. They leave the group at about age twenty-four.

The public eisaa performance takes place outside the town hall on one evening during obon. It consists of vigorous formalized dancing by young men in elaborate costumes: A few wear masks, one or two have branches on the head, some carry barrels of sake. They dance in a highly stylized and synchronized manner, punctuated by loud beating of drums and louder shouts of "Henza," "Eisaa," and "sui sa sa" (a rhythmic chant). The rhythm is quick and exciting, and the drums have an almost military flavor to them. The basic eisaa step consists of holding a drumstick overhead high in the air and then bringing it down and lunging forward with it or banging on a drum. While doing this, the dancer lifts alternate legs high in the air (with bended knee) and then stamps on the ground. Many of the hand and leg motions are similar to those of karate. The dancing is not graceful; it is vigorous and powerful. The young men are in superb physical shape. Their facial expressions are rather fierce, and sweat pours off their bodies. To my Western (and female) eye, *eisaa* dancers look the very peak of virile young manhood. Each village in Okinawa has its own dances and its own style of eisaa dancing. In some villages it is more dancelike, in some it is more athletic, in some it is more karatelike, in some it is competitive. In a few villages, thousands of people come to see the dancing; in Henza, there are as many dancers as spectators. After the formal dancing, the young men spend the night going around the village in a group, making noise, dancing, and asking for sake and food.

The year that I was in Henza, the young men began practicing eisaa several months before obon. They met late every evening on the shore, away from the village. The eisaa group is hierarchical, and the young man who brought me to the rehearsal seemed tense in the presence of the leaders. For the first hour or so each evening, experienced dancers work with younger ones, drilling them in the steps. Then the leader calls up small groups to dance, while some of the experienced dancers watch and make corrections. Later in the evening, they rehearse in larger groups. In Henza about 100 young men are involved in eisaa. The two girls who came to rehearsal the evening I was there stood at the back of the lines of dancers, and they did not hold drums.

The young man who brought me whispered confidentially that he did not like eisaa dancing and that others also felt that way but that they could not say so because the "older people" (that is, the leaders) would not like it. I asked the leader what happened if someone did not show up for practice for a few days, whether others would go to his house to get him. The leader laughed and said yes. (The leader's austerity was somewhat softened by his little daughter dancing around at his feet.) Even with the coercion involved, the atmosphere at rehearsals does not seem unpleasant, and the older members especially laugh and seem to have fun.

To summarize, Henza's eisaa is a somewhat coercive, highly hierarchical, sporadic men's activity. Rehearsals take place away from the village late at night and serve to build physical strength and self-confidence in the young men. In these ways, it is similar to young men's rituals in many other cultures, but dramatically unlike women's rituals in Henza. In common with the men's blood and death rituals discussed above, *eisaa* involves hierarchy and power—"bad things" in Henza.

The Tale of the Ashtray Rock

This story really happened, a long time ago, more than ten generations, to one from the Yamashiro family. They have three houses now over there and there and up there. In the ocean to the west of Henza Island there was a huge rock shaped like an ashtray. One time samurai from the mainland came and wanted to have a war here. They had heard that there was someone here named Henza Hatara [lit. Strong Man Henza], who is so strong that he can carry an *ito* [large measure] of rice as far as Naha [the capital]. Because he was so strong, they said, "Let's go fight him." So they came here. Henza Hatara had a younger sister, and those men asked her, "Is Henza Hatara home?" But he was in China on business. She said, "What are you here for?" They said, "In Okinawa there is no one stronger than Henza Hatara, and the three of us want to fight him." The sister said, "Just a minute, why don't you rest and have a smoke." And she brought that big ashtray-shaped rock and put it in front of them. They asked her, "Is your brother stronger than you?" "Yes, he is stronger than me." And those three people thought to themselves, "Even the sister who is a woman is strong, so Henza Hatara must be very strong." And so they said *sayonara* and left. The ashtray rock is big, made of heavy land rock, not of light ocean rock. Usually people couldn't carry it, but she carried it. The men came here to make a war but got scared because the woman who carried the rock was so strong. (composite of versions told me by two elderly Henza women).

The story of the ashtray rock is one of the very few old-time or folk stories (*mukashi banashi*) that I managed, after a great deal of asking, to elicit from villagers. It was told to me more often than any other story, and it was typically told with a great deal of animation and interest. Its prominent place in the storytelling repertoire of the village is easy to understand—the story of the ashtray rock encapsulates familiar patterns and themes in Henza life.

The main action in the story involves strangers—samurai—who come to stir up trouble on Henza Island. These samurai, fighters from an intrusive and class-based society, represent all that is anathema to yasashii Henza villagers. Despite that fact, the samurai are not presented as evil monsters in the story—oppositional themes of good guys versus bad guys are not developed. The problematic element in the story arises simply from the fact that the samurai have come to a place to which they do not belong—Henza Island. In the story, the problem is solved not by killing or vanquishing the foreigners but simply by sending them back to where they do belong. The protagonist in the story is nonconfrontational (she simply offers the invaders a smoke), yasashii, and her nonconfrontational strategy is totally successful—the foreigners leave the island without causing any trouble. In the tale of the ashtray rock the sister tells the samurai: You can't scare us with your threats of dominance because dominance isn't meaningful. See, I pick up a big rock and the story ends peacefully.

The central theme in the tale of the ashtray rock is that of a woman who protects her house, her brother, and her village. The notion of women protecting the house is ubiquitous in Henza discourse. According to Mr. Shinya, for example, "Men go everywhere, women protect the house." I particularly draw attention to the syntax in this sentence: Women are not protected by the house, but rather they protect it. Unlike in the Middle East, traditional China, and southern Europe, Okinawan women are not forbidden or discouraged from going out of the house; they are not considered vulnerable when they are in the public domain. Rather, women are described as powerful beings who are capable of protecting society's most fundamental structure.

Protecting the house encompasses both physical and spiritual endeavors. Just like the sister who lifted the ashtray rock and thereby safeguarded the island, Henza women physically take care of the house and the vegetable gardens that provide(d) most of the family's food. Simultaneously, women pray—especially at the hinu-kan—in order to spiritually protect the house. The role of the kaminchu and noro conforms to this pattern; they are often described as the ones who "take care of" the clan and village.

Another theme in the story of the ashtray rock is that of women's presence and men's absence. Note that the strong brother does not appear at all in the tale. When the samurai come to fight him and make a war in the village, he is not there to defend himself or his house. The story ends with the samurai leaving; we do not even hear what happens when (or if) the brother returns. In context after context, villagers explain that men go away and women work in the vegetable gardens, men leave and women protect the house and the island. The sister's presence and the brother's absence in the tale of the ashtray rock is central to Henza identity, a point elucidated by numerous village men and women who say that in this way Henza is different from other villages. (In fact, throughout the Ryukyu Islands, soil conditions make farming difficult; there is insufficient land for everyone to farm; the hot, humid climate makes food storage unreliable; and therefore the ocean is an attractive source of food and livelihood.)

Two other old-time stories that villagers tell also begin with foreigners, noblemen from Shuri, coming into the village and disrupting village harmony. In one story, noblemen who come to administer the land redistribution system in Henza endeavor to impose class differences in the village. A village man asks them why they are doing this unfair thing, and as a punishment for his speaking up, the noblemen exile him to the southern Ryukyus. In the other story, foreign noblemen single out one village woman for her beauty, and thereby incite the most serious social rupture imaginable—her brothers take her out to a rock in the ocean and leave her there to drown. Before she dies, she announces that all of the children born into their houses will be ugly—"and so they are until this day."

In these stories, as in the tale of the ashtray rock, the noblemen are not really evil; rather, they are foreigners who have come to a place to which they do not belong. The stories differ, however, in the strategies used to deal with the foreigners. Unlike the victorious yet nonconfrontational woman in the ashtray-rock story, in the two stories of Shuri noblemen, village men confront the foreigners, and the results are tragic. In a reversal of the ashtray-rock resolution, in the stories of the Shuri noblemen it is the villager who ends up leaving the island (through exile or through drowning), not the foreigners.

The gender of the protagonist is of consequence in these stories. In the ashtray-rock story, a woman easily and matter-of-factly protects her brother and her village. In the Shuri-noblemen stories, village men fail miserably at protecting their community. Unlike the sister who shields her brother, the brothers of the beautiful sister leave her on a rock in the ocean, unshielded and unprotected, to drown, and the outspoken man not only fails to influence the noblemen but is himself sentenced to exile—absence.

Men and Absence

Women are always home and don't do the dangerous jobs. Women are home raising vegetables and taking care of the children and the house. Men go out of the house and go to the ocean and then die, sometimes, and typhoon and die, and war and die. (village woman)

Ame tabore, shima kusara, and hama ogami have a great deal in common. All are (were) men's rituals carried out at times of communal danger. All involve killing an animal and using parts of the animal for ritual purposes. Although women could cook the meat from the animals, killing was the job of men—all rituals involving killing an animal are conducted by men. (Note that villagers do not make the categorical statement that only men kill animals or that certain rituals are men's rituals and others are women's. The entire schema that I develop here rests upon my efforts to categorize and interpret village behavior; it does not reflect any sort of ideological or even perceptual schema advanced by villagers, and it does not lead to the development of rules or taboos.)

In a very broad sense, the ritual division of labor in Henza places men in the sphere of death-related rituals and women in the sphere of life-related (and especially food) rituals.[10] We have seen that men have the key roles in burial rituals. According to Mrs. Shinzato, death rituals are carried out at low tide, whereas birth occurs at high tide. "That is nature's way that birth occurs at high tide. In those days people lived according to nature." Traditionally (and to this day), pregnant women do not attend funerals. In the past, men were not usually present at birth (although there was no prohibition involved). The noro emphasizes that she only does "the good things" and not "the bad things," and priestesses do not attend funerals.

Henza women work in agriculture, which is life-producing and a steady source of food. Men work in fishing, which involves killing and is an erratic source of food (cf. Ito 1966). Women stay in one place, doing land-based work in a culture in which the village and its environs are considered safe and healthy; men come and go, doing sea-based work in a culture in which the ocean is considered dangerous, the source of disease and typhoons. Not only typhoons but also dynamite fishing injured and killed fishermen in the past. According to one villager, "The fishermen would dive . . . without any equipment, and sometimes they wouldn't make it up when they came up to breathe, and if no one went down to help them, they died. Before the war we took the boats all the way up to the northern point of Okinawa. Sometimes people got fishhooks stuck in them. And flying fish sometimes attacked." Villagers constantly warned me to keep my children away from the beach because so many people drown, even though the water is actually very shallow for a long distance from Henza's shore.

The association of men with death and absence in Okinawan rituals is particularly striking in comparison to the common, if often unconscious, association in male-dominated Western (and some non-Western) religions between women and death (see, for example, Seremetakis 1991). According to psychologist of religion Diane Jonte-Pace, "Death, the unrepresentable, the ultimate absence, is symbolized as woman; woman becomes, through metonymy, death. Maternal absence, matricide, and castration (absence as female), are [then] negated in the religious promise of presence through eternal life and paternal love (presence as male)" (1992: 21).[11] Jonte-Pace traces the association of women with death (and death's metonym, absence) in Western thinking, citing, for example, fourth-century Church Father St. John Chrysostom, who called the female body a "white sepulcher." In contrast, Christians are truly born (or "born again") through the male body of Christ.

"This partnership of woman and death [in Western culture] articulates the gendering of absence in phallocentric culture—but it is by no means universal" (Jonte-Pace 1992: 21). What then are the sociocultural circumstances that foster the woman-death homology? The force that constructs the association between women and death is difference. According to Jonte-Pace, "The sameness of men and women is denied [in patriarchal cultures] in a discourse of difference focusing on woman as absence, a discourse which conflates woman with death and man with life" (1992: 22). This discourse is necessary, I argue, because the very meaning of patriarchy is that men procure power over women's reproductive capabilities. Patriarchy reverses nature, proclaiming that men are the life-givers; patrilineality defines the father as the relevant parent; and male creator-deities transpose birth into a male ability. In patriarchy, spiritual birth—the birthing that is done by men and male gods—becomes the true birth, the birth that saves from feminine death (see, for example, Delaney 1991). The data that I gathered in Henza validates Jonte-Pace's conviction that the woman-death homology is culture-specific.[12] As an ideological expression of difference and domination, it has no place in Henza's nonhierarchical culture.

As we have seen, however, there is in Henza some sense of an association between *men* and death or absence, and this association does demand clarification.

The interpretation given by villagers lies in men's subsistence work, which involved danger and sustained physical absence from the island. Men's absence explains, according to villagers, why men cannot manage to sustain eisaa dancing and why they do not know as much about Henza ways as do women. Men's absence is manifested in the lack of the sorts of intensive social integration that characterize women's lives. It is not uncommon to find that even when Henza men are physically present, they are spiritually absent. The high levels of sake consumption in Okinawa suggests male spiritual absence—Okinawan men usually are quiet and solitary drinkers; they typically drink alone at home and, when drunk, turn in upon themselves.

In patriarchal societies, the woman-death homology incorporates a third element —pollution or inferiority or sin—that functions to place women and death in their "proper" (subordinate) place on the moral and social ladder. This homology works because death is understood to be essentially bad (the cosmic aspiration of patriarchal Western religions is eternal life), and because patriarchy, as a hierarchical system, has a vested interest in developing compelling models of men's innate superiority and women's innate inferiority. In Henza, in contrast, life and death are not dichotomous, death is not understood to be an existentially bad state, and there is no matriarchal hierarchical ideology that can be served by promulgating a model of male inherent evil. Quite to the contrary, several villagers made a point of telling me that, unlike people in other countries, Okinawans are not afraid of death because they know that when they die they stay in the family (on the ancestor shelf and in the communal family tomb). I was also told, on a number of occasions, that it is not always clear if someone is really dead; that people assumed dead and placed in tombs "often" wake up and bang on the door of the tomb and that people who have disappeared at sea for decades "maybe are dead, but I don't know for sure." The men/absence/death complex that I have explicated, then, is mitigated by a feeling that neither death nor life is an absolute state.

In Henza discourse, women's presence and men's absence are not portrayed as either good or bad, and they carry no ideological underpinnings or hierarchical implications. Although men are provisionally associated with death and absence, no one would claim that this association is universal, eternal, or natural, and no one would claim that women are better than men. What women are is more *present* than men—an understanding offered by villagers as an empirically obvious demographic reality linked to specific subsistence conditions. When priestesses say that they do not get involved with "bad things," they do not mean evil, polluted, or inferior things; rather, they mean things that are out of place or out of equilibrium (see chapter 6). Villagers understand Henza to be a good, healthy, self-contained island. Men, however, leave the island and sometimes bring back with them disease, money, foreigners, competition, sake—all kinds of things that disrupt village harmony. Men's rituals are not existentially "bad" rituals, just as men are not existentially "bad"—neither men nor women suggest that there is any kind of gender hierarchy or ideology involved in village ritual. Rather, men—whose work is involved with absence, outsiders, danger, and killing—carry out the very few rituals that deal with disruptions of the natural and normative state of social and bodily health.

Unlike the ocean, where the men do their work,[13] the women's village is life-oriented: Violence and war are deplored, natality rates are high, virginity is not a cultural value, there are no birth or menstrual taboos, children are welcomed, life expectancy is long, and long life is celebrated at lavish rituals for people who reach their eighties and nineties. In Henza, women excel at creating the enduring social bonds that make life and culture possible. Yet, and I stress this point above all others in this chapter, what I call women's presence and men's absence is uniformly explained by villagers in terms of ecological pressures: the absence of sufficient farming land on their particular island. Women's presence and men's absence are never—at least as far as I can ascertain—interpreted as reflecting essential, existential, or universal differences between men and women. Men's fishing and women's farming, like men's ritual dealings with death and women's ritual dealings with life, are equally necessary and equally prestigious components of a cultural ethos of gender complementarity.[14] Without an ideology of difference, Henza's gendered division of labor does not develop into a hierarchical (patriarchal *or* matriarchal) cultural system.

Although women's presence does not imply gendered power, status, or authority, women's presence is understood by villagers to be associated with the benevolent presence of kami-sama. Central to Henza's immanent theology is the notion that kami-sama is present in this world, in their village, and—most visibly—in the bodies of Henza's priestesses.

PART III

SITTING IN THE SEAT OF THE GODS

SIX

Priestesses and Ritual
Feeding the Kami-sama

The use of the word priestess *is a convention begun by earlier anthropologists and should not be understood to signify what Okinawan noro and kaminchu do or are. The word most commonly used in Henza for the role that I (mis)translate into* priestess *is kami-sama.*

I had come to Okinawa to study priestesses' rituals. I had read that men are not allowed into the sacred groves, so I anticipated witnessing rituals that previous (male) ethnographers had not been able to see, but that they had considered important enough to write books and articles about. I arrived in Okinawa during a ritually dry time of year and was told by villagers and priestesses just to wait, and I would be able to see really important rituals starting in December. When I began to accompany the priestesses, I saw that on the mornings before the rituals they were excited and that after the rituals they were tired. Yet whether we were in the *utaki* (sacred grove) or at the *kami-ya* (village shrine), I found it difficult to figure out when the actual "ritual" took place or of what it consisted. Most of what the kaminchu did looked to me either like preparation for the ritual or postritual relaxation and munching.[1]

In chapter 2, I explained that Okinawan kami-sama do not really "do" or "act." Their significance is in their *presence* rather than in their authority or actions. In this chapter, we see that the same is true of priestesses. Priestesses (embodied kami-sama)—like disembodied kami-sama—emit good spiritual energy, and so villagers want to have them present at a variety of occasions. Like disembodied kami-sama, priestesses must be invited—they do not come on their own volition to rituals. Like disembodied kami-sama, priestesses' spiritual energy needs to be focused or concentrated—that is the meaning of what looked to me like preparation for the ritual. And finally, when kami-sama—embodied or disembodied—are present, they are given food.

Henza priestesses, via their divine presence, maintain their world in its natural state of equilibrium, health, and harmony. As we saw in chapter 5 in the discussion of men's rituals, and as we shall see again in chapter 10 when we discuss the role of shaman-type practitioners, priestesses refrain from becoming involved in situations in which the village's or the island's natural equilibrium has been lost. Men and shaman-type practitioners deal with the recently dead—transitional beings who are temporarily out of harmony both with the world of the living and with the world of the ancestors. After a number of years have gone by, and the dead have become ancestors/kami-sama; that is, once they have gradually moved into another state of equilibrium, the priestesses become ritually involved. This involvement, as I discuss in this chapter, is not a manipulative one but rather a matter of presence, of "being there," of embodying the spiritual energies that keep Henza in its natural state of balance.

The Ritual Is the People

SUSAN: What is the difference between *utaki mae* and *umachi?* [two rituals carried out by priestesses]?

MRS. ISHIKAWA: Utaki mae is four people, and umachi is all of these [she points to the twelve or so priestesses who were there today, an umachi day].

In this conversation I asked Mrs. Ishikawa a general question about two rituals. I had expected that she would explain how the rituals differ—that is, what is done differently at the two rituals. Her answer, however, was in terms of who comes to the rituals. Her answer suggests that the presence of specific people at the ritual *is* the ritual. My interpretation of her words is reinforced by her omission of Mr. Shibahiki, a male assistant who attends most rituals, and a woman employee from town hall who attends some rituals. Both Mr. Shibahiki and the town hall employee do important things at the rituals: He clears the path, lights the incense, and pours the sake; she provides and serves the food. But, for Mrs. Ishikawa, this *doing* is insignificant. What defines rituals is which kami-sama/priestesses are there, not what actions are performed.

SUSAN: Did the noro's job used to be bigger?

MRS. TANAHARA (with excitement): Yes!!! She did a prayer in November.

SUSAN: Did she do other kinds of things?

MRS. TANAHARA: No.

SUSAN: What does the noro do?

NORO: Do you mean what do I do each month?

SUSAN: No, I mean in general, what is the noro's job?

NORO (a pleasant and agreeable person): I will tell you what I do each month. [She gets her calendar and notebook.]

SUSAN: Before you tell me what you do each month, could you tell me in general what the noro does?

NORO: First of January—New Year's; seventh of January—all the noro [from the surrounding villages] go to Yonashiro Town and bring eggs, and they are collected there and the Yonashiro Town noro brings them to Shuri [the capital of the former Ryukyuan Kingdom]. Third of January—*hachi ubii*—*hachi mizu ugami*—first water of the new year prayer. Second of January, that is the "year of the wild boar" celebration [the first time in the new year that the day associated with the wild boar comes; each year a different animal year in the cycle is celebrated]. Fifteenth of February—that is *hachi umachi* [the first umachi ritual of the year]. We [the noro and kaminchu] go to utaki [sacred grove], to Irigusuku and Agaregusuku. About ten people from the clans go. We wear white clothes. . . . Umachi is February, March, May, June. And utaki mae is December, June, and four times. And *shinugu* is June and August.

In this conversation with the noro, we learn that the specifics of when and where the priestess goes are the substance of the role. There is no general, overarching "doing" that the always affable and obliging noro can tell me about. The priestess role is comprised of the particular occasions on which kami-sama is located in particular locations. The importance of the kami-sama's presence on these occasions also emerges in Mrs. Tanahara's emphatic statement that the noro's job used to be much bigger: She formerly prayed in November also.

SUSAN: Does the noro ever tell the clan kaminchu what to do?

MRS. ISHIKAWA: Yes.

SUSAN: What kinds of things?

MRS. ISHIKAWA: At rituals at the utaki, there are positions where each one should sit.

In this exchange, Mrs. Ishikawa has accorded a great deal of import to where the clan kaminchu sit. The seating on the stone benches at the utaki is not hierarchical; the issue of sitting is not one of status or of what they do when they sit. It is simply that where they sit *is* the ritual. Sitting is physical presence; sitting in the correct place is an expression of cosmic harmony.

Priestesses are often referred to as "sitting (*suwaru*) the position." The expression to "sit the position" refers simultaneously to the physical seat in which a particular priestess always sits when she prays in the clan house, at the kami-ya, or at the utaki and to the existential position of embodying a particular kami.[2] The priestess prays to or represents a clan ancestor. A number of years after she dies, another clan member will sit the position. Often (not always) the original ancestor (kami-sama at whose altar the priestess prays) was herself a kaminchu in the clan. Put differently, the contemporary priestess in Henza is the ancestor (kami) to whom, for whom, as whom she prays. Noriko Kawahashi explains this well:

I maintain that the divine priestess, when she makes invocations, is acting as a kami herself by asking for cooperation from other deities in order to supplement a specific *seji* [divine or spiritual] power that is lacking in her. She is more than a "priestess" who simply mediates between humans and kami. Her act of *aichee* [cooperation] with other kami is based on the very fact that she herself embodies a kami. (1992: 135)

Chris Drake (1995) argues that the identification of priestesses with deities is evident in the songs of the *Omoro Sooshi*:

The shamans [Drake uses the word shamans where I use the word priestesses] seem to be more than simply mediums through which the mother gods can appear. The great mother shaman-gods are described as coming down to earth to receive the . . . song from the earthly shamans, as if the singing shamans knew the song even more intimately than the great mother-god shaman did. The distinction between female shaman and god seems to be dependent on the shifting relations of space and time. . . . Divinity is not a thing or attribute but a moment of relationship in process. In the context of this [ritual] . . . the singers are also gods, while the gods depend on becoming (female) humans for their divinity. This mutual dependence and oscillating subject position cause severe problems for my translation, in which 'god' could equally be translated 'shaman' and in which there are few explicit subjects and the exact identity of the first-person pronouns (equally singular or plural) remains unclear. . . . The rocking, one-two rhythm of the couplets and their temporal open-endedness would be the substance of the movement by which the shamans verbally incorporate and give birth to their own mothers while they themselves are reborn from those very mothers in a circular, enfolding process. (1995: 12–13).

Village priestesses pick up, carry, and deposit spiritual energy or kami-sama with them when they go to and from the clan house and the utaki. In the next excerpt, Mrs. Shimojo explains that before she goes to the utaki she goes to the clan house in order to bring kami-sama with her to the utaki. Each kaminchu brings her own kami-sama with her; she is the only person who can bring that particular kami-sama, who can *be* that particular kami-sama. As Mrs. Adaniya puts it, "I was born to represent one particular one. Each kaminchu, her own kami-sama."

SUSAN: Which kami-sama is this that you pray to?

MRS. SHIMOJO: Mine.

SUSAN: The clan's kami-sama?

MRS. SHIMOJO: Yes. Within the clan there are several kami-sama. Each has an *uko* [incense bowl] and we are told [by the kami-sama during the preinitiation period] which uko we will sit to, and that is the one I go to. It is only that uko that I pray to. Each person has the uko that she prays to, the middle one, or that one. You are only that particular one.

SUSAN: When you pray, you only pray to your own kami-sama. Is there any name to the kami?

MRS. SHIMOJO: Yes, mine is *niisadai* [niisadai is the name of a role, not a personal name]. I am the thirteenth niisadai. For example, I pray, "Today I am going to go to the utaki, so please come with me." When I return I pray, "I went, thank you. No accident happened, the ogami [prayer] went smoothly over there, thank you." Then I pray for the clan's health.

Mrs. Shimojo herself is kami-sama; she is not a "mere mortal" who temporarily picks up kami-sama during rituals. Rather, when Mrs. Shimojo goes to the clan house to collect kami-sama before going to the utaki, she is engaged in an act of focusing more kami-sama into herself. At other occasions, such as a new-house ritual (discussed later), she engages in acts of emitting kami-sama. Seen from this perspective, there is grave importance to the specific occasions and locations in which the priestess is present.

The utaki, according to Mrs. Shimojo, is important because at the hinu-kan at the utaki "prayer goes through."[3] Six shells sit on an altar at the utaki. The shells are large conch shells, which, in the darkness of the jungle, resemble skulls (at least to my eye; see plates). Each shell has an opening into which the noro feeds cooked rice. These shells are, in some mystical way, the kaminchu's—or her clan's—double. According to Mr. Yamashiro (the noro's brother), when a priestess dies her shell turns around.[4]

MRS. ISHIKAWA: The *gusuku* [sacred grove] is spiritually high [*takai*].

SUSAN: Does takai mean that kami-sama is there?

MRS. ISHIKAWA: Yes.

SUSAN: What kami-sama?

MRS. ISHIKAWA: Susan, you went to where the shells are! There are six. Three in the front, small ones, three big ones in the back. The middle one is the noro's, and the left is mine, and right is *uchigami* [hereditary priestess role]. If one of the shells is crooked, like say the middle one, that means that in that family or clan someone will die or have an accident.

In praying at the utaki and putting rice in the conch shells, the priestesses fortify their own identity and connection to kami-sama. I will discuss this point later.

Most rituals of the noro and her associates are composed of three basic elements, almost always in this sequence: (1) lighting incense and giving rice and sake to the hinu-kan at the kami-ya; (2) donning white robes and crowns of leaves; (3) eating meals provided by the village, clan, or specific families.

By lighting incense, the kaminchu connect (*tsuujiru*) to the kami-sama, and then by sharing rice and sake they reinforce their connection with the kami-sama and the community. If the ritual goes well, this connection will be smooth (*chanto*). Priestesses often speak of their rituals and prayers as "going through smoothly" or "being smooth." The notion of "going through (*toosu*) smoothly" seems to imply that the communication and cooperation with other forms of being—ancestors or kami-sama—is easy, complete, not discordant. Kami is present in a diffuse way all the time, and offerings of incense and food serve to increase the intensity of the kami-sama's presence, to "smooth over" rough spots or gaps in the connection. This part of the sequence follows the same pattern as the offerings placed at home on the ancestral altar, where the steam of the rice, fumes of the sake, and smoke of the incense are shared with the ancestors in rites of solidarity.

In the sequence of priestess rituals, the priestess begins as a representative of the community, and on the behalf of the community she gives offerings such as incense or sake to the kami, much in the same way that the senior woman of a household does on behalf of her family. In the second stage (see the next section), by donning the white robes, the priestess fully embodies or actualizes kami-sama—her kami-nature is fully present. In the third stage, she "sits the position" and eats. By eating food and drinking sake provided by the village, the priestess receives—in the role of kami-sama—ritual offerings from the community (see the following discussion).

Wearing White

SUSAN: Why do you wear white clothes?

KAMINCHU: White clothes are for the kami-sama.

SUSAN: What are the leaves the noro and kaminchu wear on their head?

NORO: Any kind of leaves are fine. We believe that the kami-sama wear them. The kami-sama did those things, that is why we are doing it.

The noro and her associates are frequently referred to, by themselves and by others, as "the ones who wear white." They use expressions such as, "Since I began wearing white I have . . ." or, "On that day the ones who wear white go to the sacred grove." Donning the white robes is a crucial element in the priestesses' work—by donning the white they don "kami-sama-ness," or perhaps one could say that they activate the kami-sama that is already immanent within them. Putting on the white robes is an exacting and time-consuming endeavor and typically takes as long or longer than the offerings and praying in the utaki or kami-ya. The white robes consist of five parts: a skirt, blouse, undergarment, overgarment, and headband (see plates). When villagers describe visions or dreams of kami-sama, the kami-sama are typically wearing white. The crown of leaves worn by the kaminchu seems throughout the Ryukyu Islands to be a fairly widespread symbol of a deity who comes from outside to visit the village (cf. Muratake 1964/1965: 123). According to Mrs. Tanahara, an ogami person and clan kaminchu:

> For a person to become kaminchu they have to see a dream like this: a dream of wearing the [special] clothes. White clothes if it is a woman, black if it is a man. . . . I will say, "If you don't dream like that, it is improper for you to be kaminchu." . . . Because the dream shows you the clothes, so I say, "Oh, you are okay." If a woman comes, I ask, "Did you see the white clothes?" That is the first question I ask.

The tremendous importance of the white robes is demonstrated by the priestess Mrs. Ishikawa, who is crippled and cannot make the trek to the utaki in the jungle but still rides on the bus from the kami-ya with the other kaminchu. While they are walking to the utaki, she puts on the white robes and continues to sit on the bus. By doing this, she has done her job as kami-sama.

According to the noro, "Maybe I was meant to wear the white clothes because when I took a test to go to high school I didn't pass. And so I took a test to be a nurse and passed. Nurses wear white." What strikes me in this remark is that she did not say: Maybe I was meant to be kaminchu because I passed the test to be a nurse and nurses help people. For the noro, the significance of nursing vis-à-vis the kaminchu role lies in wearing white clothing, not in "doing" something.

No one else can wear a particular kaminchu's white clothes. "Each kaminchu makes the clothes one time, until she dies," says one kaminchu. According to Mrs. Shimojo, "When a kaminchu dies she takes her white clothes with her. It's buried with her."

For Henza kaminchu, white clothes are a metaphor for life and for health.

SUSAN: Is there anything the noro can't do?

NORO: I don't feel like going to funerals because at funerals they wear black clothes and I am the person who wears white clothes. The meaning of the funeral is not a good thing. I go to village celebrations or new-house celebrations. I was told [it is not clear by whom she was told] not to go to funerals because I go to village celebrations all the time. And I don't feel like going either. I only go to funerals for close family. My body feels heavy at funerals.[5]

Because the notion of priestesses being kami-sama was a difficult one for me to grasp, I became unduly obsessed with finding an example that would "prove conclusively" that in the eyes of the villagers the priestesses aren't "really gods." After a few false tries, I thought to ask the priestesses whether, when they are wearing white, they are allowed to do, or want to do, quintessentially human activities. I quote here the end of a long conversation in which I looked for something that would be absolute proof of their humanness.

SUSAN: Are there things you cannot do while wearing the white kimono, like going to the toilet?

MRS. SHIMOJO: When I wear the white kimono I am the kami-sama's representative. So I must have a clean heart to wear the white clothes. Therefore, I cannot tell lies, I cannot cheat other people. From my heart I have to pray for Henza.

Mrs. Shimojo was not evading my question. Talking about the toilet is not taboo in Okinawa, and during long rituals kaminchu will walk a few steps away from the group into a field or garden to urinate.[6] My question about the toilet was irrelevant to Mrs. Shimojo because it reflected my Western assumption that "true gods" don't go to the toilet—that gods do not share human physiological processes. I had set the dividing line between divine and human at a place that had no meaning to Mrs. Shimojo. She did not share my understanding that there must be some absolute distinction between human and divine, and that this dividing line must distinguish corporeal from incorporeal. For Mrs. Shimojo, kami-sama going to the toilet is uninteresting and nonproblematic.

Just like the need to urinate does not set people off from kami, wisdom and intelligence do not set kami off from people. One of the village priestesses is believed by the other priestesses (and indeed seems to me) to be senile; but senility does not mean that she is no longer a priestess—a kami-sama. Priestesses do not need to be intelligent, charismatic, or eloquent. They do not need to *do* anything.

SUSAN: Are there things you can't do while wearing the white kimono, like go to the toilet?

NORO: Even if you are wearing the [white] kimono, if you have to go, you go.

SUSAN: Is there anything you can't do?

NORO: No.

SUSAN: Are there some words that you can't say?

NORO: No.

SUSAN: Food that you can't eat?

NORO: No.

_____

SUSAN: Why do you go [twice a year] to wash at a sacred well before going to the utaki?

KAMINCHU: It is your real heart to clean, to clear your body, to wash off, for my heart to be like kami-sama's heart.

The notion that priestesses are kami is less fantastic than it seemed to me at the time of these conversations. For Okinawans, being kami is not extraordinary or exceptional. Kami-sama are not omnipotent, omniscient, creator, or judge. The kaminchu does not lose her human characteristics by becoming kami-sama because, in Okinawan culture, human and kami are not dichotomous. Becoming kami-sama does not endow one with superhuman powers. In fact, it is not particularly relevant to know whether the priestesses really believe that they are divinity; the point is that they experience themselves as kami-sama. My concern with whether kaminchu are really perceived by villagers to be gods is equally irrelevant; the point is that the kaminchu represent the potentiality and absolute immanence of kami-being.

The noro's answers in the preceding exchange stand in sharp contrast to descriptions of spirit possession in cultures in which it is emphasized that the possessed spirit medium does not go to the toilet, eat, yawn, or cough. In Afro-Brazilian rituals, for example, the medium acts in nonhuman ways in order to show that she has been possessed by a nonhuman entity (cf. Landes 1947: 54). Also, among the Japanese shamans described by Carmen Blacker, "behavior ordinary or human . . . [is] instantly condemned as weak and unconvincing" (1975: 277). In Henza, on the other hand, kami-sama and human are not discontinuous categories. When the noro puts on the white, she does not need to change her behavior.

If the priestess is kami-sama, and if the essence of her role is presence rather than action, we should not be surprised to find that a great deal of attention is given to personal appearance. One utaki day the noro had not come to the ritual. I stopped by her house afterward, and she told me that she had not come because "I have had a cold and my hair is messed up, and I had a blood test and my arm is red and puffy, and it is not appropriate to do be kami-sama [do kami-sama things, her language was not clear here] when you do not look nice." I asked the noro if a woman with physical deformities can be kaminchu. Her answer: "There is no one like that. Most kaminchu have a nice figure, beautiful faces."

> When you wear the white clothes they must be neat. Not hanging loosely. I don't know about other people, but I clean myself, and set my hair, and wear makeup. Like for the new-house ritual, nice hair set, makeup, clothes. (Mrs. Shimojo)

Mrs. Shimojo accords great importance to wearing nice clothes. On another occasion, we discussed how she knew she was meant to be kaminchu.

> In my case, when I was young, before the war, there was nothing [people were poor]. When I was young I told my father, I don't need to eat, but I want to buy nice clothes. At the time when people started wearing long dresses or different materials, I was always in the vanguard of fashion. Still now my children think that I only wear nice clothes. After I graduated school I did sewing jobs. My sisters always laughed at me that I cared about clothes. (Mrs. Shimojo)

Throughout much of Asia, Europe, and the United States, piety is associated with renunciation of worldly concerns. The truly devout person pays attention to matters of the spirit, sometimes treating earthly existence as a mere vehicle for spiritual advancement and sometimes actively disparaging the physicality of worldly existence. For the Okinawan kaminchu, this world—the mountain, the grove, the hearth, and above all her own body—is imbued with kami-sama. Adorning her body is a true act of piety.

Feeding the Kami-sama

On a number of occasions I asked villagers to tell me who or what a particular kami-sama is. Here is one typical exchange:

SUSAN: What is *toko no kami* [a household kami]?

MRS. ADANIYA: Only tea in the morning.

To some villagers, what differentiates one kami-sama from another is the type of food put out on the altar: tea, water, sake, rice, and so forth. In the preceding exchange, Mrs. Adaniya defined or described kami-sama in terms of ritual, in terms of an activity in which she summons kami-sama's presence, and in terms of an act in which she focuses or channels kami-sama through the fundamental action of feeding. Neither Mrs. Adaniya nor any other villager has ever suggested that a particular kami-sama likes tea better than water or sake; there is no mythological elaboration of kami-sama's idiosyncratic preferences. Rather, the ritual exchange is what defines—in the sense of delimits or demarcates— kami-sama.

By lighting incense, the priestess connects to kami-sama. Putting on the white clothes is the means by which the priestess intensifies kami-sama in her person. Once the priestess has lit incense and is wearing white, she is fully present as kami-sama. She is then ready to accept food offerings.

SUSAN: Has there been any change in the status of kaminchu?

MRS. ISHIKAWA: Yes. In the old days we were very respected.

SUSAN: How was that shown? Were people polite to you when they spoke to you on the street?

MRS. ISHIKAWA: No. When we do ogami [pray], that is when they respected us well, gave us a lot of food.

SUSAN: What has changed during the [forty-five] years that you have been kaminchu?

MRS. ISHIKAWA: A lot of differences! For example, in the old days at *shinugu* [one of the most important rituals] they served *omiki*, which isn't sake but it is made out of rice, it is white. A fermented rice drink. Mr. Shibahiki used to make it and gave it to us. Nowadays they give those little bottles of yogurt, or coffee, or soft drinks. The food is also different.

When I first had this conversation with Mrs. Ishikawa, my reaction (hopefully hidden from her) was that her answer was trivial; couldn't she come up with some more momentous changes in the priestesses' work? (I asked her whether there had been other changes but she couldn't think of any.) Surely, in the wake of World War II, the American occupation, Japanese annexation, the death of the previous noro, and the presence of a Japanese oil company renting much of the island's property, some more significant changes had occurred in the kaminchu role. Mrs. Ishikawa's answer, however, is telling. If priestesses are kami-sama, what they are given to eat has cosmic significance: There is a huge difference between giving your gods a fermented rice drink and giving them cola.

As I explained in the previous chapter, through food rituals some kind of spiritual essence or identity is exchanged. An exchange of this sort takes place when the noro at the utaki altar "feeds" the kami-sama by putting cooked rice[7] into the openings of the conch shells that are said to be kami-sama and to represent the noro and her associates (see the previous discussion). In this ritual, the noro gives food to the kami, who is really herself.

SUSAN: At the san gatsu ritual the headman served sake to the kaminchu, why?

MRS. SHIMOJO: The headman represents the people of Henza. It is like his saying, "You kaminchu do Henza's praying, and so that is why I am pouring for you."

Who provides the food is as important as who eats it. I asked Mrs. Shimojo to explain to me why the kaminchu eat two meals during the *utaki mae* (going around the sacred groves) ritual. She explained that the village provides one of the meals and a particular family provides the other.

> Over on the west side of the ocean there is a rock; it is Arakaki's [a village family]. When there was a land redistribution in Henza, that rock belonged to Mr. Arakaki—he asked please give me the rock over there. So the things that he gets from there like octopus or seaweed he brings to the kami-sama to serve to the kami-sama. That is why Arakaki's house still prepares the meal and we pray for that house first, and then for everybody. Maybe a long time ago when he asked please give me the rock, there was an arrangement that if fish or anything comes from there they will serve it to the kami-sama. The area around the rock belongs to Arakaki and if someone else would go there to try to catch fish the boat would flip over. I heard that there are some examples like that. . . . And that is why the food is given by Arakaki. . . . And we pray, "Arakaki's descendants inherited this job so please make health for their descendants."

Shinugu

MRS. SHINZATO: Shinugu [she pauses to think], that is vegetables, rice, food, agricultural products by the person who made it. Rice, wheat, sweet potato, they give the first of each harvest to the kami. For appreciation of the harvest.

SUSAN: Who does this ritual?

MRS. SHINZATO: Kaminchu—*onna no kami-sama* [women kami]. They go to the utaki to pray.

From early in my stay in Henza, I was told that I must be sure to see the shinugu ritual. The history of this ritual is complex, and various scholars and villagers offered me different and sometimes contradictory explanations (which I shall not go into here).

Several villagers' versions of the history of shinugu include a sexual or gendered theme; for example, on shinugu day, the men had to leave the house, and only women could stay inside. In this section, I shall focus upon shinugu as I saw it carried out in 1995 by the village priestesses.

> We meet at the kami-ya at 9:00. A.M. As each kaminchu enters the kami-ya, she makes a small prayer. Mr. Miyezato, a male assistant, brings yogurt,

which replaces *miki*—a mashed rice drink—as his family's offering. He lights incense and pours sake on the hinu-kan stones. They pray. The women tie on their white headbands, and they go on the bus to Irigusuku (west sacred grove). On the hike up to the sacred grove, Mr. Miyezato clears the overgrown path. While walking through the jungle, they collect various vines. At a small clearing, the women pause to put on their white clothes; the male assistants walk ahead. Arriving at Irigusuku, the women weave their crowns of leaves. Mr. Miyezato climbs a hill and waves a bundle of leaves, symbolic of the torch that used to be held up to call to Henza villagers living on a neighboring island. At the hinu-kan inside of Irigusuku the noro, Mr. Shibahiki, and Mr. Miyezato pray. They pour yogurt on the rocks (at shinugu yogurt and not sake is used). The kaminchu sit on two stone benches, and the noro holds a bundle of grass and leaves, praying in the direction of Agaregusuku (east sacred grove) and waving the bundle. They sit and rest and drink the yogurt provided by Mr. Miyezato. With Mr. Miyezato's help, each kaminchu makes a wand or bundle of branches and vines. On the way back to the bus each person holds a bundle and they chant "eh oo eh" and wave the branches at certain intervals. This is an *oharai* ("get out") against disease. Then we go to Agaregusuku for a quick prayer.

Returning to the village, we go to Mrs. Jana's house, which is the traditional stop to rest and eat food provided by her household. Mr. Miyezato passes around some more yogurt because Mrs. Jana is not well and had forgotten to prepare a meal. We rest there for quite a while because the timing of the next part of the ritual was arranged in advance, and we cannot arrive at our next destination too early.

Finally, we leave and walk along certain alleys in the village, waving the bundles of vines at every house and doing oharai. We walk to a particular spot on the road at the western edge of the village and stop to tie knots in grass stalks. Mrs. Shimojo then departs, saying that she has to "go to the ocean to catch some octopus or fish." Because Mrs. Shimojo is a male kamisama, she must leave at this point. Then we drive to a beach on the west of the island to pray to the *hama no kami sama* [beach kami-sama]. Mr. Shibahiki throws one leaf into the water as an *oharai* against bugs.

We walk to the schoolyard. Under a big special tree near a sacred well the women kaminchu sit down. This yard used to reach to the waterfront until land was filled in there. It is a hot day, and the women relax in the shade and take off some of their clothes from under the white kimonos. Mr. Miyezato sets up a "pantry" in some bushes off to the side. Mr. Umisedo drives up on a motorcycle and brings fish. Mr. Miyezato takes it from him and organizes it. Mrs. Yamashiro comes up with two big baskets of cooked rice on her head, and Mr. Miyezato puts it in his "pantry." Mrs. Shibahiki brings yogurt. Mr. Miyezato arranges the food in his pantry while the women, especially the noro, sit and boss him. There is nothing to drink, but no one goes to get anything. The noro and Mr. Shibahiki (a male assistant) stand in front of a rice basket facing to the east. The noro prays, walks around the basket, does oharai with her bundle of plants, and prays. She repeats this seven times

while Mr. Shibahiki stands off to the side. I am told that this is an oharai for
the rice harvest.

Mr. Miyezato serves yogurt. He says that he serves because he is younger
than Mr. Shibahiki (Mr. Miyezato is approximately sixty-five years old). Mr.
Shibahiki sits down, but separately from the women. Mr. Okutara (my friend
and coresearcher) joins Mr. Shibahiki, and I am also supposed to sit with the
two men and not with the kami-sama (although that morning at the kami-ya
and at most other rituals I sat with them). Mr. Tobaru's granddaughter brings
fish. I am told that she is sad because her father died recently, but her family
must still bring fish. Mr. Neho brings a third batch of yogurt. The kaminchu
sit on mats on which are placed the type of small tables that are customarily
put on the butsudan to hold offerings for the ancestors. Mr. Shibahiki does not
have such a table, and Mrs. Hamabata, a recently born kami-sama, shares a
table with Mrs. Ishikawa. The kaminchu are given dishes by Mr. Miyezato; Mr.
Shibahiki has brought his own. Mr. Miyezato brings out plates with fish and
bowls with rice and serves only the kaminchu. They pray briefly and eat. I offer to help Mr. Miyezato, who looks overworked, but he says no, that only his
family can do this job. The kaminchu clear their plates of all food. Mr.
Miyezato takes their plates and brings another serving of fish and rice. Alto-
gether he serves them seven times, and each time they say a small prayer. The
serving is done by Mr. Miyezato in a highly ritualistic manner. The fifth serving, for example, is only fish. The sixth is fish and rice. There is no other food,
no vegetables or tofu or drinks. At each round of food, the kaminchu thank
Mr. Miyezato. The women talk among themselves, and there is quite a bit of
instruction of the newest kaminchu. After the third round of serving the
kaminchu, Mr. Miyezato brings one serving to Mr. Shibahiki. After the sixth
round of food, Mr. Okutara, Mr. Miyezato, and I can eat. The kaminchu have
plastic bags for leftovers (of which there are a lot). By the end, they are putting
the food straight into their bags. It is an enormous amount of food. The kaminchu move over to a small well a few meters from where they have been sitting. There they have their seventh serving and pray one last time. They take
off their white robes and I drive them home.

Shinugu is a lengthy and complicated ritual that comprises a number of possibly unrelated elements that have, over the generations, become strung together in
the one-day ceremonial sequence described here. The first half of the day was dedicated to various kinds of oharai, in which the kaminchu (men and women, male
and female) all participated. In a classic priestly role, they actively chased out "bad
things" (bugs and disease) from the village.

The more interesting part of the ritual, to my mind, is the second half, after
Mrs. Shimojo (the male kami-sama) has left. Once the priestesses arrived at the
schoolyard, they no longer "did" anything—they just sat and ate. They no longer
included others in their party—Mr. Okutara, Mr. Shibahiki, Mr. Miyezato, and I
were clearly excluded. The time at the schoolyard was dedicated to village families
giving offerings of food for Mr. Miyezato to ritually serve to the kami-sama.

The following points distinguish these offerings from regular meals in Henza:

- The kaminchu and the noro did not share any of their food with anyone else. Normally, villagers are very generous with food; at other rituals not only did the noro and kaminchu share with me, but they also practically forced me to taste the various delicacies.
- There were no tea, seaweed, or other things that villagers usually eat in a meal. The normative Henza meal has quite a few different foods in it; just rice and fish is not considered a real meal. The food was not particularly tasty according to village human standards. Moreover, even though everyone was surely thirsty, no drinks were provided, presumably because cola or juice is not part of the traditional ritual menu. (Note that there were several soft drink machines located very near the shinugu site).
- The kaminchu were served the same food seven times in a ritualized manner; regular meals are usually served in one or, at the most, two or three courses, and the courses contain different foods.
- The quantity of food was far more than any human could eat.
- There was a total inversion of usual serving style. This is one of the only times that I have ever seen a man serving women food in Henza. This suggests that their roles have been ritually defined: Mr. Miyezato is a person (albeit a very important person), but the kaminchu are kami-sama.
- When I offered to help Mr. Miyezato, who looked tired and overworked, he refused, saying that only his family and one other family can do this job. He is not a simple waiter or host but a ritual officiant.
- The tables on which the kaminchu eat are special for shinugu; they are not used for other occasions. Nowadays, the only other place in which this type of table is used is on the butsudan, where food is placed for the ancestors and kami-sama.

Yanusuji

Henza villagers organize six rituals in the process of building a new house. Only one of these rituals—*yanusuji*—is the province of kaminchu,[8] and it is far more complex, expensive, and formal than the other five rituals, which are carried out by an ogami person or by the chief carpenter. Yanusuji is the only private ritual performed by village-level priestesses; all of their other rituals are on behalf of the village as a whole. The kaminchu told me that they do not do yanusuji at their own initiative but only at the express invitation of a family. They also repeatedly told me that yanusuji is very hard work. I was privileged to see yanusuji one time during my stay in Henza.

The ritual takes place at the new house. The family has already moved in. The *noro* and her associates dress beautifully and have their hair washed and set before the ritual. No guests or audience attend; only the homeowners and one or two close relatives are present in the house. The noro prays quietly, by herself, at the hinu-kan. Part of the ritual sequence consists of oharai for the new house, followed by a large and leisurely meal served to the kaminchu. During this meal, visitors may drop by, and as is typically done in Henza, tasty food is shared by everyone.

The central ritual begins after this meal, when more food is brought out and piled on a table on the far side of the main room, next to the kitchen.

The woman homeowner's maternal aunt and uncle have lived in Brazil for the past forty years, and they are visiting in Henza for a few months. They have been honored with the job of serving the kaminchu. The kaminchu and Mr. Shibahiki sit against the far wall in the most honored place in the house, and the aunt and uncle kneel in front of them. Uncle and aunt pour sake for the kaminchu and kaminchu pour sake for them. The woman homeowner and a woman friend shuttle plates of food from the kitchen to the aunt and uncle, who serve the food to the kaminchu. The food is formally served, brought out to the kaminchu course by course. The seven courses are served according to the noro's orders; she tells the homeowners what food to bring and when to bring it. Sometimes the kaminchu serve food back to the aunt and uncle, sometimes not, and there are constant requests to the wife to bring more sake, more food, particular pouring containers, and so forth. Each round or course of food consists of serving, praying, nibbling a bit, and putting the food in a bag to take home. Between courses, the kaminchu sing a series of songs, each round of singing lasting for about ten minutes.[9] At the end of each round of singing, they lift up either a drum or their cup and say "utooto" (the word uttered at the beginning of prayers) and murmur one or two words. With each round of singing, more sake and another course of food are brought out. They are served some of the same foods that they had been served at the first (human) meal. But now the foods are interspersed with at least two courses of soup and a bowl of pink rice. There is also a dessert course and a fruit course. The seventh and last course of food is served, and the last song is sung. The uncle and aunt say a formal thank-you, bowing low to the ground, and the kaminchu return their formal thank-you. The family joins the kaminchu for another oharai, and then everyone dances freely to a tape of lively Okinawan music [kachashi]. The kaminchu sit back down and pray a bit more. The aunt and uncle serve them hot tea, requested by the noro. Finally, the homeowners, husband and wife, come to thank them for their hard work. The kaminchu are given nicely wrapped gifts (they are also quietly paid a small sum of money), and, accompanied by a few men of the family, they go to the kami-ya to announce that the homeowners invited them and they celebrated today. They leave a bottle of sake at the kami-ya.

Later in the evening, friends and neighbors will come by and eat from a huge pot of goat soup that the homeowners have been cooking over a flame in their parking lot since the morning. The kaminchu will not return for this party.

This ritual raises a number of questions. In my earliest conversations with the noro and kaminchu, they were eager to tell me that yanusuji is an extremely long ritual and very difficult for them to perform. But when I finally was able to observe the ritual, it looked to me as if the hard work consisted of sitting around and eating for a few hours! Ritual performers cross-culturally often are proud of how hard they work at their ritual labors—a difficult and laborious ritual is more effective than an easy one. (Think, for example, of the pilgrims who crawl for kilometers on their knees to shrines in Mexico.) Yet in Henza, rituals such as *hama ogami* (beach prayer, see chapter 5), which really seemed to me to be hard work, were not described by the kaminchu as such. The only other ritual described by the kaminchu as long and hard is shinugu. And again, the hard work of shinugu seems to be sitting under a shady tree and eating!

It seems to me that both in shinugu and yanusuji the "hard work" is a metaphor for "kami-work." While in a state of enhanced kami-being, the priestesses lend their bodies to the kami-sama; by eating they quite literally feed the gods.[10] In hama ogami, elderly women traipse around in the hot sun for hours, praying along the beach fronts of Henza Island. But that "work" is nothing out of the ordinary—most Henza women are in good physical shape from gardening. The "work" of being fed seven courses at shinugu and yanusuji, in contrast, is extraordinary and therefore elicits comments from the kaminchu.

As in my analysis of shinugu, I claim that the central ritual act in yanusuji is feeding the kami-sama. What proof do I offer that the meal at yanusuji is extraordinary? First, everyone participated in the final oharai and in the first real meal, but only the kaminchu were fed the seven courses. For example, the wife's mother and Mrs. Okuda who came to help with the drumming, were served the original shrimp and tofu, but not the seven ritual courses that came afterward. Second, the noro ordered what to bring and when. The noro's bossy behavior during the meal was absolutely extraordinary for Henza, where visitors do not even help themselves to seconds of tea. Third, the amount of food served was clearly more than mere mortals could be expected to eat. The first "real" meal had been generous; the seven courses were served after everyone had already eaten their fill.

Another new-house ritual—hinu-kan transfer—had been performed for the same family by Mrs. Ikene, a local shaman-type practitioner, a month or so earlier. When I asked the woman homeowner why they needed to do two new-house rituals, she at first could not understand my question. I suspect that the source of our miscommunication was that Mrs. Ikene's and the noro's rituals seemed to her, although at that time, not to me, to be totally different. After a pause, she explained that Mrs. Ikene did oharai ("get out") and that the noro did *haitte* ("come in"). In other words, after Mrs. Ikene had ejected unwanted spirits, the kaminchu brought in something desirable. By their presence, the priestesses fill the house with kami-sama. By just being there, by sitting and eating, they diffuse a positive spiritual force. Unlike Mrs. Ikene, the kaminchu do not "do" much. The role of the kaminchu is to "be," to bring kami-sama in her body from one place to another. This is eminently suitable in a new-house ritual (particularly after the shaman-type practitioner has already taken care of any problematic spiritual entities). At yanusuji, like at shinugu and in the utaki, kami-sama sit in significant positions and are fed by the community. By their presence, kaminchu give villagers an opportunity to get close to "kami-ness," to include kami-sama in their village community.

Umachi

Similar patterns emerge in other priestess rituals. Four times each year the noro, her associates, and certain clan priestesses meet at the kami-ya for the umachi ritual; two of those times they then proceed to the utaki, twice they stay in the village square (*uchi umachi*).

At uchi umachi the priestesses pray inside the kami-ya, light incense, pour sake on the hinu-kan, and pass around a cup of sake, which each holds briefly, lifting the cup up in the direction of the altar while mumbling a short prayer, and then taking a sip. The kaminchu then go out onto the kami-ya steps, where they weave strands of straw into a crown and pick leaves from the tree next to the kami-ya to put in the crowns. Then they don their five-piece white robes. Putting on the robes and making the crowns takes about ten minutes. When the kaminchu finish dressing, Mr. Shibahiki hands a cup to each kaminchu in turn and pours sake for her. She lifts up the cup and prays briefly. While he cleans up, the kaminchu join their clan members in the village square and sit in their assigned seats in a circle on the ground under an awning; each clan has a place in the square just as each priestess has a seat in the utaki or an altar in the clan house. After everyone settles down outside, the headman, Mr. Shibahiki, and a few other men pour sake for the kaminchu. Finally, cups of sake are passed around by and to everyone.

At most Okinawan rituals, sake is passed around from hand to hand, and each person takes a sip; that is indeed what was done with the first round of sake inside the kami-ya. But in the uchi umachi ritual, a second round of sake was poured for the kaminchu, who, wearing white, were standing on the steps, just minutes after the usual round of sake had been passed around inside the kami-ya. Why did Mr. Shibahiki pour another round of sake ten minutes after the first? And why was the first round passed from hand to hand, whereas the second round was poured out individually by Mr. Shibahiki for each kaminchu?

The first round of sake, inside the kami-ya, is standard: It is a simple ritual of sharing sake among the community, the kami-sama, or the ancestors. The kaminchu pour a bit of sake on the altar and then pass around a cup from hand to hand in their role as villagers who came to pray to the village kami-sama. Their behavior inside the kami-ya is the same as the behavior of villagers at family and clan rituals in which they pray to their ancestors and then share sake or food.

At uchi umachi, following the first round of sake, the kaminchu stood on the kami-ya steps and donned their white robes and crowns. The way in which the second cup was treated suggests that the recipients of the sake had changed; instead of passing a cup of sake from hand to hand (a symbol of solidarity), Mr. Shibahiki poured a separate cup for each kaminchu (a ritual offering and a symbol of respect). The first time, they drank sake as regular humans; the second time, they drank sake as kami-sama. In the third round of sake drinking (outside in the square), the sake was once again poured individually rather than passed from hand to hand. But even more significantly, in this third round the village headman had a ritual role—as the representative of Henza he poured sake for the kami-sama.

After the formal part of the sake pouring was over, villagers—kami-sama and clan members alike—relaxed, chatted, and passed more cups of sake from hand to hand around the circle. At uchi umachi, like at shinugu and yanusuji, some of the eating and drinking is only for the priestesses and some is communal; some high-lights the "kami-ness" of the priestesses, and some highlights their humanness and solidarity with the village. The intermingling of the two styles of eating and drinking brings home the notion that the priestesses are simultaneously kami-sama and regular village women.

The year that I was in Henza, the noro had been unable to attend the June uchi umachi. During the first phase of the ritual, inside the kami-ya, one of the other priestesses informally took the absent noro's place in front of the altar. Inside the kami-ya, dressed in everyday clothes and passing sake from hand to hand, the requisite for being the noro's substitute was knowledge of how to do the ritual, and, indeed, the most knowledgeable priestess carried out the noro's tasks. Afterward, when the priestesses were wearing white, a member of the noro's clan was told to sit in the noro's place in the village square. In other words, once the kaminchu had donned their white robes and sat down to accept offerings from the village head-man, the requisite became the person's spiritual—clan—identity. (It was explained in chapter 2 that villagers sometimes speak of the clan itself as kami-sama.)

Spiritual identity should not, however, be interpreted to mean rank or status. The woman who took the noro's place was a simple shopkeeper, whose usual role in the clan is to carry the noro's mat and clothes at certain rituals. This woman sat in the noro's place not because she is the second most important or knowledgeable person in the village but rather because, as a member of the noro's clan, she also represents or embodies a particular spiritual energy whose presence is needed to make the circle complete at uchi umachi. Significantly, after the grand buildup of the white robes and crown of leaves and ritual pouring of the sake, dramatic ritual elements that serve to assure participants that the priestesses are truly kami-sama, no one is surprised, dismayed, or even interested when a simply dressed shop-keeper takes the place of the absent noro.

SEVEN

Divine Dis-order

Signs, Symptoms, and Sitting in the Right Seat

In Okinawan culture, where cosmology is unelaborated and rituals are relatively low-key, priestesses concentrate, represent, and embody divinity. The priestess is not a ritual practitioner, she is the ritual; she is not a theological expert, she is the theos. Typically, when I asked a priestess to tell me about her duties as a priestess, her answer would emphasize how she became a priestess rather than what she does. This emphasis reflects the identity and position of priestesses as manifestations of kami-sama. Because the significance of the priestess role lies in *being* rather than in doing, telling how one came to be a kami-sama is an intrinsic part of the role.

In a broad variety of cultural situations, religious autobiography is an affirmation of the integrity, sanctity, and particularity of one's life path and beliefs. Complex, bewildering, or ineffable religious truths, represented in the person of the religious narrator, become immediate, convincing, and comprehensible. In the case of religious leaders, an autobiography is also an affirmation of one's right to lead. A life story, whether oral or written, is both the calling card and the proof of authenticity of a religious leader. In short, a good (that is, convincing, dramatic, and theologically relevant) life story has the potential to establish both the credentials of the leader and the efficacy and truth of the religion. Because of the theological and social significance of religious leaders' autobiographies, "Establishing the mythical ideal, or what might better be called the biographic image, takes precedence over a simple chronicling of biographical facts" (Reynolds and Capps 1976: 4). In other words, religious leaders and experts use narrative to construct a culturally recognizable religious profile. The life story of a religious leader is often, as Laurel Kendall says regarding a Korean shaman whose initiation she has documented, "a collective enterprise with a long gestation, begun in the divination sessions when she tells her story to a shaman and is in turn told its meaning" (1996: 25).

Elaine Lawless has argued that "religion happens to be one area in which the range for creativity in personal-experience fictions is quite broad, largely because the narrator takes refuge in the fantastic world of the supernatural and/or the divine" (1991: 61). While I agree with Lawless that religious narratives, unlike many other kinds of autobiographies, are not limited to experiences that are empirically verifiable, I suspect that the extent of idiosyncratic tale-telling in religious autobiography is circumscribed by the need to tell a story that the listeners understand and accept as theologically meaningful. Religious autobiographies generally fit some sort of culturally recognized blueprint for what it means to be a religious individual of a particular type; they serve as platforms for the teller to interweave his or her own life experiences with the culturally recognized standard for religious leaders. In religious narratives, the teller typically goes to some effort to situate him or herself socially; the spiritual truth related in the story is embodied in a person of recognizable gender, class, and social position (see Kendall 1984).

In Henza priestesses' autobiographies—as in the autobiographies of many other religious leaders around the world—a most prominent theme is illness. Suffering, together with reluctance to take on the leadership role, is interpreted in many cultures as proof of a genuine spiritual calling (see Kendall 1985 on Korea). More specifically, given Henza's yasashii social ethos, there is no clear-cut mechanism for choosing or training religious leaders: Volunteering (pushing oneself forward) is not yasashii, and there is no organized body that has the power to appoint religious leaders.[1] As we shall see in this chapter, priestesses's illness narratives situate the decision to take on their role outside of either volition or institution. Requiring from priestesses a history of illness, and even more than that—the recital of a history of illness—allows the preservation of the village's broadly based yasashii and egalitarian ethos.

The conventional nature of the priestesses' narratives—the similarities that they bear to one another—suggests, as Peter Stromberg has argued regarding Christian conversion narratives, that the recitation of the narratives is a ritual performance. "Good" rituals (that is, rituals that are persuasive, interesting, and meaningful to those who participate in them) facilitate connection and communication between the canonical (enduring aspects of nature, society, or the cosmos that are encoded in stable liturgical forms) and the immediate situation of the particular individual. It is in this process of connection and communication that self-transformation and increased religious commitment take place. Stromberg suggests that the performance of conversion narratives has a profound effect not only on the audience (for whom the narrative is the most visible sign of conversion; the conversion itself is normally not witnessed by the audience) but also on the teller. Particularly regarding experiences of illness, in the course of telling and retelling the conversion story, an unarticulated and idiosyncratic bodily sensation is articulated in the form of a culturally recognized and meaningful spiritual process. As Stromberg shows, "this achievement is not a one-time event" (1993: 54). It continues to occur each time the story is told.

Autobiographic narratives are offered by Henza priestesses to elucidate the most crucial process of Okinawan religion—how a person becomes kami-sama. The construction of a "priestess-becoming" narrative is, as Yoshinobu Ota has argued, an "interpretive activity . . . by which the client [priestess-to-be] attempts to understand extraordinary life experiences" (1989: 122; also see Kawahashi 1992: 119). The narratives illustrate that what happens to the priestess's body is culturally comprehensible and of cosmic significance, that it is within the [female] body of the priestess that kami-sama is manifested in one of its most accessible forms (cf. Ota 1989).

The Priestesses' Narratives

The following narratives were offered, quite eagerly, by three Henza priestesses in answer to my question: How did you become a priestess? These narratives share many features with others that I heard from Henza priestesses.

Narrative 1—The Noro

Sickness. From fifty-five years old. Started bleeding from the nose. When we moved into this house, for two weeks I couldn't breathe. Like a mouthful of blood. Full. I went to see the doctor and he cured it. It was a dangerous condition and so the nurse didn't touch me, only the doctor himself could touch me. As soon as I arrived back home I stopped breathing again. Every day again and again. The day that we moved I couldn't do anything, so my sister had to take care of the move, and my husband was upset because I wasn't any help to him. This went on for two weeks. There is an old [male] *ekisha* [fortune-teller] in Henza, I went to him, and the ekisha told me that my [dead] aunt is behind me, following me. And the aunt [who had been the previous noro] was saying [according to the ekisha] "Who will do my job?" That is why she was following me. The ekisha told my aunt, "She will do it. Tomorrow is the new year, so go back to wherever you belong." And then he prayed and the bleeding from my nose stopped. This aunt is my father's sister. [Did you know from a young age that because your aunt was noro that you would be noro?] Not at all. We didn't know who has to do it. The kami-sama decides. I had four sisters, so we didn't know which one. I am the third daughter in the family. The ekisha told me that I have to do it. And so I went to a different ekisha also and then to more ekishas. And then I decided to do it. To become noro there is a celebration that is always in May. But on the third of March there is an ocean ritual [san gatsu] in which the noro is involved, but that year I wasn't officially noro yet, so I didn't want to be involved with it. That was my own idea. And I went to sleep that night. At 4:00 in the morning from the town hall I heard them singing the san gatsu song [she sings]. I heard it, and drums—tum tum tum—and samisen. I put on the lights and I thought the music is from the town hall. I thought there were people practicing for the March ritual. Maybe they were drunk, they were so noisy and it was so late. It was so hard to sleep with the noise. I thought to cover up my head with the blanket so I can go back to sleep. And the boom boom boom of the drum seemed so close to my ear, I could hear it right above my head. To wake me up. I felt that maybe they are trying to wake me up to prepare the meal for the third of March. Four o'clock in the morning. I thought it is a little early. But maybe not because I have to cook the meat and fish and seaweed and tofu and I have to go to the store to get the tofu. So maybe it is a good time to wake up. I was debating with myself. And I have to take a shower. Many people will come to my house to eat. And for me to be on time to go to the ocean and pray, and get dressed and made up, maybe 4:00 is a good time. *But kami-sama woke me up!*[2]

The first point I want to stress is the teller's adamant denial of any personal volition in the process of her becoming noro. A cynical outsider might suspect that the niece of the previous noro knew very well, given the hereditary nature of the position and the aunt's lack of a daughter, that she was likely to inherit the role.[3] Yet in her narrative she emphatically absolves herself of any element of choice or foreknowledge. In this instance, mysterious and dangerous bleeding from the nose leads her to visit an ekisha, and the ekisha is the one who identifies her as the noro-to-be; she herself cannot discern that she is the one. To further consolidate this point, she tells in dramatic detail how even after she had accepted the role but before she had begun to function in it, kami-sama insisted that she must act; drums banging and lights shining at 4:00 A.M.—who could shut their eyes and ears to such insistence! In another conversation, this priestess told me that kami-sama sends illness to people who must become priestesses, "Because they are scared, so if they are not made sick they won't do it." In other words, she clarifies, "don't think that I chose to do this job."

A subtext in this story is that men are the ones who identify and confirm women priestesses. Thus, although the vast majority of Okinawan shaman-type practitioners are women, the noro in this tale consulted a male ekisha.[4] Although the noro is herself a nurse by profession, her tale emphasizes that [female] nurses couldn't even touch her; only the [male] doctor could. The noro also draws our attention to the fact that her extraordinary role is constituted in the context of ordinary women's roles. She details her thoughts during the 4:00 A.M. epiphany: Maybe I should wake up and cook, buy tofu, and put on makeup. And finally, we learn that the previous noro was her father's sister; this information is relevant because Henza priestesses typically believe that the noro should inherit her position matrilineally and not patrilineally.

A further point that concerns us here is the nature of the noro's illness. Especially when we read it in comparison to the narratives of women religious practitioners in other cultures (see Finkler 1985), we see that her illness does not seem to have been very serious. The only specific feature she has mentioned is a bloody nose! This suggests that the direction of the process described by the noro is not "illness causes religious activism," but rather "religious activism demands an illness narrative." I shall return to this point later.

Narrative 2—Mrs. Shimojo

The second narrative was related to me in very similar words on three separate occasions by Mrs. Shimojo, who is popularly believed to be the most knowledgeable of all the village priestesses.

> You cannot become a kaminchu because you want to. In my case, for about twenty years I hurt here and there on my body, and we went to [a number of] yuta [shaman-type practitioners], and yuta told that I should become the replacement of the previous one [priestess who had sat the position she is now sitting]. I was young and had a job. I realized that I was the one, but I had a job, and also I was shy. I felt that I was the one to replace [her], but

I didn't want to. But the yuta told me that if I don't sit the position I will have three operations. That happened. And indeed I had three operations. First back problems, and then bleeding, and I couldn't walk. Day and night kami showed me things, the white-clothed figure. If you don't hear or don't see [kami-sama], you don't really believe it. [Did you discuss this with more experienced kaminchu?] No, if you go to two or three yuta and they say the same thing, then you feel that you must do it. I don't know about other people, but in my case [it was like this]. I was sleeping and I saw white rolled-up paper, and it went through my cheek, I was shown that. I couldn't see who did this, but then my teeth hurt because the paper was pushed through. So I went to the dentist. I was shown that, but I didn't really understand. January 4, that day I was sleeping and covered with a blanket, and then I was told "Wake up." I heard a voice saying "Wake up." I didn't know if someone was there, but I heard "Wake up." I told the one who said wake up, "My teeth hurt so I am not going to wake up." "You must wake up," that one said. I was wondering, but my teeth hurt so much. So I woke up and sat up, and the kami-sama wearing *yoroi* [samurai warrior mask] was sitting in front of me, he was chubby, that was the kami-sama. I said "Sorry, I will do it." At night the person wearing the white clothes woke me up. I could hear him saying "Wake up." [Was it a dream?] No, I could hear it. My fourth daughter was in school in Naha, and she had to leave the house to go to school at six o'clock in the morning. When I heard the voice saying wake up, I woke up. But when I woke up it was bright outside. I didn't check the clock, but it was bright. I thought, oh no, I will be late to prepare my daughter's lunch. And then I turned on the light and saw the clock and it was two o'clock in the morning. And then I saw that outside it returned to being dark. And then I thought, that is strange. I went back to sleep. And then I went to see the yuta. Yuta told me, "Are you ready, is your mind preparing?" And I said, "Yes, I will do it." And that is when I started. [Please explain the sickness.] With the sickness, for example, you don't know if you are really sick or not. You are sick, then if you go to see the yuta, but if in the clan someone who was kaminchu died, you might have some kind of idea in your brain, if you were healthy and suddenly become sick and can't walk, and you make the connection that someone in your clan who was kaminchu died, you suddenly might get that connection in your brain. And then if you go to yuta, and are told that you are the one who has to sit there, [then you know].

In this narrative, the theme of absence of individual volition is repeated. She refused to take on her role; it took three operations and a face-to-face meeting with a samurai kami-sama for her to accept her destiny. And again, despite "three operations"—one of which involved "bleeding" (a theme I return to later on)—she does not seem to have ever become unable to work or function in the house. The only detailed physical symptom is a rather minor one—toothache. The theme of night-time epiphany is also repeated, again with the detail of night turning into day, and again with a recounting of her very womanly thoughts regarding preparing her daughter's lunch. This account adds another detail of significance: the penetration of her body with the paper. I return to this point later.

Narrative 3—Mrs. Ishikawa

The third narrative was related by Mrs. Ishikawa, who has been a village priestess from a very young age and is now the most veteran of the priestesses. Although she lives outside the village, she attends most rituals. She has a problem with her legs and cannot walk more than a few steps.

> In my case when I was four years old I was weak, and my parents worried about me. On the fourteenth of the month, the day before umachi [ritual], they have a meal, rice and fish, and each time the previous kaminchu [the one in this position before me] would give me a share of the food. Otherwise, I hurt all the time, that was the only thing that made me feel better. My mother prayed, "Please let her grow up." When I became seventeen, I became kaminchu. [Who told you to become kaminchu?] Yuta, here and there. My oldest brother was in China, his family went there, he had one daughter and couldn't have any more children. And because I wasn't sitting there [in the kaminchu position], they couldn't have any more babies. After the war my brother came back and I agreed to sit there. [Was he against your becoming kaminchu?] No, he wasn't available. My parents agreed to my becoming kaminchu, but the eldest son wasn't available, so I couldn't sit, because my parents couldn't discuss it with him. And so then I agreed, and my brother agreed, and the same year his wife got pregnant. . . . If you don't do that [your kaminchu work], accidents or bad things might happen. When they say late, this means late for kami-sama's way. When my children were small, I had a burn on my elbow, and when I went to the yuta to ask why she said because I am late for *kami no michi* (kami's way). I was living in the city at the time. My husband was a veterinarian in the city, that is why we lived there. The second son's child was burned. It was hard to come here to Henza [to do the rituals] when the children were small. From the city to Henza I needed to change buses, and that was before the sea road was built [linking Henza to the main island of Okinawa].

Mrs. Ishikawa's narrative emphasizes illness less than the previous ones, most probably because in this case the priestess cannot point to her current good health as proof that her earlier illness was part of the process of her refusing to recognize and accept the priestess role. Still, we are told that eating priestess food alleviated pain during her childhood. By eating the food that was meant for her, the food of kaminchu, her illness was at least temporarily eased. This somewhat abbreviated narrative does elaborate upon the other theme we have come to expect—women's concern with men's authority; in this case she began to sit as priestess when her brother gave his approval. And finally, this narrative, like the other ones, highlights the gradual process of "priestess-becoming."

Becoming Kami-sama

In Okinawan culture the human body is seen as whole, sealed and complete. Okinawans do not express fears of bodily effluvia; there are no menstrual taboos; bodies are not seen as riddled with holes out of which and into which all kinds of physical and mystical substances flow. In Okinawa, a woman who becomes a priestess actually becomes kami-sama; priestesses gesture with their hands to the top of their heads when they talk about this—kami-sama has entered their bodies—they now possess kami-sama. (Note that my terminology here is the opposite of the usual terminology of gods possessing people; in Okinawa the priestess possesses kami-sama.) In order for this to happen, the priestess-to-be necessarily undergoes a serious personal transformation. Given that a priestess is an embodied kami-sama, no one would expect this kind of existential transformation to be incorporeal. Yet if the body is a sealed whole, there is no way for kami-sama to enter. Many of the priestesses' illness stories involve bleeding—a visible physical rupture of the body. Illness, in the case of the priestesses, opens up cracks in one's bodily integrity and allows fusion with the divine. These cracks are requisite for human and divine to interpenetrate. Significantly, the male assistants to the priestesses do not become sick or bleed. In the case of the men, it is simply the eldest son who inherits the role. These men, unlike the priestesses, are not kami-sama.

In Okinawan religion, unlike in the Western religions with which many of us are familiar, there is no notion of a powerful punishing and rewarding god who performs miracles. The priestesses do not claim that their illness is a punishment from kami-sama, nor do they claim that recovering from illness is a reward. In the priestesses' stories (not just the ones I have quoted in this chapter), the illnesses are typically rather mild (bloody nose, allergies, etc.). A cousin of the woman who spoke in narrative 3 told me that, "When she was young she was weak, that is why she became a kaminchu." That priestess herself explained to me, in a general way, the process of becoming priestess: "If a priestess in the clan dies, someone will feel sick or bleed, and that person will go to the yuta. . . . The yuta is the one who says you are the one to sit. If you feel weak, you go to yuta for this."

The husband of another clan priestess (not described here) remarked that she started to become kaminchu "about fourteen or fifteen years ago, not really sickness, more like the body felt so heavy." The brother of the noro reports that his sister "was weak, not a big sickness, like headaches. Then she went to see an *uranaisha* [fortune-teller] and was told that you have to do this position." And finally, Mrs. Hokama and Mrs. Okuda explain that "kami-sama will make her weak if that is the person kami-sama wants for the role." The theme of weakness strikes me as a significant one. The meaning of becoming kaminchu is that the woman has somehow merged with kami-sama; she has added another identity on to her own. Weakness in the preinitiation phase may well signify a weakening of individual ego boundaries and of bodily boundaries so as to facilitate this merging. I find it particularly significant that several of the priestesses report having seen at night in a vision, visitation, or dream the kami-sama on/for whom they now sit and then the next day waking up sick or weak.

I had four children and a husband, and the children were all sleeping and I was looking at the door of the room and the door was closed and I was staring at the door and it opened, and standing over there appeared the figure of the kami-sama that I am sitting on [embodying] right now, it had a knife hanging from the waist and the kami-sama tried to give it to me, to just put it next to me while I was sleeping. The next day my leg wouldn't stand up. (clan kaminchu, approx. age eighty)

In the priestesses' stories, we hear about small, symbolic illnesses but no serious psychological, physical, or social dysfunction. I had the sense that the priestesses' illnesses were an ex post facto explanation, not a true etiology. According to one informant, a woman who is both a clan priestess and a shaman-type practitioner (she diagnoses through feeling the pulse), "From the time that the baby cries it is already decided who is noro. Someone is born to become noro." The illness, therefore, is a reminder and a wedge—not a transformative experience—and hence can be gentle.[5]

The priestesses' narratives present illness as a clue that needs to be unraveled: it takes years and visits to several or many different yuta to successfully "read" the clue. Illness signals the presence of a foreign being, yet the illness is not the foreign being itself. If it were, the job of the shaman-type practitioner would be to exorcise this discomfort-causing entity and effect quick cures. But that is not what the yuta does. The role of the shaman-type practitioner in Okinawa is to teach the priestess-to-be to recognize illness as the calling card of the divine, to help her arrive at the correct interpretation of the illness. Indeed, the most common interpretation of kamidaari (divine dis-order) offered by priestesses is that it is an inkan (the signature stamp used in Japan to sign documents). In the words of one village priestess (see narrative 2), "even though you want to be kaminchu [you cannot be one], because kami-sama is the one who examines you, because kami-sama marks you, even if you don't want to be kaminchu, you have to be, because you get sick. If kami-sama says this person is it, she has to do it. Twenty years ago I had bones removed from my body, for twenty years I had suffered. And finally I said I would do it."

Several priestesses received explicit signs from kami-sama.

In my case, I didn't need to go to a yuta [to be told that I am a priestess], I knew myself because I had a stamp on my leg. It continued for about a month that in the day I went to the fields to work and then came home at night and didn't sleep and then talked. And then the next day same thing, went to the fields the morning and came home and sat, and at night talked. That scared me. I didn't go to any ekisha, I did it [figured it out] myself because I had the kami-sama's stamp on me. [What shape stamp?] A hand shape, the thumb was here [she shows us]. If you are coming from this way it is like this, but from that way the handprint is the other way around. On my left thigh a stamp [inkan] appeared. There was a black mark stamped. It is that way so that if there is a group of people it is proof that I am kaminchu. It was done by kami-sama's hand to show other people that I am kaminchu. [What did you do when you saw the inkan?] I didn't know, but when everybody got together in the clan they saw that is the mark from the kami-sama. (Mrs. Tanahara)

I asked one of the younger and more loquacious kaminchu, if she was sick before taking on the role.

I was done by kami-sama here. My chest. A stamp, like a one-yen stamp, on my chest. I asked my mother-in-law, "I have a big one-yen kind of mark here on my chest, what is this" And she said, "Maybe you scratched there." And I said, "I don't think so, it is so round like this." So she said maybe I should go to the doctor tomorrow. But then more came out all over. On my cheeks. All over my body. It didn't hurt or itch either. On my stomach. *All on places that I can see myself. There weren't any on places that I cannot see myself,* like none in the middle of my back. I was working at the time. And I prayed, "kami-sama please help, if I go to the doctor tomorrow I will fail the physical examination (and not be able to work)." And when I prayed it went away. [Do you still have this?] No. [What was this?] The inkan [stamp] that I must sit in the kami-sama's position, that I can't run away from it." (my emphasis)

Another priestess tells how, when she was six years old, she was sick, drowned, and had a rash all over her body. "That is called *kami*'s rash." Then, at age twenty-five, she vomited blood. "That is a mark from the kami-sama. That happened in the year of my *eto* [her birth year according to the Chinese calendar]. The twenty-seventh of March. I will never forget that. [She is now in her eighties.] My mother maybe knew that maybe this is kami-sama letting us know that I should be kaminchu." Reinforcing these stories of signs given directly by kami-sama is a key ritual element in the priestess accession ceremony (see chapter 8). "On the fifteenth of May at the utaki. We borrow from the noro's house a red cup, and put egg white in it, and then mix it, and stamp (in) it in the forehead. This says 'you are kami-sama's child.'"

What these stories seem to suggest, particularly in the case of the noro (narrative 1), is an effort to fit rather typical life experiences into a cultural pattern of illness as the sign of divine activity. The priestess is not more sick than other people; rather, she orally, publicly, and repeatedly interprets her illness as the priestess pedigree. As the noro explained when I asked her why someone has to get sick in order to be kaminchu: "Kami-sama uses illness to let you know." In this highly empirical society, it makes good sense for spiritual processes to take place visibly in the body. This does not, however, negate the cosmic function of illness—to weaken or open the woman's body in order to facilitate fusion with kami-sama. The physicality of the preinitiation process—the bleeding and the weakness—is necessary for disembodied kami-sama to become embodied in the body of the priestess.

Objects, Souls, Ancestors, Building Materials, and Prietesses Out of Place

The prominence of illness in the priestesses' narratives leads us to take a closer look at the meaning of illness in Henza discourse in general. In chapter 1, I explained that Henza culture does not devote much attention to the etiology of illness. Regular illnesses are understood in a rather yasashii way—neither sorcery nor any other compelling theory of illness is elaborated to explain what villagers call "real" illness. The symptoms described by the priestesses in their narratives are not, in the village view, real illness. This second category of symptoms—not "real" illness—is what I refer to as divine dis-order. The experiencing of physical symptoms on the path to sitting the priestess position is interpreted in Henza as a sign that the priestess-to-be is not situated in the seat she is meant to occupy. Although not invoked as an ideological or systematic cause of illness, a number of events and situations described to me by villagers suggest that, as in the case of the priestess-to-be, illness is sometimes precipitated as a result of a person, spirit, or object being out of place, by a kind of cosmic or spiritual dis-order.

In Henza, one often sees a few blades of grass twisted and tied into a knot. These ritual items are called *san*, or *sai*. In the old days, the sai marked the boundaries of fields. Today it is used for carrying food from place to place; the sai marks off the food as belonging to the one who is carrying it so that no one (human or spirit) will take the food. The sai is the most prevalent ritual object in Henza, and, according to villagers, possibly the most ancient. The widespread use of the sai expresses on the one hand a concern with keeping things in their proper place and on the other hand an assumption that a few twisted blades of grass are sufficient for the task.

Villagers tell a number of stories that describe illness as a result of someone taking a ritual item that does not rightfully belong to him or her. One example concerns the official necklace worn by the noro. Apparently, the necklace was once taken by some researchers, who became ill until they returned it. A second story concerns the theft of an incense bowl belonging to one of the kami-sama (Takimori) of a certain clan. Here is how a clan member tells the story:

> That person [the one who stole the bowl] said [to the rightful owner], "We are not going to give it to someone poor like you!" And then someone in the house of the person who took it died, so they brought the Takimori bowl back, but the person who had owned it before said "I don't want it," and so the ones who stole it came twice to apologize and give it back, but they [the rightful owners] said "No, you stole it from me, I don't want it." And then the one who stole it was sick day and night. And the third time they came to return it, they forgave them and took it back. After they returned the Takimori bowl, the ones who were sick in the clan got better. There was a crazy person in that clan, and that person was cured, and now is working.[6]

A spiritual item that sometimes comes out of place is a dead person's soul. Although this was not spoken about very often by villagers, one of the shaman-type practitioners explained that, "when people come to me, if they are sick, I say to go to the doctor.[7] If it is not sickness, if some dead person's soul came into the person, then I can cure. [How do you cure?] I just pray. I take the family's history, and then pray for that. I correct the troubles in the family's history by praying."

A living person's soul can also become misplaced. Okinawans recognize a condition called *mabuya*. One informant explains, "For example, I caught a cold and there was something funny about it. If there is a bad thing with you, you take a yuta [shaman] with you. If the yuta comes, she says, 'This person's soul fell off, detached.' And then you call your own mabuya [soul]." Because the illness was

caused by the soul leaving its proper place, the yuta's cure was effected by returning it to its place.

One of the more common causes of illness in Henza is an ancestor being in the
wrong place. Diagnosing these kinds of problems is the job of the yuta. The yuta
may find that troubles are being caused by an ancestor who was buried in the
wrong tomb. For example, one family in the village was having problems because,
according to the yuta, a daughter in that family had been married but was unable
to have children. She had agreed to divorce her husband so that he could marry a
fertile woman, which he did. The first wife died and was buried in the tomb belonging to her father's family. However, the yuta discovered that she should have been
buried in the tomb of her husband's family, because by divorcing him she had
facilitated his having children, and therefore the children could be considered
hers. The *yuta's* prescription was to rebury the woman in her husband's tomb. The
family's problems, then, were not caused by any inherent evil on the part of the
dead woman (or anyone else), but rather by her mistakenly having been buried in
the wrong place: "I cleared this *munchu* [sorted out the ancestral altars of this
clan] and now doctors and other important people are in this *munchu*. When I first
came to this *munchu* things were very confused, they prayed in different houses.
Everything was a mess."

Another way in which an ancestor can be in the wrong place is for his or her
ancestral accoutrements (incense bowl placed on the altar) to be located in the
wrong house. This can easily happen in families in which there is no eldest son to
inherit the butsudan. In cases like these, another son or nephew will take care of
the butsudan, but often, the yuta finds, the wrong person has received the butsudan. The yuta will then prescribe moving the incense bowl to another house.

Six distinct rituals are performed during the process of building a house. The
first involves checking with a yuta to make sure that the house is clear of malevo-
lent influences and that this year is an auspicious one for the family to build. The
second, usually led by an ogami (praying person), is done at the beginning of the
building. This prayer announces that the building will begin soon, that stray spirits
should go away, and that the family is building a new house for a good reason (for
example, their current house is too old). Part of the way through the building, the
chief carpenter conducts a small ritual when the roof is raised. When the building
is finished, the ogami person returns and prays at the corners of the property. Her
prayer goes something like this: "*Oharai kudasai* [go away please]. Lumber spirit,
tree spirit, metal spirit, cement spirit, sand spirit—go out of the house!" The ogami
person will come back a few days later, on an auspicious day, to help transfer the
hinu-kan from the old house to the new. Finally, at the conclusion of the building,
the village priestesses come for a full-day ritual called yanusuji (see chapter 6). The
chief priestess (noro) explains that this ritual is "to ask for health for the family."

The elaborate house-building ritual sequence is particularly conspicuous in
light of the minimal ritualization at most other life events. Birth is surrounded by
very few rituals, there is no traditional rite of passage or coming-of-age ritual, traditional marriages did not involve ritual (I was told that "we did not have weddings
in the old days"—this means that there was no distinct marriage ceremony). Although villagers do not explain why house building is so heavily ritualized, my

sense is that this ritualization is important because building a house involves shifting things around. In building a house, it is impossible to avoid causing things to, at least temporarily, be out of their proper places. Almost all of the house building rituals address the theme of spirits (of the building lot, the building materials), ancestors (the butsudan), or a kami-sama (such as the hearth deity) moving around. Building a house is a good thing; living in a house is a good thing; the materials that go into building a house are good. But the process of building inevitably causes objects, people, spirits, and ancestors to relocate. In a world that is naturally good and harmonious, stirring things up can lead to trouble.

Perhaps the most ritually elaborated understanding of illness is that it comes to Henza Island from the ocean or from over the ocean in boats. An annual ceremony called "beach prayer"—*hama ogami*—is performed at the end of the winter season by the priestesses and headman in order to protect the island from foreign invasion of illness. In the course of the day-long ritual, the headman constructs string arches attached to two poles at seven sites along the beach, and the priestesses pray. The headman explains that it is his job "to protect the people in the village and represent the people in the village. Hama ogami is: sickness and weakness shouldn't come to Henza, [the arches are] to keep them away at the beach, because Henza is an isolated island." The image here is that illness comes seasonally from outside of Henza Island. Illness is not inherent in the human body or even in the social body; it is an intruder of some kind, and through ritual it can be stopped. Whether the disease-carrying boats are real (it may be that at some time in history at certain seasons of the year foreign sailors bearing smallpox or other contagious illnesses indeed landed on Henza's shore) or whether they are some sort of negative spiritual entity (the ocean, under the ocean, and beyond the ocean are all sometimes considered to be the home base of kami) is not particularly relevant here (and did not seem to be relevant to those who carried out the ritual in 1995). What is relevant is the perception of illness as something exceptional and foreign, as something outside of normal Henza experience, something not "natural," and something vague—unknown and unnamed.

The underlying message in hama ogami is not that disease is something bad that should be destroyed but that disease is something that has come to a place where it does not belong. The ritual expression of this concern is oharai ("get out" or "go away") rituals. The things (usually spirit or kami) that are sent away in oharai can be good, bad, or neutral, but when they get out of place or when they intrude on others, they cause trouble—such as illness—for those around them. Health and illness, in other words, are expressions of social relationships, and not, as we might at first assume, physical characteristics.

The problem of things being out of place sounds familiar to those acquainted with Mary Douglas's (1966) notion that "matter out of place" tends to be culturally defined as pollution. Yet in the Okinawan case, it should be clarified, the "out of place" item does not cause social isolation or stigma; pollution beliefs do not exist. Henza villagers generally experience their world as a pleasant and yasashii place. Because people, spirits, and things are normally in or near places that allow their world to be a harmonious and healthy whole, there is little need for structures, institutions, ideologies, or punishments to keep people, spirits, or things in line (as we saw above, the sai—a few blades of grass—is sufficient). Villagers, like physicists, understand that change (entropy) is part of the nature of the universe and that without change there can be no growth: Birth, marriage, planting and harvest, initiation of priestesses, and building a new house all involve change, all involve things moving and shifting out of place. Even death—the ultimate change—is not understood to be intrinsically bad. When family members die, they become ancestors who look after their descendants and who, in turn, are looked after by them. Villagers explicitly say that they are not afraid to die. In general, change is experienced as something positive in Henza: I rarely heard villagers express nostalgia for the "good old days"; I was often told that life is better now, and, as I pointed out in chapter 2, there are few stories or legends that tell of an idealized past. Divine dis-order opens up cracks that allow change in an otherwise balanced society; being out of place is not intrinsically bad (although but it does need to be dealt with ritually). Indeed, as I discuss in chapter 12, too much order or structure also is experienced as problematic and also is dealt with ritually. These two themes—order and dis-order—appear in a variety of guises and intertwined with a variety of other foci in Henza religion.

This somewhat lengthy discussion of the concept of "out of place" is crucial to interpreting the priestesses' narratives. As I explained in the previous chapter, one of the most common terms to denote priestesses is "those who sit the position." The position in which priestesses sit is of cosmic importance; a particular kami-sama can only be associated with one particular priestess who sits at that kami-sama's altar and at that kami-sama's place in the sacred grove. The woman who has not yet understood that she should "sit the position" is literally sitting in the wrong place. The priestess-to-be has not recognized her true nature, and her spiritual absence causes cosmic imbalance; illness is the physical manifestation of her being existentially out of place.

Similar problems plague people who erroneously sit in the priestess role. According to one informant, "Young people sometimes say that because of sickness I will become kaminchu, but they die not reaching sixty-one years old. Someone might want to do it, but the *handan* [yuta's divination or judgment] says you cannot do it. And there are many who died." Another informant explains, "[The kaminchu role] if it is really given by kami-sama it is okay. If someone becomes kaminchu by mistake it is dangerous. The person's life will be taken." Mrs. Adaniya explains it a bit more graphically:

If your spirit [*seishin*] is bad you cannot be kaminchu. Kami-sama won't let you, won't give you permission. If you are captured by kami-sama for kami-sama's job you can't run away from it. Even if you want to quit, you can't. I started from seven or eight years old. Sometimes if you are a human being there are bad times, you have to do things that you don't like to do. You don't want to do it sometimes. I was grabbed by the hand by kami-sama. You can't pull away. But, those people who kami-sama isn't holding them, the ones who aren't supposed to be there, if those people sit there [as kaminchu], they will get kami-sama's fist. Those people who are not held by kami-sama, but say that I am the one who sits the kami-sama's seat, they will get the fist.

Another way in which a priestess can become misplaced is by sitting as kaminchu in the wrong clan. One story of this sort concerns a woman who first was told by yuta to sit as priestess in her husband's *munchu*, but she continued to get sick. After a year or so, "Another yuta told me that I am in the wrong place and to go away as quickly as possible. So now I don't do the kaminchu job, I just go to my father's father's place to pray for them. I was told you should go to your parent's parent's parent's, who gives birth to you. I thought maybe that is right. And after that I was healthier."

According to one clan kaminchu:

> To be kaminchu is given by kami-sama, that is, it is not a matter of someone being interested, it comes from kami-sama. One of my relatives, a husband and wife, came and sat in my place, the kaminchu place. Then the woman went suddenly crazy, when she was in her forties. And now she lives alone somewhere. Because she sat in a place that she is not supposed to be. You cannot sit where you want to, it is given by kami-sama. This woman tried to do it, and went crazy. You have to be given by kami-sama. And sometimes if someone sits in the wrong place they die soon after. It is not easy to become kaminchu. Even though I had been sick, my mother kept saying wait, wait take time, make sure that is really where the kami-sama wants you to sit.[8]

Illness is both a sign to become a kaminchu and a sign of sitting as a kaminchu when one is not really meant to do so. Illness, in other words, signifies cosmic misplacement or imbalance. The word used in Okinawa for the illnesses suffered by priestesses on their way to sitting the position is *kamidaari*, which is usually translated as 'possession illness' in English-language ethnographies. I propose, however, that a better translation for kamidaari is "divine dis-order"—the dis-ordering necessary for an individual to recognize her own divinity. Divine dis-order, then, is not bad; rather, it is a space in which change can happen; it is a necessary step on the path to sitting in the kami-sama's seat.

EIGHT

Born to Be Kami-sama

Initiation into the priestess role does not include either formal or informal instruction regarding ritual tasks; the essence of the priestess role is presence rather than doing. Initiation—or more properly, accession—is therefore concerned primarily with the process through which a woman recognizes, assumes, experiences, and becomes kami-sama. During the time that I was in Henza, a new village priestess, Mrs. Hamabata, began to sit in the kami-sama's seat. In this chapter I describe the process in detail.[1]

Mrs. Hamabata's Story

I spoke to Mrs. Hamabata for the first time in February, shortly after a ritual to inform the kami-sama that she will begin to sit as a priestess in May. The events that she describes in this first excerpt took place over a period of about twenty years.

SUSAN: How did you become kaminchu?

MRS. HAMABATA: A few decades ago I got sick. My legs. A couple of times I went to buy [sic] handan [judgments] from yuta, like at New Year's. That is our custom, to go to the yuta's house to buy handan for the family's health. Every New Year's I go, around February. They told me that there is some sickness in my legs but also my legs were slow [she seems to mean that her legs were slow taking her to the kaminchu "seat"].

SUSAN: Which yuta?

MRS. HAMABATA: Henza yuta, and also elsewhere several yutas.

SUSAN: Who went with you to the yuta?

MRS. HAMABATA: The old ladies who have since passed away.

SUSAN: Did your mother go?

MRS. HAMABATA: My husband's mother, also my mother. We used to go often. My legs were hurting, arthritis. I went to see the doctor, and they had so many records on me at the hospital, I went every month and they couldn't find anything, an examination of the whole body and they couldn't find anything. One hospital, Awase Hospital, I went there from when they first opened the hospital. It was so strange that I felt so bad, but they said there was nothing wrong

161

with me. Then the parents died and we moved into this house. We have been in Henza for seven years. Before that we lived in Naha.

SUSAN: How did you manage the housework?

MRS. HAMABATA: I did it. My husband and I both worked [outside the home]. I worked for thirty or thirty-five years. This past twenty, fifteen, ten years I have been sick frequently. All the time I was told that the *kami* made it happen, *kami no michi* [the kami's way or path]. My body was weak.

SUSAN: Was this kamidaari?

MRS. HAMABATA: Yes. The last ten years were the worst. After I moved to Henza, the man who pounds the *mochi* [sticky rice] was following me all the time, and he told me, "Do you know what type of birth you are?" The owner of the place that makes the mochi is the one who said this. This was Jana clan's head of the house. The man from my clan. The one responsible for the clan. He kept saying to me, "Do you know what kind of rank you are? You need to go into kami-sama's way. If something bad happens [because of your refusing the job], what will you do?" All the time, he kept telling me this. Unfortunately, my husband's mother and father died early. And now my mother died, and my grandfather, and then the deaths continued.

SUSAN: Did other clan people agree for you to become kaminchu?

MRS. HAMABATA: Yes they did. From that time I should have listened to what he said to me. I was so scared of everything to do with kami-sama's way. I was so quiet for a long time.

SUSAN: Did you have a feeling that you would be kaminchu some day?

MRS. HAMABATA: Yes. I feel like I should have done it ten years ago. Last June I had a big heart sickness. They took me in an ambulance to the hospital. I didn't pass the [doctors'] examination. The relatives, all the women, said to me that when you get sick, there is half sickness and half yuta [business]. You must try to go to yuta's house also to ask. The yuta lit incense on the altar. I took my brother's wife with me to see the yuta, and she [the yuta] banged the table and she said, "You helped your husband be successful, and your children all grew up fine, why are you so late to take the kami-sama's way?" These things were said by the kami-sama, passing through the yuta. This reprimand was given by kami-sama to me. "You have to go into the kami-sama's belief."

In this narrative, as in those in chapter 7, the dominant theme is of refusal to take up the role until harassed beyond endurance both by illness and by the [male] clan member. The priestess narrating her tale clarifies for us that she has not broken with any social norms of women's role expectations: The yuta has told her that she has been a good wife and mother, and that now that her children are grown it is appropriate for her to move into the priestess position. According to Mrs. Hamabata:

Step by step I came to this. It is not that from the beginning that I wanted to be kaminchu. This is the judgment that I got from yuta, so please understand. . . . That is why people say to buy seven handan [judgments]. And don't hurry to go into kami-sama's path [*kami no michi*], [rather] to think slowly and calmly, and sometimes you lose your life. In my case it took me twenty years. [You went to many yutas, so how did you make the final decision?] Last year, November. There is a yuta, Mrs. Uyealtari Husae, she lives right over there. She came to my house often and told me things she heard from the kami-sama. One time when I was sick in the hospital, Mrs. Uyealtari happened to go to Irigusuku [sacred grove] and she saw me with the white clothes on. Mrs. Uyealtari told me that I must think very hard about becoming kaminchu, because she saw me in the white clothes. [Did the kami-sama tell you directly?] Yes. *I dreamt of myself giving birth to a baby.* It was shown two or three times by kami-sama. If you dream that type of dream it is correct for you to be kaminchu. Other people told me that is the right dream to dream to become kaminchu. It was told by my clan's people that every time they pray, something about me comes up, so I must be the one. Now I have become this old, the time is up [so I must do it]. I said to myself, "Am I going to take my life or take the kami-sama's way? Do I have to suffer this sickness for the rest of my life? Is there any way I can cure this sickness?" That is what I asked Mrs. Uyealtari. The Takimori kami-sama [the kami-sama that Mrs. Hamabata now represents or is assimilated with] appeared in a dream at night. The kami-sama's hair was arranged in a bun and she was beautiful. I didn't see this for long, just for a second. I didn't know what that meant, so I went to see Mrs. Uyealtari. Mrs. Uyealtari also had heard from kami-sama that at the kami-ya there is a big party with drinking sake. That was a party for a baby girl who was born, and that baby girl was me. And the baby girl's face turned into my face. *So I didn't become kaminchu, I was born to be kaminchu.*" (my emphases)

Following the yuta's judgments and these spiritual encounters, Mrs. Hamabata's case was discussed in her clan, and all agreed that she was to be a clan kaminchu. In February, Mrs. Hamabata and her sister-in-law met at the kami-ya with the noro and another village priestess. According to the noro, "Today we just come here to say that she will do the [accession] celebration in May. This is an announcement prayer [*anai no negai*]. And to be healthy. This time is like registration,[2] reporting that she will become a new kaminchu." After a short prayer, the four women shared a ritual meal brought by Mrs. Hamabata. Afterwards, Mrs. Hamabata made a point of going up to the noro, bowing very low, and in a polite and quiet voice thanking her several times.

Over the next few months, Mrs. Hamabata was busy with a round of visiting relatives in the clan. According to Mrs. Hamabata (in retrospect):

Maybe that also gave me some *chikara* [power or strength][3]. . . . Each clan has places that they have to go to pray. I went to those places. That gave me [spiritual] power. I prayed at those places, that I will be kaminchu in May so please take care of me. I live in Henza at such and such address, and my husband is named such and such and my children. I went greeting and visiting the brothers and sisters of the clan kami-sama. Mrs. Uyealtari taught me those things. That gave me [spiritual] power. She told me why to go to Naki-jin and the other places, five different places. You have to have basic knowl-edge, and that gives you inner strength.

During conversations before the accession ceremony, Mrs. Hamabata reiterated that:

I don't know anything. I just started praying in the clan six months ago, and only on the first and fifteenth of each month, so I don't know much. For those things [about kami-sama] I like to look for materials [about my clan's history] to study. I come without that knowledge. I don't know why my clan came [to Henza Island], or why I have to pray here or there. I am just start-ing to learn these things, please give me time. I was just starting and I got sick in my heart, and was taken by ambulance to Chubo Hospital, and was sick for about a year. So I didn't have any time to study those things. I would like to call the village headman to get my clan's origins in the village records, so I can study this. I like to know things from the foundation. I have to know why I was given this role. Just because you are born [kaminchu], to just sit there and do what you are told, that is not the way it should be. To sit the po-sition, you should know why things are like this. That is the very meaning of my role, to know what role I am. That could be my own idea, but it is what I think.

A few weeks before the actual accession ceremony, white robes were sewn for Mrs. Hamabata. On an auspicious day according to the Chinese lunar calendar, women of her clan gathered at the clan house. Because the clothes must be sewn in one day, Mrs. Hamabata invited a professional seamstress to help with the parts that can be sewn on a machine while clanswomen sewed additional parts by hand. Before they began sewing they prayed, "We report to the kami-sama that we are go-ing to make the clothes today." The robes have to be sewn in a particular manner. "The one who starts cutting the material has to have been born in the year of the mouse. Also you have to consider the tides. You have to make it within the day. Long kimono, and bottom part and shirt. Underwear, and headband."

The final preaccession ritual is a prayer in which the previous kaminchu who had sat the position is asked to move on so that Mrs. Hamabata can take her place.

What I have to do before [beginning to sit the priestess position] is kami kuyo. [I say] "Please go peacefully to the other world so I can do this job."[4] For the person who was sitting in that position before me. I went to temple[5] to do the kuyo. To make it simple, clear. Like when you do joseki [cancellation of resi-dent's registration at the town hall], I went to do joseki for the previous kam-inchu. I went to different places to do this. The house where the previous one lived, the place where she died, I went to pray that, "I am going to do this af-ter you." The places where the previous one prayed. I went to each place where she used to pray, to do the joseki. Two days before the celebration it was shown to me that the time is ripe. I already told my husband. In the early morning I saw in a dream the noro's land, my husband was digging a hole under a tree. It was this big and many fruit came out. Ripe fruit. Lots and lots. I said, "Oh what a nice dream I had," and I thanked the kami-sama. This was at the noro's land over there [a few blocks away].

The Big Day

On the morning of May 15, Mrs. Hamabata, her sister-in-law (who served as her handmaid during the ceremonial process), and other village kaminchu gathered at the kami-ya. Several women, including the noro and Mrs. Hamabata, were wearing beautiful kimonos. All of the women had on nice clothes. Mrs. Hamabata was nervous and shy, asking people where she should sit and what she should do. She formally greeted each kaminchu with a deep bow and polite words, "How do you do?" The noro lit incense, and the kaminchu prayed and passed around a ritual cup of sake.

We boarded a bus provided by the town hall and were let off at the beginning of the trail up to the utaki. Half way up the jungle trail, at the usual place to don the white robes, the women stopped. Mrs. Hamabata was nervous and strained, did not know how to put on her clothes, and acted in a conspicuously helpless manner. Putting on the white robes was unusually time-consuming.

We walked on to the benches where the clan kaminchu sit when they go to the utaki. The noro and Mr. Shibahiki continued further in to the hinu-kan, where they poured sake and where the noro announced that Mrs. Hamabata is becoming kaminchu. While the noro prayed, Mrs. Hamabata wandered over, not seeming to know if she should be there or not, and when she saw the noro praying she knelt down in the mud, dirtying her white robes. The noro had to tell her to squat, not kneel, so as not to dirty her white kimono. Upon returning to the benches, she was shown how to make the crown of leaves worn by priestesses. Following some discussion of where Mrs. Hamabata should sit, the kaminchu prayed and passed around a cup of sake.

Mrs. Hamabata had brought with her a cup of beaten egg white. This egg white must be carried in a red cup borrowed from the noro's house. The noro put a dot of the egg white on Mrs. Hamabata's forehead, and then the other kaminchu reminded her to also put egg white on each cheek, right cheek first.[6] The kaminchu said to Mrs. Hamabata, "*Gambatte kudasai* [stand firm, hang in there]." She thanked them and asked them to please teach her, and they left the utaki. After a short hike up to Agaregusuku (the east sacred grove), the women returned to the village.

Arriving in the village square, the kaminchu were met by fifty or so clanswomen and other villagers who had spread out mats on the ground. Mrs. Hamabata's husband and one or two men stood on the edges, looking a bit uncomfortable. During the next hour, important people in Mrs. Hamabata's clan sat across from her and poured sake for her, after which she poured sake for them.[7] Then her husband poured, and people laughed and clapped and made jokes about this being a wedding ceremony.[8] Mrs. Hamabata was the center of attention, and her manner was shy, befitting a bride or young woman. She then rose and poured sake for the noro, kaminchu, and Mr. Shibahiki. Finally, men of her clan went around pouring large amounts of sake for everyone present. At the end there was a short informal prayer, and the kaminchu disrobed and hung their crowns from the nails in the village square.

In the meantime, a young clanswoman had set up food inside the kami-ya. Everyone filed into the kami-ya to look at the large quantities of food, gifts, and sake piled in front of the altar. This was provided by the clan. The noro prayed and poured sake on the hinu-kan, Mr. Shibahiki lit incense, and more sake was poured and passed around. Because the kami-ya was too crowded, mats were spread out on the porch. The noro and her associates stayed inside to eat, and everyone else sat outside and snacked. After another short prayer, each of the village priestesses was given a lovely box of cakes and a bag for leftovers.

The clanspeople—about twenty-three women and seven men—then moved on to their clan house, where the clan bookkeeper collected 200 yen per person for to-day's celebration, and a young clan woman served tea. They waited expectantly for Mrs. Hamabata, who had gone home to change from the Okinawan-style ki-mono she had been wearing earlier to a gorgeous Japanese kimono. When she ar-rived at the clan house, there was applause. The kaminchu of Mrs. Hamabata's clan prayed at the hinu-kan, then everyone prayed while the clan kaminchu knelt in front of the room, each in front of her own altar. Mrs. Hamabata cried a bit and bowed to everyone. Clan members cried out, "Gambatte kudasai (stand firm, hang in there)" and "Congratulations." Clansmen then poured sake for Mrs. Hamabata and for the other clan kaminchu, and the women reciprocated, pouring sake for the men. Cups of sake were continuously passed around the room.

Seaweed, fish, tofu, and tempura cooked by Mrs. Hamabata (and very tasty!) was served. Following the meal, several clan members performed with samisen, koto, and taiko (musical instruments), and everyone enthusiastically sang along. A distinguished clan member stood up and made a speech thanking the musicians and the kaminchu. People asked for kachashi (lively Okinawan dance) music, and a tape was found. Everyone danced enthusiastically, most making an effort to dance at least a minute with Mrs. Hamabata. After a few hours of celebrating, each clan kaminchu went to her altar to clean it up and take the food and gifts that had been placed on it. The clan members then dispersed.

It Comes Naturally

The day after the initiation, I visited Mrs. Hamabata. Her living room was still in disarray from a party that she had hosted the previous evening for a smaller group of family and friends. Her two kimonos were hanging up on display. Several women friends and relatives were in the house helping her clean up.

The change in Mrs. Hamabata was striking. The day after the initiation she was far more self-confident and spoke in a louder voice. Unlike in previous conversa-tions in which she answered many questions with "I don't know," she now gave authoritative-sounding answers to every question I asked.

SUSAN: Tell me about yesterday's ceremony.

MRS. HAMABATA: [gestures to the top of her head with her finger.]

SUSAN: The kami-sama went into your head yesterday?

MRS. HAMABATA: Yes.

SUSAN: How did it feel?

MRS. HAMABATA: I feel that each person has a *shugo-shin* [one's own guardian "god"], I felt that I have shugo-shin.

SUSAN: What did you feel at the moment of the ceremony?

MRS. HAMABATA: Spirit [*rei*] being stuck to me, like spirit covering me. My body and head were kind of floating.

SUSAN: Is the world lighter today than it was before your ceremony?

MRS. HAMABATA: Yes, very. I am in perfect health. I told my husband today. I went to the utaki yesterday and it was raining and I sat with my knees bent. Usually that would make me be sick and sleep the next day. But not today! Look, the kami-sama is protecting me. I really appreciate it. Later today I will pray at the hinu-kan "Thank you that everything went smoothly yesterday."

SUSAN: When you become kaminchu does your behavior change?

MRS. HAMABATA: Yes, there must be some change. Like how you dress, you must be careful, so that other people will make comments like "Oh yes, she must be the one!" In your personal life you must change. You must do the kami-sama's way things, and pray at the ancestral altar. There is some change. In my family, even my husband will make a small change.

SUSAN: Do you have to learn special prayers and things now that you are kaminchu?

MRS. HAMABATA: *It is not that you must learn these things, it comes naturally. If you sit in the position, the kami-sama will tell you, you don't need to study it.* (my emphasis)

Mrs. Hamabata's final comment is crucial. Recall that before her initiation she had stressed that she did not know anything, that she needed to study, that she wanted to ask the village headman for historical records of her clan.[9] Now, as a priestess, she has come to a truer understanding of the meaning of the role. She does not need to study from external sources; the source of knowledge is now inside of her.

That the kaminchu's ability to pray comes naturally is the predominant opinion in Henza. For example, according to Mrs. Shimojo, "If you sit there [in the kaminchu position], you learn what type of prayers. It comes naturally." Mrs. Adaniya explained a bit more, "I wear the kami-sama clothes on top of my own clothes. If you wear kami-sama clothes and sit there you naturally know what to say. I sit there and light incense and say that 'Today is . . .' and then the prayer naturally comes. It keeps coming. Smoothly." As outsiders, we can see of course that the new priestess had models from whom to learn at least some aspects of the role; someone taught her how to make and tie the white clothes, and she saw other priestesses praying and performing rituals. The point is the cosmological stance expressed in these remarks. Because the priestess becomes kami-sama, she now "knows"; the necessary information comes together with her new identity; she does not have to be taught.

Mrs. Ishikawa, the most veteran kaminchu in Henza today, has clear memories of *not* learning from the previous noro:

> I was seventeen and she was about sixty. If she had taught me things at that time I could have learned, but she didn't. For example, the new-house song, the noro would say, you have to have your own sense to get it, from listening. She didn't teach it. That is why I couldn't remember things. [Isn't that a rare ritual?] Yes, sometimes once a year, sometimes not. She didn't teach me anything at all.

Several villagers compared the natural knowledge of kaminchu to the learned knowledge of Buddhist or Christian priests.

> Nowadays kaminchu have a strong heart. Christians are weaker. Okinawan kaminchu don't have a training period. Neither before nor after becoming kaminchu is there training, it is just your own. Buddhist priests have training and learn how to say things. Okinawan kaminchu, no one teaches you what to say, it is from you. (a former kaminchu)

Because the kaminchu's praying comes naturally, having to make an effort to pray is a sign that one is not really kaminchu. This differs radically from mediums in many societies—including mainland Japan—who not only go through an arduous and painful period of harsh purification practices prior to their initiation but who also are expected to behave in a strange, inhuman, or violent manner when in trance (Blacker 1975). In contrast, here is how one Henza villager answered my question regarding situations in which the wrong person mistakenly becomes kaminchu:

> It happened in Nakada clan, in my clan. A woman said that she was told by yuta that she is Nakada clan's kaminchu. But the way she prayed was different from how other people prayed. She said, "I am Nakada clan's kaminchu," but the way she prayed was different. And other people said the yuta maybe made a mistake. Her prayer was strange. People were saying like that. *She was putting an effort into praying, she was working hard at the praying.* And then she got sick. Because she got sick she went to see the yuta in Kadena. The yuta said she was not supposed to be a kaminchu in Nakada clan. She was supposed to be a yuta. That is what the Kadena yuta said. She went the wrong way. (Mr. Ginjo; my emphasis)

Although becoming kaminchu is a natural process, the kaminchu's accession takes place in a communal setting after her position has been validated by a series of *yuta* and by the entire clan. Becoming a priestess is embedded within a highly social framework. And so I close this section with a reference to the communal context of the accession ritual. Note that the reciprocal pouring of sake—as at weddings and other occasions—signifies the consolidation of social relationships (this is also true in Japan).

SUSAN: Why is so much sake poured by the clan at the celebration?

KAMINCHU: It means "gambatte kudasai." Please do your best for the clan. Because, for example, if you are driving a car, you ask Mrs. Hamabata to pray for no accidents for the clan, so that is why they say "gambatte kudasai."

SUSAN: Is there meaning to two people pouring sake for each other?

KAMINCHU: In this case, "gambatte kudasai." She pours sake back to say, "I will be careful of my health so that I can pray for your health, thank you for coming today." It goes both ways.

Born to Be Kaminchu

At the beginning of this chapter, I quoted Mrs. Hamabata saying that "I didn't become kaminchu, I was born to be kaminchu." This phrasing corresponds to the understanding that one does not learn or acquire kaminchu knowledge; rather, it comes naturally.

What I have been translating throughout this chapter as "initiation" is the Japanese word *umareru*—birth. In Henza, a new kaminchu is "born."[10] The initiation process encompasses and utilizes language and symbols of birth. As we saw earlier, Mrs. Hamabata dreamed that she gave birth to a baby. The yuta Mrs. Uyealtari saw in a vision a party at the kami-ya for a baby being born, and the baby was Mrs. Hamabata. Mrs. Hamabata's fruit-tree dream can also be seen in terms of birth and fertility symbolism.[11]

I asked several women to explain to me the meaning of the three white dots, the placing of which on Mrs. Hamabata's face seemed to be the focal point of the "birth" ceremony. According to one priestess, "In the past *miki* [rice paste] was used, rather than egg white. It is a new kaminchu is born. And so they say such and such a clan, and the year of her birth, in Mrs. Hamabata's case, rabbit. When Henza people have children, they go to the river on the east side and put water on the baby in this same way." Mrs. Hamabata explains the egg white a bit differently: "They stamp it in the forehead. This says 'you are the kami-sama's child.' It is inkan [stamp] from kami-sama. You are a server of kami-sama. That is why the stamp. . . . It has to be from a red cup." And according to another kaminchu: "It should be miki (rice paste), not egg white. 'You are a kami-sama now. You are kami-sama's child.' That is the meaning."

Given the context of explicit birth language, and the emphasis on bleeding and opening the body in the narratives discussed in chapter 7, we may guess that the egg white or miki symbolizes the lochia on babies when they are born and the red[12] cup in which the egg or miki is held symbolizes the birth canal. The dots on the new priestess's face are direct parallels to the ashes from the hinu-kan and the water from the sacred well that traditionally were put on a newborn's forehead.[13] After a kaminchu is born, she will hold a series of anniversary celebrations on certain subsequent years in the same way that villagers hold celebrations every twelve years counting from one's birth year.[14]

But what does it mean for a kaminchu to be born? In his classic study of shamanism, Mircea Eliade described the paradigmatic initiation process as one of death and rebirth: The initiate dies to his old self and is reborn a shaman (1958). In the Okinawan ritual, however, I could not find any indication, symbolism, language, or hint of the initiate's death preceding her rebirth.[15] I even directly asked several of the experienced kaminchu:

SUSAN: Before a new kaminchu is born does she "die"?

MRS. ISHIKAWA: The previous one in that job died about nine years ago. [She is referring to the kaminchu who sat in the position that Mrs. Hamabata is now sitting in.]

SUSAN: I mean, are there any death symbols before being born?

MRS. ISHIKAWA: As a human being Mrs. Hamabata is not dead, it is just that as a kaminchu she was born, it is added to her character.

SUSAN: Why do they say that new kaminchu is born?

MRS. SHIMOJO: *Umarekawari*.[16] The [previous] person who died, so that is why the new one is born.

MRS. JANA [the oldest kaminchu and a close friend of the previous noro]: They [kaminchu] wear their white robes when they die. Even though they die, there [in the next world] they are doing the same way [kaminchu job].

The image suggested by Mrs. Shimojo, Mrs. Ishikawa, and Mrs. Jana is one of continuity rather than of the rupture described by Eliade.[17]

Bruce Lincoln, in *Emerging from the Chrysalis: Studies in Rituals of Women's Initiation* (1981), argues that the classic anthropological morphology of rites of passage (separation from the former status, liminality, reincorporation into the group as a person with a new status; cf. Van Gennep 1960) does not seem to fit girls' initiations, in which typically there is no separation. Unlike in a boy's initiation, the girl does not "die" to her former state in order to be "reborn" in her new state. Although I am unconvinced by Lincoln's somewhat essentialist gender analysis, his work correctly suggests that van Gennep's three-stage initiation schema may not be as universal as anthropologists have tended to assume; rather, the patterns of specific initiation processes reflect and give shape to broader cosmological understandings in specific societies. As we have seen in earlier chapters, Henza culture does not reify dichotomous categorizations (such as human and divine, or birth and death). Consistent with this ethos, initiation into the priestess role is not a matter of dying to one state and being born into another or even of transformation from one unique ontological state to another.

The illness that precedes the acceptance of the priestess role is *not*, as I argued in chapter 7, transformative; it is merely a sign that one was already born to be kami-sama. Mrs. Hambata clearly explains, "I didn't become kaminchu, I was born to be kaminchu." Mrs. Hamabata is born without dying to replace the previous one, who is dead but, in fact, is still wearing the white and doing her job in the next world. Mrs. Shimojo explains that kaminchu hold a celebration every seven years, starting from the date they began to sit the position; even after they die, they continue doing the celebration—their clan provides the food and so on.

The theme of continuity is strongly suggested in the two dreams related successively by Mrs. Hamabata: She saw herself giving birth, and her spiritual guide, Mrs. Uyealtari, saw her (Mrs. Hamabata) being born. This imagery suggests a model in which, to be born as kami-sama, a priestess gives birth to herself. If that is indeed the case, then the source of kami-sama really was "there" all the time: The initiation process did not consist of the kaminchu dying and being re-born or acquiring something—authority, knowledge, status—from outside of herself but of her coming to understand the divinity already inside her.

The Process Continues

SUSAN: Do you feel healthier now that you made the decision to become kaminchu?

MRS. HAMABATA: Still some good and some bad. For about three more years I will still not be well, it will take three years for everything to be smooth, gradually I will feel better. That is why every day I pray at the hinu-kan. Also I put sake at the hinu-kan, because I am weak, so as soon as possible to give me health. When I pray I feel so clear.[18]

Mrs. Hamabata explained that the change in health status resultant to "sitting the position" is a gradual one; the new priestess gradually moves into her new state. As I argued in chapter 7, illness is a signal to the priestess-to-be, telling her that she must begin the journey of moving into "kami-hood." After three years (three is a transitional number in Okinawa; for example, a ceremony for the dead is performed after three years), when presumably she has learned some of the priestess's roles—when she has internalized the image of herself as kami-sama—the illness can be expected to abate.

Becoming a priestess is a protracted process. Many of the priestesses report that already in childhood someone (a parent, a yuta, a relative) told them that this is their intended role, but it was not until the age of thirty or so that they began to consult yuta. Then, the process of consulting yuta took several years: Not one but many yuta are consulted. Even once the decision is made and announced to the kami-sama, several months must pass before the new priestess can "wear the white." And finally, as Mrs. Hamabata explains, the priestess expects that it will take several years to fully enter her role. Several other priestesses who began to sit at an earlier age delayed their active ritual involvement until their children grew up. According to the priestess in narrative 2 in chapter 7, "In the kaminchu's case, if you pray to the kami-sama, 'I am still young and please wait for me,' if you pray this, the kami-sama will cure you." However, untoward delay in becoming active, even after initiation, can result in repeated illness episodes.

In Henza, the new priestess does not break away from or "die" to her old identity, and the transition from the death of the previous kaminchu to the birth of the new one is gradual. According to Mrs. Shimojo, "It cannot be right away. The next one is not born right away. Even though you are the one, you don't want to be it. That is why it takes some ten years [after the previous priestess who embodied a particular kami-sama died]. Some are still not born, more than twenty years. The earliest is five or six years." According to Japanese anthropologist Yoshinobu Ota, although an Okinawan woman receives a diagnosis from a yuta, "She does not become conscious of the working of *shiji* [spiritual power] until she reorganizes her past experiences through her interaction with other villagers. *Shiji* becomes real to the woman only in the process of her self-understanding of her own past" (1989: 115).

When I attended Mrs. Hamabata's accession, I was disappointed. I had mistakenly expected that the transformation from human to kami-sama would be spectacular, sensational. Instead, I found that the actual moment of the initiation (if one can even call the dotting of Mrs. Hamabata's face with egg white the "moment" of initiation) unexciting, anticlimactic. Becoming kami-sama is not a magical moment—no bolt of lightning strikes the initiate, and no particular person or group proclaims that from this moment forth she is now a priestess. The ritual at which white is dotted onto the priestess's face should be understood as one station on a very long road of "priestess-becoming."

Looking back, I now understand that there was no need for a spectacular ceremony, because Mrs. Hamabata was kami-sama even before the initiation—she had been born to be kami-sama. The initiation was a public acknowledgment that she now understands that she is kami-sama; it was not an existential change to another order of being. For many Westerners, the distinction between human and divine is absolute; natural and supernatural, holy and profane, god and mortal, and birth and death are among the most fundamental dichotomies that organize our conceptual universe. As I discussed in chapter 2, this is not the case in Okinawa. For residents of Henza, nothing much has to happen for a kaminchu to be born, for a woman to, in Mrs. Ishikawa's words, "add to her character" kami-sama.

I asked four priestesses what they mean when they say that they are kami-sama—are they "really" gods? I quote here the four answers.

MRS. HAMABATA (the new kami-sama): The clan's kaminchu is like the clan kami's servant. The way I understand it is that I am like a bridge between the clan and the kami-sama.

MRS. HOKAMA (the local singing expert and a veteran, although rather inactive, clan priestess): Kaminchu represent kami.

SUSAN: Kami-sama means both people and invisible kami, can you explain this?

MRS. HOKAMA: Yes. Kami-sama cannot be seen. Those people are noro.

SUSAN: Is noro really kami-sama?

MRS. HOKAMA: Noro is *dairi* [representative or agent] of kami-sama. At prayer time, the noro is the one who goes in front to do the *ogami* [prayer].

SUSAN: Are you yourself kami-sama?

MRS. SHIMOJO (an active priestess for over twenty years): No.

SUSAN: Are you the one who serves kami-sama?

MRS. SHIMOJO: Yes. I am the representative of the kami-sama. When I wear the white kimono I am the kami-sama's representative . . .

SUSAN: Does the kami-sama go with you to the utaki?

MRS. SHIMOJO: Yes! We come together [to the *utaki*]. . . .

SUSAN: Does the kami-sama talk to you?

MRS. SHIMOJO: It used to be that way.

SUSAN: Kaminchu are called kami-sama, are they really kami?

MRS. ISHIKAWA: (a priestess for approximately forty years): I think it is better to understand it that way.

These four explanations reveal priestesses growing into a fuller understanding of their role. Mrs. Hamabata, the new priestess, describes herself as a bridge to kami-sama and as kami-sama's servant; both images suggest ontological separation between her and kami-sama.[19] Mrs. Hokama, although she has been a priestess for almost twenty years, is not very active in the role. She explains that the priestess is not kami-sama but rather the representative of kami-sama, an image that suggests a higher degree of identification between the priestess and the kami-sama than do the images of bridge or servant. Mrs. Shimojo, a very active and experienced priestess, adds that she not only is the representative of the kami-sama but also that she brings the kami-sama with her to the utaki. Note that she does not carry a statue or symbol of the kami-sama; rather, the kami-sama is within her. Mrs. Shimojo remarks that her relationship with the kami-sama has changed; the kami-sama used to talk to her but not any more. This change suggests that whereas the kami-sama used to be separate from her and so able to talk to her (just as kami-sama and ancestors talk to shaman-type practitioners), she and kami-sama are now sufficiently assimilated that dialogue is no longer necessary or even possible. Finally, the most experienced priestess says that it is best to understand that she *is* kami-sama. The development is quite striking: from a servant to a representative to someone who sometimes carries the kami-sama within her to being kami-sama.

Both at the ideological and the practical levels, the priestess role is not learned—it comes naturally, slowly, gradually. The role is not a series of actions that one can be taught. It comes from within, it is a matter of being. Mrs. Ishikawa has had over forty years to grow into her role, she has come to the fullest under-standing of what it means to say that the priestess is kami-sama. But I would guess that her more mature understanding does not nullify the other understandings. The priestess is simultaneously the bridge and the one who walks on it, the servant and the one who is served, the one who is born and the one who gives birth, the one who prays and the one who is prayed to, the representative and the one she represents.

Mrs. Kamura, Henza's *noro*, wearing her ritual necklace.

Three priestesses, in ritual garb, sitting on the stone benches at the *utaki* (sacred grove). Mrs. Kamura, the *noro*, is in the middle; Mrs. Tomeko sits to her right.

Mr. Shibahiki (kneeling front) and Henza's headman (kneeling rear) offer sake to the priestesses in the town square upon the priestesses' return from the *utaki* during the *umachi* ritual.

Priestesses remove and fold ritual garb in the town square at the end of the *umachi* ritual.

"Initiation" of Mrs. Hamabata (seated). The *noro* is placing dots of beaten egg white on her forehead and cheeks.

Priestesses, homeowners, and kin dance at *yanusuji* (new house) ritual.

Nakada *munchu* (clan) at s*eimeisai* (ancestor memorial day) gathering next to clan tombs on the far side of Henza Island. Mrs. Shinzato is seated on the right, holding a "San-A" bag.

Kawakami *munchu* (clan) gathering at clan house during a new year's ritual. Mrs. Adaniya is seated at the head of the table, in front of her altar.

Women sing and drum at the thirty-third anniversary of the death of Mrs. Okuda's husband. Mrs. Hokama sits second from left.

West side of town's *san gatsu* gathering. Mr. Shibahiki seated left, facing forward.

Mrs. Okuda holds a sharp spear to ritually stab fish at the central *san gatsu* ceremony held in the middle of Henza's main street.

Tug-of-war (*tsuna-hiki*).

Fitting the two *tsuna-hiki* ropes together.

Children in Henza's nursery school perform traditional Okinawan dancing and drumming at the school Christmas party. Author's son second from left.

PART IV

QUESTIONS OF POWER

NINE

The Problematics of Power

MRS. ISHIKAWA: In regular life kaminchu and other people are the same, but when it comes to *ogami* [prayer] they are different.

SUSAN: Do kaminchu behave differently from other people?

MRS. ISHIKAWA: No. Only at ogami time is there a difference.

————

FORMER KAMINCHU: When I am at clan rituals, I am the clan kaminchu, but when I go home I am just a regular person.

————

MRS. SHIMOJO: Woman who are kaminchu will not try to be over men. Being kaminchu does not give her power over men.

Power-Over and Power-From-Within

Cross-culturally, religion and religious leadership tend to be associated with or presented as manifestations of power over nature and power over people. Ceremonies that induce the soil to produce more crops or that induce the body to behave according to God's law rather than according to "natural instinct" are classic religious expressions of power over nature. Rituals of power over people include initiation ceremonies that sacralize the authority elders hold over initiates (cf. Bledsoe 1980), witchcraft accusations against individuals or groups who do not live exactly as religious authorities decree, and wedding ceremonies in which a man or his family's ownership of a woman's reproductive resources is legitimated. Religious control over people or nature by God, religion, or law often is made explicit: A prime example is the Buddhist aspiration to escape from the physical and emotional bonds that tie the soul to this world and its inhabitants (bonds which—perhaps not surprisingly—are believed to be stronger for women than for men; cf. Kirsch 1985 on Thailand).

Power over people and power over nature tend to coincide in male-dominated religions. Sherry Ortner, in her now-classic 1974 essay "Is Female to Male as Nature is to Culture?" argued that human culture is constituted through defining itself in opposition to nature—nature is, by cultural definition, what is not culture. According to Ortner, nature and culture not only stand in binary opposition to one another, they also stand in a conceptual relationship of hierarchy: Culture is seen as superior to nature because it is understood to be what conquers nature. Ortner further suggested that in many if not all human societies, women—because of childbirth and child rearing—are perceived as more associated with nature and therefore inferior to men and culture. In her recent writings, Ortner has clarified this argument, underscoring the importance of religion in the patriarchal enterprise.

> The logic that de Beauvoir first put her finger on—that men get to be in the business of trying to transcend species-being [making culture], while women, seen as mired in species-being [nature], tend to drag men down— still seems to me enormously widespread, and hardly an invention of "Western culture." From a range of tribal societies with male-only rituals and practices that would be spoiled by women's gaze, to so-called high religions, both Western and non-Western, that exclude women from their higher practices, the basic logic shows up. (1996: 180)

Religion is an especially effective and widespread tool for asserting that the power of culture over nature—and of men over women—is necessary, good, and right. By positing a source of authority that is outside of nature, *supernatural*, religion can legitimize and sacralize human domination of nature and male domination of women.[1]

In many societies, a role of religious leaders is to teach, encourage, or force the laity to behave in compliance with what is culturally understood to be supernatural law or wish. The leader, whether shaman, priest, minister, or rabbi, becomes the arbiter of divine decree. The leader possesses knowledge of what God wants, and the leader has the socially recognized authority to construct society in accordance with God's rule. The religious leader is the embodied model of domination: Just like culture dominates nature and men dominate women, God dominates his creation and the leader dominates his flock.

When we look at religious leadership, then, we expect to find that the leader has some sort of power: Power to teach people what to do and to punish them for not doing so, power to effect change or movement within the human world and within the divine world, and power over nature or natural processes. *The kaminchu— priestesses—in Henza do not hold, use, or symbolize power.* They do not preside at life-cycle rituals[2]—that is, they do not cause or proclaim changes in status of villagers, and they do not officiate at weddings or other "rites of passage." They do not lay claim to special knowledge or the power that results from esoteric or arcane knowledge—that is, they do not preside at rituals of divination or fortune-telling. They do not harness supernatural power in order to heal or otherwise effect changes in villagers' destinies. They do not perform rituals that express power over nature—kami-sama is immanent in nature, and priestesses refrain from participating in rituals that effect change in nature (such as rain rituals in years of drought). They do not teach villagers rules of social behavior or even rules of ritual behavior. And they do not proclaim that one gender is better than the other at embodying or communicating with deities: Henza priestesses do not dominate men, seek to dominate men, or propagate an ideology of female dominance and male inferiority (see chapter 11 on gender ideology). In these respects, kaminchu behave like other (Okinawan) kami-sama. As discussed in chapter 2, kami-sama do not create the world, give laws, or punish and reward human beings. Neither embodied nor disembodied kami-sama "do" anything in the sense that priests or gods "do" in many other religions.

Although I do not believe that ecological conditions or subsistence technologies necessarily lead to particular forms of social organization or cultural ideologies, they are part of the multidimensional whole that we call culture; the relationships that societies develop with their physical surroundings reflect and enhance other cultural patterns. In fishing societies, or at least in Henza, people do not own or control nature the way they do in agricultural societies where power over the land can, so it seems, be obtained. One can buy more land and protect its borders with stronger armies; one can plow the earth a little deeper; one can spray stronger pesticides and herbicides; one can tear up jungle and forest and replace variegated plant life with a lucrative cash-crop; one can mobilize peasant labor to build irrigation systems, which are then controlled by the government or the landed elite; one can import cheap, migrant labor to work longer hours in the fields; and one can store surplus food and sell it for higher profits during times of scarcity.[3] In ocean fishing societies, in contrast, the relationship with the source of subsistence is more ephemeral. Fish cannot easily be stored for long—without labor-intensive work of salting or smoking, it rots quickly; the ocean ecosystem cannot (at least not until recently) be radically modified to grow more or grow only certain kinds of foods; and until the advent of substantial motor-powered ocean liners, the sea could not be counted on not to drown trespassers. Fishing—with the cultural implications that I have just presented—is not the only subsistence source in Henza; traditionally (and still today), more food has been provided through women's foraging and horticulture than through men's fishing. Women who forage along the seashore of Henza pick up whatever the tide happens to have brought them that day. Foraging does not involve efforts to dominate or permanently alter the ecosystem. The kind of horticulture practiced in Henza also has minimal impact on the environment; in Okinawa's hot, humid climate, gardens are quickly overrun by jungle—villagers' plots are not the neat, orderly gardens we know in Europe and the United States. Henza horticulture does not conquer nature, it is part of nature. Characteristically, in the *oharai* ('go away' ritual) for bugs on the crops (see *shinugu* in chapter 6), the priestesses send the bugs away, they do not conquer or kill them. Again, I emphasize that the pattern I have summarized here is multidirectional: Both Henza Island's topography and Henza villagers' attitudes, history, beliefs, and preferences encourage certain sorts of subsistence work—which in turn affects the ecosystem in particular ways and encourages particular sorts of attitudes, beliefs, rituals, and so on.

This brief overview calls to mind Peggy Sanday's cross-cultural study of the status of women in horticultural societies (1981). Sanday has found that in horticultural societies a relatively high status for women is correlated with both a view of nature as beneficent and a cosmology that includes female deities—a constellation that certainly characterizes Henza. The dimension of power that I have introduced in this chapter serves to refine Sanday's model. The natural world of Henza is understood to be essentially good, and human nature is understood to be yasashii;[4] control of any kind—whether over people or over nature—is seen as pointless; men and male institutions do not seek to control that natural resource known as women, and priestesses do not seek to control or dominate men; women embody both male and female deities; and the status of both men and women is relatively high. Just as the relationship with nature is one of accommodation and balance rather than one of domination in Henza, so are the relationships among people. (I make no claim regarding causal order: Relationships with nature and with people mutually reflect one another; one does not cause the other.) In Henza, religion does not function to glorify, mystify, or sacralize domination either of people or of nature.

I opened this chapter with a general discussion of power as the ability to control nature or people. In those conceptual terms, Henza priestesses are not powerful. The question I wish to raise now is whether there are other ways of thinking about power. In an analysis of the meaning of power in island Southeast Asia, Shelly Errington argues that power in the Western sense of economic control and coercive force "reveals a lack of spiritual power . . . and consequently diminishes prestige" (1990: 5). Power, or as Errington prefers to call it, "potency," in Southeast Asia is conceptualized as an intangible, mysterious energy which animates the universe. Unlike Western "power," Southeast Asian "potency" is not exercised or used; it simply "is." In making this distinction, Errington's understanding of power in Southeast Asia sounds a great deal like kami-sama in Okinawa.

However, unlike in Okinawa, Southeast Asian "potency" is accumulated.

> It seems that a good part of the indigenous politics and symbolic forms in this area have as their intention to tap the energy and effectiveness of this invisible realm, from the seances of shamans in remote mountain settlements, to the trance-dances of lowland peoples, to the asceticism and meditation of the indicized hierarchical courts of Java and elsewhere. . . . The signs of potency in persons include large amounts of wealth and substantial numbers of followers. . . . The periphery around a potent center consists of its entourage or audience, which both signifies and bears witness to the presence of potency. . . . Individuals who aspire to tap potency and gain prestige must attract audiences. (Errington 1990: 42–44).

Therefore, Errington explains, the performing arts are so important in island Southeast Asia in general and in the religion in particular (cf. Atkinson 1989 on Wana shamanism). Moreover, according to Errington, in island Southeast Asia, women are often associated with worldly power and men with spiritual potency. "Women in many of these societies are assumed to be more calculating, instrumental, and direct than men, and their very control of practical matters and money, their economic "power," may be the opposite of the kind of "power" or spiritual potency that brings the greatest prestige; it may assure them of lower rather than higher prestige" (1990: 5–7).

In Henza cosmology, kami-sama cannot be accumulated. One priestess is associated with (amalgamated with) one kami-sama. She cannot acquire more potency by praying at another altar, by ascetic practices, or by learning new rituals. The lesson of initiation (see chapter 8) is that kami-sama cannot be acquired at all—the initiate discovers that kami-sama was, in fact, there all the time. Priestesses do not acquire prestige or followers because of kami-sama. Henza's cosmology functions to constrain both the motive for and the practice of power (in the sense of domination). The religious worldview in Henza village is an egalitarian one, just as is the social worldview. Kaminchu, like other kami-sama, do not have entourages of followers; if one did, villagers would probably suspect that she is not really a kaminchu.

Although Southeast Asian "potency" as described by Errington may originate in a different source than Western "power" and may be used for different purposes than Western "power," its meaning is really quite similar. Both are acquired and accumulated, and both involve hierarchy—especially gender hierarchy. Both are what spiritual feminist writer Starhawk calls "power-over," in contrast to the "power-from-within" that, it seems to me, characterizes Henza's kaminchu.

> Power-over is linked to domination and control; power-from-within is linked to the mysteries that awaken our deepest abilities and potential. . . . Power-over . . . is the consciousness modeled on the God who stands outside the world, outside nature, who must be appeased, placated, feared, and above all, obeyed. . . . In its clearest form, power-over is the power of the prison guard, of the gun, power that is ultimately backed by force. Power-over enables one individual or group to make the decisions that affect others, and to enforce control. . . . Power-from-within is akin to the sense of mastery we develop as young children with each new unfolding ability: the exhilaration of standing erect, of walking, of speaking the magic words that convey our needs and thoughts. But power-from-within is also akin to something deeper. It arises from our sense of connection, our bonding with other human beings, and with the environment. (Starhawk 1987: 9–19)

Power-from-within is nonhierarchical. It arises from authentic connections between beings and with nature, not from the performing arts, and it does not translate into gendered superiority for those who develop it. Starhawk's notion of "power-from-within" fits well with the meaning of being kaminchu in Henza village. This kind of power cannot be used, accumulated, or validated by an audience of followers. The initiation process, as I argued in chapter 8, is a process of discovery, of unfolding, of learning to recognize the divinity that was really there all the time, of giving birth to oneself as a more spiritually aware being. The initiate does not acquire knowledge or authority; neither priestesses—nor anyone else in Henza—function as "leaders."

In the remainder of this chapter, we shall look at some of the ways and contexts in which questions of power touch upon the experiences of Henza priestesses.[5]

Deconstructing Leadership

"As many scholars have pointed out, the hierarchical principle permeates Japanese society, from political life to family and individual life. . . . Since all folk religion is strongly influenced by this social requirement, it is noticeable that Japanese folk religion in particular has played an important role in maintaining this system" (Hori

1968: 29). Masao Miyoshi has observed that throughout the Tokugawa period, rituals and ceremonies provided the hierarchical framework of Japanese society. "In the great chain of being that—theoretically—connects the Emperor to the humblest laborers via the Shogun, lords and myriad rank of samurai, farmers, artisans, and merchants, all must perform ceremony so that order may be maintained throughout" (cited in Smith 1983: 37). Much of Okinawan ritual, in contrast, serves to "dis-order" hierarchical notions and structures. Henza rituals tend to deconstruct cultural categories: to show that cultural constructs—and hierarchial constructs in particular—are artificial.[6] Because the kaminchu are embodied kami-sama, the "threat" of hierarchy could be quite real. A variety of rituals decompose that threat through underscoring the flexibility of kami-sama, that a person or thing both is and is not kami-sama, becomes and then unbecomes kami-sama.

As we saw in chapter 6, the priestesses wear impressive crowns of leaves and sparkling clean five-piece white robes when they perform rituals in which they embody or represent kami-sama. (These robes must have been even more impressive in the days—until quite recently—in which regular village clothing was scanty). The priestesses's rituals are surrounded with mystery: The sacred groves are located deep in the tangled, dark jungle; the kami-ya is in the midst of the village, but until recently spectators were not allowed to enter.

At a number of rituals (such as umachi), priestesses dressed in regular clothes pray in the kami-ya while clan members slowly gather in the village square. The priestesses then go on a bus that takes them to the jungle trail leading to the utaki. While in the jungle, they change into their white robes, weave and put on crowns of leaves, pray and eat, and then return to the village by a different path from the one they took when they left. The aesthetic and spiritual impact of the kami-sama returning to village is impressive; they look holy and exotic. They come from an unexpected direction, not from the direction in which the village women had exited; they are wearing kami-sama clothes, not the clothes which the village women had worn. Clan members waiting in the village square rise to greet the kami-sama; they spread out mats for the kami-sama, pour them sake, and serve them.

Yet, and this is the point that interests me, when the kami-sama and clan members finish drinking and eating, the kami-sama simply stand up and take off their white robes, fold them and put them in bags, and hang up their crowns to disintegrate on nails that protrude from a wooden frame in the village square. Then in their everyday clothes they walk back to their homes. I can't help but compare this to Eastern Orthodox or Roman Catholic priests who never take off their exotic clothes in public—their special clothes create an illusion of power and existential difference. The priestesses' disrobing in the village square, on the other hand, makes a public, playful statement: Okay, now we're done being kami-sama and you can all come and see that we are just plain people.

In the priestesses' ritual sequence, they begin by intensifying their "kami-sama-ness," after which they engage in ritually "being there"—sitting in the utaki and accepting food offerings from villagers. Yet they end their impressive rituals by showing everyone that being kami-sama is a cultural construction: Put on some clothes and you are kami; take them off and you are a village housewife. The ritual sequence of the priestesses deconstructs the notion that there is a discrete category of divinity—kami-sama—that is above or beyond human experience.

The ritual sequence of the priestesses deconstructs still another cultural category which, in many societies, becomes reified. That category is leadership. Because of the nature of leadership—that leaders need followers—leaders often present themselves as "natural" leaders, as special, as different from "just plain folk." That priestesses end an impressive ritual by publicly taking off their robes and walking home to do house and garden work dramatizes and concretizes the message that leadership is not immutable—that the priestess role is limited to very specific activities and places. This message, of course, fits well with the rotating system of village headmanship; no one remains a leader for very long, and, in fact, someone who really acts "like a leader" is not well liked or respected.

Moreover, given that male dominance characterizes, to lesser or greater degrees, most known society (a fact of which Henza villagers are aware), a cultural arrangement in which women publicly embody deity is a particularly compelling way to demonstrate that hierarchy is meaningless and unwanted, that power is valueless and undesirable, and that even God is neither omnipotent nor above the natural world. When the dominant sex monopolizes roles of spiritual leadership, hierarchy is enhanced, intensified, and mystified. Because women are not dominant—in Okinawa or any other known society—the very fact that they represent and incarnate divinity weakens any budding connection between secular power, divine power, and gender.

For people to develop a clear and critical conception of hierarchical authority, and thereby to demystify it, they tend to need to experience more than one kind of authority. Otherwise, authority appears to be part of an immutable, natural order. The reality of Okinawa having experienced, simultaneously and sequentially, various sources of foreign domination (historically by Japan and by China, and more recently by Japan and by the United States) certainly can be construed as contributing to a cultural ethos in which no single source of authority is recognized as inherently and legitimately authoritative. But also on a more immediate village level, it seems to me that the customary distinction between religious and political authority has the same effect. The association of women with religious leadership and of men with political leadership means that the two most culturally salient forms of authority are not only institutionally but also empirically separate.[7] This division in and of itself serves to deconstruct power and authority.

Problems of Power

The fact that power and hierarchy need to be ritually deconstructed suggests that, in the eyes of villagers, they pose problems of one kind or another. We shall turn now to a few arenas in which issues of power threaten to become problematic and to the solutions that village culture offers to the threat of the accumulation of power.

Succession of Priestesses

In a society in which both structure and leadership are undeveloped, succession of priestesses poses a thorny problem. Putting oneself forward as a priestess would probably be interpreted as proof that one is *not* born to be a priestess, yet there is no public mechanism for appointing priestesses. The previous priestess does not select or train her successor; the potential priestess herself cannot know that she is destined for the role; a number of different yuta are asked for their opinions (no one of which is binding); and the clan which she represents has no clear role in deciding that a particular woman is the one who should sit the position. In one clan, the current (very elderly and veteran) priestess is said, by some villagers, to actually be the sister of the true priestess (the sister left Okinawa for "Canada or Peru"). The current priestess, who is not very popular, "is sitting representing her sister," a state of affairs that is far from ideal. However, when I asked, "So she wears white clothes but she isn't a real kaminchu?" I was told, "Well, yes, uh uh, once she sits there [in the priestess position] . . . [voice trails off]." The implication, then, is that once she sits the position she does in some way embody kami-sama or (and) that once she sits the position, no one is empowered to tell her not to.

The following comments demonstrate that the process of succession is characterized by a flexible construction of reality that leaves a great deal of room for negotiation and change. Power is not vested in any one party.

SUSAN: Did the previous noro tell Mrs. Kamura [the current noro] that "you will be noro after I die?"

MR. YAMASHIRO: No, she didn't say that. There is nothing like her saying "you do it." Because she was still doing the job, she could not say that to the next one.

––––––––––

SUSAN: Kaminchu and yuta are different, so why do kaminchu have to go to yuta to find out that they should be kaminchu?

MRS. ISHIKAWA: We cannot know by ourselves whether we can sit as kaminchu or not, whether to sit is good or bad. Four yuta have to say the same thing. From olden days this has been the same way.

––––––––––

SUSAN: So the yuta decides if you become kaminchu?

MRS. IKEDA: No! You need to go to many yuta. If they all say yes, it is okay. But if one says yes and one says no, it is no. We go to four or five different yuta. . . . We do *kome kuji* (rice divination) to get an answer. When you are on the way to sitting the position, you can't do it yourself, someone else has to do it.

––––––––––

SUSAN: So who has the final authority to say who will be kaminchu?

MR. MASAMITSU (*sekininsha*—administrative head—of a large clan): If the person comes with a *handan* [yuta's judgment], then the clan says, "Okay, you have a handan." We would not say you are not the one. However, they come to us.

SUSAN: Everyone agrees together?

MR. MASAMITSU: Yes, everybody. Everyone has to hear the story about the handan. The clan people get together, and she says "I was given by kami-sama to become kaminchu"—she tells this to everyone and then asks, "Please let me be kaminchu, this was given by kami-sama." It is not that easy to say, "you yes, you no, you are, you are not." We cannot say things like that.

————

SUSAN: Does it ever happen that someone says that she went to three yuta and all said she should sit the position, but the other kaminchu know that this woman isn't appropriate?

MRS. SHIMOJO: Yes. A person in the clan says no sometimes. For example, maybe I am the one that the *kami-ban* [divination] yuta said should be kaminchu, but when I went to the clan one of the clan people says "No, you are not the one." What I will do then is pray to kami-sama and say, "When I went to kami-ban yuta they told me that I am the one who is supposed to sit that seat, but one in the clan won't let me do it. So would you do something about it. Please cooperate with me." That is what I would pray to the kami-sama. And then the person who said no, if something happens to her, like getting sick, or something happens to her children, they of course go to see the yuta. Maybe then they find out through the yuta that because she said no, that is why this happened.

————

SUSAN: Were you headman when Mrs. Kamura became noro?

MR. TAMURA: Yes.

SUSAN: If someone strange or inappropriate had been suggested for noro, what could the town hall have done?

MR. TAMURA: Nothing.

The fuzziness of the succession process underscores the lack of any kind of "power-over." Neither the clan nor the headman has power over the priestess, the priestess does not have power over the headman or the clan, the yuta does not have power over the priestess, and the priestess does not have power over the yuta.[8]

To my mind, one of the more interesting aspects of Henza religion is that there typically is a lengthy gap between the death of a previous priestess and the initiation of the next one to sit in her position.

SUSAN: There is a gap of seven years after one noro dies and before the new one sits the position, isn't there?

MRS. SHIMOJO: No. We don't know how long it will take. There is no set time. Within the clan they don't know who, it can take ten years or twenty years.

SUSAN: When the position is vacant, does someone else do the job?

MRS. SHIMOJO: No.

SUSAN: Has it ever happened that there was a big gap between one noro and the next?

MRS. SHIMOJO: Yes. For the current noro to be born [take on the role], it took about ten years.

SUSAN: So who did the prayers in that time?

MRS. SHIMOJO: Everybody, even without noro the kaminchu go to the utaki to pray. Only the noro seat was vacant.

SUSAN: Usually noro is the one who prays, so who prays then?

MRS. SHIMOJO: Everyone. There are ten kami-sama, so everybody prays.

SUSAN: For example, does it ever happen that during the gap between noro someone else sort of takes over the job and becomes in charge of this thing, and then the noro is born and there might be different opinions?

MRS. SHIMOJO: If the noro is born, everyone will cooperate with the new noro. There is no conflict.[9] If the new noro is born, everyone prays that a new noro is born and a celebration is held.

The time gap in succession between noro or kaminchu has a profound effect on the degree of authority inherent in the role. Following a period (which can be twenty years or more) in which the position is unfilled, the community becomes accustomed to managing without the priestess. When a priestess is born, she must, to some extent, create the position anew. On the one hand, this arrangement allows for some measure of individual creativity—the new kaminchu has not been trained by her predecessor. On the other hand, it means that she does not benefit from whatever power her successor had accumulated, and she is highly dependent upon the other kaminchu to show her the ropes. The extended gap between kaminchu also can be seen as a symbolic expression of the kaminchu's role coming naturally (see chapter 8). The gap between kaminchu is a clear, public statement that the kaminchu does what she does not because she was taught and not because she was appointed but because she has a source of spiritual strength within herself.[10]

I found it surprising that villagers and clan members are not anxious about the long gap between kaminchu. In contrast to the Catholic Church, where the entire Catholic world waits with baited breath for a new pope to be declared immediately following the death of the previous one, Henza villagers insist that there always must be a gap. Given that each kaminchu is a particular kami-sama, we might think that when there is no kaminchu to sit a position, a unique form of spiritual energy is missing from the village. Yet this is not what villagers say: They are absolutely unconcerned about the gap. I suspect that because priestesses are embodied kami-sama, the fact that a priestess has not been born does not mean that kami-sama is absent but rather that kami-sama is temporarily unembodied (or semiembodied, because the previous one takes her white robes with her to the grave). In general, present and absent are less dichotomous for Henza villagers than for Westerners (see chapter 5). A clan without a kaminchu or a village without a noro is not like a flock without a shepherd; the priestess does not lead the villagers—either with a stick or with a carrot. Villagers and clan members rejoice when a kaminchu or noro is born because embodied kami-sama is a wonderful presence, not because they were lost sheep without her.

The Link to Shuri

In many religious situations, a leader gains power or prestige because of his or her link to a central institution or association. The leader, having access to resources and sanctions controlled by that central organization, is treated by laity as an embodiment of the power held by that institution.

During the time of the Ryukyuan Kingdom, the noro functioned as Shuri's representative in the villages, and the noro were given symbols of status by the Shuri government (for example, a special necklace).[11] At least within the memories of Henza villagers, any power or rank held by the noro resulted from her connections with the Shuri government, and villagers express ambivalent feelings about these connections. Leadership today in Okinawan religion is decentralized and nonauthoritarian; the centralized, hierarchical noro system instituted by Shuri collapsed with Japanese political annexation of Okinawa. In the absence of strong political inducements, village priestesses do not tend to organize structures that reflect or bolster power over others.[12]

KAMINCHU: The noro was not really high rank; she was only serving people above her.

MRS. HOKAMA: When my husband was still alive he went to Tokyo to research what noro is, and [he found out that] the noro is not really a great person. The noro is the person who was told her duty. They would tell her: You don't marry, we will give you land so that you can support yourself and pray for the whole village.

MR. GINJO: In the old days the king appointed the noro, so she was respected. But nowadays, no. The olden days when the noro was appointed by the king, she was a bit of a snob.

MR. TAMURA: Before the headman system started—eighty-six years ago, the noro was the main one. That was the noro system. A person appointed by Shuri came once or twice a year, and they would tell the village men to cooperate with the noro.

The theme in all of these comments is that the noro did not have any independent authority; whatever authority she had was given her by the men from Shuri. The ambivalence with which villagers speak about the noro's status seems to be related to several factors. First, the entire Shuri government system is understood by villagers as foreign. Historically, each Okinawan village (and particularly island) was an independent entity. Gradually, they became consolidated into a series of small chiefdoms and then a kingdom, yet villages tended to maintain distinct identities—a fact that Henzans reiterated to me in many different contexts. Henza clans originated in a variety of sections of Okinawa, and most villagers speak of a sense of identification with Nakijin (in the north) rather than Shuri (in the south-central part of Okinawa's main island). I was told by villagers that the noro system only reached Henza in the eighteenth century, and by the end of the nineteenth century it was disbanded. The noro as part of a national network of political-religious leaders linked to the central government in Shuri lacks historical depth in Henza.

Second, as I discussed in chapter 1, leadership in Henza generally tends to be yasashii. The clan kaminchu fit well into this pattern. They do not lead the clan as much as they embody certain spiritual energies that the clan wishes to summon on ritual occasions. Only the Shuri-style noro diverged (in the past) from this pattern, a divergence that makes villagers a bit uncomfortable.

And third, a great deal of evidence suggests that women cross-culturally are disinterested in religious centralization. In *Priestess, Mother, Sacred Sister: Religions Dominated by Women* (1994), I showed that although women-led religions do have internal role differentiation and rank, these are within particular chapters or congregations. Almost all women's religions are independent of a centralized power structure. In the few instances in which there is a central governing body, it is organized and run by men. This was the case for North American Spiritualism and is still true for Afro-Brazilian religions (also see Cosentino 1982: 23 on women's Sande and men's Poro in West Africa; Breidenbach 1979: 111 on men and women leaders of the Harrist Movement in Ghana; Jacobs and Kaslow 1991: 184 on the Black Spiritual churches of New Orleans). In the Okinawan case, not only was the centralization of noro instituted and organized by men, but even today attempts to organize yuta associations are male endeavors, and the "yuta school" that opened in Naha (the capital of Okinawa Prefecture) a few years ago is run by men, although almost all Okinawan yuta are women. Neither Henza priestesses nor Henza yuta seek the authority that comes from association with religious leaders in other communities.

Religious centralization tends to be linked to several other religious patterns—transcendence, obligatory rituals, sacred scripture, and uniform dogma—and to several rather obvious political patterns such as expansion, domination, and imperialism (cf. Eisenstadt 1982), patterns that are often detrimental to women's religious and secular autonomy (cf. Frymer-Kensky 1992 on the ancient Near East; Silverblatt 1980 on the Andes). The "power-over" mode that characterizes religious centralization is a poor fit for Henza's diffuse understanding of kami-sama and disinterest in power relationships—including gendered ones.

Liturgical Leadership

While we were living in Henza, an Okinawan pop star invited a Shinto priestess[13] from a shrine in Naha to carry out a boat launching ceremony.[14] At this ritual, while dozens of villagers looked on, the Shinto priestess spread impressive quantities of food and other ritual items on tables at the beach. She shook a large handful of sheaves and used the sheaves to sweep the area. She picked up and put down various ritual objects. She clapped her hands. And finally she motioned to all participants and onlookers to remain silent while she prayed out loud at some length. The meanings of her theatrical ceremonial actions seemed clear: She swept in order to purify the area of malignant spiritual forces, she picked up the foods to show the kami-sama her offerings, and she prayed for the safety of the new boat. In this public ceremony, she functioned as an intermediary between the boat owner and kami-sama, and she presented herself as a leader of the community.

I cite this description by way of contrast to the rituals in which Henza priestesses are involved. The rituals carried out by the noro and kaminchu are low-keyed. There is no loud singing, no dramatic manipulation of unusual ritual objects, no drumming or music, no complicated hand gestures or body movements, no speeches or loud prayers, no animal sacrifice, no prostrating or extravagant genuflection, no clapping or bell-ringing, no blowing of the ram's horn, no theatrical liturgy sanctified by ancient tradition, no melodramatic confessions or exorcisms. I am convinced that the Shinto priestess was busy and active because she does things for or to kami-sama and her audience; her rituals are an expression of power-over. The Henza priestess, on the other hand, *is* kami-sama, and her rituals are an expression of power-from-within.

Henza villagers are quite familiar with the model of a religious leader who stands in front of a congregation and leads prayers or rituals. On a regular basis, they see the Buddhist priest who conducts burial services. When he prays, everyone is quiet, he tells people where to stand and what to do, he is clearly in charge. Kaminchu do not lead prayer in the way that priests, ministers, or rabbis do. They do not pray out loud, and they do not tell people how or what to pray. When they are in small groups, the noro kneels or squats to pray, and the other kaminchu then follow her example; but when they are in the larger context of clan gatherings, someone else, often a man, informally will call out words like "everyone, pray time" and then "finished now." I have never seen a group of people praying in unison; each villager or priestess says his or her own prayer. This easygoing arrangement gives the impression that, although the kaminchu are ritually proficient and preeminent, they are not in charge.

Instruction and Admonishment

The fact that priestesses are kami-sama does not mean they have special knowledge that translates into the right or the responsibility to tell villagers or other priestesses what to do. I will suggest in the next chapter that it is precisely because yuta do have special knowledge that villagers feel ambivalent about them.

SUSAN: Do people ask kaminchu their opinions about things?

MR. GINJO: No. Of course they go to learn from the yuta.

———

SUSAN: Is it the kaminchu's job to teach people?

MR. IKEDA: No, that is yuta. Yuta is the one who teaches.

SUSAN: For example, does the kaminchu teach children not to do bad things like steal?

MR. IKEDA: Kaminchu pray for health. Kaminchu don't do things like that. Each individual house has to do this, to teach the children. If you are kaminchu you [only] teach your own children to be good.

The occasional kaminchu who tells people what to do is suspected of being a yuta rather than a kaminchu. According to the noro: "I think it is not good that women now go to Nanza Island during the san gatsu festival . . . [but] I can't tell women not to go there. They might call me *yuta-gwa* [a disrespectful term for yuta—the suffix *gwa* means 'just' or 'only'].

The male assistants to the priestesses clear the path in the jungle, carry the priestesses' parcels into the sacred grove, and clean up after them. These men inherit their important ritual roles from their fathers. One of the current male assistants is a drunkard and often shows up inebriated at rituals. He is not a quiet drunk, and in the wake of drinking sake he can be quite disruptive. I asked both the noro and the village headman why they do not tell him to stop coming drunk to rituals. Both gave me the same answer: That is not something I can do.

SUSAN: Is there anybody who has the right to ask the male assistant to stop drinking?

KAMINCHU: I think if someone says such a thing he'll give some funny answer like, "I am drinking, why aren't you drinking too?"

SUSAN: Can't the headman or someone tell him?

KAMINCHU: I don't know about other people, but I myself can say that he irritates my kami-sama.

SUSAN: Can the noro tell him to stop drinking?

KAMINCHU: No, he'll just say, "I am the one who is drinking [it's none of your business.]"

This particular kaminchu seems to be the only kaminchu in Henza who is willing to confront the male assistant (although she herself is a relatively inexperienced kaminchu). Perhaps not surprisingly, I have heard a number of other kaminchu say that they suspect that she may be sitting the kami-sama position by mistake, and that she is really a yuta. Here is how an elderly priestess in her own clan speaks about her:

That one is from my clan, but that person is too much. Frightening. She talks the way the yuta talks. The clan said to her: "Do yuta things at home, this is the clan kaminchu's place." Everyone is against her. That person is frightening. She is violent. Five years ago [when she began sitting the position], she didn't talk to the clan. Two or three people were against her sitting on the kami-sama, but she sat anyway. She didn't discuss it with the clan, no talk, she just sat. That is how she sat. That person, she doesn't talk my clan's kami-sama talk, she talks yuta talk. We are all against her. But I won't say anything [tell her she should stop being a priestess]. Nobody will say. Even though they think in their minds, they cannot say, she is so violent.

This kaminchu is not really violent. Her colleague uses the word "violent" as a metaphor for assertive, garrulous, pushy, and opinionated. What we learn from this excerpt is that initiative, verbal skills, and ambition—the very character traits that make up leadership in the West—are in Okinawa proof that one is not really kaminchu. Note also that the elderly priestess who in this excerpt accused the other of being yuta is herself mother-in-law to a yuta whom she highly respects. In other words, her problem is not with yuta, but with people who sit in the "wrong position," and with kaminchu who express "power-over."

The Division of Ritual Labor

The clan is primarily a ritual group, yet clan kaminchu do not have any particular authority within the clan. For example, the clan has an annual budget made up of money given as dues by clan members, but the kaminchu do not decide how the money is spent, even though the money is spent on rituals that they carry out.

SUSAN: Do the kaminchu have any power in the clan, for example, to tell the administrative head of the clan what to do?

MR. IKEDA: If it is things that she can say [the things in her sphere], she can say.

SUSAN to MRS. IKEDA (clan kaminchu): Have you ever done that?

MRS. IKEDA: No. Our clan doesn't have those things.

SUSAN: Does the clan ever ask the kaminchu for their opinion?

MRS. IKEDA: No.

SUSAN: Do people respect kaminchu?

MR. GINJO: Actually, there is no rank among them. It is not like government officials with hierarchy, with section chiefs and so on. They are like volunteer workers for the kami's duty. Just try to clean the altars, first and fifteenth of the month they put tea on the altars. People appreciate that they do that. There is no real rank involved. Within the clan maybe they will say that she is our clan's *ukuringwa* [clan priestess], maybe there is a little respect for that.

Although it may look as if the noro is "higher" than other priestesses, in actuality the categories of priestesses are not woven into an overarching hierarchy. The regular clan priestesses, for example, have no reason to be in contact with the noro. She is not their boss, she does not instruct them or tell them what to do, and she does not supervise them. One reason that the priestess roles do not develop into a hierarchical order, I suggest, is because the kami-sama that the various priestesses embody are themselves dis-ordered. Because the cosmos is not imaged in terms of order, rank, or power-over, particular pieces of the cosmos, such as ritual experts in a given village, experience no cosmic push toward hierarchy (see chapter 2).

SUSAN: Is your rank lower than noro or same rank?

MR. UMISEDO (an assistant to the priestesses, his family traditionally is in charge of providing fish at rituals): I think this is a difference at rituals [we do different jobs at rituals]. I don't think there is above or below. Ogami is ogami, we have different roles.

The men who clear the jungle trail for the priestesses and who bring them food offerings are not understood to be "below" the priestesses. I have chosen to refer to these men as "assistants" because, from my point of view, their role looks to be one of providing services to the priestesses. From their point of view, however, it would probably be more accurate to refer to them as "male ritual practitioners" or "male kami-sama."

The nonhierarchical ritual division of labor is particularly noticeable when dates are set for ceremonies.

SUSAN: Who says when to do a ceremony?

MR. YAMASHIRO (noro's brother): It is already known what to do at the events, but the date is decided by the town hall.

SUSAN: In the old days, who set the date?

MR. YAMASHIRO: Mr. Shibahiki and Mr. Umisedo, old men, about four or five men, set the date, before there was a town hall. On the second day of New Year they got together here [in his house which traditionally was the noro's house] to talk about the dates.

Mrs. Shimojo confirms that this is indeed the procedure. "I don't know which day exactly, the town hall will contact me and tell me. And the town hall provides all the expenses. The day we go to the utaki the town hall . . . provides a bus. If I want to go to the utaki I have to tell the town hall and they arrange it. And they pay me 3500 yen for the New Year prayer." This should not, however, be taken to mean that the "real" power lies with town hall, Mr. Shibahiki, or the other old men. The situation is far fuzzier. As Mrs. Shimojo explained to me in a conversation about cleaning the utaki, "Mr. Shibahiki's younger sister and I went to a yuta together, and she said because I belong to the seven kami-sama [village kami-sama] I shouldn't do the cleaning there. I am a real kami-sama, but Mr. Shibahiki is asked by the village, so he can do the cleaning things." In ritual contexts, the headman and Mr. Shibahiki (and other men with similar roles), are—in Mr. Shibahiki's words—"representatives of Henza." The kaminchu, in ritual contexts, are representatives or embodiments of kami-sama. Yet it is crucial to understand that village and kami-sama do not stand in a relationship of hierarchy.

SUSAN: What is the relationship between the headman and the noro?

MR. TAMURA (former headman): In Henza the noro is the kami who protects Henza. So the person who becomes headman has to cooperate with the noro. The noro is above the headman. This was in the old days. Because she is a woman, she cannot order what to do for each event [such as, order the bus, tell the town hall to provide sake, and so on]. So that is why the headman is important. As headman you have to know about the noro festivals, and about haari, umachi, and so on.

Mr. Tamura paints a picture of a division of labor in which a variety of ritual actors interdependently ensure the health of Henza. Neither the noro nor the village headman can protect the village without the cooperation of the other. Because ritual roles are divided between men and women and between elected individuals, individuals chosen by kami-sama, and individuals who inherit their position, power cannot accumulate in the hands of one person or group. Priestesses—flanked on one side by the yuta who are needed to ascertain who is born to the role, and on the other side by the village headman who is the one who can organize and set the date for ceremonies—share a ritual field populated by many other ritual experts.

TEN

Priestesses, Yuta, and Ogami People

The priestesses of Henza are not the only ritual experts on the scene. A variety of categories of religious specialists accomplish in Henza what in many other cultures is accomplished by one category—or by an ordered hierarchy—of experts. Aside from religious leaders who identify themselves as associated with another religious tradition (for example, the Buddhist priests who come to the village from the main island in order to officiate at funerals), Henza is home to at least twenty different ritual-specialist roles. Many of these roles are limited: A particular person or family is responsible for a shrine or for bringing a certain type of food to rituals. Together with the priestesses, the ritual experts most salient in the lives of villagers are yuta and ogami [prayer] people—almost all of whom are women. In previous chapters, in order to discourage readers from assuming that the content of these roles is the same as that of shamans in other better-known societies, I have chosen to translate both of these words ambiguously as "shaman-type practitioners"; in this chapter I shall explain how these roles are understood in Henza.

Most previous studies of Okinawan religion have treated yuta as part of a different ritual framework from that of the priestesses and have given very little attention to ogami people (see W. Lebra 1966; Matsui et al. 1980; Sakumichi et al. 1984; Kamata 1966; Ohashi et al. 1984). This treatment does not fit the current reality of Henza, where yuta are believed to have the spiritual insight to know who should be initiated as a priestess and where villagers have as much or more contact with ogami people than they do with yuta and priestesses. I suspect that the discreprency between my findings and those of earlier researchers reflects both the unique characteristics of each Okinawan village and broader realignments in religious roles in the wake of rapid urbanization of the main island.

Following an introduction to yuta and ogami people, I turn to how these roles differ from, and intersect with, the priestess role. Central to this discussion are the ways in which power is diffused, distributed, and decentralized through the work of the several categories of ritual specialists.

Yuta

"Yuta" has been translated as "shaman" in the English-language ethnographic literature. The word "shaman" is one that Western scholars choose (sometimes fairly arbitrarily) to apply to a wide range of ritual experts in diverse cultures. In this chapter, I shall try to take a clean look at yuta, recognizing that the yuta role is currently in a state of transformation and that it is probably quite different in the cities than it is in a small village like Henza (for excellent discussions of yuta, see Ohashi et al. 1984; Randall et al. 1989).[1]

The yuta's role is multifaceted, but I think that the best way to sum it up is to say that she mediates between villagers and other aspects of the cosmos. She knows how to ask the kami-sama whether a particular woman should be a priestess or a yuta, she is able to transmit messages from deceased ancestors to living descendants, she is able to discern the reasons for misfortune, and she can tell if an upcoming move or change is a good one or not. She knows how to consult books that tell whether certain days or years are auspicious and in which directions graves should be built to face. It is routine to consult a yuta after a death, to ask if the dead person is comfortable, if she or he wants to tell the living person something. "Maybe the yuta will say the dead one is unhappy because no one brought flowers to his tomb. The yuta connects between the dead person and you." It is common to consult the yuta regularly, perhaps once each year shortly after the New Year to ask the family's fortune for the year, much in the same way that many of us visit a physician each year for tests and screening. The fortune is not etched in stone—the purpose of the consultation is both to find out if there are problems and to use ritual means to clear them up. The yuta's work is called "doing handan" (*hanji* in Okinawan dialect). *Handan* denotes judgments and connotes diagnosis.

Most villagers bring someone with them when they visit the yuta. Families often come as a group, though it is usual for only the oldest woman to actually speak to the yuta; everyone else kneels quietly in the background. When clients enter the room, they bow to the yuta. The yuta may or may not wear a special jacket or robe. As in many other cultural settings, the shaman-type practitioner seems to work by the "law of accumulation"—collecting many and diverse ritual objects in order to maximize her efficacy (cf. Bastide 1978: 278). The yuta's altar will be full of pictures, statues, a crystal ball, incense bowls, and amulets from various Buddhist and Shinto shrines.

A typical ritual at the yuta's house begins with lighting incense. Then the yuta asks the client for a list of family members, including the *eto* (birth year) of each one. The yuta writes these down on a piece of paper. She may eliminate names of people who are not living in the house or who are not part of the client's close lineage. The yuta is careful to get the client's exact house address and the correct *kanji* (Chinese character) for the family name. During the session, the yuta repeatedly consults the paper with this information. The ritual continues with the yuta saying "*utooto*" (the way any prayer begins) and then reciting family names and dates. Different yuta have different techniques, but a common one is to pick up pinches of rice while chanting in a monotonous voice. The yuta then counts the grains of rice to see if she received a positive or negative answer. She will repeat the chanting and rice counting possibly a dozen or more times in one session. During the session, her voice subtly alternates between her own prayer-chant and the information she is passing on from the kami-sama or ancestor. She may occasionally stop her chanting to ask the client a brief question. On her table she will have a book of calendrical information based on the Chinese calendar. This book will be used at the end, when she tells the client what and when to pray in order to clear up problems. The session may end with the yuta making a date to accompany the client to a grave or a shrine. The client hands the yuta money (typically 3000 yen) and leaves, bowing deeply.

Unlike the performance skills that are, according to Kendall (1996), de rigueur for Korean shamans, the performance skills of Okinawan yuta take a distant second place to their divination skills. Whereas Korean shamans wear fabulous costumes, dance, and dramatize figures from their shared cultural repertoire, yuta wear plain white jackets, sit still, and murmur quietly. Kendall explains that in Korea women, "become great shamans through their command of ritual knowledge and performance skills acquired during an onerous apprenticeship" (1996: 21).[2] Okinawan yuta are more likely to gain a great reputation for their "go through" (*toosu*) ability; that is, their ability to communicate with deities and ancestors. This ability, according to villagers, is a matter of having a "clean heart" and of being born with the predisposition to "go through"; acquired skills—and especially performative skills—are of minor importance and perhaps even frowned upon.

Each yuta has one or more kami-sama with whom she communicates regularly. She will probably have an altar for that kami-sama. Her special kami-sama will pass on to her information about clients' ancestors. The yuta can see things that ordinary people cannot see. This ability allows her to predict the future and to find and bring back lost souls. It also allows her to see if a foreign spirit, perhaps a dead grandmother, is "attached" to the client and thereby causing illness. Because the yuta can communicate with ancestors, she can "calm them down," and she can tell descendants about unfinished business that the ancestor had on earth, especially bad acts that need to be cleared up. Clearing up refers both to ancestral lines that became confused and need to be sorted out properly and to mistakes made in the past that left a messy trail behind them. In the case of ancestors who did something bad, their behavior will affect the descendants unless the descendants clear things up. Illness in the broad sense discussed in chapter 7 is probably the most frequent manifestation of dis-order that needs to be cleared up. Yuta distinguish between real illness, which necessitates a doctor, and ancestral dis-order, which is their sphere of expertise.

Okinawan yuta do not fit most classic descriptions of shamanism found in the academic literature: Yuta do not lose consciousness, travel up to the sky in ecstatic journeys, experience a significant initiation ritual characterized by themes of death and rebirth, summon spirit familiars, or directly heal patients (Eliade 1964; cf. Hori 1968: 203–205 on Japanese shamans). Unlike shamans in many cultures, yuta do not seem to have much power either over people or over spirits (although villagers may not always recognize that this is the case). The role of yuta is to transmit information and help people (dead and alive) negotiate better relationships; the yuta does not manipulate either spirits or people to the extent that shamans in many other cultural settings do.

A recurrent theme in the literature on women shamans and spirit mediums cross-culturally is that they offer their largely female clientele a supportive framework in which to tell their problems and receive advice, support, and sympathy from other women (Kendall 1985: 74). In Okinawa, although the yuta's waiting room may be jam-packed, she sees each client individually either in a separate room or alcove or behind a screen. The client does not discuss her problems with the other women in the waiting room, although she may well wait five or more hours to see the yuta. Yuta do not usually give the client much time to talk. Most of the yuta–client interaction consists of divining the source of problems, not discussing the content of the problems. In contrast to Brazilian Candomble priestesses who help clients network with one another (to everyone's mutual advantage; see Lerch 1980), a visit to the Okinawan yuta does not result in any kind of networking. I suspect that the high degree of social integration among Okinawan women, and especially among village women (see chapter 4), obviates the need to make connections through a shaman's practice. Still, it is likely that the simple presence of so many other clients in the waiting room conveys the feeling that "I am not the only one who has problems." This feeling is strengthened by the yuta in conversations like this one:

CLIENT: Maybe my two sons aren't married because we haven't done right by the ancestors. One son is in Tokyo and one is still at home. I told my son to find someone to marry.

YUTA: That is how young people are nowadays, they don't get married so quickly, and if they marry, the man worries that the wife will run away. Don't worry, you are not the only one to worry about your children. [She then picked up her notebook with records of other clients and looked through it as proof that others ask about this problem.]

In some contemporary cultural situations, the shaman role is a revolutionary one. The shaman, as a charismatic practitioner who is in direct contact with the gods or spirits, can offer women, low-caste people, and the disprivileged an interpretation of reality that is different from the dominant, often oppressive, one (Sered 1994: 115ff.). For example, Laurel Kendall (1985) found that Korean shamans suggest to women a worldview more matricentric than the highly patriarchal mainstream Confucian worldview. Whereas Confucian ancestor worship only acknowledges official, patrilineal ancestors, Korean shamans encourage women also to relate to matrilineal ancestors and unofficial ancestors (for example, people who died young and so did not leave descendants to worship them). Okinawan yuta, in contrast, generally bolster the most narrow patrilineal interpretations of kinship and ancestor worship. On several occasions, I heard yuta tell clients that their misfortunes were caused by the presence in their butsudan of a beloved relative who, according to strict patrilineal kinship rules should not be there. Unlike Korean shamans, yuta come down on the side of "correct" succession rather than of emotional ties. Ironically, whereas Henza kinship arrangements are quite flexible, even leaning toward matrifocality, and the noro's succession is officially matrilineal, the yuta—who are outside the patrilineal clan system—are the spokespeople of patrilineality. I strongly agree with Professor Tsuha of the University of the Ryukyus that yuta teach mainstream or even elite cultural values to the common people.

The yuta is not a social misfit. The yuta's houses that I visited looked like normal Okinawan houses. Although this may not be entirely typical, it does seem that the husbands of yuta are more involved with their wives' work than are other Okinawan husbands. The three yuta whom I met were articulate, pleasant, attractive, hospitable, and intelligent women. Some of the kaminchu whom I met seemed less socially integrated than the yuta did.

I close this section with an excerpt from a conversation with one yuta living in Henza in order to illustrate the following points: The yuta feels that she is respected by villagers and her role is higher than that of the noro, and she sees herself as having an ongoing public role.

SUSAN: Do you feel that yuta are respected?

MRS. UYEALTARI: Yes, I think so, you need to do ancestor prayers so yuta is respected. If people ask me to go and pray, I do whatever kami-sama tells me to do. Also when I pray at the hinu-kan, I pray in the words I am told [by kami-sama] to pray. . . .

SUSAN: So yuta is very high?

MRS. UYEALTARI: Yes, above noro. Noro will not receive teaching [from kami-sama]. I think noro goes to yuta to buy the learning, I am not sure, but I think so. Yuta existed before noro. From the time of one of the Ryukyuan kings yuta were oppressed by the king.

SUSAN: Do you ever pray in a public place or just in houses?

MRS. UYEALTARI: Yes, I did a new building ritual and ogami for the bridge from Henza to Hamahiga Island. The two companies building the bridge asked me to do this. . . . Usually they ask a Shinto priest to do that, but they asked me. That was the first time that I did ogami like that. Now I am responsible for that, so on the first and fifteenth of each month I will pray for them too. Every time I have *hatsu ogami* [first prayer of the year] I pray for them to build the bridge safely, I feel responsible.

Ogami (Prayer) People

In the ethnographic literature that I had read before coming to Okinawa, I saw repeated mentions of yuta and priestesses, and I felt that I had some understanding of what these roles mean. Shortly after arriving in Henza, I attended a large ritual led by a woman named Mrs. Ikene. I asked the people standing near me:

SUSAN: Who is that woman in the front praying?

VILLAGER: Mrs. Ikene.

SUSAN: Is she a priestess?

VILLAGER: No, not a priestess.

SUSAN: Is she a yuta?

VILLAGER: No, not a yuta.

SUSAN: So what is she?

VILLAGER: Ha ha, she is an ogami [prayer].

ANOTHER VILLAGER: She is like *skoshi yuta* [a little bit of a yuta].

I learned that there are other villagers known for their ogami. One of these women is Mrs. Yae Yasamura, and so the next week I set out to talk to her. Streets in Henza do not have names, and my usual working method was to wander around the village asking people where so-and-so lives, getting closer and closer to the house, until finally someone would walk me over and introduce me. On this day, I asked villagers where Mrs. Yasamura lives, but Yasamura is a very common name in the village, and people did not know which Yasamura house I was looking for. After a few false starts, I learned how to ask for her: To hold my hands together in the gesture for praying. That morning I learned that *ogami* is indeed an appropriate title for these ritual practitioners.[3] Although I do not wish to push the point too far, I do find it interesting that villagers typically refer to these women simply as ogami (a noun meaning prayer) without the words *suru hito* (person who makes).

Unlike the priestess, who is an embodiment of kami-sama, and the yuta, who may speak for the ancestors, the ogami person is a representative of the family or household. Much of what is now done by an ogami person used to be done by *obaasan-tachi* (old women, grandmothers). According to Mr. Tamura, it used to be that "they didn't have yuta, they were called *tooto obaa* [praying grandmothers]. These were not really special woman, just neighborhood *obaasan* [old women, grandmothers]. Now there are people, yuta, who do this. It used to be that they didn't have money, so they just served a meal to the person who does good ogami. Before the war there wasn't much money."[4]

Even today the ogami people are seen as regular folk rather than full-time professionals. When I asked one villager to tell me who Mrs. Ikene (the most popular village ogami person) was, she answered me, "Mrs. Ikene grows potatoes and she is good at ogami." Here is how Mrs. Shimojo explains the role: "If you can't do the ogami yourself, you can ask someone like Mrs. Ikene to do ogami for you. It doesn't have to be Mrs. Ikene, anyone that you think can do the ogami you can ask to do it. Kaminchu usually do their own ogami for their own houses. But some kaminchu ask someone to do it."

Mrs. Kauwajo explains about ogami people: "These people who are good at words, the words come directly to their heads." Villagers have varying amounts of contact with ogami people; some villagers invite an ogami person to make the bimonthly prayer at the hinu-kan, and other villagers meet ogami people only at special events. An important role for ogami people is to help families with funeral rituals. Because priestesses do not become involved in death-related matters, and because the Buddhist priest who conducts the funeral lives off the island and comes only once for the main burial service, ogami people are kept busy with the many postfuneral rituals carried out for the ancestors.

Although there is no formal ranking among the ogami people, some are more respected than others. Mrs. Ikene, especially, "is like the chief of the ogami people, she does ogami for the village, while the others just do ogami for private individuals." Having discovered that there is no real name for this role, I then found that many villagers simply spoke about "ones like Mrs. Ikene." Ogami people have a variety of styles and specialties. Mrs. Chibana, for example, does not hear words from the kami-sama but rather songs in Okinawan dialect.

Ogami people seem to gradually move into their roles. Some start off by praying informally for friends and relatives and later begin to receive money for their praying. Some only do ogami and some also do handan (judgments or divination), especially of fortunes for the New Year. Ogami people can be seen as constituting a continuum ranging from regular folk to yuta. According to Mrs. Shimojo, "Among yuta some can do handan and some cannot. So when you go to a yuta, the yuta will ask for the address and name and tell the fortune, but some yuta cannot do that, they don't have the ability to do that, so those ones will only do ogami." Other villagers have clarified that the yuta is the one who diagnoses the source of a problem (does handan), and then tells the client to pray to clear the problem up. The ogami person may then be turned to for help in praying.

Villagers are somewhat concerned with distinguishing between ogami people and yuta, and sometimes a practitioner pointed out to me as a yuta would tell me that she is not yuta but an ogami person. The issue may be one of social status: yuta is a somewhat problematic role socially, whereas ogami person is not (cf. Wilson's discussion of the two words for Korean shamans: *mansin* and *mudang*; 1983: 126). Or the claim to be an ogami person rather than a yuta may simply reflect the typical Henza aversion to bragging or putting oneself forward: Because yuta have more skills than ogami people, a practitioner who does not want to boast may say that she is "only" an ogami person and not a full-fledged yuta.

Priestesses and Yuta: Differences

I asked villagers—including priestesses, yuta, and ogami people—how yuta and priestesses differ.[5] Having read a great deal about cultures in which official (male) religious leaders discredit or persecute unofficial (female) shamans, I had expected to find the differences between yuta and priestesses defined, at least by non-yuta, in ways that are pejorative to yuta. In the United States, Korea, and Myanmar, to take just a few examples, women shamans and shaman-type practitioners have been accused of charlatanism, insanity, promiscuity, witchcraft, and greed (Moore 1977; Wilson 1983; Spiro 1967). To my surprise, I did not hear any of this sort of rhetoric in Henza.

It is useful to look at the axes around which villagers organize the similarities and differences between yuta and priestesses. Because the villagers feel strongly that the two roles are distinct (but equally necessary), understanding what they see as the salient differences offers important insight into Henza's religious worldview.

We Are Born Differently

The most important point, and one that is made both by priestesses and by yuta, is that the two roles are existentially different; the "brains" of priestesses and yuta are different, and the kami-sama of priestesses and yuta are different.

SUSAN: You are priestess and your daughter-in-law is yuta. What is the difference?

MRS. ADANIYA (kaminchu): My brain and her brain are different. . . . I am an inherited kami-sama, not like yuta. I was born to sit in the clan's kami-sama, the yuta is different. . . . The yuta does not come from particular families. Each is on her own.

———

SUSAN: Is the same person ever both yuta and kaminchu?

MRS. UYEALTARI (yuta): I think the way they are born is different to become kaminchu and yuta. We are not clan kaminchu, it is separate. Only one kami-sama comes to you, you can't have two kami-sama. If you are a clan kaminchu you have the clan's kami-sama; but yuta has yuta's kami-sama. It is individual. Only one kami-sama will come to you.

———

SUSAN: Do yuta and kaminchu tend to have different personalities or, for example, more or less education?

NORO: It has nothing to do with education or anything like that. Yuta and kaminchu are born that way, and kami-sama directs you to become that one.

The priestess is the embodiment of one particular kami-sama; she has a lifetime association or amalgamation with that kami-sama. Yuta and ogami people, in contrast, can contact many different kami-sama, ancestors, and spirits. Yuta hear and see various entities, but they are not possessed by them.[6] To the contrary, possession is the domain of priestesses and to some extent ogami people. This is illustrated graphically by the custom of priestesses and ogami people pointing with their finger to the top of their head to explain what their ritual role is.

Mrs. Ikene, the ogami person, explains the difference between possession (what happens to her) and what happens to yuta: "When a person dies and if a yuta goes there will be somebody else and they will speak through the yuta. But my job is different, it is that the dead soul itself is in me and then I feel pain."

Kaminchu explain that they do not converse with kami-sama. It may be that the priestesses' kami-sama do not talk to kaminchu because the kaminchu *is* the kami-sama, or it may be that they do not talk because there is no reason for the kami-sama to pass on information to the kaminchu—there is nothing she needs the information for. The yuta, on the other hand, maintains an existential separation from the kami-sama (although she sometimes speaks in the kami-sama's or ancestor's voice); therefore, she can hear and see kami-sama.

The priestess is the kami-sama; once she understands that, the ability to sit the kami-sama's seat comes naturally. The spiritual gifts of the yuta, on the other hand, can be developed and improved on. Yuta, for example, use books in their ritual practice, whereas priestesses do not. Here is how the noro explains it:

> I never studied. That is why my older brother told me to go to the school in the south that yuta go to. He said, "The yuta is good at talking, right, and if you go there and study it will be better, the yuta goes there also to learn. They pay thousands of yen each month to study. That is why they are so good at it, at talking. So go there and study." That is what my brother said. [But] I don't want to go to school and become a kaminchu in that way! Kami-sama teaches me how, just the main summary [of prayers].

Mrs. Ikene, the ogami person, makes a similar distinction, but in her case it functions to align ogami people with kaminchu (who do things naturally) rather than yuta (who have to learn their job): "When I do ogami I don't think; they [the words] just come through my mouth. The yuta was taught, thinks. I can't stop the kami-sama's words, they just keep coming. Until the kami-sama says stop it can't stop. . . . My job is ordered by the kami-sama how to help people, that is what I do."

Yuta's and Kaminchu's Autobiographies Compared

The following excerpt is from a narrative told to me by a yuta in a neighboring village. This woman is a native of Henza and counts many Henza villagers among her clients. She is an attractive and competent woman, now in her mid-sixties.

Narrative A

About twenty years ago I got crazy. For one week I didn't eat but only drank. The two sides of my head were doing different things, one was crazy but one remembered. My legs swelled up. [At this point her husband joined the conversation and they talked at length about how crazy she was, and her husband said that he left the house to get away from her.] People would stare at the leaves on trees when I went by in order not to look at me, I was so crazy. I went to the hospital but the doctor didn't know what was wrong. But I figured out what was wrong when the kami-sama of Henza, the water kami, told me that I should be a yuta, that I should buy the book [a fortune-teller, geomancy book that she identifies as Chinese.]

The next narrative was related by Henza's one male yuta. Although his services are utilized by villagers, he is less respected than other (female) ritual practitioners.

Narrative B

I drank a lot of sake from seventeen to thirty-seven years old. From morning to evening I drank sake. I didn't know that I had this role of kami-sama's path. . . . I felt pain all over my body. I went to see the doctor, at least five different doctors each day to see what is wrong with me. I got shots, and one doctor said to me that this is rheumatism so you won't be cured until you die. Even though then I didn't know what this illness meant. And then sometimes I would faint and have to go by ambulance to the hospital. And I had stomach cancer and they said to prepare the operation. My wife's friend knew about this side of things [kami's way] but I didn't know about this and I believed there was not such a thing in the world. I didn't believe any of it. . . . Finally I asked a yuta to pray for me. Then at Chuba Hospital they said I am not sick, there is no cancer. So I went back to work and a few months later I fainted again, and this time the doctors said it is lung cancer. So I asked an ogami person to pray for me. And then went to see the doctor again and he said there is no lung cancer and sent me back home. And the third time that I fainted again they said it was intestinal cancer. And again I asked the ogami person to pray for me, and then the doctor said again there is no cancer. The doctor asked me if I took some [illegal] drugs. I told the doctor that I am an engineer and I can tell what is wrong with equipment, so how come you are a doctor and can't tell me what's wrong with me. Then I went to the hospital in Naha and they laughed and said, what, first stomach and then lung and then intestinal cancer? They let me stay in the hospital for two months to find out what is wrong, but they couldn't find it. . . . Since I accepted what kami-sama said I don't have these illnesses. . . . Also, before I became an ogami person my paycheck money would just disappear. Now I manage to make money for my daily life. But I don't do this job in order to make money.

The illnesses described by yuta and ogami people are far more severe, debilitating, and socially stigmatizing than those described by priestesses (see chapter 7). Whereas illness narratives of priestesses answer the question of how a person comes to recognize her true "kami-ness," illness for yuta and ogami people answers the question of why or what caused them to take on this ritual profession. "Why" is primarily a sociological or psychological question, and the answer lies in the social or psychological experiences of the religious activist. "How," in contrast, is a theological or cosmological question, and the answer lies in the meaning of being human and divine.

Yuta's and ogami people's narratives, unlike the priestesses' narratives, do bear a certain resemblance to well-known social scientific models of women, illness, and religion (cf. Finkler 1985; Lewis 1975). Unlike priestesses, yuta and ogami people describe long illnesses that made them chronically dysfunctional and into social outcasts; religious involvement functions to ameliorate their illness and rehabilitate their social standing. Yuta (and to a lesser degree ogami people) need a great deal of persuasion to take on a role that is seen as strenuous, somewhat dangerous, and of ambiguous social status. Priestess, on the other hand, is a semi-inherited role, and the preinitiation illness is mild—a mark or a stamp. A particular woman may not know from childhood that she will be priestess, but she knows that the chances are high: Her mother, aunt, or grandmother have been priestesses before her. Priestesses, unlike yuta and ogami people, do not act "crazy," lose their jobs, or receive diagnoses of cancer. Becoming a yuta or an ogami person is a meaningful social and economic realignment; becoming a priestess is a spiritual realignment. While priestesses' narratives describe episodes of weakness and bleeding (which I interpreted in chapter 7 as facilitating merger with deity), yuta-to-be tend to suffer from problems with their heads—an appropriate training ground for a ritual expert whose work involves speaking with and hearing deities and ancestors.

Yuta and ogami people work outside of any kind of larger system or organization, and illness is the way in which they become socially recognized ritual practitioners. As experts in human misfortune, a personal history of having overcome terrible illness and suffering is the best possible proof of their own ritual efficacy. Illness is their training, their university; through illness they learn their role. Priestesses, on the other hand, work within the clan system; they have no need to attract clientele or to show off their skills; and there is no suggestion that suffering makes them into "good" priestesses. All that the priestess needs is to prove that she is indeed the one who was born to sit in the kaminchu's place. A visible sign—an *inkan* or a nose bleed—suits that purpose admirably. Moreover, and this point is crucial, the priestess is kami-sama. The essence of her role is not that she suffers more than other people but that she is more kami-sama. Too much illness, and especially illness that leads to socially inappropriate behavior, would be poor proof of divinity.

Priestesses Only Deal with "Good Things"; Yuta Also Deal with "Bad Things"

SUSAN: If accidents happen, do you pray?

MRS. SHIMOJO (priestess): No, yuta does. Noro prays only for good things. Yuta does *oharai* ['go away' rituals].

The implication here is not that yuta are evil, but rather that yuta can deal with bad spirits, the bodies of the dead, and other unpleasantness. Priestesses keep the world harmonious; yuta (and men) deal with disruptions in harmony. This point is clarified in the next excerpt from a priestess:

MRS. TANAHARA: Even though I don't think the words, the words come out from my mouth. . . . Because I have kami-sama, I don't do the ogami for a house that had a death in the family. I don't do the grave ogami. I only do happiness things. I don't do suffering things. Even if I wanted to go there [to suffering or death places] I am not able to go.

Priestesses Take Care of Communal Matters; Yuta Take Care of Private Ones

SUSAN: Why do people have two rituals when they finish building a house, one with an ogami person and one with priestesses? [see chapter 6]

MRS. SHINYASHIKI (she invited an ogami person to perform a new house ritual): I brought Mrs. Ikene to do ogami because I myself don't know how to pray so well.

MIDDLE-AGED MAN: Actually, the noro must do the ritual because she is the only one who can report to the [village] kami-ya (shrine).

In the eyes of villagers, the very definition of priestess is that "she does for the clan" (or in the case of the noro and her associates, that "they do for the village"), whereas the yuta "only does for the one house [family]." The priestess's geographical sphere of action is limited to the village; the yuta's is wider. Thus the noro tells us that, unlike the yuta, she did not pray for the road or bridge linking Henza Island to other islands because her work is "only Henza's work." Each priestess is associated with one kami-sama, and that kami-sama is the spiritual manifestation of a particular village or clan. Although the definition of her role is a communal one, she has no role outside of her own village or clan. When I asked the noro why she had not prayed at the public ceremony organized by a rock star to launch his new boat from Henza (a Shinto priestess had come from Naha to pray; see chapter 9) she answered, "Because the ship is supposed to go to the mainland so it is better that a big priest does this and not only Henza's kami-sama. This boat isn't only for Henza." The noro explained that she cannot leave the village for more than about two weeks (there is no institution that keeps her in the village nor is there a formal rule; she is referring to her own feeling that she cannot leave). Similarly, a clan *umei* (servant or assistant to kaminchu—*umei* is a spiritual role, and the process of discovering that one is born to be umei is the same as the process of discovering that one is born to be kaminchu) related that once she had gone to live in Tokyo, but within one year a strange rash came out all over her body, and "everyone" told her that she had to come back to Henza. Since then, she has never missed a ritual, and the rash has not returned. Yuta, in contrast, work with individual clients and can contact a variety of spirits in a variety of places; therefore, they are capable of extending their ritual arenas.

The Status of Yuta and Ogami People

SUSAN: Do Henza people respect Mrs. Ikene's work?

MRS. HOKAMA: Instead of respect I would say they need her for ogami, she is necessary.

My sense is that many villagers have ambivalent feelings about yuta (somewhat less about ogami people)[7] and that this ambivalence is connected to fear: fear of the yuta's spiritual gifts (she can see the dead and other frightening powers) and fear of her ability to access intimate knowledge of the problems of village families. Villagers say that they prefer to go to a yuta who does not know them, someone outside the village. The fear is not that the yuta will use her knowledge to do harm but rather a vague uneasiness with the power represented by the yuta's knowledge. Put in terms of the typology of power introduced in the previous chapter, villagers feel more comfortable with a relationship of power-from-within (kaminchu) than a relationship of power-over (yuta). Many are eager to point out that "Henza is a noro village," whereas "Yakena [a nearby village] is a yuta village."

The preference for a yuta from another village also reflects villagers' interest in empirical proof of spiritual matters. A yuta who can discern specifics about people she does not know is more likely to be respected. Some villagers make a distinction between real yuta ("go through yuta"—yuta who "go through" to the ancestors or kami-ama) and fakes (especially those who only know what they read in books). Their scorn is limited to the latter. As I explained in chapter 1, villagers respect individual's talents; what they disdain is showing off. Ogami people and yuta understand that villagers appraise their ability.

SUSAN: Is ogami people's advice listened to in Henza?

MRS. IKENE (ogami person): Yes.

SUSAN: How about nonclients?

MRS. IKENE: People who like the way the way things [that I pray] go through [to kami-sama] come to me; other people might not and go to another place. They choose. Sometimes I can't do this [connect to the kami-sama], and then the customer goes to another place.

It is common for villagers to consult more than one yuta. This custom significantly lessens the power of the yuta; no one yuta can obtain real control over the lives of her clients.

MRS. IKEDA: I haven't been to yuta since becoming kaminchu. I don't believe yuta.

SUSAN: You don't believe in yuta, but you believe in them when they say to become kaminchu?

MRS. IKEDA: Yes. They tell lies sometimes. One yuta could be telling lies, that is why you have to go to many different yuta to see that they are all saying the same thing.

The status of the one male yuta in Henza is more problematic (see narrative B).[8] According to village gossip, this man is the black sheep of an important family, and he has made himself into an outsider in his own clan by criticizing the way they do things and for having "too many new ideas about how things should be in the clan." He is rather disheveled looking, and lives on the outskirts of the village. One villager explained,

People say he is knowledgeable and intelligent, but he doesn't get along with people and he keeps himself separate from the community. For example, in each [of the village's five] district they take turns giving out fliers from the town hall, but he refuses to take his turn. He is divorced because of this yuta business, but still maintains contact with his ex-wife who now lives in

Gushikawa. He calls her when he needs her, and he has been known to threaten her.

Unlike the priestesses and the female yuta and ogami people, the one male yuta refuses to do the kinds of mundane tasks incumbent on all members of the community. Perhaps the gravest accusation against him is that he has ties to a literate spiritual circle in Shuri. Thus his yuta knowledge was not acquired either "naturally" or locally, but from foreign books. In contrast to the female yuta and ogami people, who generally uphold standard village behavioral norms both in their own lifestyles and in their judgments and teachings, he has broken with community traditions. Finally, I wish to raise, although not answer (because I do not have the data to do so), the question that being male makes his community status even more problematic.

Despite a certain amount of disdain for fake yuta or social misfits like the male yuta just portrayed, Henza villagers respect the yuta's word. This attitude is also true of the men who run the secular affairs of the village. Here is Mr. Tamura's story: "Before, when I was headman, someone from Hamahiga Island who is not yuta but can see things, came and told me to do some kind of prayer, with seven people. Because that person is someone who can see things, I listened. So I used my own money to coordinate with seven people to go to Naha and other places to do ogami and what I was told to do."

Yuta Take Money for Their Work

FORMER KAMINCHU: Yuta are above kaminchu because they see and hear. That is why we pay the yuta.

MR. IKEDA: Yuta is a business person.

Another source of ambivalence regarding yuta is the issue of money. I discussed this matter with Mr. Shibahiki, a male assistant to the priestesses:

My work is the representation of Henza. The lives of the 5000 [sic] people of Henza are in my hands. That is okay, for everyone to be healthy, that is our way of thinking. It's not good to receive money and then pray. The money won't help connect through [to the kami]. It's like if you get money it is like a loan shark. That type of attitude is not good. To give your heart to the kami-sama is, my own, to open up everything of your heart. You have to think that there is nothing wrong, my heart is clean, and then pray, otherwise you won't connect to the kami-sama. Kami-sama won't receive you if you are like that [taking money to pray].

Despite Mr. Shibahiki's comments, I never heard a villager accuse a particular yuta or yuta in general of charlatanism or of being in it just for the money. Material aspects of existence, such as money, are not looked down upon by villagers in the way that they may be, for instance, in some Buddhist societies. The village priestesses are also paid in cash for their work at rituals, but the payment is made quietly, unlike the yuta, for whom the cash payment is made openly. A finer distinction is that a yuta can, if she is popular, make a living from her work; it is a full-time occupation. Priestesses, on the other hand, only receive sporadic remuneration for their ritual work.

The noro believes that some villagers invite an ogami person or yuta rather than priestesses to a new house ritual because the yuta costs less. (In fact, yuta are often paid a great deal of money.) "To a yuta you only need to pay a little money. At the large celebration that we went to they had to prepare a lot of food, seven meals, and we sing a lot of songs." What I understand here is that the payment of the yuta is a business transaction, whereas the food given to the priestesses is an offering. These two things are ontologically different, and whereas the money payment may be treated with some slight ambivalence in a society in which the use of cash is fairly new and perhaps associated with the economic imperialism of America and Japan, giving food to the kami-sama is ancient and venerable. The food given to the priestesses *is* the ritual; the money given to the yuta is payment for the ritual. Significantly, the yuta is paid with "naked" money (plain, unwrapped bills) in a society in which money given on ritual occasions (such as funerals, weddings, etc.) is always wrapped in a decorative envelope.[9]

Priestesses and Yuta: Intersection of the Roles

SUSAN: Who does the prayer for the oil company [that rents land on Henza Island]?

MRS. SHIMOJO (priestess): The noro is supposed to do it. Actually, if she cannot do it, a yuta does it.

———

SUSAN: In the past were there ogami people?

MRS. KAUWAJO: Yes, many. Clan priestesses are good at it.

In keeping with the yasashii ethos that characterizes Henza, the division of labor between yuta/ogami people and priestesses is not absolute, and some jobs are done by more than one kind of ritual practitioner. If a villager is facing a difficult situation (school exam, a trip abroad), she or he could ask either a clan kaminchu or a yuta or ogami person to pray. Villagers often speak about all three types of ritual experts in analogous ways:

SUSAN: Who is Mrs. Ikene?

MRS. MIYEZATO (wife of assistant to noro): Yuta. She is born like this. She can't learn it. No one teaches her. . . . The kami-sama taught her what to say. Mrs. Ikene comes here twice each year to pray at my *hinu kami-sama* [hinu-kan]. She takes care of Henza.

What strikes me in Mrs. Miyezato's words is the likeness to descriptions of priestesses. We see here the same emphasis on the ability to do the job coming naturally rather than being taught, of her "being born like this." Like a priestess, Mrs. Ikene's ritual role is a regular biannual one (rather than last-resort help in times of misfortune), and, like the noro, she "takes care" of the village. The issue of taking care is an important one; that is the essence of the noro's role (and a generally admirable character trait in Henza). Thus I was interested to hear the noro say to a yuta in the next village: "Please live a long life so that you can take care of us." Significantly, the yuta's reply is a carbon copy of how a kaminchu would have spoken: "I don't need to [have a long life] because another [yuta] will be born when I die."

Many ogami people and yuta have a special relationship with their clan kami-sama. Although villagers say that ideally an individual cannot be both a yuta and a kaminchu, there are some women who are both. Mrs. Tanahara, for example, is both "skoshi yuta" (slightly yuta) and a clan kaminchu. Other anthropologists have found that it is not uncommon for a woman to be both a priestess and a yuta (usually in two different villages; cf. Yoshida 1990; Kamata 1966: 66).

SUSAN: Are you yuta, kaminchu, or ogami person?

MRS. TANAHARA (kaminchu and ogami person): My *first* thoughts are kaminchu.

On one occasion, I saw a former village resident who is now a popular yuta on another island (see narrative A) return to Henza and fill in for the kaminchu in her clan during a clan pilgrimage.

SUSAN: Why did Mrs. Kawakami do this job?

MRS. SHIMOJO (village priestess): She is a clan member.

SUSAN: But there are lots of people in her clan, why her?

MRS. SHIMOJO: She gets electric waves (*dempa*). That is why she represents the clan.

Ogami people and yuta are interested in spiritual matters in general, including clan ritual. For example, the ogami person Mrs. Ikene lives in the main house of her husband's clan. She is now a widow, but the clan altars are still in her house, and she takes care of them. Given the uncodified nature of Okinawan religion, a great many decisions regarding who does what are made on the basis of who feels an affinity for the role, who has the time to take on the role, and who is willing to put him- or herself forward and volunteer for the role. My sense is that a person who wants to take an active part in rituals tends to drift into it, perhaps in several different contexts.

Priestesses and yuta visit many of the same sacred sites, including the utaki, and they sometimes run into each other at the kami-ya or on the path to or from the utaki. None of the priestesses sees this as problematic (although Mr. Shibahiki, the male assistant, does), and the two groups typically greet each other in a collegial manner.

SUSAN: Do you let yuta use the kami-ya?

NORO: It is good that many people pray there. . . . Before the war it was hard, people other than kaminchu could not go in there. But now there are many Henza people who have moved on to the main island [Okinawa], and there are yuta on the main island, and the yuta told the Henza people that they are originally from Henza and so they must come here to do ogami.

When I asked village yuta and ogami people if in their opinion Henza's priestesses are doing a good job, the answers were uniformly positive. Yuta may back up kaminchu in situations in which villagers have become slack about traditional rituals. For example, the Arakaki family traditionally brought food to the priestesses four times each year. Not so long ago, the current Mrs. Arakaki became busy and stopped bringing food. An Arakaki family member—who also happens to be the sister of Mrs. Shimojo (a priestess)—is, in Mrs. Shimojo's words, a nervous person, and so she went to a yuta. The yuta said that the Arakaki family must continue bringing the food, and so they have. The point I wish to emphasize here is that the yuta and ogami people may see themselves and may be seen by others as part of the village ritual system and not as marginal or solitary practitioners.

The primary intersection of the yuta and priestess is over the decision to become priestess. The relationship is interactive rather than purely hierarchical. According to a former kaminchu:

Yuta have to be above clan kaminchu. Yuta are the ones who tell you to become a kaminchu, and once you are told you think and worry. Yuta can see, can hear, that is why they tell us. The yuta has a big responsibility. Among yuta not many can say correctly what is the answer. Some are wrong and say wrong things. *And then the person who receives the information from the yuta has to think herself.* (my emphasis)

Yuta not only identify potential priestesses but may also go around with them and pray together with them during the process of becoming priestess. We saw in chapter 8 that Mrs. Hamabata (the new kaminchu) considers the yuta Mrs. Uyealtari to be her mentor. Similarly, the noro told me that "this yuta [one whom I visited together with her] has very high spiritual feelings. Four or five times we went together to do ogami. . . . Sometimes when I go to Agaregusuku or Irigusuku with a yuta I can hear something, sometimes. Like songs. I asked a yuta how come I can hear this song. The yuta said because a long time ago this song was sung here, that is why you can hear it."

Mrs. Shimojo offers additional insight into how priestesses and yuta work together: "If there is some problem and I don't know what to do, I pray and say that I will go to such and such a yuta, so will you please tell the yuta so that I can hear the answer." On another occasion, Mrs. Shimojo and I had this exchange:

SUSAN: People on Okinawa seem to say that yuta are bad, but you seem to respect them?

MRS. SHIMOJO (village priestess): We have to judge whether this particular yuta is good or bad. The yuta should give an answer that is close to what you are thinking.

The picture that I have painted of Henza is of a society in which there is not one official truth that everyone is expected to share. Decisions ideally are reached through consensus rather than through exerting power.

MRS. CHIBANA (yuta): Even though there are many yuta, each has different words to say. So please check, and don't go only to one yuta.

SUSAN: Is the basic thought of different yuta the same?

MRS. CHIBANA: No. It depends on the person. I have my own way.

The yuta Mrs. Uyealtari made the same point: "If there is not a match with the customer and me, I tell them to go to other yuta and if it seems like it matches, ask that yuta to do ogami for you."

Each yuta has her own words, and each priestess has (is) her own kami-sama. The fact that different people have different spiritual abilities and that the different abilities are needed on various occasions is explained by Mrs. Kauwajo, who recently retired from her job at town hall:

SUSAN: If a lot of bad things happen, do people blame the noro, that her praying wasn't very good?

MRS. KAUWAJO: No, I don't think they think that way. But if a lot of bad things happen, they might ask another person to pray for them [because the first prayer didn't go through].

Yuta, ogami person, and priestess are complementary roles; each needs the other for the jobs that the other performs best. All three groups accept the same moral and cosmological worldview. Almost all Henza ritual practitioners are middle-aged women, all use the same ritual accoutrements (rice, sake, incense), all "take care of" the same villagers, and all tell stories of illness to explain how or why they had entered the role. All attend the same village festivals and many of the same ceremonies and celebrations. Cross-culturally, we can come up with many examples of societies in which two or more kinds of ritual experts coexist. However, in many (if not most) of these situations we find hierarchy, competition, or conflict among the different practitioners, especially if the different practitioners are in close contact with one another. Examples that come to mind include the tension between priests and prophets in the Old Testament and tension between mystics and ordained clergy in the medieval Church. In Henza, in contrast, we find that the various kinds of ritual specialists praise each other's work and avail themselves of each other's expertise.

The relationships among the various kinds of ritual specialists in Henza are an expression of divine dis-order. Their overlapping presences embody the notion that there is not only one kami-sama, no one path to kami-sama, and no one category of people who have a monopoly on kami-sama. In a society characterized by a yasashii ethos and an aversion to hierarchy, religious leadership could be a sticky problem. Because religious leaders have special knowledge, power, or potency, religious leadership often tends to become hierarchical and reified. In Henza, the coexistence of various kinds of ritual experts diffuses power and deconstructs hierarchy. Ogami people, at one end of a continuum, are regular village women who are a bit more gifted at speaking than other villagers (the "praying grandmothers" of the previous generation). At the other end of the continuum, the ogami role shades into the yuta role: They are professionals who are paid for their work and consulted by clients from all over Okinawa. Priestesses, at one end of a continuum, are born to be embodied kami-sama; at the other end of the continuum, they are recognized or selected by yuta, who may be seen either as more professional versions of "praying grandmothers" or as being entrepreneurs or frauds. These kinds of cross-cutting understandings mitigate against an accumulation of power in the hands of any one group.

PART V

DECONSTRUCTING GENDER

ELEVEN

Un-gendering
Religious Discourse

When you are born the kami-sama pick certain people and put a stamp [inkan] on them, and it doesn't matter whether they are male or female. (male yuta)

———

SUSAN: Why in Okinawa are women the religious leaders?

VILLAGE PRIESTESS: I don't know.

SUSAN: Why are women more involved in religion?

VILLAGE PRIESTESS: I don't know.

SUSAN: Are there male kaminchu?

VILLAGE PRIESTESS: Three or four.

SUSAN: Are all clan kaminchu women?

VILLAGE PRIESTESS: Yes, all women.

SUSAN: Do you think that women's religious position gives them a higher status here?

VILLAGE PRIESTESS: Only when it comes to ogami. In Okinawa, all festival activities are done by women, the number of men is small in these things. I also wonder why women do this!

———

SUSAN: In Okinawa, are women higher in religious matters?

PRIESTESS/OGAMI WOMAN: In Okinawa, men and women have the same status.

SUSAN: Are women closer to the kami-sama?

PRIESTESS/OGAMI WOMAN: Ha ha ha!

Conversations with Village Sociologists

In light of the attitude toward power and authority that characterizes Henza's cultural ethos, it is not surprising to find that the statement "women dominate Okinawan religion" is not articulated by villagers. Rather, it is an assessment made by

215

scholars, most of whom are Japanese, American, or European. In numerous conversations, I asked villagers why their religious leaders are women. As we see in the following pages, the most common initial response was: "Are they?" If I insisted on continuing the conversation (by saying "yes, they are"), villagers typically offered sociological explanations ranging from demography (counting off the religious leaders in order to verify that they are indeed all women), localizing and temporalizing (explaining that women's religious leadership is limited to specific times and locations in which particular social or historical forces have caused this to be so), social-role theory (men's and women's subsistence work leads to certain religious roles), distinguishing between description and prescription (between what happens to be the case and what should be the case), analysis of confounding variables (factors other than gender that confound easy interpretations of behaviors as gender-linked), and socialization theory (women are not innately more religiously gifted, but rather they are educated to know the correct rituals). Taken together, these sociological theories proclaim that gendered religious behavior is not universal, not absolute, not immutable, not particularly desirable, and not natural.[1]

The nonrecognition of and disinterest in the category of women's religious leadership is part of an Okinawan inclination to think in terms of role-based rather than existential gender identities. Igor Kopytoff explains the difference in this way: "Some social identities are culturally defined as having to do with what people 'are' in a fundamental sense, indicating a state of being (for example, in the West, father, woman, or priest). This is in contrast to social identities that are culturally perceived as being derived from what people 'do' that is, identities based on their roles (for example, teacher, physician, policeman)" (1990: 79–80). In the Okinawan case, it is useful to modify this schema somewhat, because the key ritual roles are states of being: The priestesses *are* kami-sama, they do not *do* kami-jobs. However, when gender is introduced into the discussion, priestesses and nonpriestesses alike typically move to a role-based perspective: They maintain that there is no existential link between womanhood and priestesshood and that any association that seems to be there is a function of what men and women do in specific contexts and not of what men and women are.

Demography

SUSAN: Are Okinawan rituals carried out only by women?

MR. YAMASHIRO: No, there are also men.

SUSAN: But I went to the sacred grove with the noro and her associates, and only women were there.

MR. YAMASHIRO: Well, there are men but they don't come, just once in a while.

In Henza, approximately sixteen priestesses have roles in village events. At many of these events, one or two men assist the priestesses by clearing the path through the jungle, pouring sake, and carrying bundles of food and ritual items. Although the priestesses themselves treat these men as helpers rather than as fellow priests, some villagers classify these men together with the noro and her associates. This leads to conversations like the following one:

SUSAN: In Henza why are only women kami-sama?

MRS. HOKAMA: There are men kami-sama, but men usually won't put in ogami. There is a man, two, already there, Mr. Shibahiki, Mr. Miyezato. Women kaminchu are Mrs. Kamura and Mrs. Jana. Two women, two men. Also Mrs. Tomeko and Mrs. Ishikawa.

Despite the auxiliary role of the male assistants, when I asked villagers if priestesses are always women, these men sometimes were mentioned as "proof" that priestesshood is not gender-linked. I am particularly impressed with Mrs. Hokama's initial effort to show that the number of men and women is balanced, a stance she had to back down from when she began to list the other kaminchu, all of whom are women.

Clan kaminchu represent the clan to the kami-sama, and they pray on behalf of individual clan members who have personal problems. In a number of conversations, villagers told me, in the face of conspicuous empirical evidence to the contrary, that not all clan kaminchu are women. For instance, I asked the sister of Henza's leading male ritual assistant (Mr. Shibahiki), "Are all clan kaminchu women?" Her answer consisted of a lengthy list of names of and anecdotes about women kaminchu in the various clans. Like many other informants, she avoided explaining why kaminchu are women or even saying that all kaminchu are women. She offered me a list of specific names rather than a global statement. Other villagers resolved the paradox between the ideological stance that "clan kaminchu is not an intrinsically gender-linked role" and the empirical observation that "all Henza clan kaminchu are women" with a compromise statement using the word *most*—"most clan kaminchu are women." In reply to my question regarding whether Okinawan prayer is always done by women, Mrs. Shinzato replied, "Yes, only. Men go sometimes to pray, but most of the time women."

Localizing and Temporalizing

SUSAN: Why are women the religious leaders in Okinawa?

NORO: Before the Sho King era, before then I think, men did the main part of the rituals. Every day they would fight and drink and fight, and the king said if men do the rituals Okinawa will go bad. So give the women property so women will not need to marry and they can make a living out of the property. And I was given my house, and Mrs. Jana's property, and the other clans also. That's why the property was given.

SUSAN: Do you think it is better that women do the rituals?

NORO: I don't know, but women are so busy I would prefer a man to do the job. January is so busy, January first. I have to prepare meals for visitors. I only get a couple hours' sleep that night, I am preparing for guests to come. It doesn't feel like New Year's.

SUSAN: Do you think women have a better relationship with the kami-sama?

NORO: In mainland Japan men do it [rituals], only in Okinawa it is women. That is why the scholars come to do research here. Ha ha ha.

As we have already seen, Henza villagers are reluctant to reify social or cognitive categories. Blurring and indeterminateness characterize their discourse of kami-sama, of social roles, of leadership, and of gender. *Temporalizing* and *localizing* are two of many rhetorical strategies that allow villagers to avoid describing their universe in absolute terms.

The following example underscores villagers' resistance to gendered discourse. I attended a ritual meal held after the clan priestesses pray at the sacred groves. All those who attended the meal were middle-aged and elderly women. I asked a kaminchu why only women came to the meal today. "Old men used to come. People who don't have jobs come." In this exchange, we hear both the device of temporalization—men used to come but not anymore—and the linkage of religious participation to social roles, in this case employment. (Actually, in the age group of people who attend rituals, women tend to be far busier and work harder than men.)

We now turn to a somewhat different example of temporalization. At the san gatsu festival, after the ritual spearing of a fish, villagers, with the exception of the group of women who had constituted the core ritual group, began a parade down the main street toward Nanza Island, carrying banners and drumming and singing (see description of san gatsu in chapter 5). When it came time to wade to Nanza Island, only a small handful of women continued on with the large group of men. I asked the core ritual group several times if only men go to Nanza Island. The women insisted, "Anyone can go to Nanza Island." When I pressed the point, asking why they were not going, they explained, "Because our legs now aren't strong enough to walk." Although I had joined these women many times in hikes through the jungle to the sacred grove (a walk at least as difficult as the one to Nanza Island), they insisted that what stopped them from going to Nanza Island was a recent physical weakness and not any sort of gender-linked prohibition. They called upon an idiosyncratic, nonintrinsic, temporal factor (weak legs) rather than a permanent or ideological one.

One village priestess answered my inquiry regarding women going to Nanza Island with an explanation that took into account social change and interpreted gendered religious behavior in terms of temporary fashion: "It used to be that women didn't go. The reason is that they wore kimonos, and when they went into the ocean it was not pleasant with kimono, they didn't like it. They would take a boat instead. But now because [she points to her Western clothes] it is for the whole village, everyone goes. It used to be that only fishermen went."

Praying at the hinu-kan, according to many informants, is explicitly associated with women; villagers often call the hinu-kan "onna no kami sama" (women's kami-sama). I asked Mrs. Adaniya, an elderly woman respected by other villagers for her ritual knowledge, if only women pray at the hinu-kan. Her reply: "Yes. Truthfully, men also should, but they don't, at least in Henza. It's not just for women, but in Henza only women do."

We see here a pattern of localizing; in Mrs. Adoniya's remarks, discourse was narrowed down from the global to "in Henza." The significance of localizing is that it shifts the meaning of gendered behavior from the realm of the natural or universal to the realm of the specific or incidental.

Henza headmen (the Japanese word—ku-choo—is ungendered) have been men since the headman system was instituted approximately one hundred years ago, yet villagers are adamant that this is not a necessary situation. The temporal and localized aspects of this role are clarified by the woman who owns Henza's beauty parlor. I asked, "Is the headman always a man?" Her reply: "Until now. But women could be. There is an election and a woman could run. But Henza's headman job is very busy, there are so many village events. Compared to other villages, Henza's headman is busy. For that reason it is hard for women to do the job."

The beauty parlor owner tells us that in general women can be headmen, but in the specific, local case of Henza the role would be difficult (not impossible) for a woman. This point is developed further in the following conversation with an elderly woman and her daughter-in-law:

SUSAN: In Okinawa, is the headman always male?

DAUGHTER-IN-LAW: No, women can do it too.

MOTHER-IN-LAW: Either woman or man, whoever wants.

DAUGHTER-IN-LAW: Yes, a woman can become headman.

MOTHER-IN-LAW: In modern society, there is no distinction between men and women.

DAUGHTER-IN-LAW: That's right. In a village in Gushikawa, there is a woman headman [not far from Henza, Gushikawa is a medium-sized town where many village women go to shop for items that are unavailable on Henza].

In this exchange, we see both localization (in Henza there is no woman headman, but there is in Gushikawa) and temporalization (in modern society, all roles are open to women and men). Daughter-in-law and mother-in-law reiterated that the real issue is one of volition: Whoever wants to be headman can; there are no social rules limiting candidacy to men.[2] We will examine the issue of gender and headmen further in the next section.

Social Roles

SUSAN: Could a man be a clan kaminchu?

MRS. IKEDA: He could but he wouldn't want to.

SUSAN: Why not?

MRS. IKEDA: Mmh, maybe, because he is busy.

I quote now at length from Mrs. Shinzato, the wife of one of Henza's leading citizens and a woman highly respected for her skills at running a household. Please note the parallel ways in which she deals with the question of gender in the case of priestess and in the case of headman.

SUSAN: Is the headman always a man?

MRS. SHINZATO: I wanted to be headman (laugh). But I have to take care of my husband and give respect to my husband, I can't neglect the house and go there (to town hall). If you are headman, you can't do your house things. Men usually don't help women. In your case, Susan, your husband helps, but my husband doesn't help. Washing clothes, cooking, raising children—women do alone. So I couldn't become headman.

SUSAN: Why are noro and other kaminchu always women?

MRS. SHINZATO: In the old days, men were busy. Every day outside. And they went to foreign countries, America, Hawaii, Brazil. If they get on the boat one month or one year they don't come home. They did this to earn money. Women had free time because men went away for a long time. Men go away like to foreign countries, the woman always prayed for her husband to be healthy. Every day. For her father, husband, brothers, older and younger brothers—they should have health and long life. To protect them from dangerous jobs, the women always pray. In the main island [Okinawa], there was more property, so men could do farming jobs, too. [But] Henza is surrounded by the ocean and there aren't enough farms to make money, and that is why men had to go to the ocean to do their jobs.

In this conversation, Mrs. Shinzato accounts for the absence of men priestesses and the absence of women headmen in the same terms: busyness. Women cannot be headmen because they are too busy with their household tasks. Men cannot be priestesses because they are too busy with their boats and fishing. I stress that this explanation is above all a sociological one. She does not tell us that women cannot be headmen because women tend to react emotionally and not analytically; she does not tell us that men cannot be priestesses because semen is polluting or because men do not give birth. Her explanations are rooted in culture rather than in nature and thus allow a cognizance both that gender roles can be arranged differently from how they are arranged in Henza and that even in Henza gender roles can change.

I discussed the question of gender and religious roles with the local headman:

HEADMAN: The Ryukyus differ from mainland Japan in that here women are noro.

SUSAN: Why are women noro here?

HEADMAN: The system is that men go to war and women stay home, take care of the family, take care of health, and so pray. This is the system that was institutionalized, and it is okay.

In this conversation the headman—a very good sociologist—explicity construed women's religious leadership in terms of social roles, pointed out that these social roles are not universal, and identified the existence of social processes by which social roles are institutionalized. Let us now listen to a conversation with a former village headman:

SUSAN: Are there are any rituals that only men do?

MR. TAMURA: No.

SUSAN: What about ama goi [rain ritual performed by men; see chapter 5]?

MR. TAMURA: They did ama goi three or four times since the war. Not since I became headman.

SUSAN: Why do only men do this ritual?

MR. TAMURA: I don't know the real reason. Ama goi's kami-sama doesn't hate women, but—mmh—That is why ama goi is only men. Even the noro doesn't go. Women are the ones who work in the kitchen and use water. Women use water to do their job. Men go outside to do their work. So only men do this ritual.

A number of points here merit mention. First, we note his noncognizance of the category "rituals performed by men." Then, when offered a specific example of a ritual in which only men participate and asked why women don't participate, this very thoughtful and knowledgeable informant had no ready ideological answer and even negated the one possible ideological answer that occurred to him ("the kami-sama does not hate women"). At the end, the reason that he came up with is a sociological one having to do with the division of labor in the village.

Acquired Knowledge

At village funerals, after the hired male Buddhist priest leaves the cemetery, elderly women sit across from the tomb and sing traditional Okinawan-language lamentations (*wakareru utta*). Men do not sing these songs, and, moreover, while the women are singing, men either leave the cemetery or help (noisily) to take down the awning that had been erected in front of the tomb during the Buddhist funeral service. On several occasions, I asked villagers why only women sing these songs:

SUSAN: What are wakareru utta?

FISHERMAN: I don't know. These are old women's songs.

SUSAN: Do men sing these songs?

FISHERMAN: Men can sing these songs, but here in Henza the old women are the ones who know them.

_____

SUSAN: Do only women sing wakareru utta?

PRIESTESS: Yes.

SUSAN: Why don't men sing them?

PRIESTESS: They don't know the songs. Even some women don't know the songs.

Similar comments were offered by villagers regarding the song sung at the ritual held thirty-three years after a death of a family member. At a ritual of this sort that I attended for Mrs. Okuda's late husband, the first part of the event consisted of guests and family members lighting incense and saying prayers at the ancestral altar. Afterward, middle-aged and elderly women sat in a circle on the porch next to the main room of the house. Drums were distributed, and women began to sing a special song. At one point in the singing, Mrs. Okuda got up and danced. The only man present in the room was a grandson, who photographed the event. The next day I asked the school principal, a self-professed aficionado of local culture, whether the song for the thirty-third anniversary after a death is a women's song. "No," he said, "Everyone can sing these songs." Later, I asked the widow who had danced whether this singing is only for women. "Yes," she said. "Why?" I asked. Her reply, "Men could sing but they don't know the songs."

All of these speakers utilized references to socially acquired knowledge to loosen the perceived link between women and funeral songs. Men can sing the songs, but they don't know them. Especially in the conversation with the priestess, we see that although she began with an empirical statement that only women sing the songs, she then backed up, suggesting that women do not sing the songs just because they are women and men are not prevented from singing because they are men; only people who are knowledgeable sing.

Confounding Variables: Age

In a variety of contexts, villagers introduced age as a variable that confounds the connection between gender and ritual: Women qua women are not religiously active or knowledgeable; rather, age is the real issue.

Villagers explain that old people are more active in ritual than young people and that because in the over-seventy age group women outnumber men, women predominate at ritual events. Religious involvement, then, is not linked to gender but to age.

SUSAN: Are any old men involved in kami-sama things?

MRS. HIROMI: No. Men die earlier than women.

Significantly, villagers also proffer social rather than inherent reasons for old people's greater religious interest and activism. According to one middle-aged woman, "It is not that all people who do kami-sama things are old. It is just that the younger ones go to work. I am married to a first son of a family and I have an altar and I do the things I have to do, to prepare the tea at the butsudan."

Old people, villagers say, have seen rituals more times, so they are more likely to remember how things are done.[3]

SUSAN: Who sings the wakareru utta (funeral songs), only women?

MRS. HOKAMA: Everyone who attends the funeral will sing.

SUSAN: Is it true that only old women sing these songs?

MRS. HOKAMA: Yes, men don't sing.

SUSAN: Do all women sing or only old women?

MRS. HOKAMA: Everyone who attends the funeral who knows the songs sings. But the younger generation doesn't know the songs. That is why they don't sing. Every time you go to funerals you hear those songs, so naturally you remember those songs. When you reach the age of forty or fifty you have attended lots of funerals so you know. People who attend funerals naturally remember the songs.

In this passage, Mrs. Hokama explicitly linked old people's greater religious activism to their greater acquired knowledge of ritual matters. This point is particularly important, because as Errington (1990: 47ff.) has shown, in much of Southeast Asia gender hierarchies are weak precisely because age hierarchies are so strong. And it is indeed the case that age—on the surface—seems to be a salient hierarchical construct in Henza. Beginning at age eighty-five, villagers are treated to increasingly expensive and impressive birthday celebrations, at which songs are sung praising the elderly person's age and wisdom.[4] At Mrs. Okuda's eighty-fifth birthday, for example, her family spent (according to her) some $40,000 on a party equal in size and ostentation to a wedding. She herself wore several different gorgeous gowns during the party, every hour or so leaving to change from a Spanish flamenco gown to a beautiful Japanese kimono to a Western-style wedding dress.

At age ninety-nine, the villager is given a spectacular celebration with a parade around the island. This series of rituals, combined with the village system of age-cohort social and ceremonial activity, could easily lead one to believe that age is a meaningful and natural social category (cf. Katata 1992). At the final shindig—the ninety-nine-years-old party (kajimaya)—two songs are sung. One of the songs goes like this: "Seven small celebrations have passed [each twelve years.] You went through those years, and to have this kajimaya celebration you are becoming kami-sama."[5] This song seems to suggest that old age is indeed ontologically significant—that old people's status changes to kami. However, and this is the point I was leading up to, the other song goes like this: "The wind-turning flower toy, if it doesn't have the wind it won't turn, and when you reach this age you are like a child and you play with the grandchildren." The message made explicit in the second song is: So you thought that age means social status but really it means nothing. You who have reached the great age of ninety-nine have once again become a child. Significantly, the truly extravagant parade and celebration are held not when the villager is eighty-five or eighty-eight and likely to still be functioning well and able to exert some sort of authority in the village or the household, but at ninety-nine, an age at which most celebrants are incapacitated and living in old-age homes. Age, then, like gender, is ritually and discursively deconstructed just when it seems like it might become something real.

In sum, although villagers use age as an explanatory factor that deconstructs the (what is to me) prima facie association of women and religious activism, they do not replace that association with a natural or immutable correlation between age and religious activism. Age, like gender, carries religious significance as a role-based rather than an existential matter.

Confounding Variables: Place of Origin

In Henza all ogami people are women, and, indeed, some informants refer to these practitioners as "praying grandmothers." Still, when I asked villagers why ogami people are women, the typical answer was, "Men can be ogami people." In the following conversation, I spoke to the most prominent ogami woman in the village.

SUSAN: Are ogami people always women?

MRS. IKENE: No, there are many men.

SUSAN: Do male and female ogami people pray the same way?

MRS. IKENE: They should be the same, but the words [that they say] are different. *Each individual is different.* I was from Shuri-udun so it used to be that I used the Shuri dialect in ogami, but now I have been here I have acquired the Henza accent. When I did ogami, Shuri dialect would come out from me and customers would say why do you talk like that, and I would say that I am originally from Shuri. [my emphasis][6]

In this conversation, Mrs. Ikene resisted my use of gender as a relevant category and instead shifted the focus away from gender to another (confounding) variable: location. We learn from her that men and women pray the same way but that people from different parts of Okinawa pray differently. Mrs. Ikene endeavored to move the level of discourse from the categorical (women vs. men) to the individual ("I myself pray . . ."). In this, her perspective is identical to that of the teachers who were quoted in chapter 3: Significant differences are not between men and women but among individuals—each individual is unique and should be treated accordingly. Mrs. Ikene and the village teachers defy Western sociology's need to sort phenomena and people into discrete categories. If the bottom line is that each individual is different, any empirically noticeable tendency for men's or women's behavior to cluster in particular ways is inherently meaningless.

SUSAN: Do men and women have the same or different ways of thinking?

MRS. ADANIYA: Same. But it depends on the human being. Maybe your thinking and my thinking could be different.

Description versus Prescription

The difference between description and prescription is that the first tells how things are, whereas the second tells how they should be. The first is a discourse of social reality, whereas the second is a discourse of existential or cosmological ideal. This distinction emerges clearly in the following conversation. I was discussing men's ritual activities with a divorced man in his sixties. Note here his eagerness to seize on means to avoid giving me a categorical answer.

SUSAN: In rituals, whenever an animal is killed, does a man do it?

MR. HIKOSKI: But today we buy meat at the supermarket so we don't need to kill like before.

SUSAN: In the old days was it forbidden for women to kill animals?

MR. HIKOSKI: No, not forbidden but it wasn't the custom, men killed animals.

This distinction between description and prescription emerges even more explicitly in the context of a conversation about incense. At Henza rituals attended by both men and women, men consistently light the incense that is placed on the altar. In the course of my fieldwork, I saw this dozens of times—men light the incense. Yet when I asked villagers why men always light the incense, they invariably evinced surprise and denied that this is true. One villager insisted to me that lighting incense is not gender-linked and that if I had seen men lighting incense I should understand that this is a trend and not a rule (custom and not law). "If it were a man's job, then widows would have to ask a man to light, but they don't!"

Sociological, Not Ideological

In Henza, women are associated with land-based work and men with sea-based work, a division of labor that is reflected in religious rituals, household arrangements, and a range of other cultural patterns. Yet unlike in many other fishing cultures, Henza villagers offer little or no ideological exegesis of or justification for men's fishing and women's horticultural work.[7] The division of labor is seen by villagers as rooted in subsistence needs, not in human nature or divine order. I asked one elderly fisherman if in the old days Henza men ever worked in the gardens: "No no no! Henza is only four kilometers wide, so there is not enough land to make enough money to support the family. So men go to other places, Singapore, Philippines. So women stayed in Henza but men went to other countries." His claim is not that women work in gardens because they are forbidden to go to sea or that men go to sea because garden work is beneath their dignity. Rather, he explains that because there was not enough land on Henza, men were compelled to go to sea to earn a living.

I was told by several villagers that women cannot go on fishing boats.[8] When I asked why, I found that most of their explanations had to do with social roles: "Women are too busy with other things." Although two informants fleetingly mentioned menstruation as a possible reason for women not going on fishing boats, neither speaker elaborated on the matter, and, in fact, women sometimes do go out on boats. According to one of the few active fishermen still in Henza: "Women can go on boats if they are members of the fishermen's association. Nowadays, they can go into the boats. Sometimes the wife of a member goes also. They can use a net." Women often help out on the boats, painting, loading and unloading, making repairs, and managing the nets; and women can go on transport boats. One woman, who is now in her late seventies, knows how to pilot a boat and has a boat license. In the old days, she often accompanied her husband on trips and once even sailed the boat by herself to some faraway village.

I cite here a conversation with an elderly man:

SUSAN: Is it true that if you saw a woman in the morning on the way to the boat you would not go fishing that day?

MR. MASAMITSU: Yes. There are some people in both the east and west [sides of Henza] who had this custom.

SUSAN: Would women have to stay in the house in the morning?

MR. MASAMITSU: No, we cannot say to a woman not to go out because we are going to fish. But sometimes by chance we would happen to see a woman. If you met a man it was okay, just a woman you couldn't meet. Those people who believed this, they would say that today is not a good day for fishing, if they met a woman.

SUSAN: Did all men have this belief?

MR. MASAMITSU: Not all, some. There were particular people in east and west [sides of the village]. Not many.

SUSAN: Where did those people get that belief from?

MR. MASAMITSU: It was told from a long time ago, that a man who saw a woman didn't do well fishing. The fisherman himself would understand that this is why he didn't catch fish [because he had seen a woman], but the woman or other people would not know that this was going on.

This conversation is particularly rich. Mr. Masamitsu makes clear that the custom regarding seeing a woman is idiosyncratic and not systematic: It is not associated with east or west Henza, but with some few people in each area. Only those people who believed it would say that if they met a woman it was not a good day for fishing. I particularly call attention to the point of view of the speaker: He is describing this custom from the outside ("those people" and "they would say"). He does not see the bad luck ensuing from seeing a woman as being real—rather, he sees it as "people's belief." It was a custom, not a rule, and it was individual rather than communal ("the woman or other people would not know that this was going on.") There was no coercion involved: "We cannot say to a woman not to go out because we are going to fish." Finally, there was no ideological substructure to this custom—it was merely empirical: The fisherman himself would see that he didn't catch fish after he had seen a woman.

We find a similar discourse in our next example. Henza's public, communal New Year rituals are to a large extent patterned after Japanese and Chinese rituals which are dominated by men. In Henza, the main lunar New Year celebration takes place in the morning in the square across from the kami-ya. The year that I was in Henza, about one hundred men, dressed in suits and carrying offerings of sake, gathered in the square while the noro and a few other priestesses, the head-man, and several male dignitaries prayed inside the kami-ya. The men then sat down outside on mats, and, to the accompaniment of a samisen, began dancing, eating oranges, making speeches, and drinking sake. The party moved to the town hall, where the men were served plates of sashimi (raw fish) and large quantities of sake and beer.

Traditionally, on New Year's morning, men go out of the house before women. According to Mr. Ginjo (an elderly man):

> Women don't go out on New Year's morning. Blood [he points to his foot]. Blood is a negative symbol, and women menstruate and so they don't want women to go out first. But noro and kaminchu are women and they also menstruate [but they pray at the kami-ya on New Year's morning], and so this doesn't make sense. Because New Year, up till 10:00 in the morning, girls don't go out, but I don't really agree with this. In my case if the neighbor's boy comes in people say this will be a good year, but if the girl comes in people will say this won't be a good year [laughs]. This is probably from China. In Itoman and Henza this thought is strong, because of the ocean contacts. Mainland Japan taught that man is above women. But Americans came in and taught ladies first, so the thought reversed. Okinawan education and religion traditionally were mainly from China. It went first to Okinawa and then to mainland Japan.

Mr. Ginjo's explanation of the custom of women not going out on New Year's morning fits well with the kinds of discourse we have already seen. He acknowledges that this is indeed the custom, he points to some inconsistency in the custom (that some women do go out in the morning), he notes that this custom is not universal (not even throughout Okinawa), he laughs a bit at the custom, and then he explains it in terms of historical processes and not in terms of ideology. In a variety of contexts, villagers gave me to understand that they realize that other societies (especially Japan and China) are more highly gendered than theirs.

According to Mrs. Hokama, "On New Year's men go first to do the greetings [of neighbors], women try to go second. For example, I might want to go greeting the neighbors first, but there is a proverb hina gu gasachi bai [women shouldn't go ahead]. I accept this because I was raised that way, I was told to do this by the elders when I was small." Again I draw attention to the lack of any kind of essentialist statement: She acknowledges the difference between a cultural expectation and her own individual inclination—I might want to go greeting the neighbors first, but I don't—and she roots her acceptance of this custom in the socialization process ("I accept this because I was raised that way.") It is interesting to add here that she is one of the many women who told me that she did not raise her eight children in the way that she herself was raised, that nowadays women can have jobs and support themselves and so they are stronger, and that two of her daughters, both in their thirties, are unmarried.

I asked two elderly women why women do not go out on New Year's morning. "It used to be [that way], but now they have to go out to school [Okinawan schools run on the Japanese solar calendar, not on the Okinawan lunar one]. It was thought to be bad luck for women to go out. Because visitors will come to the house, women have to stay in the house to serve them. That is what I think. They needed someone to host visitors." What these women seem to be saying is, first, that the custom was limited to a particular historical period, and, second, that it was not a real prohibition but rather a social arrangement that allowed visitors to be hosted. Showing that the issue here is not one of a taboo or true ritual prohibition, informants do not in any way suggest that there may be problems or misfortune nowadays caused by schoolgirls going out on New Year's morning.

Henza's sociological discourse is particularly striking when we look at the essentialist discourses found in many other cultures. In the Embrees' 1935 study of the Japanese village Suye Mura, for instance, we read that "the view of women held by village men was less than flattering in all its details, and the women themselves frequently commented on what they interpreted as the frailties peculiar to their sex" (Smith and Wiswell 1982: 2). In Suye Mura cultural thought, "There was a darker side to women's nature that went well beyond the negative characteristics normally attributed to them. . . . The villagers believed that only women were witches" (Smith and Wiswell 1982: 170). Putting curses on others was believed to be done only by women, "because they harbor deep and longer grudges" (Smith and Wiswell 1982: 272). Exemplary of the negative view of women in Suye Mura are the practices of brides wearing the *tsuno kakushi* (horn cover headdress) and women blackening their teeth at marriage. According to a [man] informant, "Both indicate the sinfulness of women. Because she is sinful, woman must be deprived of the possibility of biting others, and the concoction used to blacken the teeth serves much the same function as the bit in a horse's mouth" (Smith and Wiswell 1982: 2).

Gender and Religious Ideology

We have seen in this chapter that although Henza men and women (like men and women in many other societies) tend to engage in different ritual activities, Henza's division of labor is not explicated or naturalized by any sort of gendered discursive frame. In the course of dozens of conversations and interactions, I never heard even a hint of the kinds of gendered ideological assertions or analogies that characterize Suye Mura (Japan) and so many other societies. I suspect that it is the absence of gender as a significant symbolic category, more than the absence of gender as a pragmatic category, that reflects, reinforces, and grows out of women's religious preeminence in Henza.[9]

Religions in which men are structurally dominant have developed elaborate ideologies to explain, justify, cause, or apologize for women's subordinate status. Examples of these ideologies include claims that women are more prone to sin, especially sexual sin; that woman (Eve) brought sin into the world; that women's souls or intelligences are inferior to men's; and that God chose to become incarnate as a male. As the Vatican Congregation for the Doctrine of the Faith succinctly declared in 1977, there is a "sacramental bond between Christ, maleness and priesthood" (quoted in Iadarola 1985: 469). The pattern of male religious leadership explained and justified on ideological, cosmological, or mythological grounds is a common one cross-culturally (Uchino 1987; Lacks 1980). Feminist philosophers and theologians have explained the ubiquitousness of these kinds of ideological stances as part of the patriarchal package deal: "The symbol of the Father God . . . sustained as plausible by patriarchy, has in turn rendered service to this type of society by making its mechanisms for the oppression of women appear right and fitting" (Daly 1973: 13).

In a similar vein, almost all of the small number of known religions that are led by women explain women's religious leadership in essentialist, ideological, or mythological terms (Sered 1994). For example, nineteenth-century Spiritualism "made the delicate constitution and nervous excitability commonly attributed to femininity a qualification for religious leadership. If women had special spiritual sensitivities, then it followed that they could sense spirits, which is precisely what mediums did" (Braude 1985: 422). In the Tres Personas Solo Dios religious movement, a syncretic religion including elements of both Catholicism and indigenous Filipino beliefs, "Some time in the 1960's this community decided to have only women as priests, based on their view that males were not able to remain celibate" (Ruether, n.d.: 2–3). In Northern Thai matrilineal spirit cults, women predominate as mediums, and women are believed to have a sort of "soft soul" that makes them more susceptible to the effects of spirits (Tanabe 1991: 189; see also Tambiah 1970: 283). Similarly, in certain new Japanese religions, "Women are more fitted to be mediums than men, because they have stronger feelings, better intuition, and more sensitive emotions" (Offner and Van Straelen 1963: 124). And to take one last example, the Shakers believed that founder Ann Lee's gender was an inherent and necessary precondition for her role in redemption (Procter-Smith 1985: 6). Not only was Ann Lee's femaleness seen to complement Jesus's maleness, but also men and women were seen to possess different natures—women more spiritual, nurturing, emotional, and affectionate, and men more worldly, physical, rational, and intellectual (Bednarowski 1980: 211; Brewer 1992; Kern 1981).

Because these women-led religions are not situated in societies that are dominated by women (unlike men-led religions which are situated in societies dominated by men), the gender ideologies offered to explain women's religious leadership cannot be understood as part of a matriarchal cultural complex or as the ideological underpinnings to matriarchal social institutions (in the way men-led religions can be understood as part of a patriarchal cultural complex and as the ideological underpinnings to patriarchal social institutions). With the important exception of Okinawan religion, religions led by women are never (at least within historical times) the official or main religion of the societies in which they are situated (Sered 1994). Explicitly gendered religious ideologies in religions led by women, therefore, must be understood as reflecting some sort of interaction with the dominant, men-led religion. And, indeed, we find that ideologies of male superiority either infiltrate into women-led religions or that women's religions invest a great deal of energy in challenging dominant ideologies of male superiority via the construction of parallel ideologies of female superiority. Perhaps the most consistent pattern of gender beliefs in women-led religions is apparent acceptance of widespread essentialist, patriarchal ideas concerning women's nature and role. These ideas are, however, reinterpreted as evidence of women's greater interest in, or talent for, religious activity.

To recap, whereas religions led by men typically propagate ideologies that sanctify men's leadership as part of a general enterprise that reflects and strengthens other patriarchal social institutions, religions led by women typically propagate explicit gender ideologies that defend women's religious leadership in response to cultural situations in which women dominate neither the society at large nor the mainstream religious traditions. Although these two sets of discourses seem to be contrary to one another, in fact, both utilize the same set of discursive parameters— the essential difference between men and women and the cosmological "rightness" of gender as a determinant of religious role. Both are discourses of difference.

In Okinawa, the women-led religion is the mainstream religion. This religion (for as long as we have historical documentation) did not develop in response to, under the auspices of, or in the shadows of a men-led religion. Neither in need of countering a mainstream male-dominant religious ideology nor concerned with upholding other social institutions featuring gender hierarchy, Okinawan priestesses have no reason to elaborate a gendered religious discourse.

TWELVE

Gender Bending(?) and Ritual Deconstruction

In chapter 1, I portrayed Henza social life as characterized by yasashii interactions and social categories. Because of extensive contact with foreign cultures (Japanese, Chinese, American, Philippine, and others), Henza villagers are aware that other people live differently, yet it is rare to hear villagers say that their own ways are better. Henza villagers seldom reify their own social arrangements or institutions. Nevertheless, social organization does tend to generate a force or stamina of its own. Even when there is little or no ideological bolstering or justification for particular social patterns, just the fact that "this is how things are and how they have been for a long time" may tend to make them appear immutable and necessary.

Anthropologists explain that rituals function to convince participants that their cultural norms and organization are good, true, and eternal; through religious ritual people worship their own social structure (Durkheim 1915, Geertz 1969). Even rituals that seem on the surface to turn normal social arrangements upside down—so-called rites of reversal (Gluckman 1965)—actually serve to prove to participants that their ordinary social arrangements are necessary; disorder is fun for a few hours but untenable as a permanent lifestyle. In the anthropological literature, rites of reversal defuse potentially disruptive social forces via temporary inversions that set conflict within a ritual discourse that neutralizes the threat and therefore results in the continuation of the status quo. In this model, ritual liminality ("time-out" from normal cultural demands and structures; see esp. Turner 1981: 159–160) is followed by reintegration—by putting things back together again.

As in the classic anthropological model, Henza's ritual repertoire includes rites of reversal that move from the status quo to its opposite and back to the status quo; these rituals defuse potentially disruptive social forces and demonstrate for villagers that the status quo is really quite desirable. The difference between the rituals described in the literature and Henza's rites of reversal lies in the structure (or nonstructure) of the ritual and the status quo: Certain Henza rituals fabricate order, competition, structure, dualism, and hierarchy and then expose them as artificial, synthetic, and not particularly desirable constructs (cf. Lincoln 1989: 89ff.). In contrast to Victor Turner's model of ritual as beginning with structure, moving to antistructure, and then returning to structure, many Henza rituals begin with nonstructure, exaggerate and play around with structure, and then return to nonstructure. A pervasive theme in Henza ritual is the ceremonial, often dramatic, exposure of the artificiality, temporality, and optionality of village social categories—what I call ritual deconstruction.

Cross-culturally, gender is one of the most ubiquitously reified social categories. Because gender "looks" as if it is a function of biological sex, its cognitive hold is particularly strong. Gender hierarchy threatens ideological and structural egalitarianism in a particularly potent manner precisely because gender differences often seem so natural—they seem to be rooted in biology. In different cultures, a variety of practices serve to make gender seem real. These practices are what is known as "gender performativity" in recent anthropological literature (Morris 1995: 569). In this theoretical framework, gender is not a fact or an essence but rather a set of acts that produce the effect or appearance of a coherent substance. Gender is something that people do rather than a quality that they possess. It derives its compulsive force when people mistake the acts for the essence and come to believe that they are mandatory. The effect of gender performatives is to compel certain kinds of behavior by hiding the fact that there is no essential natural sex to which gender can refer as its starting point (Butler 1993). Significantly, Okinawan culture seems to include rather few gender performatives, and those that we find actually seem to deconstruct rather than construct gender. Most noticeably in the realm of ritual, gender performatives tend to follow the nonstructure-structure-nonstructure formula that I discussed above; ritual performatives in Henza expose the fact that there is no essential natural sex to which gender can refer.

Although Okinawa is one of the more egalitarian cultures with which anthropologists are acquainted, men and women are not equal. Both an ideology of male superiority (most probably imported from China) and a political structure run by men are present, albeit weakly. I am convinced that in Henza the visible presence of kami-sama who are embodied in female form helps deconstruct one of the world's most prevalent and tenacious patterns of power—"natural" male leadership. The engendering of kami-sama as women, especially in a society in which the headman and government are men, subverts incipient hierarchies of gendered authority (see chapter 9). A number of Henza's ritual practices can be seen as additional forums for deconstructing gender categories.

Ritual Deconstruction

Tug-of-War

Henza's most visibly public ritual—*tsuna-hiki* (tug-of-war)—structures and exaggerates gender dichotomy, only to reveal gender to be, in the end, an artificial category.

Throughout the Ryukyu Islands (as elsewhere in East and Southeast Asia), villages perform annual ritual tugs-of-war. The tsuna-hiki is linked to the agricultural harvest. Two enormous ropes made out of rice straw are joined by thick loops through which a stick is placed. Teams then pull at the ropes; the team that succeeds in moving the stick to their side wins. This tug-of-war has been described in the ethnographic literature as one in which male and female compete; women should win for there to be a good harvest (see Muratake 1964/1965; Mabuchi 1968: 129). Apparently, in some villages in the Ryukyu Islands, the competition is between human men and human women; in some villages, it is between a symbolic female rope and a symbolic male rope. But in either case, as I understand the literature, the ritual has to do with cosmic tension between male and female principals, tension that should be resolved in favor of the female principal in order for the world to regenerate annually. Competition—and gender, from this perspective—seem to be something "real": Gendered competition gives birth to fertility.

Following is a description of the tsuna-hiki in Henza in 1995.

Preparing the large, heavy ropes for the tsuna-hiki begins weeks in advance. Village men spend hours sitting on the porch and then in the parking lot of the town hall braiding by hand and machine the gargantuan ropes. On the day of the tug, villagers gather on the main street, where the two ropes are joined together with a large log. A man with a loudspeaker announces that there will be three tugs, boys versus girls, men versus women, and east village versus west village. The girls start out on the east and boys on the west. It is a tie, with neither side strong enough to budge the rope. Then women and men are told to join the boys and girls. Everyone pulls and shouts and strains with all their might, while some of the older villagers bang drums on the sidelines to help boost the tuggers' spirits. The boys win—budging the rope an inch or two to their side. When the men and boys begin to beat the women and girls noticeably, some men go over to the girls' side to help pull. The two teams then switch sides of the rope, and again the men win, but the announcer makes a pronounced point of reiterating that there are more men than women, which is why the men won (to my eye it is not at all clear that there are more men than women). After this rather intense competition between men and women, the announcer calls out that the next tug will be between east and west side residents of the village. The sides reshuffle: Men and women who moments before had been situated in a dramatic setting of gender competition now pull cooperatively on east and west teams. After the first east-west tug, the two teams switch sides, with the east side of the village moving to the west side of the rope and the west side of the village moving to the east side of the rope. The minute the last tug is over, the two "halves" of the village mingle, and women hack the "gendered" ropes to bits in order to take small pieces as charms and to take big pieces as compost for their vegetable gardens.

In Henza's tug-of-war, the drama and buildup of the men-versus-women tug—the illusion that men and women constitute opposing "teams"—falls apart the moment that villagers reassemble for the east-versus-west tug. The message of the Henza tsuna-hiki seems to be: You thought that gender was a meaningful category? Well, look at this, it takes us about two minutes to unravel it. Given villagers' non-cognizance of gender as a natural principle of social or ritual organization (see chapter 11), in an unusual variation on classic anthropological models of rites of reversal, the Henza tsuna-hiki creates categories where there were none and then publicly and spectacularly dissolves them.

The success of the tsuna-hiki ritual deconstruction is demonstrated in conversations that I had with villagers on the subject of the previous year's tsuna-hiki. When I spoke to villagers, they were uninterested in, or unaware of, gender symbolism related to the tug. Here is a conversation with one of the few villagers who even understood my question:

SUSAN: Why is tsuna hiki done? Is it just for fun?

MRS. ADANIYA: In the old days in the village they raised rice, so the tsuna-hiki is to bring the villagers together as one. And wish for a rich harvest year.

SUSAN: Is one side supposed to win?

MRS. ADANIYA: Maybe this year east, next year west.

SUSAN: In the tsuna-hiki, who is stronger, men or women?

MRS. ADANIYA: There are more women than men, so I think women are stronger. Last year women won.

SUSAN: When women are stronger, is there a good harvest?

MRS. ADANIYA: There are more women, so they are stronger.

Two points should be noted here. First, we see a rhetorical device that we met earlier—temporalizing. By answering my general question with the words, "Last year women won," Mrs. Adaniya avoided making a blanket declaration about who should or does win the tsuna-hiki. Second, we see a clear statement that women qua women are not stronger; rather, women won because they were more numerous. Mrs. Adaniya interprets women's victory in a specific year in terms of demography and not cosmology or biology.

Mrs. Adaniya's approach was atypical in that she even related seriously to my question. The most common response to my questions about previous years' tsuna-hiki was confusion: No one seemed to remember who had won, and villagers seemed surprised that I would ask about it. Most typical was this conversation with Mr. Yamashiro, the brother of the noro.

MR. OKUTARA: Susan and I read that at tsuna-hiki men are on the east and women are on the west, and if women win there will be a good harvest.

MR. YAMASHIRO: (laughs). I think that tsuna-hiki has no meaning.

Shifting Dualism

When I first saw the ropes used for the tsuna-hiki I felt confused: Although I had read in the literature that there is a male rope and a female rope, the two ropes looked to me to be identical (in fact, the loop at the end of one rope is very slightly larger because the two loops need to fit one inside the other). Given that village men work at braiding these undifferentiated "male" and "female" ropes for several weeks on the porch and then the parking lot of the town hall, I would go so far as to argue that, at least on one level, the meaning of tsuna-hiki is that gender distinctions are manufactured by human hands and really rather minimal. The tsuna-hiki is the antithesis of gender performatives that hide the fact that there is no necessary connection between gender and sex. Instead, Henza's tsuna-hiki is an "un-gendering" performative that exposes the connection between gender and sex to be artificial, minimal, and "man-made."

In Henza, both gender dualism and geographic dualism seem to be manufactured in specific situations only, such as the tsuna-hiki ritual. In reality, Henza is *not* divided into two halves, east and west. Traditionally, there were three sections to the village (east, west, center), as there still are for the purpose of *usudeku*. Politically, the village is divided into five hamlets. The division of the village into two sides during tsuna-hiki should not be understood as reflecting social structure or organization (for example, there are no marriage rules or class differences associated with east and west). East and west have no significance outside of a few very specific ritual contexts. As Professor Yoshida suggests, "The idea that a certain thing is always valuable does not exist [in Okinawa]. . . . East and west in the village seem to be relevant only for tsuna-hiki" (personal communication). Thus a more useful way to think about village culture may be in terms of shifting or situational dualisms.[1]

The analysis that I offer here builds upon Toichi Mabuchi's crucial insight that in Ryukyuan cosmology appositions such as east-west, right-left, male-female, upper-lower, sea-land are

> combined with each other in various ways, *but not necessarily in consistent ways:* for example, the sea may be combined either with the upper or with the lower *according to the situation,* while leading to a transposition of its partner, the land. Such a state of things would result in what may be called the *shifting dualism* in which the ways of combining these sets are *not constant,* though apposition and combination as such remain ever-present. Meanwhile, this kind of dualism seems to have developed bipartition here and there into tripartition. *This depends largely on the situation.* (1968: 139; emphases mine)

Although Henza (like other Okinawan villages) plays around with geographic and gender dualisms, these dualisms not naturalized, idealized, or stable. This fact mitigates against the development of essentialist understandings of social categories.[2]

My analysis, as I said earlier, builds upon Mabuchi's conceptualization, yet I recognize that Mabuchi, like many other scholars, imputed more weight to dualisms in Okinawan cosmology than I found to be the case in Henza. Although the discrepancy between my observations and those of certain other scholars (especially Muratake 1964/1965) may be attributed to regional variations and to cultural changes that have taken place during the past thirty years, it is also possible that the discrepancy reflects the kind of data we collected. Scholars who treated dualisms as fundamentally important in Ryukyuan culture have looked primarily (of course, not solely) at myths, rituals, and symbols, many of which the anthropologist himself interpreted within a theoretical framework explicitly drawing upon Levi-Strauss's structuralism. My work focused more on village discourse and interactions and on villagers' own interpretations of rituals, even if those interpretations were idiosyncratic and transient. In Henza, geographic dualisms, for instance, are vaguely known at a ritual level, but they most emphatically are not considered relevant either at the level of daily life and role or at the level of immediate or conscious interpretation. Although labels like "east" and "west" and "male" and "female" are certainly used in the context of tsuna-hiki, the more important issue (to me) is whether these labels are understood by villagers to have any sort of ontological meaning or significance; and to that question the answer is "no." The salience of Henza's tsuna-hiki does not lie in the sanctification or ritualization of gender or geographic dualisms. At least in Henza, the salience lies in the fact that at the end of the ritual all of these oppositions are experienced as manufactured and ephemeral, male and female and east and west join together, and villagers explicitly interpret the ritual as one that builds village unity. (In Mrs. Adaniya's words, "to bring the villagers together as one.")

Gender roles and geographical units do exist in Henza. I suggest that tsuna-hiki deters them from becoming too real by exaggerating them; tsuna-hiki allows villagers to see that if men and women compete—pull their very hardest against each other—a rice straw rope can be budged but a few inches, and that is all. In tsuna-hiki victory is not very substantial; the hard competitive work of tsuna-hiki bears far fewer empirically observable fruits than does the hard cooperative work of men and women in daily life. The tsuna-hiki, then, can be seen as defusing not only gender and geography but also competition in a wider sense. In tsuna-hiki, competition, a minor yet potentially disruptive undercurrent in Henza's egalitarian village ethos is exaggerated and played around with and seen to be a difficult and inefficient way for getting things done.

Given the artificiality and contextuality of the dualisms in tsuna-hiki, and given the village interpretation of tsuna-hiki as fostering unity, I think it is most helpful to treat the tsuna-hiki as a ritual expression of balanced or egalitarian complementarity. There can be no tsuna-hiki if men and women do not agree to cooperate in carrying out the ritual; there can be no unity if one side is naturally and immutably stronger than the other; fertility, good harvests, village unity (or whatever other good things the tsuna-hiki is understood to promote) are only possible when men and women are rather equally matched and willing to collaborate with one another. The message of complementarity is, to my eyes, symbolized by the fact that it is village men who spend weeks making the rope and village women whose gardens will benefit in the months to come from the pieces of rope that they take home when the half-day ritual is over.

In Henza, the clearly artificial ritual construction and deconstruction of dualisms help mitigate against the development of permanent and compelling power or status hierarchies. On the one hand, structures and order in a society function as safeguards against the chaos that allows strong, violent, fortunate, or charismatic individuals to grab power or prestige. On the other hand, structures and order tend to become reified and compulsory, thus preserving power or prestige in the hands of certain groups or categories. The shifting dualisms and ritual constructions and deconstructions of Henza constitute a means of representing and dealing with structure and power that is neither chaotic nor reified and therefore eminently suited to a society committed to an egalitarian "yasashii" ethos.

Cross-Dressing?

At village rituals there are two men, Mr. Miyagi and Mr. Arakaki, who sometimes wear women's clothing.[3] I am sure that there are many ways for anthropologists to analyze this phenomenon. What is most interesting to me is the response of Henza villagers. Their reaction is, quite simply, nonexistent. In order to ask people why these men wear women's clothes, I first had to dedicate quite a bit of time to clarifying to whom I was referring.

At the haari ritual boat race, a man in women's clothing was standing at the edge of the pier next to the headman. The next day I asked a villager:

SUSAN: Who is that man who was wearing a woman's dress?

VILLAGER: What man?

SUSAN: The man with the woman's dress.

VILLAGER: Oh, there was a man with a woman's dress?

SUSAN: Yes, the man in the bright red dress, blond wig, and padded bra. You know, the man who stood right up in front of the entire audience at the edge of the dock and danced with the master of ceremonies during the climax of the race.

VILLAGER: Oh, you mean Mr. Miyagi.

SUSAN: That's right. Who is he?

VILLAGER: A bus driver.

SUSAN: Why does he wear women's clothes?

VILLAGER: He likes to make people happy at festivals.

SUSAN: Does his wife mind that he wears women's clothes?

VILLAGER: Oh, his wife, she is the one with the garden next to your house.

SUSAN: Well, what do people in the village think of a man who wears women's clothes?

VILLAGER: He likes to make people happy at festivals.

SUSAN: Were there traditionally men who wore women's clothes at festivals?

VILLAGER: I don't think so, I don't know.

At the san gatsu ritual, a man named Mr. Arakaki wore a woman's bodice and a long red loincloth between his legs. Afterward, my conversations with villagers were similar to the conversation about Mr. Miyagi. The only difference was when I asked:

SUSAN: Who is he?

VILLAGER: Mr. Arakaki.

SUSAN: Who is Mr. Arakaki?

VILLAGER: He is a schoolteacher.

SUSAN: Oh.

VILLAGER: But that isn't why he wore those clothes. Teachers don't have to wear those clothes.

Sometime after these events I turned to one of my best informants, a woman who has worked at the town hall for many years.

SUSAN: Who is Mr. Miyagi, who wears women's clothes at haari?

MRS. KAUWAJO: That is his habit.

SUSAN: How about Mr. Arakaki, who wore women's clothes at san gatsu?

MRS. KAUWAJO: He is a village council member and it is his hobby to decorate himself. There is no meaning to this. Just to cheer everyone up, to get people into the mood.

SUSAN: In my country if a man wears women's clothes people would say he is strange.

MRS. KAUWAJO: That is just his hobby.

These dialogues, similar to several other conversations held with both men and women villagers, can serve as an introductory lesson in how *not* to do anthropological fieldwork. It is a great credit to Henzans that they were able to withstand my persistent efforts to put words into their mouths and to force them to share my own cultural categories. What is clear in these exchanges is that the notion of a man wearing women's clothes is not at all interesting to Henza villagers. No one remarked on it without my asking, no one drew my attention to it at the festival, no one even realized who I was asking about until I repeated my question several times, and no one understood why I was interested in asking about this topic. A man wearing women's clothes, publicly and flamboyantly, is of no particular interest to villagers. Whereas to my Western eyes these men were crossing gender categories, in the eyes of villagers they simply wore clothes that usually are worn by women but that have no inherent or permanent gendered attributes. Wearing women's clothes does not turn a man into a gender bender; it is simply a way to raise people's spirits at a village event.

We turn now to a somewhat different example of a man who sometimes wears women's clothing. Many Henza women belong to one of three neighborhood usudeku groups (see chapter 4). These are groups that practice and then perform elaborate traditional dances at the obon festival. Although these are all-woman groups, a ninety-two-year-old man has joined one of the groups. At meetings, he sits quietly in the farthest right corner of the room next to the *toko no ma* (the traditional place for men to sit in Okinawan houses). The women do not relate to him very much but they do seem to like him and expect him to dance. He was pointed out to me in the context of several women telling me with pride that there are many very old people in their group (all the others, of course, were women); his age rather than his gender elicited comment in this all-women's group. The women told me that at san gatsu festival he dressed up in women's clothes and made merry for the people in the old-age home. I asked why and was told, "Because he likes to, and because he has his late wife's clothes. He put on makeup and a complicated kimono by himself. He has pictures. His wife died when she was seventy-one years old. She did usudeku until she was sixty-five, and he used to like to watch it." At this point he joined the conversation: "Because my wife died I take her to the san gatsu by wearing her clothes."

Marjorie Garber argues that transvestism ultimately reinforces gender divisions (1992; cf. Bateson's 1958 classic discussion of transvestism as marking difference between the sexes in *naven* ceremonies). In the West, when a man dresses like a woman and passes, he is gender bending. If he does not pass, or if he deliberately shows a male trait (such as hair on his chest), the incongruity of his appearance strengthens the belief that the two genders are polar opposites. Either way, the obvious transvestite makes people uncomfortable: This is because in the West gender is understood to be naturally and existentially connected to sex. The absolute identification of gender with sex in the West means that an individual who mixes the "wrong" gender with the "wrong" sex draws attention to the "naturalness" of the gender-sex association and the "unnaturalness" of detaching that association. And so the man who wears women's clothes is categorized as pathological, unnatural, bizarre. By setting him off from what is "normal" and "natural," the gender-sex categories are sustained as "real."

In Okinawa, on the other hand, gender—like other social categories—is loosely constructed, the connection between sex and gender is tenuous, and cross-dressing elicits almost no interest from onlookers: A man dressed in women's clothing presents no paradox, challenges no worldview, is given no label or diagnosis, and invokes no emotional reaction.[4]

Weston (1993), Morris (1995: 583) and Murray (1996), in contrast to Garber, argue that berdache and other instances of transgendering are forms of double mimesis in which individuals parody the society's representations of ideal gender. By making gender so fabulously artificial, drag performances show up the artifice of gender. The Okinawan case certainly seems more in keeping with this latter view. I would suggest, however, that the best analysis may lie in a synthesis of these two interpretations. In cultures in which gender and sex are experienced as a natural unity, cross-dressing is not sufficiently strong to unravel the gender-sex complex and instead "looks" pathological, or, at the very least, meaningful.[5] In cultures like Okinawa, in which there is cognitive space to decompose the sex-gender complex, cross-dressing can be enjoyed, laughed at, or simply ignored.[6]

A question that begs to be raised is, if it is so easy to cross gender lines in Okinawa, if no one cares about men dressing in women's clothing, why do Mr. Arakaki and Mr. Miyagi bother to do so (and to do so in very public contexts)? To solve these puzzles, we return to the description of the clothes worn by Mr. Miyagi and Mr. Arakaki (especially Mr. Miyagi). Both of these men dressed in stereotypical Western women's clothing (one even wore a blonde wig) and *not* traditional Okinawan women's clothing. In Okinawan culture, as I said in chapter 3, women's and men's clothes are only slightly differentiated—traditional Okinawan dress does not accentuate secondary sex characteristics or draw attention to sexuality. Now let us step back a moment and recall the argument I made earlier regarding the tug-of-war and other ritual competitions in Henza. In these events, I argued, villagers exaggerate normally undeveloped social structures, play around with them, and in the end defuse them through inversion. I would suggest that we are seeing a similar process at work in the case of the men in women's clothing. The bright red Western women's dresses and bodices that they wear function to take clothing norms out of the drawer of the taken-for-granted and relocate them to the front window display case. By dressing up in caricatured foreign women's clothes, these men's bodies proclaim that strong expressions of gender difference are unnatural (foreign). What they are playing with here, I believe, is not the idea of crossing gender boundaries but rather the idea of constructing gender boundaries. The women's clothing worn by Mr. Miyagi and Mr. Arakaki serves to deconstruct gender in much the same way that the tug-of-war does. An alien social trait (in this case the alien social trait is the notion that gender is something "real") is exaggerated, caricatured, played around with, seen for what it is—a social construct rather than a natural order—and finally deconstructed when villagers go back to regular, everyday social patterns.

The ninety-two-year-old man who wears customary Okinawan women's clothing (his late wife's kimono) in order to bring his wife with him to celebrations embodies another means for deconstructing gender difference. By wearing his wife's kimono, he is not being outrageous but rather, in his own quiet manner, demonstrating or embodying the continuity between men and women (and between life and death). All a man has to do, he tells us, is put on a woman's kimono and he can add on to himself another aspect of being, in this case a female aspect. This man's actions are exactly parallel to those of the priestesses, who, as we saw in chapter 8, "add to their character" an aspect of kami-sama and "bring kami-sama" with them—in their bodies—from the clan house to the utaki.

Gender Bending?

When gender ideology is loose and unelaborated, an individual who wants to enact a role usually associated with the opposite gender does not need to change very much about his or her appearance or behavior. Thus, for example, the climax of the san gatsu festival involves the ritual spearing of a fish, meant to elicit a good fish harvest in the coming year. The person who spears the fish is always a woman dressed in a lovely kimono, although in Henza fishermen are almost always men. According to one of the women who sometimes fills this role, the woman in this ritual "represents" men, yet she does not need to dress like a man in order to do so.[7]

Like tsuna-hiki, san gatsu is a dramatic and public ritual. When I first came to Henza, villagers made a point of encouraging me to stay long enough to see san gatsu; they told me that other villages do not do the fish-spearing ritual on san gatsu, that only Henza does, and that is why so many scholars and newspaper reporters come to see it. In other words, villagers understand san gatsu to be a ritual that in some way encapsulates their communal identity. Undoubtedly, san gatsu is important to their communal identity because so many village men went to sea. However, I suspect that something additional is happening at san gatsu: Precisely because men doing ocean-based work and women doing land-based work seems to be one of the more stable organizing principles of Henza society, one could easily think that men are "naturally" fishers and that women are "naturally" gardeners. When the beautiful Mrs. Okuda, dressed in a gorgeous kimono, gets up in the center of the main street of the village and spears a fish in the context of one of the most popular and visible village rituals, she embodies the message that there is nothing "natural" about commonplace social roles. Given the fact that villagers do not interpret women's ritual fish-spearing as exemplifying gender reversal, we can treat Mrs. Okuda's ritual role as a kind of un-gendering performative.

We turn now to a few brief examples of situations in which an individual has easily, and without arousing village interest, taken on a role usually associated with the other gender.

In each clan, a woman or a few women tend to take responsibility for caring for the clan house in which the clan's altars are located. In one clan, a man in his seventies has taken upon himself the role of living in and keeping up the clan house. Here is my conversation with that man:

SUSAN: Isn't it usually women who do this kind of job?

MALE CLAN HOUSE CUSTODIAN: A man can do it. Other clans all have women, but I can get through [to the kami-sama].

In another clan, the *sekininsha* (person who is in charge of clan secular matters) died, and his widow took over the job, although in all other clans a man holds that position. Again, no one in Henza seems to find the switch particularly noteworthy.

Clan priestesses, as we have said, are women. At the New Year ritual in which the clans visit Henza's sacred spring, I watched each clan approach the spring, and I watched each clan's kaminchu pray in front of the spring. When it came time for the Shibahiki clan to pray, a man—Mr. Shibahiki—knelt down to pray. I asked people why he seemed to be doing the job of clan priestess. One reply:

MRS. SHIMOJO: He is the kaminchu of Shibahiki clan.

SUSAN: He is a man, so is he a real kaminchu?

MRS. SHIMOJO: He is a real kaminchu.

At this like at other ritual events, men of the various clans carried and spread out the mats on which the kaminchu knelt to pray, and men scooped up water from the sacred spring. In a few clans, however, women carried and spread out the mats, and women scooped up water from the sacred spring. When I asked onlookers why women were doing a job usually done by men, my questions were met with incomprehension: Ritual roles are neither rigidly nor consiously gendered. Neither a woman carrying a mat nor a man kneeling to pray at the spring is perceived to be a "gender bender."

The senior woman in each household is responsible for praying at the hinu-kan. In Henza, there is a man who prays at the hinu-kan. He is about sixty-five years old and the brother of Mrs. Shimojo, the village priestess. He has been divorced since his early thirties and lives alone in a large, lovely, clean, and rather empty house. He told me that he prays at the hinu-kan for his children and grandchildren. He also cleans and cooks for himself, and because he is not good at talking to people (in his opinion), he has chosen to work in jobs that necessitate little social contact: porter and vegetable gardening (gardening is usually women's work). On a clan pilgrimage, he chose to sit on the bus for part of the way with women and part of the way with men. Despite his living a lifestyle that more closely resembles a typical woman's than a typical man's lifestyle, and although he performs a ritual almost always performed by women (praying at the hinu-kan, the onna no kami-sama—women's kami-sama), no one in the village (except the visiting anthropologist) finds this man especially interesting.

To take another example, on Ancestors' New Year, men usually visit the houses of their kinfolk:

MS. KUMI YAMADA: Tomorrow I have to come to Henza to go around to relatives' houses.

SUSAN: But you just told me that this is something men do, that the women stay at home and serve food.

MS. KUMI YAMADA: Well yes, but in my case my eldest brother doesn't live in Okinawa, so I have to do this instead of him.

In fact, in her family there is another brother, married with children, who does live in Okinawa. Yet he did not take over the eldest brother's role; she did, and no one seemed to find this situation in need of justification, explanation, apology, or rationalization.

My final example returns us to the kaminchu-feeding rituals discussed in chapter 6. Recall that it is the role of a village man, Mr. Miyezato, to prepare the trays and serve the food to the kaminchu at shinugu. Yet, as we saw in chapter 5, food preparation and service are typically women's tasks in Henza. When Mr. Miyezato serves food to the priestesses, he does not do so in a carnival-like atmosphere of reversal—the message is not "look how silly it is for a man to serve food to women." Quite to the contrary, he is competent and matter-of-fact, as are the kaminchu. One (albeit not the primary) message of this very public, very ritualized meal is: Food service is not an existentially female task.

Back to the Priestesses

Shortly after arriving in Henza, I met Mrs. Shimojo, the woman whom everyone had told me is the most knowledgeable priestess. Early in our conversation, she explained to me that she is a male kami-sama. I found her claim enigmatic: I could not see that she did, said, or wore anything that looked "male." To the contrary, Mrs. Shimojo was one of the most "feminine" women (by Japanese and Western standards) in Henza.

Both male and female kami-sama are embodied by women kaminchu in Okinawa. This seems to indicate that gender categories are accorded some significance (otherwise, there seems no reason to use a discourse and cosmology of gendered kami-sama). On the other hand, the difference between a male kami-sama and a female kami-sama is minimal. The priestesses know who is a male kami-sama and who is a female kami-sama. But when I asked questions such as, When you are a male kami-sama, do you talk in a deeper voice? or do you do "male" things such as smoke? the answer consistently was that they do not.

SUSAN: You are a male kami-sama?

MRS. SHIMOJO: I am female but I represent male. That is why I tie the white headband in the front [when wearing kaminchu white robes].

SUSAN: Was it always that a woman represented the male kami-sama?

MRS. SHIMOJO: Yes, I think so. I am Uezato [from Uezato family—Uezato is her maiden name], I am a woman but I sit for a man kami-sama.

SUSAN: At rituals do you speak in a male voice?

MRS. SHIMOJO: No.

SUSAN: When you say that your kami-sama is a male kami-sama and the noro's kami-sama is a female kami-sama, what does that mean exactly?

MRS. SHIMOJO: There are people who wear white clothes [kaminchu], I sit in the middle [at the utaki], I am a female but my kami-sama is male. Because of the way we wear the clothes, it is different from others. Usually, the female wears the kimono like this but I wear it like that. Also the way the headband is tied. I tie the headband in front because I am a man kami-sama.

As can be seen in the plates, the priestesses wear a five-piece white outfit. Male and female kami-sama have the same five pieces, but the male kami-sama fold the skirt slightly differently, a difference that is not readily apparent to observers. Also, the female kami-sama tie their headbands with the knot in the back of their heads, whereas the male kami-sama tie the knot in the front. A question that intrigued me throughout my stay in the field is why they go to the trouble of making the distinction between female and male kami-sama if male and female kami-sama do not behave differently, look different, or carry out different tasks.[8] The answer, I suspect, lies in a vague belief in the equality and complementarity of the sexes. Priestesses' kami-sama are ancestors who came to Henza Island and begat the clans; this begatting was physical, not mystical, and—logically enough—the clan ancestors are both male and female. In general, the world comprises both males and females, and kami-sama—who are very much part of the world—are both male and female. At the same time, male and female, from a Henza perspective, are not highly elaborated cultural categories—not much needs to be done to "do" gender (Lorber 1994; Morris 1995). Both on human and cosmic planes, differences between male and female are slight. A woman who embodies a male kami-sama is neither transformed in any very substantial way nor does she elicit any sort of attention for gender bending.

I would now like to turn away from Mrs. Shimojo, a woman whom villagers respect as an especially knowledgeable and skilled priestess, and attend instead to the kaminchu we met in chapter 9 who was willing to confront the drunk male ritual assistant, and whom her clan colleague assessed as "violent." This woman is a clan priestess, but some people in the village believe that she really is "born" to be a yuta and not a priestess. In the first part of our conversation, she mentioned several times that she was born outside of Okinawa: Her father had left Henza, married a foreign woman, and later returned to Henza. She herself moved to Henza in her late teens.

My kami-sama is a male kami-sama, so he lets me drink one big bottle of sake. That was my first time [drinking] since I was born. I don't drink [but my kami-sama does]. Usually I sit like this [like a woman, with knees to the side] but when my kami-sama rides me [norikakaru, like riding a horse] I sit like this [like a man]. When I go home [after a ritual], I think to myself, "Why did I say that?" I myself don't smoke, but the kami-sama naturally has me smoke. It used to be that they had a long tobacco pipe. Kami-sama smokes tobacco, but not cigarettes, kami-sama smokes the old kind of pipe. Naturally it comes to me, because he wants to drink and smoke. It is not that I want to, it just happens. I don't know when kami-sama wants it. I sit like a man [she demonstrates sitting with one leg in a squat and one knee up]. I am kind of ashamed to sit like this. Also [I get] a red face. And [I hold] a cup in my hand. I say to the person who doesn't believe, "I am going to throw this cup here to you, and if this cup breaks you will lose your life, and if it doesn't break, you should think that you are lucky. Do you want me to try it?" That is what I say. I don't know how, I am a woman, but when I sit like a man at a table my right leg pushes the table. I don't know how a woman can be strong enough to do that. So I will say, "Do you want me to do like I am doing to the table?" That is my kami-sama's character. [She bangs the table.] If I bang like that on the table, I make a hole, but I don't feel any pain, and there is no bruise. I am a regular person, but when I go to the kami-ya, kami-sama rides me. Once I leave the kami-ya to go home, I am a regular person. . . . Everybody says, "You are not a male kami-sama, the one before you in that position was a female kami-sama, why from you should it become a male kami-sama?" But my cousin who sat in this position before me wore a black mantle and pants that are connected to shoes [like construction workers], and a stick and pointed hat. I think that her clothes looked like male clothes. Like a crazy person, she went around and said "I am a man." And when the noro and her associates went to pray, they wouldn't summon my cousin, but she would hear from kami-sama and climb up the tree and speak ill of the noro and her associates, saying "Why don't you take me? The meal that you are preparing, even if you do ogami, won't pass through to kami-sama, because you don't take me." She acted like a man, but she wore white robes [was a female kami-sama]. But in her sixties she died. I feel sorry for her. The kami-sama was telling her that he is a male kami-sama, but my cousin didn't get the meaning of that. After that it all came to me.

This kaminchu's self-portrayal is reminiscent of descriptions of women possessed by male spirits in Afro-Brazilian religions, North American and British Spiritualism, and African zar cults (Leacock and Leacock 1972; Skultans 1983; Boddy 1988). Those women, like the kaminchu whose story we just heard, are possessed; that is, they temporarily empty themselves of their own personality and are "ridden" by a foreign being.

In this excerpt, the speaker makes it clear that her behavior is an aberration in Henza and that it is not welcomed. She draws our attention both to her clan's stubborn refusal to listen to her gendered message and to the fact that she was born in a foreign country and that she is an outsider in Henza. Her self-assessment helps us understand why another kaminchu in her clan considers her to be "violent."

What is the difference between the esteemed Mrs. Shimojo, a male kami-sama whose maleness is barely discernible, and the unpopular kaminchu who smokes, drinks, and exhibits physical strength when she is possessed by a male kami-sama? My sense is that this kaminchu has failed to grasp the overarching cosmology of Henza priestesses. That cosmology, expressed both verbally and through ritual, is one of absolute immanence. The male kami-sama is already there in the female person who is a male kami-sama. There is no need for bizarre clothes or "masculine" behaviors.[9] Nothing needs to happen for a woman to become a man, just like nothing needs to happen for a person to become a kami-sama. Actively doing gender—like actively doing "kami-ness"—is a proclamation of difference, of categories, of bounded cultural structures, all of which are anathema to Henza's ethos of *tege* and being *yasashii*. All that a woman has to do to be a male kami-sama is don the white kimono and then tie her white headband and robe a bit differently, an act that she knows is a symbolic one rather than a transformative one. To do more than that, the way that the "violent" kaminchu does, is to impose binary structures on a cultural setting uninterested in naturalizing social or cosmological differences.

Conclusion

Religion, Power, and the Sanctification of Gender

The question that inspired this study is whether women, in situations of autonomy, make different religious choices than do men. In the only known case of a mainstream religion led by women, does the religion differ significantly from other religions with which we are acquainted? The ethnography and interpretations offered in this book suggest two answers. The first is *no:* Women, like men, engage in a variety of religious rituals as ways of experiencing, contacting, expressing, thanking, enjoying, beseeching, embodying, warding off, communicating with, and influencing the divine. Not surprisingly, Okinawan religion bears certain resemblances to other East and Southeast Asian religions, most especially Japanese Shinto. The second answer is *yes:* Because the reification of patriarchy (that is, of ideologies and structures of male dominance) is a central mythological, ritual, theological, moral, organizational, or symbolic theme in almost all known religions—certainly in all world religions (Sharma 1987; Atkinson, Buchanan and Miles 1985) and seemingly in most tribal religions (Young 1994; Lepowsky 1993; Dugan 1994; Hackett 1994)—the absence of a cosmology and an ideology of gender difference in Henza is surely significant.

Religions cross-culturally seem to pay enormous attention to the "problem of women"; religions mystify, sanctify, and ideologize women's subordination; religions work hard to present the spurious and unnatural link between sex and gender as true and natural; religions are among the most compelling ideological glues that bind gender to sex (Daly 1978). In Henza, in contrast, the bond between sex and gender is thin. Although certain social roles are commonly carried out mostly by men or mostly by women, villagers profess no ideology that makes the commonplace necessary or good. Parents and teachers invest little energy in gender socialization. When villagers are confronted with a situation in which only men or only women fill a particular role, they endeavor to interpret that situation as a temporary and local quirk of chance or choice. When individuals deviate from common social arrangements or enter the space usually occupied by the other gender, no one cares very much—these individuals are not seen as threatening the "natural order" of things.

Without an ideology of difference, there can be no sustainable hierarchy. An ideology of gender difference is what converts a society in which a variety of peo-

246

ple engage in a variety of tasks into a society in which there is only one right way for men to behave and one right way for women to behave. An ideology of gender difference is what makes one of those ways better than, in charge of, or superordinate to the other way. In Henza, I saw no evidence that villagers propound an ideology of difference; to the contrary, they use rituals to deconstruct differences that threaten to become too solid, too reified, too "real." The only bits of an ideology of difference that we find—for example, the mild belief that men should go out first on New Year's—are clearly understood by villagers to be foreign, and not particularly valuable or sensible, imports. In many conversational contexts, villagers introduced sociological discourses of temporality, localization, acquired knowledge, social role, socialization, and demography, discourses that deconstruct and de-essentialize gender (and other) differences that they understood that I had (mistakenly) perceived as "real."

The shifting or contextual dualisms of certain Henza rituals are key parts of a cultural constellation that preserves gender complementarity through deconstructing and denaturalizing the gender-sex link. True gender complementarity cannot be built upon a foundation of essential difference, because, as I have argued, essential difference is the bedrock of hierarchy. Hierarchical relationships are often characterized by mutual dependence in the form of service and patronage (a model I am familiar with from my research in the Middle East), but that is *not* true complementarity. In Henza, ritual and discourse reflect and enhance gender equality and balance—that is, social patterns in which men and women, and men's and women's endeavors, are equally valuable and valued, and therefore neither gendered roles nor gender separation become reified or rigid.

In many societies, essentialized differences are constructed by means of a religious ideology (Bynum, Harrell, and Richman 1986). Because the dominant gender has such a great interest in perpetuating the perception of gender hierarchy as natural, religion and ritual—with their uniquely persuasive ability to present ideas as true and their special expertise in dealing with the "ultimate conditions of existence" (Geertz 1969)—are called into service to present gender differences as existentially and cosmically authentic, legitimate, and certain.[1] Because, as Bruce Lincoln explains, hierarchies and the inequalities they engender are always subject to contestation, they are defended "above all, through those discourses [ritual and myth] that legitimate or mystify their structures, premises, and workings" (1989: 173). Ritual and mythic discourse obviate the need for the direct use of coercive force, which anyway remains "a stopgap measure: effective in the short run, unworkable over the long haul," and transform simple power into legitimate authority (1989: 4–5). Gendered rituals and myths, I would add, are particularly potent means for legitimating power: By pinning power and hierarchy on something that "looks" natural, power itself becomes naturalized.[2]

Ideologies, including religious ideologies, are themselves cultural constructs associated with specific social structures; in particular, structures in which one group seeks to obtain or sustain power over others (Lerner 1986; Leacock 1986; Moghadam 1994). In hierarchical societies, ideology arises through the efforts of groups, often elite groups, to protect and legitimize their interests. Concurrently, hierarchical ideologies construct the sorts of reified differences that lead to the maintenance of ongoing social hierarchies. In a society like Henza, where power in terms of social institutions and power as a personality trait is unelaborated, un-celebrated, and unwelcome, any kind of social hierarchy tends to be minor, loose, temporary, and inconsequential. In the absence of power interests—and especially of gender-related power interests—gender differences are not necessarily codified, mystified, legislated, or enforced. In the absence of inequality, neither the reifica-tion nor the mystification of gender differences (through, for example, mythology) serves any meaningful cultural function. Possibly because of ecological limita-tions, possibly because of a deep-seated cultural ethos of being "yasashii," possibly because of spiritual experiences that have led to a cosmology of absolute imma-nence, possibly because of a long history of conquest and accommodation, Henza never developed a group of people interested in creating, spreading, or enforcing an ideology of difference.

As I said, in Henza the ideological link between sex and gender is thin; there is no vigorous gender ideology, even though there are gender roles. One suspects that in the absence of a male elite, rigid (religious) gender ideologies do not develop, and in the absence of a patriarchal gender ideology, women can hold on to (reli-gious) leadership. The conditions that, in Henza, mediate against the ascension of a male elite and of a rigid patriarchal gender ideology include an especially high level of social integration among women (women's "presence"); matrifocality; the economic centrality of women's subsistence work; a substantially longer life ex-pectancy for women; village endogamy; extended male absenteeism (men's "ab-sence"); a lack of substantial land to conquer and control or to pass on as inheri-tance (and therefore no reason to control women's movements in order to ensure that descendants are true patrilineal offspring); an inheritance pattern that en-courages younger sons to live with their wives' families or in nuclear households or to emigrate (and that makes it highly unlikely for a group of brothers to live to-gether); an aversion to aggression and authority of all kinds; a series of rituals that deconstruct power and competition; and nonrigid, nonhierarchical cosmologies. This configuration is a poor fit for a patriarchal elite that justifies and sacralizes its own dominance by preaching about an all-powerful Father in Heaven represented by powerful priests on earth.

Whereas male-dominated religions are associated with patriarchal social insti-tutions, the one known example of a mainstream religion led by women is situated in a society that is neither patriarchal nor matriarchal. Male deities in patriarchal cultures typically embody values of "power-over" and conquest, and the gender-ing of the deity reinforces social-gender hierarchy. The myths and laws of gods, priests, and secular leaders—all of whom are male—forge an illusion that domi-nance and power are natural, inevitable, immutable, and gender-linked. In Oki-nawa, the "power-from-within" presence of priestesses and kami-sama—in the context of a social structure that is matrifocal but self-consciously, ideologically, and adamantly *not* matriarchal—mitigates against any such illusion.

APPENDIX 1
Glossary of Japanese and Okinawan Words

Agaregusuku	east sacred grove
ame tabore (ama goi)	"please give us rain" ritual
butsudan	ancestor shelf on which the *ihai* are placed
eisaa	traditional young men's dancing at obon
ekisha (uranai-sha)	fortune-teller
eto	birth year in twelve-year Chinese animal-cycle system
fujinkai	women's association
genki	lively
gusuku	holy place, grove, or castle
haari	boat racing ritual
hama ogami	beach prayer
handan (hanji)	judgment (yuta's diagnosis)
hinu-kan	hearth deity (three stones placed in the kitchen and on other altars)
ichigomui	"first talking" marriage ritual
ihai	ancestor tablets
inkan (in)	stamp, signature stamp
Irigusuku	west sacred grove
kachashi	lively dance usually done at the end of parties or celebrations
kajimaya	party at age ninety-nine years
kami	deity, god or spiritual being; priestess
kami no michi	kami's way
kami ban yuta	yuta who specializes in divination
kami-sama	deity, god or spiritual being; priestess; *sama* is an honorific suffix
kami-ya	"god house"; building in the center of town where the noro and other priestesses carry out rituals
kamidaari	illness on the path to becoming priestess
kaminchu	priestess
kiyomeru	to clean
kome kuji	rice divination ritual
mabuya	life-force, soul
mo-ai	mutual loan group
mochi	sticky rice cake
munchu	clan
nibichi	wedding procession
noro	village priestess traditionally appointed by Shuri government (phonologically, *nuru* is a more correct spelling, but *noro* has become conventionalized among scholars)

249

nunduruchi	noro's house
obon; bon	late summer festival in which ancestors return home for three days
ogami (ugami)	prayer (villagers use it in a broader sense to mean ritual); person who is an expert at doing ogami
oharai	"go away" rituals
omiki; miki	traditional rice drink
Omoro Sooshi	collection of Okinawan songs and rituals, written down during the sixteenth and seventeenth centuries
onna no kami-sama	women's kami-sama or women kami-sama
rei	spirit or spiritual thing
roojinkai	senior citizens' club
samisen	stringed instrument
san (sai)	twisted grass used to mark off property or objects
san gatsu	third-month ocean and fishing ritual
sekininsha	secular administrator of clan
seimeisai (shiimi)	ancestor memorial day
seinenkai	young adults' association
Shibahiki	man's hereditary ritual role
shiji (seji)	spiritual power
shima kusara	winter ritual
shinugu	ritual carried out by priestesses
tege (tege yasa)	"whatever, it's okay"
ten	sky; heaven
tengoku	heaven
Tobaru	man's hereditary ritual role
tsuna-hiki	tug-of-war
uchi umachi	"home" *umachi* ritual for priestesses
uchigami	priestess role
uko	incense bowl
ukuringwa	clan priestess
umachi	agricultural ritual
umareru	to be born
umei	woman ritual servant to priestess
umi ogami	ocean ritual
Umisedo	man's hereditary ritual role
usande	taking food off an altar
usudeku	women's dancing for obon
utaki	sacred grove
utaki mae	ritual in which priestesses go to the utaki
utooto	word to begin prayers
utooto-obaa; tooto-obaa	praying old women
utushi	"go through" praying place
wakareru utta	lamentations
warui koto; warui mono	bad things
yanusuji	new house ritual performed by priestesses
yasashii	easygoing, easy
yuta	shaman-type practitioner

APPENDIX 2
Dramatis Personae

This list includes only those Henza villagers who appear often in the book.

Mrs. Adaniya: Mrs. Adaniya, eighty-two years old when I arrived in Henza, is known for her ability to remember and tell old-time stories and events. She is a widow, living with her son, daughter-in-law, grandchildren, and (during the year I was in Henza) granddaughter's baby. Mrs. Adaniya experiences periodic pain and weakness in her legs, and so generally stays home, where she helps with the baby, talks to her daughter-in-law, and receives a steady stream of informal visits from friends and relatives. Mrs. Adaniya is a clan kaminchu.

Mrs. Noriko Goeku: Noriko is in her late thirties, married, and mother to four children. She was born and raised in Naha (the capital of Okinawa) and came to Henza about ten years ago with her husband (whose family is from Henza). Noriko is a very dedicated mother and is determined that her children will attend good high schools and universities. To that end, she spends a great deal of time supervising their homework and arranging private tutoring for them. In the past two years, since her youngest son has started school, she has opened a fish retail business at the port of Yakena (the village that is closest to Henza on the main island of Okinawa). Her husband owns a fishing boat docked in Yakena. Mrs. Adaniya is his aunt.

Mrs. Hokama: Mrs. Hokama, in her seventies, is a former school teacher and is now known as the local song expert. Since retiring, she has learned to play the *koto* (string instrument) and has prepared a collection of traditional Henza songs. She also is a clan kaminchu. Mrs. Hokama is a widow who lives alone and spends a great deal of her time out of the house at senior citizens' club activities and other social and cultural events. Her children, some of whom attended college, live off of Henza.

Mrs. Ikene: Mrs. Ikene, in her seventies, is the best-known ogami person in Henza. Villagers say that her prayers "go through" particularly well. She is also an active farmer, and when she is not doing ogami work, she can usually be found in her vegetable garden hoeing the weeds or harvesting carrots. Especially around the New Year, clients come to her almost every day. In her role as ogami person, she carries out rituals both at her house and at shrines and tombs around Okinawa. She was born in the Shuri area but came to Henza at age ten (her father is from Henza). She suffered many years of pain and illness and lost two of her chil-

251

dren, all of which prepared her to take on the ogami role. Today she is a widow, has six surviving children, and lives in a lovely house that the kami-sama told her to build.

Mrs. Kamura: Mrs. Kamura, in her early seventies, is the noro. She has been sitting this position for only about ten years and often consults more veteran kaminchu regarding rituals. She lives with her husband, one of the more distinguished village men, in a big and lovely house, where her grandchildren often come to visit. When Mrs. Kamura is not busy with noro work, she tends her large and unusually orderly vegetable garden.

Mrs. Okuda: Mrs. Okuda, eighty-six years old when I arrived in Okinawa, was famous in Henza for her dancing. She danced on the main island of Okinawa and even in her eighties continued to dance at most village events. Because she spent time off of Henza, she was also quite knowledgeable about the outside world. She was especially known for her role as the ritual fish-spearer in the san gatsu ceremony. She lived with her son, daughter-in-law, and grandchildren. She and Mrs. Adaniya were cousins and close friends. Sadly, Mrs. Okuda passed away before this book was published.

Mr. Okutara: Mr. Okutara, now eighty, is a native of Henza but moved to Hawaii as a youth in order to make a living. He is married to Kuni, who comes from mainland Japan, and they lived together in Chicago for thirty years. They returned to Henza about fifteen years ago in order to take care of his aging widowed mother (who has long since passed away). Mr. Okutara is self-educated and an expert in Okinawan folklore. He has published several books and pamphlets on the subject of Henza's customs.

Mrs. Shimojo: Mrs. Shimojo, a priestess in her early seventies, embodies a male kami-sama. She is also unusually feminine in her dress and demeanor. Mrs. Shimojo is probably the most articulate of the village priestesses and highly involved in village ritual. Many villagers seem to consult with her informally regarding how and when to carry out rituals. She is now a widow and lives with her son, daughter-in-law, and grandchildren. She has remained healthy and continues to do a great deal of the housework.

Notes

Introduction

1. There may be other examples of women-led religions that have not yet been documented. A great deal has been written recently regarding preliterate societies in which women may possibly have had important religious roles (Stone 1976). The kinds of evidence available for reconstructing preliterate societies allow only tentative glimpses into such intangibles as beliefs, rituals, and social structure (Gimbutas 1974).

2. In Korea, Confucianism is the mainstream religion; in Thailand and Myanmar, it is Buddhism. *Zar* religion is a marginalized and sometimes persecuted ritual stream in Muslim and Coptic Christian societies. Both the Brazilian and the Central American women's religions are situated in societies in which the official, high-prestige religion is Catholicism. The North American women's religions are all minor, and, indeed, are typically referred to as cults. Sande secret societies of west Africa cannot be considered fringe or unofficial, yet unlike in Okinawa, where both men and women participate in the women-led religion, the Sande groups are only for women. Women's religions have typically been treated in the scholarly literature as artificial, reactive, synthetic, politically motivated, or a mere escape valve for repressed and frustrated women (Lewis 1975).

3. The following schema is my own, although it is consistent with the recent thinking of most feminist anthropologists on sex and gender.

4. As Lorber (1994) argues, not only gender but also sex is culturally rather than absolutely constructed. Humans do not fit into two neat and undisputed categories of male and female.

5. In much of the contemporary Western world, public avowals of gender and race equality are contradicted by ideologies of psychological or cognitive difference (for example, "whites have higher IQ's," "men are better at math," "women care more about relationships").

6. Ortner explains that in debates about the universality of male dominance three different issues are looked at: prestige, power, and dominance. Authors who claim that gender asymmetry is universal have—appropriately—based their argument primarily upon prestige: "That it was in some sense culturally accepted in every known society that men have greater prestige and/or status, whether or not they exert dominance over women and whether or not women have a great deal of official or unofficial power. . . . Without cultural prestige, female power is not fully legitimate and can only be exercised in hidden and/or distorted ('manipulative') ways" (1996: 141–142).

7. Other anthropologists have dealt with this ritual differently. I do not see our various interpretations as mutually exclusive, but rather as highlighting different aspects of the ritual. See chapter 12 for a more detailed discussion.

8. Because Okinawa has been a Japanese prefecture since the early 1970s and because there are so many similarities between the two societies, I wish to clarify from the outset that the status of women in Okinawan religion is significantly different from the status of women in mainland Japanese religion. Although a number of writers have suggested that in the distant past priestesses were important religious leaders in Japan, there does not seem to be much concrete evidence for this claim; rather, historical hints have been based on, for instance, possible Chinese mispronunciations and misspellings of Japanese names (Ellwood 1986). The sources that are cited are typically allusions found in myths, and myths, as scholars of religion know, do not necessarily constitute a reliable historical record. On the other hand, scholars such as Michiko Yusa offer abundant and convincing evidence of women's inferior position from the seventh century onward, a position reinforced under the Tokugawa Shogunate—1603–1867 (1994: esp. p. 96). The *saigu*—royal princesses who lived in seclusion—should not, as far as I can see, be construed as parallel to the powerful, public Okinawan priestesses. According to Carmen Blacker, Buddhist influence resulted in the elevation of the role of the male ascetic and the degradation of the role of the female medium in Japan (1975: 278; see also Paulson 1976 for a discussion of the influence of Buddhism on the status of women in Japan). The Japanese model of a woman shamaness and man priest or Buddhist mountain ascetic who work together, with the shamaness going into trance and her priest/husband interpreting the content of her trance and then exorcising evil spirits (cf. Hori 1968: 78, 200) is unknown on Okinawa and in no way analogous to any religious structure that I have seen in Okinawa. Even in the new Japanese religions, many of which were founded by women, women do not sustain leadership roles for more than one or two generations (Hardacre 1994; Nakamura 1980). In short, even if one could make a convincing case regarding women's religious dominance in early Japanese culture (and despite my skepticism about the proof for this, I do think that it is a distinct possibility), there is no doubt that for many centuries men have dominated Japanese religious life.

9. However, I do wish to clarify that the driving force behind this project has been, and continues to be, my ongoing interest in situations in which women obtain and hold onto religious autonomy. The theoretical literature that provides the intellectual nourishment for this study is, above all, literature on gender and religion. I remain intrigued with the variety of symbol systems generated by men and by women, and by the power of religion cross-culturally both to legitimate oppression of women and to offer women avenues for personal expression and communal empowerment.

Prologue

1. The primary Chinese influence on Japan came from northern China, whereas in Okinawa it came from southern China (Haring 1964: 40).

2. For example, the Satsuma passed a decree in 1611 stating that the kingdom should not give emoluments to women. The women this decree referred to were the priestesses who traditionally were given land and stipends. The order was never fully carried out, and many priestesses continued to receive emoluments (see Kawahashi 1992: 47 for translations of the original citations).

3. Yoshida (1990), for example, explains the preservation of women's religious dominance in Okinawa in terms of Buddhism's singular lack of success in reaching out to the Okinawan population. Because Okinawa, unlike the rest of East and Southeast

Asia, did not embrace Buddhism, Buddhism was not able to undermine women's religious dominance.

4. According to Marvin Harris, when state-level societies impinge upon smaller-scale societies, the degree of centralization of the small-scale society is one determinant of its ability to maintain its own cultural patterns and identity (1985: 356ff.).

5. In Okinawa, as in Japan and other parts of East Asia, individuals and communities rather easily adopt and identify with elements of more than one religious tradition. Given Okinawa's history of conquest, one wonders whether the current division of labor, by which men carry out many of the Chinese-style ancestral rituals and Buddhist funeral rites whereas women carry out the indigenous kami-oriented rituals, might be an expression of accommodation.

6. On the main island of Okinawa, men work in agriculture, especially sugarcane and pineapple cash crops. The land on Henza is not appropriate for large agricultural enterprises. According to Professor Takara, in the distant past, Okinawan men were split between seafaring and farming. Because of taxation under the Satsuma, men were forced or encouraged to move into agriculture, but before that time the traditional pattern on Henza (men go to sea and women farm) was probably typical throughout Okinawa.

7. The Okinawan butsudan and ceremonies surrounding the butsudan are very similar to the Japanese ceremonies.

8. Villagers, in their typically empirical manner, explain that the lunar calendar is more appropriate for fishermen.

9. Both Ouwehand (1985) and W. Lebra (1966) constructed schema for organizing Ryukyuan rituals. In W. Lebra's schema, Okinawan rituals take place at the level of the family, clan, village, and (formerly) the kingdom. Ouwehand, in a study of one of the Yaeyama Islands in the southern Ryukyus, ordered the complex ritual life by objective (agricultural, announcement, etc.). Neither schema reflects the divine dis-order of Henza's ritual life.

10. In other Okinawan villages, the headman may perform the role performed by the male assistants in Henza.

11. The names of these roles are *uchigami, wakanoro, negami,* and *niisadai.* Mrs. Ishikawa, the negami, explains that negami is the original village priestess and that her clan is the biggest, but in Henza people think the noro is above the negami. According to Professor Takara of the University of the Ryukyus, in pre-Shuri days the negami was an independent leader, not linked to a central government. Professor Akamine of the University of the Ryukyus believes that usually negami and noro are the same rank. Not every village had a noro, but every village had a negami. Henza's system, in which the negami is one of the noro's helpers, is not typical.

12. Even if these dates are inaccurate, the villagers' comments indicate that in their eyes the centralized noro system was only temporary in Henza and not a deeply rooted institution. According to Patrick Beillevaire, it is unlikely that the noro system was introduced into the region that late; rather, noro were in charge of several villages, and so possibly began to be chosen from a Henza house at about that time (private communication).

13. It is common in Okinawa, as in Japan, for villages to publish village histories and collections of village customs and folklore. Henza even has a small museum in the yard of its school. The museum contains examples of traditional clothing, tools, and children's toys and written descriptions of prewar life in the village.

14. Noriko Kawahashi (1992) also uses the term *divine priestess* to capture both the human and the divine aspects of these women.

Chapter 1

1. Linda Angst shows that Okinawans tend to be portrayed in Japanese discourse as gentle, peace-loving, primitive fisherfolk, "an image which is problematically adopted today by Okinawan leaders in rhetoric defining Okinawan ethnic identity" (1996: 4). In light of Angst's analysis, I would suggest that villagers' *yasashii* self-portrayal be taken with a grain of salt.

2. Not even samurai swords or bows and arrows. The older boys do play video arcade games in which there is "virtual" fighting.

3. Before establishment of the Ryukyu Kingdom there apparently was a great deal of warring (Sakihara 1981).

4. Most Henza villagers do not seem to hold strong opinions in the matter of American military presence. No Henza land has been taken over for American military use; a few villagers have reaped certain economic benefits from the American presence.

5. Kerr cites sources commenting on Okinawan people's love for performing arts. These comments were made by visitors to Okinawa over the course of several centuries (1957: 223–224).

6. Maretzki and Maretzki (1966), in their classic study of childhood in a northern Okinawan village in the 1960s, also witnessed the easygoing nature of social interactions. Much of what I describe here is similar or identical to Maretzki and Maretzki's findings. The similarity of our findings suggests that these easygoing social patterns are widespread throughout Okinawa. I will not cite each of the parallels, but I highly recommend their detailed book to those interested in learning more about Okinawan childhood and child rearing.

7. Of course, some children and adults are more talented and enthusiastic performers than others. Most village children and adults do seem comfortable singing or dancing on the stage.

8. They are also taught self-control and the ability to concentrate, which are the bases of school learning in Japanese schools (see Ben-Ari 1996 on Japanese day-care centers). Please note that much of the nursery school curriculum is not Henza's choice but rather is directed by the Japanese Education Ministry. On the other hand, local attitudes do color what happens in the school.

9. Disagreeing with what one's conversational partner says is a typical conversational mode in Israeli culture. This is true within families, in chance encounters at shops, in the parliament, and in the traditional Eastern European *yeshivot* (religious academies), where study of sacred texts customarily involved incessant, even ritualistic, arguing over points of law and interpretation.

10. Teigo Yoshida has also noticed that Okinawans seem puzzled when asked about opposites (personal communication). I find it intriguing that, in his analysis of the ancient Okinawan liturgical poems recorded in the *Omoro sooshi*, Chris Drake notes: "The Ryukyuan couplets perform a loose narrative, they foreground contiguity as similarity, while Anglo-Saxon rhetoric, as perhaps befits a warrior-centered culture, privileges negation, irony, antithesis, confrontation, and contrast as agonistic conflict between incompatible alternatives. Ryukyuan shamanic couplets appear more interested in muted or delicate contrasts; they seem . . . to stress repetition not as reduplication but as similarity with a slight, though marked and almost echoic difference. To make a rather speculative hypothesis, this might suggest that in the discourse of these songs . . . not only are the singers usually plural, but the realities they attempt to both construct and reconstruct by the singing of the song are perhaps regarded as similarly plural, although within definite parameters" (1995: 6).

11. This dispute involved two brothers, one of whom had left the island and the other of whom had stayed to take care of their elderly parents and then inherited the house.

12. This is, of course, very similar to Japan. According to Smith, much of the definition of a "good person" in Japan "involves restraint in the expression of personal desires and opinions, empathy for the feelings and situation of others, and the practice of civility" (1983: 45).

13. Although I did not hear of any such cases, I do assume that as a last resort villagers would report violent crimes to the police and commit a violent "crazy" family member to a mental hospital.

14. Institutionalized hierarchy is an integral part of Japanese history and culture. Feudal society and its cultural legacy are firmly based on the theory of hierarchical distinctions (Smith 1983: 38). The traditional Japanese hierarchy—nobility, samurai, peasants, artisans, merchants, outcasts—is not found in Okinawa. "Everyone [in Japan in the period before the Meiji Restoration] was supposed to remain within their own class, continue the work of their forebears and marry within their own social category. Samurai warriors were empowered to take immediate retaliation in the case of overt expressions of rebellion against the system by using the swords that they always carried to decapitate the offender" (Hendry 1995: 80). Smith (1983) argues that Japanese hierarchy is not as clear-cut as it seems on the surface, yet as I understand Smith's analysis, hierarchy—whether of status or function—is indeed an ethos that permeates almost all areas of life. Moreover, social stratification has been described as rigid and persistent, even in rural villages that in many other ways resemble Henza (cf. Smith and Wiswell 1982, drawing upon the Embrees' observations in Suye Mura in 1935). Hendry points out that hierarchy is less central to Japanese women's social interactions than to those of men. Women who meet in a variety of social contexts tend to have reciprocal rather than hierarchical relationships (1995: 90).

15. Tsugiko Taira, an Okinawan folklorist, explains that Okinawans feel that there is nothing to acquire money for. The only desired acquisition is land, and with American military bases occupying so much of Okinawan territory, there simply is no land available.

16. I am aware that remarks like these reflect an egalitarian ideological stance rather than detailed proof that families never consider the status of potential in-laws. However, I believe that this kind of ideological ethos in fact filters down into the ways in which people actually live their lives.

17. He said main island (Okinawa), but I think he meant mainland (Japan).

18. The rejection of ethical absolutes seems to be deeply rooted in Okinawan culture. Gregory Smits (1996) has shown that what he calls "situational weighing" of appropriate behavior characterized the philosophy of the great Ryukyuan Confucian thinker and political reformer Sai On (1682–1761). Smits explains that Chinese and Japanese Confucian philosophers of Sai On's period were ambivalent about *quan* (expediency) as a value in political decision making, praising instead *jing* (established norms). In the context of Ryukyu's precarious political position vis-à-vis China and Japan and in a reversal of the mainstream Confucian view, Sai On used "the widely accepted notion that change lies at the heart of the cosmos, to require and authorize frequent use of *quan*. In his view, *jing*, taken as the rough equivalent of *li* (social norms, ritual forms, rules of behavior, etc.), serves as a temporary expedient for those not yet sufficiently advanced in moral cultivation to employ *quan*" (Smits 1996: 474).

19. My approach to what constitutes morality in Henza is similar in this respect to what writers have observed in mainland Japan. "For the Japanese, goodness or badness

is a relative matter, relative to social situation and impact, whose complexity may often be beyond any judge's comprehension" (T. Lebra 1976: 11). In the same vein, according to Milton Creighton, "[Unlike Western culture] Japanese culture does not emphasize restraining the inherent evil basic to human nature, but rather shaping human beings into a socially desirable form. . . . Japanese morality tends to judge the value of an act in a situational context based on its impact on significant relationships" (1990: 297; see also Rohlen 1989: 13).

20. My findings concerning "pollution" and "taboos" differ from W. Lebra's (1966: 49ff.). It may be that these matters vary from village to village, or it may be that Lebra and I interpret similar matters in different ways or use the same terms in different ways.

21. According to Maretzki and Maretzki, in the Okinawan village of Taira, a husband may be present at childbirth, especially the birth of the first child; and in the old days, a birthing woman was supported by her husband or someone else in a half-sitting position (1966: 91). Thus there does not seem to be a taboo on men coming in contact with childbirth blood. In contrast to Okinawa, Japanese women seem to follow a number of taboos during pregnancy, and, in some parts of Japan, the mother and baby are regarded as polluted after the birth for a period of about one month (Hendry 1995: 134; on mainland Japanese attitudes toward menstruation, see Yusa 1994: 115ff.; Blacker 1975: 42). According to T. Lebra, in Japan, both Buddhism and Shinto imposed a variety of taboos upon women; women's bodies are believed to be dirtier than men's; and men in certain professions (for example, brewery) avoided contact with women because of pollution beliefs (1984: 126–127). Ohnuki-Tierney notes that mainland Japanese women abstain from bathing and washing their hair during menstruation (1984: 28). According to the Embrees, in Suye Mura (Japan) in the 1930s, "They also said that in theory a menstruating women should not visit [Shinto] shrines, but that they actually do. . . . [One woman] said that indeed menstruating women cannot go to the kamisama, but can visit the Buddhist temples. 'The same is true of people in mourning during the first forty-nine days after a death,' she added" (Smith and Wiswell 1982: 85).

22. When I asked villagers how they say *kiyomeru* (Japanese for purification) in Okinawan dialect, they were stumped. One suggestion offered was *oharai*, which, as discussed in chapter 7, means 'go away' but not 'purification'. The concept of pollution does not seem to exist in Henza, and the word *kiyomeru* is usually used by villagers to mean physical washing.

23. My sense is that villagers are willing to eat all digestible, nonpoisonous fish, plants, and animals, although some are considered preferable to others. Potential foods that they do not eat are rejected because of taste, not because of religious sanctions or village identity.

24. This information is taken from the *Okinawa Prefecture's Annual Population Abstract* of 1993, 37th edition, published by the Prefectural Government.

25. This is one of many themes common to both Okinawan and Shinto belief. "Shinto maintains the worldview that human beings are basically good, sharing the goodness of *kami* deities, and that the world in which we live is a good place, where we ought to pursue happiness and prosperity, and establish peace" (Yusa 1994: 94; see Hori 1968 on Japanese folk religion).

26. Emiko Ohnuki-Tierney analyzes the intensive and extensive attention shown by Japanese to illness, causes of illness, and cures for illness. Japanese tend to see the outside world as impure, dirty, and a potential source of disease. Thus, for example, Japanese do not like to use secondhand clothing. (In contrast, Henza villagers often

pass clothing from one household to another.) Japanese, unlike Okinawans, believe in humoral imbalance as an illness etiology. Ohnuki-Tierney discusses the Japanese (not Okinawan) notions of *jibyoo* ('my very own illness') and the individual's inborn constitution as framing much of the Japanese discourse of illness. "With their persistent emphasis on hygiene, one might expect that the Japanese would perceive themselves as clean and healthy; after all, they try so hard to avoid contamination with cultural germs. But the opposite is actually true: Many Japanese regard themselves as somewhat less than healthy, if not sickly. Conversations and greeting frequently relate to the topic of illness, either of the participants or of mutual acquaintances. . . ." (1984: 51).

27. This pattern does not seem to be limited to urban Japan: the Embrees noted, in the Japanese village of Suye Mura in the 1930s, that "the doctor's offices are always crowded with women" (Smith and Wiswell 1982: 96) and that villagers attribute women's illnesses to their work overload and to venereal diseases passed on to women by their husbands.

28. Prayer at the *hinu-kan* (hearth deity), the *butsudan* (ancestral altar), and the *utaki* (sacred grove) is consistently described as being for health. Prayer at new or foreign shrines such as Futemma (a Shinto shrine on the main island) is not usually described as health-oriented. For example, villagers tell me they go to Futemma to get amulets to avoid car accidents.

29. In many ways, Vanatinai culture differs drastically from Henza culture. Until recently, Vanatinai men were involved in frequent warfare. In Vanatinai gender ideology, men's power as killers and destroyers gives them an advantage over women in the key ritual sequences of exchange and mortuary ceremonies. Vanatinai men and women exhibit a constant fear of sorcery, and the sorcerer is the epitome of maleness—taker of life (Lepowsky 1993: 302). There seems to be a fair amount of tension between men and women (or at least between male and female symbols): There are menstrual taboos, and "women are forbidden by custom to hunt, fish, or make war spears" (1993: 289).

Chapter 2

1. It is possible that Okinawan and mainland Japanese cultures developed from at least some of the same early sources. The best English-language overview of Ryukyuan cosmology is Kreiner (1968).

2. Although there are certain similarities between Japanese and Okinawan religion, the differences are equally extensive and significant. To name just a few, such Japanese institutions as mountain priests or ascetics, traveling priests, arctic-style shamanism in which the initiate makes a mystical journey to the other world, ascetic practices, concern with ritual purity, elaborate mythology, sacred texts, and the cult of the emperor and royal family are totally absent from Okinawan religion. Many of the differences between Okinawan and Japanese religion reflect the strong influence of Buddhism in Japan and its almost negligible influence in Okinawa. Kitagawa has summarized what he ses as the two main threads of Japanese Buddhism (neither of which, I add, is present in Okinawa): (1) "national" Buddhism, which tends to depend on, ally with, and accept the control of the ruling regime, and (2) "folk" Buddhism, which presents itself as a gospel of salvation and a religion of compassion for the oppressed and downtrodden (1987: 209).

3. See Kitagawa (1987: 121) on the power of beautiful words to bring about good and of ugly words to bring about evil.

4. One woman told me that in the old days there were "bad things" (she used both *warui mono* and *aku no kami-sama*—bad kami-sama) that would sometimes follow one home at night; but they could be gotten rid of by the villager walking first to the pig house because the pig's oinking noises chase the bad things away. The expression *aku no kami-sama* is not used by many villagers. When I asked the noro about aku no kami-sama she said, "There are none. All are good."

5. *Rei* means 'spiritual thing'; here is seems to mean an accident caused for spiritual reasons.

6. Haring argues that kami corresponds to the *mana* of ethnology; that is, impersonal mystical power resident in gods, trees, men, nature, and so forth (1964: 44).

7. My intention here is to pick up on one particular strand of ritual meaning; there are many other strands, some of which I deal with in chapter 6 and chapter 12.

8. This kind of understanding can be found in other cultures as well. For example, according to Cutler, "For Hindus, divinity is essentially a process rather than a thing, a becoming rather than a static being" (1985: 164).

9. The notion that the entire universe is permeated with kami is also a feature of early Japanese religion (Kitagawa 1987: 70).

10. Mabuchi cites the priestesses of the Okinawan village of Kabira as explaining that "the sea, heaven, and land—these are one and the same thing" (1968: 35).

11. The continuity between human and divine and the easy deification of human beings is another area in which Japanese and Okinawan religion are similar (cf. Hori 1968: 13).

12. In Professor Takara's opinion, the Okinawan idea is that god comes to people called *kami-sama*. The old word for priestess was indeed *kami*; the old word for god was *nushi*. I have chosen not to use the word "incarnation" to refer to priestesses/kami-sama because incarnation—the divine temporarily taking human form (or "descent" of the deity, in the Hindu case)—presupposes that between good and human there is an ontological distinction that can be bridged in certain exceptional circumstances. In the Okinawan case, it is not at all clear that such ontological distinctions exist: The difference between "unembodied" kami-sama, "embodied" kami-sama, and all people is far from clear.

13. The word *kami* sometimes is used in Japan and in Okinawa to refer to important people. I never heard it used this way in Henza.

14. Mr. Okutara elaborates a bit more: "Takahara Aji was the last chieftain of Henza. . . . In approximately 1450 when Katsuren Castle was conquered . . . he had to escape. He went to Izena Island. Later he returned to Henza . . . He changed his name to Izena Ounushi, and when he died he was buried under Irigusuku castle."

15. Mabuchi notes that, "It is theoretically important to distinguish ancestor worship from the worship of the dead, but in the Ryukyus the real situation is too subtle to draw a clear line of demarcation between these two" (1976b: 109).

16. Similarly, Kitagawa writes regarding Japan, "There is no indication . . . that the *kami* were thought to have any supramundane qualities until after the introduction of Chinese civilization and Buddhism" (1987: 120), and Pelzel notes that in Japanese mythology, "There is no hint that such cosmic forces as do exist can overpower life as man proposes to live it. The gods do not have arbitrary powers" (1974: 15).

17. In Christianity, Hinduism, and Buddhism, the mission of the incarnate deity reflects the cosmic importance of salvation. Embodied deities in Okinawa—like other Okinawan deities and people—are simply *present*. They have no special mission because there is no sacred history or eschatology.

18. In contrast, mainland Japanese kami are associated with rich mythologies (see, for example, Hori 1968; Kitagawa 1987). W. Lebra writes that "In most respects . . .

the Okinawan kami seem less personalized and even more vague than those of the Japanese pantheon. . . . It is true that myths relating to the lives of kami are notably few and simple, even when compared with the Japanese system" (1966: 21). In Okinawa, he continues, there is, "A striking paucity of any highly developed mythology. Culture hero myths, accounts of mythical epochs, or myths relating to the principal deities are notably absent or but weakly developed" (1966: 43).

19. According to W. Lebra, "Okinawa abounds in etiological myths. One may record within a single village several different myths explaining the same custom" (1966: 43). I interpret Lebra's observation regarding the variety of myths that explain the same custom as further indication of the absence of a cultural ideal of one "right way" of thinking.

20. A small repertoire of folktales could be taken as a sign that the traditional stories are no longer known in the village. However, most of my best informants were elderly women who had lived on the island their entire lives and who were extremely well informed about social arrangements, technology, songs, and dances from the old days.

21. Hendry cites surveys estimating that between 60 and 80 percent of Japanese households have a Shinto god shelf associated with Amaterasu (1995: 30).

22. Sometimes, when those places are unavailable, villagers will pray via an *utushi*, a 'go-through' place; that is, a place from which prayer will go through to the place at which the kami-sama can hear the prayer.

23. What she means is that in the past each family buried its own dead, but now the village and the government have a larger role in people's lives, and cemeteries have become regulated. Also, people have become too weak to stand outside in the hot sun or the rain at funerals, and, therefore, the village council decided to build a hall with a roof and chairs at the village cemetery.

24. My argument here recalls Swanson's cross-cultural analysis of religious beliefs, in which he found that monotheism is positively related to the presence of a hierarchy of three or more sovereign groups in a society, and that societies with social classes are significantly more likely than others to possess a belief in superior gods (1960: 81, 96).

25. The plethora of deities in women-led religions in Southeast Asia (especially the *nat* religion of Myanmar and Northern Thai matrilineal spirit cults) is particularly suggestive against the background of Buddhist (in theory) nondeistic cosmology. Similarly, ethnographers around the world have been struck by the predominance of Jewish, Christian, and Muslim women at shrines of saints (Sered 1994).

26. Lepowsky makes the important point that feminine and couple origin myths (which according to Sanday [1981] are especially common in the Insular Pacific region) seem to be associated with cultures that are highly concerned with female reproduction, that hold an ideology of male dominance and female pollution, and that are characterized by men's rituals that emulate, control, or appropriate female reproductive powers. "Couple or feminine origin myths in these Pacific societies may therefore symbolize not an egalitarian ideology of gender but male preoccupation with female power and the ritual means through which it may be assimilated by men, who thereby become ideologically dominant over women and children" (1990: 198). This entire constellation is absent from Henza.

Chapter 3

1. Ortner goes on to say that "you can call such societies 'gender egalitarian' if you want, and you would not exactly be wrong, but the egalitarianism is complex, inconsistent, and—to some extent—fragile" (1996: 175).

2. While we were in Henza, my daughter—who turned four during the year we were there—was perfectly content to wear shorts, a T-shirt, and cropped hair like the other children. When we returned to Israel, it took her about three days to figure out that she only wanted to wear dresses and that her hair was too short and to ask if I could please buy her some stick-on earrings! In other words, gender socialization happens even faster than recovery from jet lag! Also in Henza things seem to be changing. The year that my children attended the nursery school, boys and girls both wore shorts. When I returned for a short visit one year later, several of the girls were wearing cotton dresses, indicating that Japanese and American fashions are influencing the older ungendered clothing styles.

3. In this respect, Henza villagers sound quite similar to Westerners who believe that gender equality has already been achieved. Any instances of gender inequality are then written off as exceptions rather than seriously addressed as systematic problems.

4. Most of the comments here were made by the local English teacher, who is not a native of Henza (although he is Okinawan), and the principal, who is a native.

5. Anthropologists who carried out fieldwork in Okinawa in the 1950s were impressed with the important role that older siblings (including brothers) had in caring for younger siblings (Maretzki and Maretzki 1966). One of the old village midwives told me that she became a midwife because her mother had many babies who died, and, as the oldest sister in the family, she felt responsible for her younger siblings, for helping her mother raise them. She also took care of the bodies of the babies who died. She was only about ten at the time. The expectation that older siblings will spend hours each day looking after younger ones has declined as children begin to attend school earlier and continue to attend school longer.

6. This couple did not know that I was researching gender; they were simply telling me about their children.

7. In contrast, the men who organize modern Japanese-style rituals do endeavor to appeal to children. This was evident, for example, at the solar New Year's kite-flying contest organized by the village headman.

8. Okinawan women, unlike their Japanese counterparts, do not wear spike-heeled shoes or talk in artificially high, sweet voices.

9. In the mid-nineteenth century, when Commodore Perry visited Okinawa, he also noticed that men and women wear very similar clothes (Hokama 1974: 36). He and his party saw few women during their visit, and those they saw were "strikingly unhandsome" (Hokama 1974: 198). My guess is that the lack of gender-enhancing practices made Okinawan women appear unattractive to Commodore Perry and his friends. Perry also wrote that the status of Okinawan women was like "mere slave or chattel, and always slighted by the men, who seem hardly to notice her, either in the houses or in the streets" (Hokama 1974: 370). His observations differed from those of most other visitors to Okinawa, who commented upon women's freedom and strength. It should be noted that Perry's contact was mostly with upper-class men, and he did notice that "the women are kept so secluded, *particularly those of the higher rank*" (1974: 368, my emphases).

10. According to Mrs. Hokama, who is in her late seventies, there were no menarche rituals in her youth. She had heard that recently there have been menarche rituals "to be glad that your daughter has become an adult." According to Mr. Shinya (the school principal), in the old days married women were marked with a kind of tattoo, but the only woman I saw in Henza with a tattoo was one very old woman who was tattooed as part of a medical treatment. When I asked about tattoos, I was told that married women were sometimes tattooed to make them ugly so that Japanese men wouldn't carry them off.

11. Japanese cosmetic companies in Okinawa invite girls who have recently graduated high school to meetings where they teach them how to use cosmetics and give them free samples.

12. According to T. Lebra, in postwar Japan "the coeducational system has liberated sex. Heterosexual intimacy in class has become a common phenomenon which no longer arouses curiosity or excitement" (1984: 71). In Henza, boys and girls remain rather separate, and I was told that if a "couple" forms during junior high or high school, they will hide their relationship from their friends because of embarrassment.

13. I unfortunately have no information about attitudes toward homosexuality.

14. At weddings, relatives and friends perform songs, dances, and humorous skits. In one such skit performed at a village wedding, fifteen or so male friends of the groom executed a dance that ended with one of the men holding a bottle between his legs and the other holding a cup. They mimed sexual intercourse, wiped off the bottle and cup with a towel, and then again mimed intercourse, this time from behind. The audience did not seem perturbed, except for some of the young women, who looked a bit embarrassed.

15. I asked one of the older women about Henza food production. "Seasonal things are once a year each. If you put daikon [large radish] and next a leaf vegetable like cabbage, you can usually have it twice. The daikon I am cutting now I planted in October. This is the second one of this year. But after this there is no more daikon. The land will be too dry for daikon. And then goes to cucumber. Then a few kinds of pumpkins and *gooya* [gourd] type things. But I don't have as much space as I used to. I have a little bit there and here for a garden, but some people don't have property for this." I asked, In Okinawa is there always some kind of vegetable in season? "Yes, throughout the year." Traditionally, women also took care of the pigs that were owned by the family. During the American occupation, Okinawans were encouraged to give up their pigs.

16. Some Okinawan men (not in Henza) have moved into cash-crop agriculture, such as sugarcane.

17. Women even own and run large businesses and factories in Okinawa, although probably not to the extent that men do. Japanese businessmen reputedly are taken aback by the prominent role of Okinawan women in commerce.

18. In the middle of the century, Hopkins noticed that in Okinawa "there was man's work and there was woman's work, but either might be obliged to cross the line" (1951: 181).

19. In contrast, regarding Suye Mura (Japan) in the 1930s, the Embrees noted that one woman "created a mild sensation by having special trousers made which she will wear for ploughing, for she does not like to get her bare legs and kimono skirts wet. Lacking any men in the house, she has to plough her own fields" (Smith and Wiswell 1982: 256).

20. Lock points out that recent studies show that large numbers of Japanese women "are bored, lonely, frustrated, and retain a strong feeling that they have no sense of personal identity or fulfillment" (1987: 146).

21. The Japanese ideal type, like ideal types in many societies, seems not to be fully realized in outlying villages and among the nonelite. For example, in Suye Mura in 1935, "Officially, as all over Japan, they [women] occupied a subordinate position, but they did not always act as if they did. It is true that women had no role in village administrative affairs and that at home they followed the standard pattern of subservience to the husband, but in day-to-day gatherings, their drinking, and their outspokenness, they certainly acted with much greater freedom than any Japanese female city-dweller" (Smith and Wiswell 1982: xxxvii).

22. The data I present here are based upon an analysis of Henza's population records for 1993, as registered in the local town hall. This analysis was carried out together with Professor Yoshimi Ando of the University of the Ryukyus.

23. In Henza's population records, most women aged through approximately seventy years are listed as "spouse of the head." This echoes the fact that the Japanese census automatically records the husband as household head, thus this terminology should not be seen as reflecting actual household arrangements. When Yoshimi Ando and I studied village population records, we noticed that in some families a middle-aged son is listed as head of household and his widowed mother as "mother of household head," whereas in others the widowed mother is listed as the head and her son as "son of household head." I asked the town hall secretary about one case in which an elderly mother was listed as the head and was told that the reason was that the middle-aged son had never married. These inconsistencies in listing head of household reflect tension between Okinawan ideology, Okinawan reality, changing times, and Japanese governmental requirements.

24. According to T. Lebra, in Japan also prewedding cohabitation was acceptable prior to the absorption of samurai values (1984: 106). This is yet another example in which a significant difference between Okinawan and Japanese culture seems to pivot upon samurai cultural patterns (see Hendry 1981: 24ff. for a discussion of the spread of the samurai ethic). For a discussion of the absence of stigma attached to unmarried motherhood in another maritime community, see Cole (1991: 62). For a feminist analysis of virginity and patriarchal control of women's social and sexual lives, see Ortner (1996: 43–58).

25. According to Takenori Noguchi, the practice of a husband temporarily staying with his wife's family is still common on at least some of the Ryukyu Islands (1966: 27).

26. Traditionally, weddings seem to have been far more elaborate in rural Japan than in Okinawa. Bernstein notes that "in the old days—and as late as the 1960s in some areas—rural [Japanese] weddings were elaborate and costly affairs: three days were spent feasting at the groom's house and paying formal visits to the neighbors of the groom's family in order to introduce the bride into her new community" (1983: 158).

27. According to T. Lebra, in prewar Japan it was not uncommon for fathers to coerce daughters into marriage (1984: 89).

28. In a study of a village on the main island of Okinawa, Tanaka found that the rate of endogamy in marriages is 84 percent, and in marriages contracted before 1950 it was 93 percent (1977: 34). I did not compile precise figures for Henza, but my guess is that the rate is about the same.

29. She does not mean that individuals were forcibly restrained from leaving but rather that it was strongly frowned upon to leave.

30. In the old days, this could be problematic when her natal family was not able economically to provide for her.

31. I was also told by Mrs. Nakamura that people in Henza think it is admirable for a widow not to remarry, primarily because a second marriage would be difficult for the children. My sense, however, is that most young widows do and did remarry.

32. I would draw attention here to Mabuchi's comments regarding cult-group affiliation in the southern Ryukyus. He found that affiliation is sometimes patrilineal, sometimes matrilineal, sometimes matrilineal for daughters and patrilineal for sons, and sometimes optional. In writing about the succession of priestesses, he noted that "the various ways of succession of the priestesshood mentioned above further lead to multidirectional deviation from the ideal pattern in question" (1964: 85).

33. One of the very old local midwives told me that abortions traditionally were available in Henza.

34. The typical financial arrangement nowadays is that the groom pays three months' salary as a sort of gift to the bride and her family, and the bride's family buys furniture and household goods.

35. Unlike in many other East and Southeast Asian countries, almost no Amerasian babies are put up for adoption in Okinawa, although, due to the large American military presence, many are born. Okinawan women usually are able to raise their children with the help of relatives.

36. Mrs. Nakamura (in her late seventies), who married into a well-to-do family, explains that women in poorer families did not have to work as hard as women in better-off families because the latter had more land to farm and that women who married an eldest son and lived with his parents would not have been given as much food as a woman who continued to eat at her own mother's house.

37. According to Patrick Beillevaire, patrilineal succession at the domestic level, and specifically inheritance by the eldest son, are stricter in Okinawa than in Japan (personal communication).

38. In Japan also older women have more freedom and mobility (see Embree 1964: 172). However, upon retirement Japanese men may become excessively dependent upon their wives and insist that they always be present to do the husband's slightest bidding (Lock 1987: 148). This does not seem to be the case in Henza. Women told me that their husbands expect them to prepare food in advance if they leave the house, but I did not hear of women whose husbands expected them to stay home all day to serve them.

39. In the Portuguese maritime community that Sally Cole studied, it is common for sons and daughters to say that "the house is my mother's" and not "the house is my parents'" or "the house is my father's," even in cases in which the father actually owns the house. Cole explains this locution in terms of men's extended absenteeism at sea and women's role in supporting the family during the long absences (1991: 58).

40. Professor Takara believes it likely that in the past also Okinawan women lived longer than men. Of the nineteen kings in the Ryukyu dynasty, quite a large number died and were succeeded by their wives, who lived about twenty years longer. Also, in records of gifts given by and to the kings, there are many references to old women (personal communication).

41. According to the noro, her husband also resents that she does not go to funerals and that he has to go instead of her.

42. In contrast, in Japan, the photographs that adorn houses tend to be of male relatives. Gail Bernstein writes, "In every other farm house I visited, I would find similarly sober, unsmiling patriarchs, dressed in black robes and peering down on guests from their perches below the ceiling" (1983: 7).

43. This is in contrast to drinking among Mexican men, which is considered inherent to maleness—as part of the machismo complex.

44. According to Professor Higa, in traditional Okinawan society wife beating was very rare, but if it existed it was found in the upper class rather than in the peasant class (personal communication). Although my informants in Henza do report that men would sometimes beat their wives, Professor Higa's belief that this was limited to the upper class is interesting. In general, upper-class women were less autonomous than village women, and the upper class was more influenced by Chinese ideologies of male dominance.

45. This seems to be different from the case in traditional rural Japanese villages (cf. Embree 1964: 175).

46. Okinawan women's organizations are well aware of these issues. See, for example, *The Ryukyuanist*, 1996, newsletter no. 34, p. 3, where it is noted that women's voting rate exceeded that of men in the recent referendum regarding American military presence. Also, Okinawa seems to be ahead of most of the rest of Japan in appointing women to key political positions. Mrs. Hiroko Sho is a vice-governor of the Okinawa Prefecture and the second woman vice-governor in all of Japan (*Shimpo Weekly News*, August 20, 1991). A woman has also been appointed presiding judge of the Naha District Court; she is the third woman in Japan to receive so senior an appointment (*Shimpo Weekly News*, January 5, 1991).

47. The contrast between Henza and Suye Mura (Japan) is striking in this matter. According to the Embrees (in the 1930s), women had no formal authority in Japanese village affairs because the men and perhaps most of the women "simply assumed that women could not run their own affairs, much less those of a more public nature. The headship of the Suye Women's Association was assumed by a man from the village office. . . . Even the account books of some of the revolving credit associations formed by and for women were handled by men at the members' request because, the women said, they had no head for figures. The production of silk was almost entirely in the hands of women, but few were allowed to keep the money earned by its sale" (Smith and Wiswell 1982: 273). Japanese patterns regarding gender and family finances vary from village to village. According to Bernstein, "Not only do most of the farm women surveyed keep the wages they earn and spend them as they see fit, but a great many of them manage their husband's salary as well, doling out an allowance to him" (1983: 169).

48. I am not saying that women in patriarchal societies do not use all sorts of "weak" strategies such as trickery, lying, petty stealing, and quiet mockery (when no men are present). My claim is that these do not constitute significant and sustained resistance to patriarchy (cf. Morris 1995).

Chapter 4

1. I have chosen to use the term *separation* rather than *segregation* because the latter term implies a more extensive and formalized separation than is the case in Henza.

2. His estimate is based on approximately 150 *senbaru* boats, which took about five men each.

3. This seems to differ from the employment pattern of Japanese women of the same generation. According to T. Lebra, for prewar Japanese women, "maid-apprenticeship [was] one of the few accepted options to fill the interval between school graduation and marriage" (1984: 74–75).

4. Glacken, who studied both fishing and agriculture villages in Okinawa, found that "one observes more daytime visiting among [fishing village women] than among the women of the agricultural villages" (1951: 173). T. Lebra has noted that also in mainland Japan seamen's wives are thought to be stronger and more autonomous than women married to men who work on land (1984: 136).

5. According to Bernstein, in Japanese villages at funerals, "women serve as caterers, donning white smocklike aprons over dark slacks and preparing food for the family of the deceased, while their husbands, dressed in western suits, white shirts, and ties formally represent their household as mourners" (1983: 131). In Henza, both men and women attend funerals and pay visits to the homes of mourners. Some women, as in Japan, cook for the family of the deceased.

6. In contrast, according to Bernstein, in rural Japan women "do not participate in hamlet festival activities except as spectators" (1983: 130).

7. Potter's (1977) study of the Northern Thai provides an interesting parallel. Potter argues that many previous researchers have mistaken Northern Thai's matrifocal social bonds for an absence of social structure or for a "loose" social structure. Her analysis suggests, moreover, that a loose social structure may be a good fit for matrifocality. Significantly, Northern Thai matriclans are also ritual units in which women hold the key leadership positions (see Turton 1984).

8. For a general discussion of how men's prolonged absences in fishing communities and women's role in fish processing and marketing can lead to the possibility of more power for women both in the home and the community, see Thompson (1985). Thompson makes the important point that the model of male absence–female independence is too simplistic. Because fishing economies—at least nowadays and frequently in the past—are part of larger global economies, there are differences in the extent to which fishing families control their own labor. Through a discussion of Newfoundland, Norwegian, and other fishing societies, Thompson argues that when the men are exploited by merchants or employers, they may be driven toward compensating self-indulgence and "assertion of their own male authority when they return home" (1985: 22). It is important to note that this was not the case in Henza.

9. Tea was made with the umbilical cord as a cure for stomachaches.

10. One woman told me that when she was young she lived with her husband's family and "It was so terrible I didn't want to go home, so I would stay and work in the fields until dark so as not to have to see his parents. They were rich and had rice paddies." These sorts of ornery in-laws seem to have been more typical among better-off families and far more typical in mainland Japan (T. Lebra 1984: 145–146).

11. See Clark (1996) on lifelong relationships among sisters in a mainland Japanese family. Clark shows outmarrying women who continue to think of their natal families as their "other house." The women whom he interviewed maintain extensive, multidimensional relationships with their adult sisters.

12. The absence of emphasis upon the brother-sister relationship differs significantly from earlier reports of the "spiritual predominance of the sister." The sister was believed to be a guardian spirit (unari-gami) for her brother, and he was obligated to help and protect her (Mabuchi 1964; Haring 1964). My guess is that the decline of the brother-sister relationship is a fairly recent phenomenon and does not characterize all Okinawan villages. Regarding a village in the north of Okinawa, Kawahashi writes that "to this day the brother-sister relationship in Okinawa has remained a very intimate and warm one, which appears to observers from mainland Japan a novel characteristic, distinguishing Okinawa from the visitor's native culture. I myself have had the experience of mistaking my informant's brother for her husband as he was making regular visits to her house during lunch hours" (1992: 84).

13. I was told that in the east and west neighborhoods, women stay in the group located in the neighborhood of their natal households; women born in the center neighborhood join the group located in the neighborhood of their husband's household (although some variation on the basis of personal preference is possible). This may be related to the fact that more center neighborhood families had Shuri connections.

14. Villagers try to stay home as much as possible for the first year after the death of a family member. Women more than men seem to abide by this practice.

15. In Henza, the munchu system is incorporated into the village cult organization but in a manner that does not seem to have a great deal of meaning. According to Pro-

fessor Akamine, on outlying islands such as Kudaka Island the village religious structure is basically unrelated to the munchu system (personal communication).

16. According to Professor Akamine, the munchu system was established on Okinawa at the end of the seventeenth century among the upper classes and only later spread to the rural areas (personal communication).

17. Adult men living together and constituting a corporate group is one of the key markers of true patrilocality in classic anthropological schema. According to Tanaka, in some Okinawan villages, there is an actual rule against two adult, married brothers living in the same house or being enshrined in the same ancestral altar (1977: 41). Adult women may live with adult brothers or sisters (1977: 42).

18. I did not collect information on this point in Henza, but according to Glacken's study of another Okinawan village (Minatogawa), fishermen avoid teamwork among close relatives; members of the immediate family will not go out on the same fishing boat (1955: 161). In contrast, women relatives do a great deal of their work in groups.

19. In recent years, a few young women have joined. They are not particularly active in the association.

20. Old men also work at making the tug-of-war rope, helping out especially in the first stages, in which the rope is not yet too heavy or thick.

21. Okinawan men generally do not have the strong company loyalty and identity that is common in Japan.

22. Mrs. Kuni Okutara, who was born in Japan and now lives in Henza, says that gift giving is also common in Japan, but not to the extent that it is done in Henza—"on every little occasion." On gift giving in Japan, see Befu (1974).

23. In a similar vein, Ram, writing about Mukkavar fishing communities, comments that "Women utilize social and ritual bonds, established through marriage, work, neighborhood and fictive kin relationships, to undertake financial transactions which owe little to male intervention, which blur any clear distinction between domestic and extra-domestic worlds, and which are recognized as vital to the daily and seasonal survival of households" (1991: 162).

24. Of course, men's social ties are also cross-cutting in endogamous villages like Henza.

25. Margaret Lock explains that "in societies where [women's] social participation in ritual events is commonplace, there is the opportunity for women to readily discover that their distress is shared by others, . . . and articulation of social problems can then be facilitated through collective ritual performance. [In Japan] the alienation of middle-class urban dwellers is increased by isolation, and there is no opportunity to understand how common their problems are nor to appreciate their social rather than personal origins" (1987: 153).

Chapter 5

1. Today the big open air markets in Itoman and Naha are still dominated by women food sellers and buyers.

2. As I argued in *Priestess, Mother, Sacred Sister,* elaborate food preparation is common in women's religions (1994: 133–138). For a detailed description of foods rituals on Hateruma Island (a southern Ryukyu Island), see Ouwehand (1985: 132ff.). On Hateruma Island, a larger variety of foods is prepared for rituals than in Henza. A great deal has been written about food in Japanese rituals. For one example, see Ashkenazi (1983: 85ff.). I also refer the reader to Caroline Bynum's fascinating discussion of food rituals among medieval Christian women (1987, esp. pp. 189–194).

3. Other villagers told me that they do not especially put out foods that the deceased liked, although, as one explained, they do joke about it sometimes. I was told that they try to give favorite foods to recently deceased relatives.

4. Contrary to the usual village pattern, I was told by one woman that the food that is put on the ancestor's altar (*butsudan*) at home is changed on the first and fifteenth of each month and that it must be thrown away—it is forbidden to be eaten.

5. Befu explains that in Japan the contemporary custom of offering foods, sake, and the first crop of the field to gods, ancestors, neighbors, and relatives is historically related to *naorai*, the custom according to which gods and mortals shared foods together. "In the original form of naorai, offerings to gods were gifts to gods, and these gifts were returned by gods as their gifts for mortals to share with them, so that the mortals might partake of the divine power of the gods to whom the gifts were originally offered. . . . It is because communion with supernatural beings was achieved primarily through commensality that offerings to gods were, and still are, largely foodstuff, and also that even now food is considered the traditional type of gift in Japan and that in fact is the most popular type of gift. In the past, commensality was not only a device for transferring supernatural power to man, but also a means by which members of the community could partake in one another's power and be brought into a mystical union" (Befu 1974: 210–211).

6. Most of the examples of symbolic foods that villagers could think of are Japanese, not Okinawan. One Okinawan holiday-related food is *popo*—a barley pancake that is eaten at san gatsu. Another calendrically associated food is the special *mochi* (rice cake) wrapped in a leaf from the wild ginger plant. This is eaten in the twelfth month, shortly before New Year's. According to Mrs. Adaniya, "We serve *imo* (sweet potatoes) at New Year because it has a lot of roots and so you will have a lot of grandchildren." Of course, sake is used in rituals. I was told that "we need sake to connect to kami-sama." I have also seen miso placed on the ritual tray at a new house ritual because "this is what we need to live."

7. One informant said that it has been done only four or five times in the past sixty-five years, but another informant said that it is done more often because droughts are frequent on the island.

8. The human sacrifice motif seems obvious to me, but I never heard a villager suggest that line of interpretation.

9. Eisaa, like many Okinawan rituals, is historically dense, and different people explain its meaning in different ways. One of the older men of the village told me that it is a Buddhist dance and that it is not native to Henza. In one version told to me, eisaa dancing began with poor people going through town begging; it probably had a Japanese Buddhist origin. Other people have told me that eisaa is probably an old Okinawan custom, which later became attached to obon. Eisaa dancing is done to make the ancestors happy when they come during obon.

10. This pattern may also hold true for symbolic objects. I was told that the goat used in the men's ame tabore ritual (performed in times of severe drought) is traditionally a male goat; in another context entirely, I was told that the goat eaten at housewarming rituals (a "good thing" attended by priestesses) is traditionally a female goat. These may, however, have been random comments with no meaning.

11. An association of women with death or absence is also expressed in psychoanalytic theories. "Female genitals in Freud's analysis . . . are a gap, a lack, an absence: the female acknowledges the fact of her castration, and with it, too, the superiority of the male and her own inferiority" (Jonte-Pace 1992: 20). Winnicott, according to Jonte-Pace, somewhat softens the equation of women and absence yet does not elimi-

nate it: Winnicott writes that when the mother is away the child perceives her as dead—the mother's absence is the very meaning of death. Julia Kristeva maintains the homology of women and death: The feminine as the image of death is a screen for both the fear of castration and for the matricide that is necessary for the individual to become autonomous. Jonte-Pace makes clear that association between women and death in Western thinking is not always explicit or visible; to the contrary, the public discourse in the West tends to be that of "woman as life-bearer." This discourse, however, is also used to restrict women's freedom and social power.

12. Cross-culturally, in a number of women-led religious frameworks, women are associated with food, fertility, and abundance and men are in charge of animal sacrifice and associated with death symbolism (see Sered 1994; see also Jay 1992 on gender and sacrifice). This point comes across dramatically in Shigeharu Tanabe's (1991) description of an elaborate ritual of a large Northern Thai matrilineal descent group. The space inside the sanctuary where the ritual takes place is divided into female and male sides. The polluted (in Thai terms) animal sacrifice takes place on the male side, while the female side remains pure. An equally striking instance is provided by the Tetum, among whom women preside at almost all religious rituals. The one significant exception is death rituals, at which men are more active than women. The most dramatic figure in death rituals is the "lord of death," who is a senior male of the dead person's hamlet (Hicks 1984, 120–121).

13. The ocean also is both dangerous and purifying. Things from the sea (salt, salt water, octopus, fish, stones from the sea) are used for oharai of various kinds.

14. Unlike Kawahashi (1992), I never heard any informant suggest that women are priestesses because they have the innate ability to give birth.

Chapter 6

1. The discussion in this chapter focuses upon the noro and her associates—the village kaminchu—but much of what I describe here is also true of clan kaminchu. In the past, the priestess role varied, as it does today on different islands. For example, nowadays Henza priestesses do not use a formal liturgy; their prayers are spontaneous ("natural" is the word they use to describe how they pray). But they know that in the past there was some formal liturgy. See Ouwehand (1985: 140ff.) for liturgical texts from the southern Ryukyus and W. Lebra (1966) for descriptions of rituals in other Okinawan villages.

2. I asked Mrs. Shimojo what would happen if a kaminchu sat in the wrong seat on the benches in the utaki. She replied with a laugh that they never sit in the wrong seat.

3. In Henza, there does not seem to be any particular association between priestesses and the hearth god (hinu-kan). To the contrary, villagers told me that yuta are the ones who know about hinu-kan. Also Kreiner argues that it is inaccurate to speak of a cult of "holy fire" as the center of the noro religion (1968: 110).

4. According to Mrs. Shinzato, this kind of shell was hung on the pig house in the old days when a child was ill or to keep away the aku no kami-sama ('bad gods').

5. Throughout much of Asia, death is seen as polluting, and it is often the case that local religious leaders do not perform funerary rituals (Buddhist monks or priests take care of the bodies of the dead in many Asian societies). In Okinawa, there is no notion that death is polluting, and the idea that kaminchu do not attend funerals is not absolute. Henza priestesses attend funerals of close relatives; the Nakijin noro told

me that she only avoids funerals close to the dates on which she goes to the sacred grove.

6. It is not permitted to urinate in the utaki.

7. Raw rice is usually sprinkled on the hinu-kan or other altars. At the utaki altar, the priestesses first sprinkle raw rice and spill sake, then they pray, then the noro "feeds" the cooked rice into the conch shells.

8. In some villages, priestesses do not perform new-house rituals. Henza may be somewhat exceptional in this matter.

9. I was told some of the words: "The pole of the east side and west side and then the roof on the top, now let's have a celebration." One of the kaminchu told me that she prays that the couple will have a long life together, happiness, and health.

10. I thank Starhawk for helping me formulate this analysis.

Chapter 7

1. During the time of the Ryukyuan Kingdom, before the noro died, she would suggest a replacement. When she died the villagers would write to Shuri, reporting her death and naming her replacement, who would, as a matter of course, receive official appointment from Shuri. (Villagers showed me one of these letters.) Since the Shuri government no longer exists, Henza's noro is now chosen in the same way that clan kaminchu traditionally have been. According to Yoshida (1990), in some villages priestesses are selected by lottery from among several candidates. The system on the Yaeyama Islands seems to be rather different (see Ouwehand 1985: 127ff.).

2. That this epiphany occurred on the morning of san gatsu may be related to an old idea that on certain holidays the kami comes to cohabitate with the priestess.

3. Clan membership goes through the male line; thus—with the exception of the noro—a woman is more likely to be a priestess in her father's clan than in her mother's. Throughout Okinawa, there are different customs regarding the succession of the noro, and in Henza there was a change from matrilineal to patrilineal succession with the current noro. Josef Kreiner has found that with the exception of the noro, the succession of priestesses is bilateral (1968: 106).

4. *Ekisha* are literate fortune-tellers. Their system came from outside of Okinawa. Ekisha are usually men, and they are ranked among themselves.

5. In a narrative cited by Ota (1989: 117), the priestess used the word *shirashi* or notification (sent by the god). Kawahashi also notes that the illnesses can be minor. She gives an example of a priestess-to-be whose illness consisted of a carbuncle on the tip of her finger. The priestess explained, "This time, the message seemed obvious to me: I had a swollen index finger because the deity was pointing at me" (1992: 125; also see pages 128ff.). Kawahashi cites another priestess who interpreted her illnesses as manifestations of the village's neglect of ritual responsibilities (1992: 130–131).

6. I was told the following story by the local English teacher: Once a relative was having bad headaches. The yuta asked if he had taken something from Hamagawa Island. "Hamagawa Island is a mysterious place," he said, "and you are not allowed to take any natural thing (rock or tree) from it. These things belong to the kami-sama." It turned out that he had taken a stone from Hamagawa Island. "When he returned it to the kami-sama of Hamagawa Island, his headaches went away."

7. Yuta do not see their services as competing with those of physicians but rather as complementary (cf. Sakumichi et al. 1984).

8. I suspect that the slow process of becoming a priestess allows the really dysfunctional candidates to be screened out.

Chapter 8

1. The full ceremony for priestess initiation is rare; only the priestesses who go to the sacred grove experience the entire accession process. Clan priestesses undergo an abbreviated version of the accession described in this chapter. Initiation rituals vary greatly from island to island. For a very different description, see Kamata (1966: 65).

2. *Todoke* is a Japanese word that is used, for example, to register a new baby at city hall. Mrs. Hamabata used the word *shoomei*—a Japanese term used bureaucratically to mean verification—to describe her sister-in-law's witnessing the yuta's judgment, and she also makes reference to *inkan* (stamp that is used to sign official documents).

3. By *chikara* she means spiritual power or strength, not authority or domination. Mrs. Hamabata uses more Japanese religious terminology than do the other priestesses. Much of her spiritual jargon has been picked up from her mentor, the yuta Mrs. Uyealtari.

4. *Kami kuyo* is Japanese, and I never heard the word used by anyone in Henza except for Mrs. Hamabata. What Mrs. Hamabata describes as kami kuyo is usually referred to in Henza as either *futuchigwan* or *nujiha*. According to Mrs. Shimojo, "For example, the previous noro died. Now she is not kami-sama anymore. To go to heaven, please let her go to heaven. They do nujiha [take out, remove]. When she was alive she was kami-sama, and she passed away. For example, if I am her replacement, please nujiha and let her go to heaven [*tengoku*], that is the ogami I would make." Mrs. Tanahara explains it a bit differently: "Nujiha is to pray out the previous kaminchu. Nujiha is an ogami to say that the next person is here so the previous one please step down."

5. She is probably referring to a Buddhist temple on the main island of Okinawa.

6. The ritual was so brief that I asked whether it was longer in the past. According to Mrs. Shimojo, it was always like this.

7. In general, a lower ranking person pours sake first and a higher ranking person pours second, if that person chooses to. It is rare for a man to pour for women.

8. Analogous to brides at wedding ceremonies, the "star" wore pretty clothes and was the center of attention. However, unlike for Japanese women ritual practitioners, there is no hint in village discourse or ritual that priestesses are understood to be brides of the kami-sama (cf. Blacker 1975: 118ff.; 146ff.).

9. Similarly, Kendall cites a Korean shaman initiate as insisting that she "really didn't know anything" (1996: 23).

10. The word *umareru* (birth) is also used for a ship-making ritual (but not for a new-house ritual).

11. Portentous dreams are central in the initiation narratives of shamans in many cultures. See, for example, Kendall (1996: 23).

12. Red is generally an auspicious color in Okinawa.

13. Traditionally, soon after a baby was born, the midwife took ashes from the bottom of the pot on the hinu-kan, put them on the baby's forehead, and gave the baby its name. At New Year's water from a special spring was put on the baby's head three times.

14. Mrs. Shimojo told me that celebrations are held on the first and second year after accession and every seven years thereafter.

15. Death and resurrection symbols and myths are especially common in agricultural societies and regions in which there is a season during which there is no crop

growth. In Okinawa (subtropics), there are harvests all year, and the central religious imagery does not portray death as preceding birth—new births are added on to previous births just like in village gardens. Also, I would tentatively suggest that whereas men would be likely to see birth from one perspective, that of the born, women would see birth from two perspectives, of the giver of birth and of the born. From the perspective of the born, perhaps death does precede birth; the baby is torn from—dies to—its uterine world and is born into the outside world. From the perspective of the birth giver, however, birth is one step along a continuum of relationship and nurture that begins with conception (or even before) and, at least in religious contexts, continues even beyond death.

16. *Kawari* means replace, *umare* means born; this is used, for example, in saying that a child is the *umarekawari* of a dead great-grandparent, a vague sort of reincarnation.

17. In contrast, Blacker describes the initiation of the medium in mainland Japan in these terms: "Dying to her old self, she is reborn in the dazzling garb of the bride of the deity implanted in her at the moment of death and with whom she will henceforth stand in close tutelary relationship" (1975: 147). The Okinawan priestess does not die to her old self, nor does she marry the deity or have the deity implanted in her. In Okinawa, unlike in Japan, there is no tutelary relationship with the deity.

18. Mrs. Hamabata uses the word *sukkiri*—relief. According to my Okinawan friend and interpreter, this word "describes how you feel if you really need to go to the bathroom and then you go."

19. The language of serving as a bridge is common among shamans cross-culturally; see, for example, Atkinson (1989: 286).

Chapter 9

1. This analysis fits well with feminist analyses that treat power and hierarchy as rooted in men's efforts to control the means of reproduction and in men's need to renounce the natural female world in which they were nurtured but from which they feel they must separate in order to construct a cultured male identity (Rubin 1975; Chodorow 1974).

2. In this they differ considerably from Shinto priests. Nowadays, Henza villagers who wish to have a modern wedding may well have a Shinto ceremony at a wedding hall on the main island. Some villagers celebrate the Japanese three-five-seven (year-old) ceremonies, but the priestesses have no part in this, either. Some few villagers may take their children to a Shinto shrine on the main island at these ages.

3. I find it interesting that Hori interprets certain core components of Japanese religious thinking in terms of agriculture (1968: 20).

4. Although Henza, like the rest of Okinawa, experiences typhoons, some of which are quite dangerous. In the past, village men would sometimes drown in typhoons at sea.

5. My sense is that power relationships are quite different in Okinawa than in Japan. In this context, it is interesting to consider Rohlen's discussion of the view among Japanologists that the organization of power in Japan presents a "portrait of the center as a focus of legitimacy and balance, but not one in which great authority and power are united. . . . A structural approach that equates hierarchy with power is somewhat misleading" (1989: 16–17). However, Rohlen argues, the fact that teachers, bosses, government, and so on frequently step back from a direct leadership role does not mean that they lack power or authority. To the contrary, they can do so precisely because "authority is not weak or uncertain of its ultimate power to mobilize social

forces. This reserve has the further consequence of protecting authority from appearing coercive and it helps maintain the legitimacy of the office" (1989: 31). In other words, power and authority in Japan are significant and meaningful, but manifested in indirect or disguised ways.

6. I do not argue that this is the sole or, from a historical perspective, the most salient function of these rituals. It is, however, a pervasive theme in Henza ritual.

7. The separation of church and state is of course one of the trademarks of modern democracies.

8. Two kaminchu told me that they did the lots (*kome kuji*) by themselves and decided on their own that they are kaminchu. On the one hand, this suggests that the communal process or the yuta's role may not be totally necessary. On the other hand, both of these kaminchu seem a bit unpopular. In other villages, the succession issue is dealt with by carrying out a lottery among the potential candidates from the clan (see Kawahashi 1992).

9. Of course, this might not really be the case. I get the impression that one of the other village kaminchu had taken on some additional responsibilities after the previous noro died and that this kaminchu does seem to resent the current noro (but that may be because she had been very close friends with the previous noro).

10. Most people I asked did not know (or did not offer to me) a reason for waiting several years between kaminchu. Mrs. Kamura told me that "you can't do it right away because the person who was doing it before just died, and so you must wait for the celebration, so as not to do a celebration right after a funeral." Her explanation does not, however, explain a ten- or twenty-year gap.

11. This necklace includes a *magatama*—a semiprecious kidney-shaped stone that, according to Haring, is found in archeological digs throughout the Ryukyus and is believed to be a repository of "mana" (1964: 43–44).

12. This is another area in which Okinawan religion differs from Japanese (see Hori 1968: 59).

13. In Japan, of course, Shinto priests are men.

14. The pop star, Shoukichi Kina, had commissioned a traditional boat from local craftsmen. The boat was to be used to sail on a mission of peace to Hiroshima, Nagasaki, and further ports. Shoukichi Kina performs with his sisters and other musicians in Okinawa, Japan, and internationally. His performances combine traditional Okinawan singing and dancing with contemporary rock and roll.

Chapter 10

1. According to Kerr, during the late seventeenth century some Chinese Taoist practices crept into Okinawa's cultural repertoire. Specifically, "Fortunetellers known as yuta began to rival the noro priestesses in the eyes of the townsmen" (1958: 219). According to Professor Akamine, there is a debate in the literature regarding the role of yuta in previous times. On Miyako Islands today and also on Kudaka (but not Yaeyama), the yuta is a member of the village cult organization in her role as yuta. According to Professor Takara, there are names of yuta in historical records as early as 600 years ago.

2. Kendall does cite other Korean ethnographers who have found that shamans commonly deny that they learned to perform their rituals from other shamans (1996: 53).

3. The word *ogami-san* (or *ogamiya-sama*) is used in Japan (cf. Blacker 1975: 154). I never heard the full word ogamiya-sama or ogami-san used in Henza. Henza villagers

simply call these practitioners *ogami* which means prayer. The term "ogami" for these practitioners is relatively new in the village.

4. According to Professor Takara, although the role of what is today called ogami people did exist during the Ryukyuan Kingdom, there was no official name for the role. The scanty historical evidence suggests that about 10 percent were men (personal communication).

5. I refer the reader to Kawahashi's (1992) detailed discussion of the relationship between yuta and kaminchu.

6. Yuta use various ritual techniques. Once when I accompanied a friend from Henza on a visit to a neighboring island (Yabuchi Island) where there is a sacred cave frequented by yuta, we saw a yuta with clients pray for about five minutes and then lean forward and gasp or yawn approximately ten times, after which she began to speak in a different sort of voice. When she had finished speaking in what I assume is the ancestor's or kami's voice, she repeated the gasps or yawns one or two times. Afterward she knew what the kami-sama had said.

7. Okinawan yuta bear a long history of oppression (Ohashi et al. 1984: 72). During the Ryukyuan Kingdom, from about 1650, the upper classes persecuted yuta, claiming that yuta lie. According to Kerr, in 1736 yuta were forbidden to represent themselves as healers of the sick. In 1884, yuta were forbidden to "offer to relieve pain and sickness by incantations and spells" (Kerr 1958: 402). In the 1940s Garland Hopkins saw that yuta practiced clandestinely (1951: 184).

8. Haring writes that in the Amami Islands (north of Okinawa), there are male fortune-tellers and diviners, but they talk and dress like women when carrying out professional duties (1964: 44).

9. Aside from obvious business transactions in stores and the like, Japanese and Okinawans prefer to give money in an envelope.

Chapter 11

1. My findings regarding this matter in Henza probably are typical of Okinawa as a whole. For example, the noro of Nakijin (one of the most important holy sites in Okinawa) told me that she does not know why in Okinawa women are the priestesses. When I asked her if it is because women are closer to kami-sama, she replied, "See, Susan, in your country [where men are the rabbis] then it would be that men are closer to kami, so I don't think you can really say who is closer to kami."

2. In contrast, Bernstein writes regarding rural Japan that in recent years, because many farm men work in the towns and cities, traditional attitudes toward the role of women in the public and social lives of the village are being eroded. "For example, women may now go in place of their absent husbands to the hamlet council meetings, which traditionally *they were prohibited from attending*" (1983: 164; my emphasis). In Henza, no one ever insinuated that women are prohibited from participating in the town council.

3. Henza villagers, both men and women, tell me that this has always been the case. According to W. Lebra (1966: 77), the association of religious activism with age is not a new phenomenon in Okinawa and does not reflect a dwindling of interest in religion in modern times. Rather, this seems to be a traditional pattern.

4. Also in Japan there are parties for old people at certain ages—seventy-seven, eighty-eight, and ninety-nine (Hendry 1995: 143).

5. These songs were given me by my neighbor, an elderly fisherman and *samisen* player.

6. Shuri dialect is seen by some people as higher status (more polite).

7. For example, in writing about Mukkuvar fishing communities, Ram notes that Mukkuvars describe the rigid sexual division of labor (men fish and women do land-based work), "in terms of the violating of cultural values entailed in permitting women to engage in work in male-dominated spaces without suitable safeguards. It is not merely that the violation of such cultural norms would be dangerous for women. Women themselves are seen as dangerous—to men . . . women as a category share the stigma of being designated dangerous, particularly to the male pursuit of hazardous activities such as fishing" (1991: 50).

8. According to Professor Akamine, in Japan there is a taboo on women going on fishing boats; in Okinawa this idea is recent, probably only since ships with engines have been in use (personal communication).

9. My argument in this section, that villagers do not offer ideological interpretations of gender roles, runs counter to Noriko Kawahashi's analysis. For instance, Kawahashi explains women's role as priestess in terms of the fact that women are mothers, whereas I never heard this sentiment expressed or even hinted at in Henza. Kawahashi also writes in her conclusion, "I described more than one way in which a female is closer to kami than is a male" (1992: 197). Again, this is a sentiment that I never heard expressed in Henza. Given the autonomy of Okinawan villages, our findings may reflect different social realities in different villages. On the other hand, much of Kawahashi's argument seems to be based on interpretations that she did not receive directly from villagers. For example, "The divine priestesses prayed for abundance of rice and wheat crops. We may extrapolate from this that the kingdom recognized an explicit connection between the earth's fertility and women's reproductive fertility, and was utilizing the forces of nature which they believed to be sacralized in women" (1992: 46). To my mind, her extrapolation here constitutes a rather large leap in interpretation. Because no ethnographic work is ever free from the perceptions of the particular researcher, I assume that Kawahashi and I look at issues of gender from different perspectives.

Chapter 12

1. Patrick Beillevaire made similar observations in Tarama Village: "Dignity seems to be attached to the north-east corner, but in Tarama *there is some ambiguity* between the north-east and south-east corners" (1986: 78). Later on Beillevaire notes that the east side is superior to the west, but in the case of "certain rituals" he finds "an instance of *hierarchical reversal.*" And again, "contrary to Muratake's own opinion concerning Tarama, the *north is not superior to the south in* every *ritual context*" (1986: 81; all emphases are mine). If I may rephrase Beillevaire's findings, east, west, north, and south are certainly part of village cosmology, but their meanings and their ritual uses are not immutable. Summarizing the shifting dualisms of indigenous geography, Beillevaire explains that cosmic life originates in the east or in the southeast, whereas human life (childbirth) starts from the west. "However, during a person's lifetime, his or her vital principle belongs to the eastern part of the house. Death is followed by a movement back to the west, but gradually the ancestor, unless reborn, moves east again" (1986: 80). In Maesato Village (in the southern part of the main island), where I also saw the *tsuna-hiki* the ritual was far more competitive than in Henza: The two teams pulled with passion and were not rescrambled in the middle, and the tug was followed by some quite violent stick-fighting displays. Still most villagers did not seem to know which team was supposed to be male and which team female. It was ex-

plained to me that the east team is male one year and female the next, and vice versa for the west team, a situation of shifting dualisms.

2. The only time that I ever heard a categorical statement about people from the west versus people from the east was in the context of Mrs. Adaniya's talking to me about various springs and water sources in the village. According to Mrs. Adaniya, people in the west side of the village are bigger "because the water from the spring over there makes them bigger." When I asked, she explained that if people move from one side of the village to the other, their size changes.

3. I am not referring here to men playing the part of women in all-male cast plays or court dancing. I am referring to men who sometimes choose, for their own reasons, to wear women's clothes. Note that men in women's clothing are also found in mainland Japanese rituals.

4. Atkinson similarly found among the Indonesian Wana that "because notions of gender are constructed as a continuum rather than as a set of dichotomies, shamans can exploit a range of behavioral styles without couching their actions in transvestite imagery" (1989: 283).

5. Looking at societies in which gender is a highly marked category is instructive. Murray, for instance, describes cross-dressing men at Martinique's carnival, where some of the men wear padding on their chests or buttocks: "The padding is often exaggerated or purposefully visible. And in a few cases, there is another form of padding around the genital areas, where either a tampon is visible sticking out from a woman's bathing suit, or a mophead has been inserted through the crotch of a woman's one-piece lycra workout bodysuit, so that the hanging strings resemble unshorn pubic hairs" (1996: 3). Another example of this sort can be found in the Embrees' description of a celebration in Suye Mura (Japan) in the 1930s: "Some of the old women dressed in men's clothing ran about and danced like youngsters. They generally acted in complete accordance with the assumed sex, making passes at all the girls and women" (Smith and Wiswell 1982: 80). Similarly, Hauser-Schaublin shows that at certain ceremonies among the Iatmul of Melanesia, women dress in men's costumes and hit the other women participants with sticks as a means of mocking men's aggressive behavior toward women (1995: 48–49). What she found among the Iatmul is women dressing like men, acting like men, and using dress and behavior to express gender conflict. Significantly, scholars of Melanesian ritual have convincingly argued that initiation rites—including elements of transvestism—are fundamentally concerned with the creation and maintenance of separation between the sexes (cf. Allen 1967; Lutkehaus and Roscoe 1995). And finally, according to James Peacock, male transvestites in Java, many of whom play in the theater, appropriate female attributes in as complete and conspicuous a way as possible. Peacock argues that the division between male and female is a fundamental and extraordinarily salient principle of Javanese culture, and even more broadly, that Javanese culture is permeated with the very idea of classification. "Even in daily life, the transvestite is not interested merely in imitating women, but in classifying himself in the category 'female'" (1978: 216–217). Peacock concludes that "given their concern with cosmic order, the Javanese get a peculiar charge out of abnormal combinations that connote disorder. . . . They get excited at viewing peculiar combinations of male and female qualities represented by the transvestite on the stage, and they continuously remind themselves of the mix. . . . If the transvestite should spoil the illusion by a stiff or coarse gesture that permits maleness to show through, the audience responds with disgust" (1978: 217–218).

6. As Murray (1996) argues, these two stances are not necessarily static, and the same event of cross-dressing can encompass both kinds of meanings.

7. Even among the relatively egalitarian Vanatinai of New Guinea, women who practice sorcery—which is considered a men's role—dress in traditional men's dress (Lepowsky 1990: 184). There is some evidence that formerly when Okinawan men entered the sacred groves (a rare event) they would wear women's clothes.

8. The only ritual difference between the male kami-sama and her female counterparts is that at the *shinugu* ritual she does not accompany the others to the ritual meal but leaves them halfway through the day, announcing that she has to go catch some octopus or fish. I did, however, notice that Mrs. Shimojo (the male kami-sama) tends to act more assertively at rituals, and when Mr. Shibahiki—the male assistant—is absent, she is likely to take over some of the tasks that he normally does (such as walk first up the trail through the jungle or light the incense). The noro and Mrs. Shimojo herself, however, assure me that Mrs. Shimojo does not act differently than female kami-sama and that the only difference is in how she ties her headband and skirt.

9. An interesting contrast to Mrs. Shimojo are the women chiefs in traditional Polynesian society. These women, situated in a society that was clearly not egalitarian, either remained virgins (those were the sacred chiefs) or became gendered men—headmen. In other words, gender was extremely relevant—women qua women could not be sacred chiefs or headmen. Niel Gunson shows that women chiefs were typically portrayed as aggressive, masculine in appearance, and very large in size (1987).

Conclusion

1. What I am presenting here is, of course, the Durkheimian model, in which religion is a means by which a society worships itself and its own social institutions. A corollary is that religious leadership, and especially institutionalized leadership, is in the hands of those who have an interest in sustaining the society's institutions (see also Eisenstadt 1982). I realize that my model privileges religion, a privileging that I feel is justified, in many instances, given the role of religion in explaining and manipulating gender patterns (Geertz 1969).

2. Race and age like gender, are examples of culturally defined categories that, because they "look natural," can be used to naturalize hierarchy (cf. Yanagisako and Delaney 1995).

References

Allen, Michael. 1967. *Male Cults and Secret Initiations in Melanesia*. Victoria: Melbourne University Press.

Angst, Linda. 1996. Gendered Nationalism: The Himeyuri Story and Okinawan Identity in Postwar Japan. Paper presented at the American Anthropological Association Annual Meeting. San Francisco.

Anzai, Shin. 1976. Newly-Adopted Religions and Social Change on the Ryukyu Islands (Japan). *Social Compass* 23(1):57–70.

Ashkenazi, Michael. 1983. Festival Change and Continuity in a Japanese Town. Ph.D. diss., Yale University, New Haven.

Atkinson, Clarissa, Constance Buchanan, and Margaret Miles (Eds.) 1985. *Immaculate and Powerful: The Female in Sacred Image and Social Reality*. Boston: Beacon.

Atkinson, Jane Monnig. 1989. *The Art and Politics of Wana Shamanism*. Berkeley: University of California Press.

Bastide, Roger. 1978. *The African Religions of Brazil*. 1960. Baltimore: Johns Hopkins University Press.

Bateson, Gregory. 1958 [1936]. *Naven*. Stanford: Stanford University Press.

Bednarowski, Mary Farrell. 1980. Outside the Mainstream: Women's Religion and Women Religious Leaders in Nineteenth-century America. *Journal of the American Academy of Religion* 48(2):207–231.

Befu, Harumi. 1974. Gift-Giving in Modernizing Japan. In *Japanese Culture and Behavior: Selected Readings*, ed. Takie Sugiyama Lebra, 208–224. Honolulu: University of Hawaii Press.

Beillevaire, Patrick. 1986. Spatial Characterization of Human Temporality in the Ryukyus. In *Interpreting Japanese Society: Anthropological Approaches*, ed. Joy Hendry and Jonathan Webber, 76–87. Oxford: JASO.

Ben-Ari, Eyal. 1996. From Mothering to Othering: Organization, Culture, and Nap Time in a Japanese Day-Care Center. *Ethos* 24(1):136–164.

Bernstein, Gail Lee. 1983. *Haruko's World*. Stanford: Stanford University Press.

Blacker, Carmen. 1975. *The Catalpa Bow: A Study of Shamanistic Practices in Japan*. London: George Allen and Unwin.

Bledsoe, Caroline H. 1980. *Women and Marriage in Kpelle Society*. Stanford: Stanford University Press.

Bleier, Ruth. 1984. *Science and Gender*. New York: Pergamon.

Boddy, Janice. 1988. Spirits and Selves in Northern Sudan: The Cultural Therapeutics of Possession and Trance. *American Ethnologist* 15(1):4–27.

Braude, Ann D. 1985. Spirits Defend the Rights of Women: Spiritualism and Changing Sex Roles in Nineteenth-Century America. In *Women, Religion and Social Change*, ed. Yvonne Yazbeck Haddad and Ellison Banks Findley, 419–432. Albany: State University of New York Press.

Breidenbach, Paul. 1979. The Woman on the Beach and the Man in the Bush: Leadership and Adepthood in the Twelve Apostles Movement of Ghana. In *The New Religions of Africa*, ed. Bennetta Jules-Rosette, 99–126. Norwood, N. J.: Ablex.

Brewer, Priscilla J. 1992. "Tho' of the Weaker Sex": A Reassessment of Gender Equality among the Shakers. *Signs* 17 (3): 609–635.

Burdick, John. 1990. Gossip and Secrecy: Women's Articulation of Domestic Conflict in Three Religions of Urban Brazil. *Sociological Analysis* 50(2):153–170.

Butler, J. 1993. *Bodies That Matter: On the Discursive Limits of "Sex."* New York: Routledge.

Bynum, Caroline Walker. 1987. *Holy Feast and Holy Fast*. Berkeley: University of California Press.

Bynum, Caroline Walker, Stevan Harrell, and Paula Richman (Eds.) 1986. *Gender and Religion: On the Complexity of Symbols*. Boston: Beacon.

Chodorow, Nancy. 1974. Family Structure and Feminine Personality. In *Women, Culture, and Society*, ed. Michelle Z. Rosaldo and Louise Lamphere, 43–66. Stanford: Stanford University Press.

Christian, William. 1972. *Person and God in a Spanish Valley*. New York: Seminar Press.

Clark, Scott. 1996. My Other House: Lifelong Relationships between Sisters of the Hayashi Family. Paper presented at the American Anthropological Association Annual Meeting, San Francisco.

Cohen, Paul T., and Gehan Wijeyewardene. 1984. Introduction. *Mankind* 14(4):249–262.

Cole, Sally. 1991. *Women of the Praia: Work and Lives in a Portuguese Coastal Community*. Princeton: Princeton University Press.

Colson, Elizabeth. 1993. A Note on the Discussions at Mijas. In *Sex and Gender Hierarchies*, ed. Barbara Diane Miller, xv–xix. Cambridge: Cambridge University Press.

Connell, R.W. 1987. *Gender and Power*. Stanford: Stanford University Press.

Cosentino, Donald. 1982. *Defiant Maids and Stubborn Farmers: Tradition and Invention in Mende Story Performance*. Cambridge: Cambridge University Press.

Creighton, Milton R. 1990. Revisiting Shame and Guilt Cultures: A Forty-Year Pilgrimage. *Ethos* 18(3):279–307.

Cutler, Norman. 1985. Conclusion. In *Gods of Flesh / Gods of Stone: The Embodiment of Divinity in India*, ed. Joanne Punzo Waghorne and Norman Cutler, 159–170. Chambersburg, Pa.: Anima.

Daly, Mary. 1973. *Beyond God the Father*. Boston: Beacon.

———. 1978. *Gyn/Ecology: The Metaethics of Radical Feminism*. Boston: Beacon.

Delaney, Carol. 1991. *The Seed and the Soil: Gender and Cosmology in Turkish Village Society*. Berkeley: University of California Press.

Desroche, Henri. 1971 [1955]. *The American Shakers: From Neo-Christianity to Presocialism*. Amherst: University of Massachusetts Press.

Douglas, Mary. 1966. *Purity and Danger*. London: Pelican.

———. 1970. *Natural Symbols: Explorations in Cosmology*. London: Barrie and Rockcliffe.

Drake, Chris. 1995. Questions of Gender in the *Omoro sooshi*. *Rikkyo Review: Arts and Letters* 55:1–34.

Dugan, Kathleen M. 1994. At the Beginning Was Woman: Women in Native American Religious Traditions. In *Religion and Women*, ed. Arvind Sharma and Katherine K. Young, 39–60. Albany: State University of New York Press.

Dumont, Louis. 1970. *Homo Hierarchicus: The Caste System and Its Implications*. Trans. Mark Sainsbury. Chicago: University of Chicago Press.

Durkheim, Emile. 1915. *The Elementary Forms of the Religious Life*. London: Allen and Unwin.

———. 1963 [1898]. *Incest: The Nature and Origin of the Taboo*. New York: Lyle Stuart.

Ehrenreich, Barbara, and Deidre English. 1979. *For Her Own Good: 150 Years of the Experts Advice to Women*. Garden City, New York: Anchor Press/ Doubleday.

Eisenstadt, Shmuel. 1982. The Axial Age: The Emergence of Transcendental Visions and the Rise of Clerics. *Archives Europeennes de Sociologie* 23(1):294–314.

Eliade, Mircea. 1958. *Rites and Symbols of Initiation*. New York: Harper and Row.

———. 1964 [1951]. *Shamanism: Archaic Techniques of Ecstacy*. Trans. Willard R. Trask. Princeton: Princeton University Press.

Ellwood, Robert S. 1986. Patriarchal Revolution in Ancient Japan: From the *Nihonshoki Suujin Chronicle*. *Journal of Feminist Studies in Religion* 2(2):23–38.

Embree, John F. 1964 (1939). *Suye Mura: A Japanese Village*. Chicago: University of Chicago Press.

Errington, Shelly. 1990. Recasting Sex, Gender, and Power: A Theoretical and Regional Overview. In *Power and Difference: Gender in Island Southeast Asia*, ed. Jane Monnig Atkinson and Shelley Errington, 1–58. Stanford: Stanford University Press.

Finkler, Kaja. 1985. *Spiritualist Healers in Mexico*. South Hadley, Massachusetts: Bergin and Garvey.

———. 1994. *Women in Pain: Gender and Morbidity in Mexico*. Philadelphia: University of Pennsylvania Press.

Frymer-Kensky, Tikva. 1992. *In the Wake of the Goddess: Women, Culture, and the Biblical Transformation of Pagan Myth*. New York: Free Press.

Furnivall, I. C. S. 1911. Matriarchal Vestiges in Burma. *Journal of the Burma Research Society* 1:15–30.

Gable, Eric. 1995. The Decolonization of Consciousness: Local Skeptics and the "Will to be Modern" in a West African Village. *American Ethnologist* 22(2):242–257.

Garber, Marjorie. 1992. *Vested Interests: Cross-dressing and Cultural Anxiety*. New York and London: Routledge.

Geertz, Clifford. 1969. Religion as a Cultural System. In *Anthropological Approaches to the Study of Religion*, ed. Michael Banton. London: Tavistock Publications.

———. 1973. *The Interpretation of Cultures*. New York: Basic Books.

Gilligan, Carol. 1982. *In a Different Voice*. Cambridge: Harvard University Press.

Gimbutas. 1974. *The Gods and Goddesses of Old Europe*. London: Thames and Hudson.

Glacken, Clarence J. 1955. *The Great Loochoo: A Study of Okinawan Village Life*. Berkeley and Los Angeles: University of California Press.

Gluckman, Max. 1965. *Custom and Conflict in Africa*. Oxford: Basil Blackwell.

Godelier, Maurice. 1986 [1982]. *The Making of Great Men: Male Domination and Power Among the New Guinea Baruya*. Trans. Rupert Swyer. Cambridge: Cambridge University Press and Editions de la Maison des Sciences de l'Homme.

Gray, John. 1992. *Men Are from Mars, Women Are from Venus: A Practical Guide for Improving Communication and Getting What You Want in Your Relationship*. New York: HarperCollins.

Gunson, Niel. 1987. Sacred Women Chiefs and Female "Headmen" in Polynesian History. *Journal of Pacific History* 22(3):139–171.

Gutmann, David. 1977. The Cross-Cultural Perspective: Notes Toward a Comparative Psychology of Aging. In *Handbook of the Psychology of Aging*, ed. James Birren and K. Schaie, 302–326. New York: Van Nostrand Reinhold.

Hackett, Rosalind I. J. 1994. Women in African Religions. In *Religion and Women*, ed.

Arvind Sharma and Katherine K. Young, 61–92. Albany: State University of New York Press.

Hardacre, Helen. 1994. Japanese New Religions: Profiles in Gender. In *Fundamentalism and Gender*, ed. John Stratton Hawley, 111–136. New York: Oxford University Press.

Harding, Sandra. 1986. *The Science Question in Feminism*. New York: Cornell University Press.

Haring, Douglas G. 1964. Chinese and Japanese Influences. In *Ryukyuan Culture and Society*, ed. Allan H. Smith, 39–55. Honolulu: University of Hawaii Press.

Harris, Marvin. 1985. *Culture, People, Nature: An Introduction to General Anthropology*. 4th ed. New York: Harper and Row.

Hauser-Schaublin, Brigitta. 1995. Puberty Rites, Women's *Naven*, and Initiation: Women's Rituals of Transition in Abelam and Iatmul Culture. In *Gender Rituals: Female Initiation in Melanesia*, ed. Nancy Lutkehaus and Paul Roscoe, 33–54. New York: Routledge.

Hawkesworth, Mary. 1990. *Beyond Oppression: Feminist Theory and Political Strategy*. New York: Continuum.

Hawley, John, (Ed.) 1994. *Fundamentalism and Gender*. New York: Oxford University Press.

Hendry, Joy. 1981. *Marriage in Changing Japan*. Rutland, Vermont and Tokyo: Charles E. Tuttle.

———. 1995 [1987]. *Understanding Japanese Society*. 2nd ed. London: Routledge.

Hick, John. 1993. *The Metaphor of God Incarnate*. London: SCM Press.

Hicks, David. 1984. *A Maternal Religion: The Role of Women in Tetum Myth and Ritual*. Monograph Series on Southeast Asia. Northern Illinois University: Center for Southeast Asian Studies.

Hokama, Seisho (Ed.) 1974. *Commodore Perry's Visit to Okinawa, 1853–1854*. Rev. ed. Naha, Okinawa: Ryuyodoshobo.

Hopkins, Garland Evans. 1951. Okinawa Religion. *International Review of Missions* 40:179–184.

Hori, Ichiro. 1968. *Folk Religion in Japan: Continuity and Change*. Chicago: University of Chicago Press.

Iadarola, Antoinette. 1985. The American Catholic Bishops and Woman: From the Nineteenth Amendment to ERA. In *Women, Religion and Social Change*, ed. Yvonne Yazbeck Haddad and Ellison Banks Findly, 457–476. Albany: State University of New York Press.

Ito, Mikiharu. 1966. Rice Rites in Japan Proper and the Ryukyus: A Comparative Study. In *Folk Cultures of Japan and East Asia*, 37–55. Monumenta Nipponica Monographs, no. 25. Tokyo: Sophia University Press.

Jacobs, Claude F., and Andrew J. Kaslow. 1991. *The Spiritual Churches of New Orleans*. Knoxville: University of Tennessee Press.

Janeway, Elizabeth. 1981. *Powers of the Weak*. New York: Morrow Quill.

Jay, Nancy. 1992. *Throughout Your Generations Forever: Sacrifice, Religion and Paternity*. Chicago: University of Chicago Press.

Jonte-Pace, Diane. 1992. Situating Kristeva Differently: Psychoanalytic Readings of Women and Religion. In *Body/Text in Julia Kristeva: Religion, Woman, Psychoanalysis*, ed. David Crownfield, 1–22. Albany: State University of New York Press.

Kamata, Hisako. 1966. Daughters of the Gods: Shaman Priestesses in Japan and Okinawa. In *Folk Cultures of Japan and East Asia*, 56–73. Monumenta Nipponica Monographs, no. 25. Tokyo: Sophia University Press.

Karim, Wazir Jahan. 1995. Introduction: Genderising Anthropology in Southeast Asia. In *"Male" and "Female" in Developing Southeast Asia*, ed. Wazir Jahan Karim, 11–43. Cross-Cultural Perspectives on Women. Oxford: Berg.

Katata, Jun. 1992. Longevity Culture in Okinawa, Japan. *Korean Journal of Research in Gerontology.*

Kawahashi, Noriko. 1992. *Kaminchu: Divine Women of Okinawa.* Ph.D. diss. Princeton University, Princeton.

Kendall, Laurel. 1984. Korean Shamanism: Women's Rites and a Chinese Comparison. In *Religion and the Family in East Asia*, ed. George A. De Vos and Takao Sofue, 57–73. Berkeley: University of California Press.

———. 1985. *Shamans, Housewives, and Other Restless Spirits: Women in Korean Ritual Life.* Honolulu: University of Hawaii Press.

———. 1996. Initiating Performance: The Story of Chini, A Korean Shaman. In *Performance of Healing*, ed. Carol Laderman and Marina Roseman, 17–58. New York: Routledge.

Kern, Louis J. 1981. *An Ordered Love: Sex Roles and Sexuality in Victorian Utopias—the Shakers, the Mormons, and the Oneida Community.* Chapel Hill: University of North Carolina Press.

Kerns, Virginia. 1983. *Women and the Ancestors: Black Carib Kinship and Ritual.* Urbana: University of Illinois Press.

Kerr, George H. 1958. *Okinawa: The History of an Island People.* Rutland, Vermont: Charles E. Tuttle Company.

Kim, Yung-Chung (Ed.) 1982. *Women of Korea: A History from Ancient Times to 1945.* Seoul: Ewha Women's Press.

Kirsch, A. Thomas. 1985. Text and Context: Buddhist Sex Roles/Culture of Gender Revisited. *American Ethnologist* 12(2):302–320.

Kitagawa, Joseph M. 1987. *On Understanding Japanese Religion.* Princeton: Princeton University Press.

Kohlberg, Lawrence. 1981. *The Philosophy of Moral Development.* San Francisco: Harper and Row.

Kopytoff, Igor. 1990. Women's Roles and Existential Identities. In *Beyond the Second Sex: New Directions in the Anthropology of Gender*, ed. Peggy Reeves Sanday and Ruth Gallagher Goodenough, 75–98. Philadelphia: University of Pennsylvania.

Kraemer, Ross Shepard. 1992. *Her Share of the Blessings: Women's Religions Among Pagans, Jews, and Christians in the Greco-Roman World.* New York: Oxford University Press.

Kreiner, Josef. 1968. Some Problems of Folk-Religion in the Southwest Islands (Ryukyu). In *Folk Religion and the Worldview in the Southwestern Pacific*, ed. N. Matsumoto and T. Mabuchi, 101–118. Tokyo: Keio University.

Lacks, Roslyn. 1980. *Women and Judaism: Myth, History, and Struggle.* New York: Doubleday.

Landes, Ruth. 1947. *City of Women.* New York: Macmillan.

Lawless, Elaine. 1991. Rescripting their Lives and Narratives: Spiritual Life Stories of Pentecostal Women Preachers. *Journal of Feminist Studies in Religion* 7(1):53–71.

Leacock, Seth, and Ruth Leacock. 1972. *Spirits of the Deep: A Study of an Afro-Brazilian Cult.* New York: Double Day Natural History Press.

Leacock, Eleanor. 1986. Women, Power and Authority. In *Visibility and Power: Essays on Women in Society and Development*, ed. Leela Dube, Eleanor Leacock, and Shirley Ardener, 107–135. Delhi: Oxford University Press.

Lebra, Takie Sugiyama. 1976. *Japanese Patterns of Behavior*. Honolulu: University of Hawaii Press.

———. 1984. *Japanese Women: Constraint and Fulfillment*. Honolulu: University of Hawaii Press.

Lebra, William P. 1966. *Okinawan Religion*. Honolulu: University of Hawaii Press.

Lepowsky, Maria. 1990. Gender in an Egalitarian Society: A Case Study from the Coral Sea. In *Beyond the Second Sex: New Directions in the Anthropology of Gender*, ed. Peggy Reeves Sanday and Ruth Gallagher Goodenough, 169–224. Philadelphia: University of Pennsylvania.

———. 1993. *Fruit of the Motherland: Gender in an Egalitarian Society*. New York: Columbia University Press.

Lerch, Patricia. 1980. Spirit Mediums in Umbanda Evangelizada of Porto Alegre, Brazil: Dimensions of Power and Authority. In *A World of Women*, ed. Erika Bourguignon, 129–159. New York: Praeger.

———. 1982. An Explanation for the Predominance of Women in the Umbanda Cults of Porto Alegre, Brazil. *Urban Anthropology* 11(2):237-261.

Lerner, Gerda. 1986. *The Creation of Patriarchy*. New York: Oxford University Press.

Lewis, I. M. 1975. *Ecstatic Religion*. 1971. Harmondsworth, England: Penguin Books.

Lincoln, Bruce. 1981. *Emerging from the Chrysalis: Studies in Rituals of Women's Initiation*. Cambridge: Harvard University Press.

———. 1989. *Discourse and the Construction of Society: Comparative Studies of Myth, Ritual, and Classification*. New York: Oxford University Press.

Lock, Margaret. 1987. Protests of a Good Wife and Wise Mother: The Medicalization of Distress in Japan. In *Health, Illness, and Medical Care in Japan*, ed. Edward Norbeck and Margaret Lock, 130–157. Honolulu: University of Hawaii Press.

Long, Susan Orpett. 1996. Nurturing and Femininity: The Ideal of Caregiving in Postwar Japan. In *Re-Imaging Japanese Women*, ed. Anne E. Imamura, 156–176. Berkeley: University of California Press.

Lorber, Judith. 1994. *Paradoxes of Gender*. New Haven: Yale University Press.

Lutkehaus, Nancy, and Paul Roscoe (Eds.) 1995. *Gender Rituals: Female Initiation in Melanesia*. New York: Routledge.

Mabuchi, Toichi. 1964. Spiritual Predominance of the Sister. In *Ryukyuan Culture and Society*, ed. Allan H. Smith, 79–91. Honolulu: University of Hawaii Press.

———. 1968. Toward the Reconstruction of Ryukyuan Cosmology. In *Folk Religion and the Worldview in the Southwestern Pacific*, ed. N. Matsumoto and T. Mabuchi, 119–140. Tokyo: Keio University.

———. 1976a. A Note on Ancestor Worship in "Cognatic" Societies. In *Ancestors*, ed. William H. Newell, 105–117. The Hague: Mouton.

———. 1976b. Optional Cult Group Affiliation Among the Puyama and the Miyako Islanders. In *Ancestors*, ed. William H. Newell, 91–103. The Hague: Mouton.

Maretzki, Thomas, and Hatsumi Maretzki. 1966. *Taira: An Okinawan Village*. Six Cultures Series, vol. 7. New York: John Wiley and Sons.

Matsui, Hiroko, Kazuya Horike, and Hideshi Ohashi. 1980. Rorschach Responses of Okinawan Shamans "Yuta." *Tohoku Psychologica Folia* 39(1–4):61–78.

Matsuzono, Makio. 1976. A Note on the Enshrinement of Ancestral Tablets at Zamami Island, Okinawa. In *Ancestors*, ed. William H. Newell, 231–240. The Hague: Mouton.

Moghadam, Valentine. 1994. Introduction: Women and Identity Politics in Theoretical and Comparative Perspective. In *Identity Politics and Women: Cultural Reassertions and Feminisms in International Perspective*, ed. Valentine Moghadam, 3–26. Boulder, Colorado: Westview Press.

Moore, R. Laurence. 1977. *In Search of White Crows: Spiritualism, Parapsychology, and American Culture*. New York: Oxford University Press.

Morris, Rosalind C. 1995. All Made Up: Performance Theory and the New Anthropology of Sex and Gender. *Annual Review of Anthropology* 24:567–592.

Muratake, Seichi. 1964/1965. Dualism in the Southern Ryukyus. *Archiv für Völkerkunde* 19:120–128.

Murray, David A. B. 1996. Undressing Crossdressing at Martinique's Carnival. Paper presented at American Anthropological Association Annual Meeting, San Francisco.

Nadel-Klein, Jane, and Dona Lee Davis. 1988. Introduction: Gender in the Maritime Arena. In *To Work and to Weep: Women in Fishing Economies*, ed. Jane Nadel-Klein and Dona Lee Davis, 1–17. St. John's, Newfoundland, Canada: Memorial University of Newfoundland.

Nakamura, Kyoko Motomochi. 1980. No Women's Liberation: The Heritage of a Woman Prophet in Modern Japan. In *Unspoken Worlds: Women's Religious Lives in Non-Western Cultures*, ed. Nancy Falk and Rita Gross, 174–190. San Francisco: Harper and Row.

Noguchi, Takenori. 1966. The Japanese Kinship System. In *Folk Cultures of Japan and East Asia*, 16–36. Monumenta Nipponica Monographs, no. 25. Tokyo: Sophia University Press.

Ochshorn, Judith. 1981. *The Female Experience and the Nature of the Divine*. Bloomington: University of Indiana Press.

Offner, Clark, and Henry Van Straelen. 1963. *Modern Japanese Religion*. Leiden: E. J. Brill.

Ohashi, Hideshi, Shinsuke Sakumichi, and Kazuya Horike. 1984. A Social Psychological Study of Okinawan Shamanism (I): Approach and Some Findings. *Tohoku Psychologica Folia* 43(1–4):66–79.

Ohnuki-Tierney, Emiko. 1984. *Illness and Culture in Contemporary Japan*. Cambridge: Cambridge University Press.

Okinawa Prefectural Government. 1993. *The Basic Plan for the Site Utilization of the Lands Currently Used by the U.S. Military in Okinawa*. Naha, Okinawa.

Okinawa Prefectural Office. 1993. *Okinawa Prefecture's Annual Population Abstract*.

Okinawa Prefectural Office. 1994. *Okinawa Women's Report*. Naha, Okinawa.

Ortner, Sherry. 1974. Is Female to Male as Nature Is to Culture? In *Women, Culture and Society*, ed. Michelle Zimbalist Rosaldo and Louise Lamphere, 67–88. Stanford: Stanford University Press.

———. 1996. *Making Gender: The Politics and Erotics of Culture*. Boston: Beacon Press.

Ota, Yoshinobu. 1989. Creating the Experience of a Sacred Elite: An Examination of the Concept of *Shiji* in Southern Ryukyuan Religion. *Contributions to Southeast Asian Ethnography* 8:111–125.

Ouwehand, C. 1985. *Hateruma: Socio-Religious Aspects of a South-Ryukyuan Island Culture*. Leiden: E. J. Brill.

Paige, Karen Ericksen, and Jeffrey M. Paige. 1981. *The Politics of Reproductive Ritual*. Berkeley: University of California Press.

Parrinder, Geoffrey. 1982. *Avatar and Incarnation*. New York: Oxford University Press.

Paulson, Joy. 1976. Evolution of the Feminine Ideal. In *Women in Changing Japan*, ed. Joyce Lebra, Joy Paulson, and Elizabeth Powers, 1–24. Boulder, CO: Westview Press.

Peacock, James L. 1978. Symbolic Reversal and Social History: Transvestites and Clowns of Java. In *Reversible World: Symbolic Inversion in Art and Society*, ed. Barbara A. Babcock, 209-224. Ithaca: Cornell University Press.

Pelzel, John C. 1974. Human Nature in Japanese Myths. In *Japanese Culture and Behavior: Selected Readings*, ed. Takie Sugiyama Lebra, 3–26. Honolulu: University of Hawaii Press.

Potter, Shulamith. 1977. *Family Life in a Northern Thai Village: A Study in the Structural Significance of Women*. Berkeley: University of California Press.

Powers, John. 1995. *Introduction to Tibetan Buddhism*. Ithaca, New York: Snow Lion Publications.

Procter-Smith. 1985. *Women in Shaker Community and Worship: A Feminist Analysis of the Uses of Religious Symbolism*. Lewiston, New York: Edwin Mellen.

Ram, Kalpana. 1991. *Mukkuvar Women: Gender, Hegemony and Capitalist Transformation in a South Indian Fishing Community*. London: Zed.

Randall, Maxine, Koichi Naka, Aiko Ikei, Hiroshi Ishizu, William Randall, and Toshihiro Takaishi. 1989. High Spirit Rank Birth (*Saadaka Unmari*) in Okinawa: Toward a Medical Anthropological Approach to Mental Health. Paper presented at the World Congress for Mental Health. Auckland, New Zealand.

Reiter, Rayna R. 1975. Men and Women in the South of France: Public and Private Domains. In *Toward an Anthropology of Women*, ed. Rayna Reiter, 252–282. New York: Monthly Review Press.

Reynolds, Frank E., and Donald Capps. 1976. Introduction. In *The Biographical Process: Studies in the History and Psychology of Religion*, ed. Frank. E. Reynolds and Donald Capps, 1–33. The Hague: Mouton.

Riesman, Paul. 1992. *First Find Your Child a Good Mother: The Construction of Self in Two African Communities*. New Brunswick: Rutgers University Press.

Rohlen, Thomas P. 1989. Order in Japanese Society: Attachment, Authority, and Routine. *Journal of Japanese Studies* 15(1):5–40.

Rosaldo, Michelle Zimbalist. 1974. Women, Culture, and Society: A Theoretical Overview. In *Women, Culture, and Society*, ed. Michelle Zimbalist Rosaldo and Louise Lamphere, 17–42. Stanford: Stanford University Press.

Roscoe, Paul. 1995. "Initiation" in Cross-Cultural Perspective. In *Gender Rituals: Female Initiation in Melanesia*, ed. Nancy Lutkehaus and Paul Roscoe, 219–238. New York: Routledge.

Rubin, Gayle. 1975. The Traffic in Women: Notes on the "Political Economy" of Sex. In *Toward an Anthropology of Women*, ed. Rayna Reiter, 157-210. New York: Monthly Review Press.

Ruether, Rosemary Radford. n.d. In the Mountains of Banahaw Padre is a Woman. unpublished essay.

Sacks, Karen. 1979. *Sisters and Wives*. Westport, Connecticut: Greenwood Press.

Sakihara, Mitsugu. 1981. History of Okinawa. In *Uchinanchu: A History of Okinawans in Hawaii*. Honolulu: University of Hawaii at Manoa Ethnic Studies Program.

Sakumichi, Shinsuke, Hideshi Ohashi, Hiroko Horike, and Nobuya Tohyama. 1984. A Social Psychological Study of Okinawan Shamanism (II): An Investigation of the Health-Seeking Process in the Traditional Society Under the Infiltration of Modern Western Culture. *Tohoku Psychologica Folia* 43(1–4):80–90.

Sanday, Peggy Reeves. 1981. *Female Power and Male Dominance: On the Origins of Sexual Inequality*. Cambridge: Cambridge University Press.

———. 1990. Introduction. In *Beyond the Second Sex: New Directions in the Anthropol-*

ogy of Gender, ed. Peggy Reeves Sanday and Ruth Gallagher Goodenough, 1–20. Philadelphia: University of Pennsylvania Press.

Sasaki, Kokan. 1984. Spirit Possession as an Indigenous Religion in Japan and Okinawa. In *Religion and the Family in East Asia*, ed. George A. De Vos and Takao Sofue, 75–84. Berkeley: University of California Press.

Sered, Susan Starr. 1992. *Women as Ritual Experts: The Religious Lives of Elderly Jewish Women in Jerusalem*. New York: Oxford University Press.

———. 1994. *Priestess, Mother, Sacred Sister: Religions Dominated by Women*. New York: Oxford University Press.

Seremetakis, C. Nadia. 1991. *The Last Word: Women, Death and Divination in Inner Mani*. Chicago: University of Chicago Press.

Sharma, Arvind (Ed.) 1987. *Women in World Religions*. Albany: State University of New York Press.

Silverblatt, Irene. 1980. Andean Women under Spanish Rule. In *Women and Colonization: Anthropological Perspectives*, ed. Mona Etienne and Eleanor Leacock, 149–185. New York: J. F. Bergin.

Skinner, G. William. 1993. Conjugal Power in Tokugawa Japanese Families: A Matter of Life or Death. In *Sex and Gender Hierarchies*, ed. Barbara Diane Miller, 236–270. Cambridge: Cambridge University Press.

Skultans, Vieda. 1983. Mediums, Controls and Eminent Men. In *Women's Religious Experience*, ed. Pat Holden, 15–26. London: Croom Helm.

Smith, Robert J. 1983. *Japanese Society: Tradition, Self and the Social Order*. Cambridge: Cambridge University Press.

Smith, Robert J., and Ella Lury Wiswell. 1982. *The Women of Suye Mura*. Chicago: University of Chicago Press.

Smits, Gregory. 1996. The Intersection of Politics and Thought in Ryukyuan Confucianism: Sai On's Uses of *Quan*. *Harvard Journal of Asiatic Studies* 56(2): 443–477.

Spiro, Melford. 1967. *Burmese Supernaturalism*. Englewood Cliffs, N.J.: Prentice-Hall.

Starhawk. 1987. *Truth or Dare*. New York: Harper and Row.

Stone, Merlin. 1976. *When God Was A Woman*. New York: Harvest/HBJ.

Stover, Ronald, and Christine Hope. 1984. Monotheism and Gender Status: A Cross-Societal Study. *Social Forces* 63(2):335–348.

Stromberg, Peter G. 1993. *Language and Self-Transformation: A Study of the Christian Conversion Narrative*. Cambridge: Cambridge University Press.

Swanson, Guy E. 1960. *Birth of the Gods: The Origin of Primitive Beliefs*. Ann Arbor: University of Michigan Press.

Swartz, M. J., V. Turner, and A. Tuden (Eds.) 1966. *Political Anthropology*. Chicago: Aldine.

Taeuber, Irene B. 1955. The Population of the Ryukyu Islands. In *Population Index*, vol. 21, no. 4, ed. Frank W. Notestein and Dorothy Good, 233–257. Princeton, N.J.: Office of Population Research, Woodrow Wilson School of Public and International Affairs, Princeton University; Population Association of America, Inc.

Taira, Koji. 1997. Troubled National Identity: The Ryukyuans/Okinawans. In *Japan's Minorities: The Illusion of Homogeneity*, ed. Michael Weiner, 140–177. London and New York: Routledge.

Takara, Kurayoshi. 1994. King and Priestess: Spiritual and Political Power in Ancient Ryukyu. Paper presented at the International Society for Ryukyuan Studies. Harvard University, Reischauer Institute.

Tambiah, S. J. 1970. *Buddhism and the Spirit Cults in North-East Thailand*. Cambridge: Cambridge University Press.

Tanabe, Shigeharu. 1991. Spirits, Power, and the Discourse of Female Gender: The Phi Meng Cult in Northern Thailand. In *Thai Constructions of Knowledge*, ed. Manas Chitakasem and Andrew Turton, 183–212. London: School of Oriental and African Studies.

Tanaka, Masako. 1977. Categories of Okinawan "Ancestors" and the Kinship System. *Asian Folklore Studies* 36(2):31-64.

Tanner, Nancy. 1974. Matrifocality in Indonesia and Africa and Among Black Americans. In *Women, Culture, and Society*, ed. Michelle Z. Rosaldo and Louise Lamphere, 129–156. Stanford: Stanford University Press.

Thompson, Paul. 1985. Women in the Fishing: The Roots of Power Between the Sexes. *Comparative Studies in Society and History* 27(1):3–32.

Turner, Victor. 1969. *The Ritual Process: Structure and Anti-Structure*. Chicago: Aldine.

———. 1981. Social Dramas and Stories About Them. In *On Narrative*, ed. W. J. T. Mitchell, 137–164. Chicago: University of Chicago Press.

Turton, Andrew. 1984. People of the Same Spirit: Local Matrikin Groups and their Cults. *Mankind* 14(4):272–285.

Uchino, Kumiko. 1987. The Status Elevation Process of Soto Sect Nuns in Modern Japan. In *Speaking of Faith: Global Perspectives on Women, Religion, and Social Change*, ed. Diana Eck and Devaki Jain, 159–173. Philadelphia: New Society Publishers.

Van Gennep, Arnold. 1960 [1909]. *Rites of Passage*. Chicago: University of Chicago Press.

Weston, K. 1993. Lesbian/Gay Studies in the House of Anthropology. *Annual Review of Anthropology* 22:339–367.

Williams, Raymond B. 1985. The Holy Man as the Abode of God in the Swaminarayan Religion. In *Gods of Flesh/Gods of Stone: The Embodiment of Divinity in India*, ed. Joanne Punzo Waghorne and Norman Cutler, 143–157. Chambersburg, Pennsylvania: Anima.

Wilson, Brian. 1983. The Korean Shaman: Image and Reality. In *Korean Women, View from the Inner Room*, ed. Laurel Kendall and Mark Peterson, 113–128. New Haven: East Rock Press.

Yanagisako, Sylvia, and Carol Delaney. 1995. Naturalizing Power. In *Naturalizing Power*, ed. Sylvia Yanagisako and Carol Delaney, 1–22. New York: Routledge.

Yoshida, Teigo. 1990. The Feminine in Japanese Folk Religion: Polluted or Divine? In *Unwrapping Japan*, ed. Eyal Ben-Ari, Brian Moeran, and James Valentine, 58–77. Honolulu: University of Hawaii Press.

Young, Katherine K. 1994. Introduction. In *Religion and Women*, ed. Arvind Sharma and Katherine K. Young, 1–38. Albany: State University of New York Press.

Yusa, Michiko. 1994. Women in Shinto: Images Remembered. In *Religion and Women*, ed. Arvind Sharma and Katherine K. Young, 93–120. Albany: State University of New York Press.

Index